The Journal of a Civil War Surgeon

J. Franklin Dyer

THE JOURNAL
OF A CIVIL WAR
SURGEON

EDITED BY

Michael B. Chesson

University of Nebraska Press

Lincoln and London

LIBRARY OF CONGRESS CATALOGING-IN-PUBLICATION DATA
Dyer, J. Franklin (Jonah Franklin), 1826–1879.
The journal of a Civil War surgeon / J. Franklin
Dyer ; edited by Michael B. Chesson.
p. cm.
Includes bibliographical references and index.
ISBN 0-8032-6637-5 (paperback : alkaline paper)
1. Dyer, J. Franklin (Jonah Franklin), 1826–1879 –
Correspondence. 2. United States. Army. Massa-
chusetts Infantry Regiment, 19th (1861–1865).
3. United States – History – Civil War, 1861–1865 –
Medical care. 4. United States – History – Civil War,
1861–1865 – Personal narratives. 5. Massachusetts –
History – Civil War, 1861–1865 – Personal narra-
tives. 6. United States – History – Civil War, 1861–
1865 – Regimental histories. 7. Massachusetts –
History – Civil War, 1861–1865 – Regimental
histories. 8. United States. Army – Surgeons –
Correspondence. 9. Surgeons – Massachusetts –
Correspondence. I. Chesson, Michael B., 1947-.
II. Title.
E513.5 19th .D94 2003 973.7'75'092—dc21 [B]
2002032484

For George Burton Dyer, 1905–1990

  Who preserved this record of the Civil War

Contents

.

Illustrations

Acknowledgments

Like the men and women who experienced it, those who study the war never know what to expect. Some years ago Gerald Murphy, a student in my undergraduate course on the Civil War and Reconstruction, asked if I would be interested in looking at some family papers. I said that I would, without knowing what awaited me. Dr. J. Franklin Dyer's journal was fascinating, but still I sought the opinion of my staunch Salem friend from graduate-school days at Johns Hopkins, Charles A. Michaud, director of the Turner Free Library in Randolph, Massachusetts. His ancestors served in the Seventeenth and Twentieth Massachusetts, and like many buffs he knows "the real war," particularly the Union side in the East, and especially Gettysburg (his college town), better than many academics. After reading Dyer's stirring account of the battle, he recommended the project and has generously assisted this descendant of Confederates since I began it. Without his strong endorsement, I would not have undertaken the task of editing Dr. Dyer.

The letters from the Gettysburg campaign to November 1864 that have survived were made available after I became interested in Dyer and proved to be even more rewarding than the journal based upon them. I contacted Gerry's aunt, Mrs. Nancy D. Witmer of South Carolina, who graciously consented to allow me to edit the material and try to find a publisher. She and her mother own both the manuscripts and Dr. Dyer's medical instruments, sword, uniform, and photographs of him and the Annisquam house. Gerry's own grandmother, Mrs. Mildred G. Dyer, the widow of George B. Dyer, provided additional material, as did Gerry, who took photographs of the house as it looks today. Barbara Skinner of the Annisquam Historical Society provided Gerry with copies of items relating to Dr. Dyer, his wife Maria, and their house.

On the North Shore in Gloucester, I am particularly grateful to Sarah V. Dunlap, Priscilla Kippen, Mary and Alan Ray, Janie Walsh, and the other volunteers on the Archives Committee of the City of

Acknowledgments

Gloucester, as well as Judy Peterson, archivist and records clerk; Barbara Lambert and Ellen Nelson at the Cape Ann Historical Association; Director David McArdle, reference librarians Tom Madden and Judith Oski, and the other fine professionals of the Sawyer Free Library; and George Belezos, overseer of Oak Grove Cemetery. The archivists at the Phillips Library of the Peabody Essex Museum in Salem were tireless in tracking down relevant collections, particularly those of men who served in the Nineteenth Massachusetts or who lived in Gloucester and Annisquam. These scholars provided invaluable assistance in finding details on Dr. Dyer's life before and after the war, as well as during it. I thank Bruce H. Tobey, former mayor of Gloucester, for permission to publish a photograph of the official portrait of Mayor Dyer, recently discovered by members of the Archives Committee hidden away in City Hall, as well as Judy Ryan of his office. I am indebted to David Stotzer, Cape Ann Photography, and his production assistant Pam Ash for their professional services and to Shawn McNiff, the current owner of Dyer's house, for permission to use a picture of his home.

A fellow history major and Civil War student, Dorothy Amichetti, volunteered to serve as a research assistant with Gerry on the project. Both completed independent research for academic credit under my direction. They pursued biographical details on Dyer and wrote a sketch of his life. Dorothy, a legal secretary, transcribed the letters, a particularly laborious task, for many were pasted and taped in scrapbooks at odd angles. Without such capable assistants this project would not have been completed at all. Few teachers are as fortunate in their pupils as I have been at the University of Massachusetts–Boston.

In the course of my own research, I was also assisted by Harold L. Miller of the State Historical Society of Wisconsin. Erik C. Jorgensen, executive director of the Pejepscot Historical Society, Brunswick, Maine, sent a copy of the alumni records confirming Dr. Dyer's graduation from the Medical School of Maine and his son Franklin's enrollment at Bowdoin. He also put me in touch with Susan Ravdin, then the assistant curator for Special Collections, at the Bowdoin College library. She provided two letters by Dyer to Maj. Gen. O. O. Howard, documents from the medical school, and a wealth of other important items that helped fill in vital aspects of the doctor's life before and after the war. Sean M. Monahan,

Acknowledgments

Special Collections and Archives assistant, provided some last-minute help in my attempt to identify a member of O. O. Howard's staff.

Bradley Finfrock, staff assistant, American Battlefield Protection Plan, National Park Service, and Terry Reimer, researcher at the National Museum of Civil War Medicine, provided essential details on Dr. Dyer's service at Antietam. The staff of the Boston Public Library, especially the music department; Widener, Houghton, and Lamont Libraries and the Loeb Music Library at Harvard University; the National Archives and Records Administration in Waltham; the Massachusetts State Archives; and the state Registry of Vital Records and Statistics provided invaluable assistance. Valerie McKay at the State Library of Massachusetts, Boston, and Karen Adler Abramson and Mary Bicknell of the library's Special Collections Department helped me pin down Dyer's comments about the capture of the Nineteenth Massachusetts below Petersburg in 1864 and newspaper coverage of the event. Without archivists, librarians, and the staff of historical societies, few Civil War historians would be able to gain, much less hold, a foot of ground.

Edward L. Ayers, Richard Maxwell Brown, Charles B. Dew, David Herbert Donald, Eric Foner, and James I. Robertson all read the manuscript at an early stage and gave me support that was critical, as did my colleagues in the Department of History at the University of Massachusetts–Boston: Spencer M. DiScala, Clive E. Foss, Lester A. Segal, Julie Winch, Woodruff D. Smith (then dean of the College of Arts and Sciences), and our chairman, Paul G. Faler. I am indebted most of all to William A. Percy, a fellow Southerner, for years of advice and encouragement while I worked on a Union surgeon's papers. Daniel J. J. Ross, originally the history editor and former director of the University of Nebraska Press, and the acquisitions staff at the press have supported this project over a number of years, most importantly with their wise and warm counsel. I am also indebted to two anonymous readers for the press for their perceptive and generous criticisms of the manuscript.

My wife, Jane B. Sherwin, contributed in ways too numerous to list, not least with her computing skills. Miss Helen Sherwin added to my knowledge of Walt Whitman's hospital service. Our children, Mark and Virginia, have patiently borne their father's absence while he spent many hours with Dr. Dyer and the war that transformed

Acknowledgments

America. My parents, W. E. and Mrs. Virginia Chesson; my brother, Mark W. Chesson, and his wife, Nancy; and my wife's parents, Mr. and Mrs. Sidney A. Sherwin, all gave me essential support.

The greatest debt of all is owed to Mr. George B. Dyer, Mrs. Witmer's father. Maria Dyer left the Annisquam house at her death to Franklin G. Dyer, her husband's nephew, who was George Dyer's father. Franklin G. Dyer began the compilation of the family genealogy that George continued. About 1934 he and his family moved into the vacant house to maintain it and lived there for several years during the Depression. In Dr. Dyer's study and in the attic, George Dyer found the major's papers, letters, and medical instruments, left largely untouched by his widow. Although financial conditions finally forced him to sell the house, he collected and preserved all of the material belonging to Dr. Dyer. In later years he enjoyed showing the memorabilia to his children and grandchildren as they became old enough to appreciate the significance of the items. The manuscript journal and letters and the major's medical kits, sword, and other uniform items were given by Nancy Dyer Witmer to the Peabody Essex Museum in Salem, Massachusetts. The sword and medical kits are valuable artifacts for Civil War collectors, but the manuscripts are far more precious. Without George B. Dyer's concern for his family's heritage and our country's history, this story would not have been told.

Introduction

Jonah Franklin Dyer, the surgeon of the Nineteenth Regiment of Massachusetts Volunteer Infantry, surgeon in chief of the Second Division, and acting medical director of the II Corps, Army of the Potomac, was born April 15, 1826, in Eastport, Maine, a town with fewer than 2,500 residents.[1] He was the fourth of seven children of Charles Dyer, a Maine native, and Hannah Snow, who was born in Granville, Nova Scotia. His roots went back to the founding of New England, with military forebears on both sides of his family over several generations. The future Union surgeon was named for his grandfather, Capt. Jonah Dyer, who fought in the American Revolution, was held prisoner by the British, and settled after his release in Gorham, Maine. A more distant relative, the Quaker Mary Dyer, was hanged on Boston Common in 1660.[2]

Dyer's maternal line descended from Nicholas Snow, a passenger to Plymouth Plantation on the ship *Anne* in 1623, who married Constance Hopkins. She was the daughter of Stephen Hopkins. Both had come over on the *Mayflower*, and Hopkins later served under Capt. Myles Standish. The couple had twelve children. Their descendants were in provincial forces that invaded Canada and in the French and Indian War. At least two Snow families lived in Eastport during Frank Dyer's youth, possibly maternal cousins.[3]

Charles Dyer (b. 1793) died in 1844, when Jonah was eighteen.[4] Charles Henry Dyer (1821–1906), about to embark on the career that would make him a prosperous Eastport merchant, was still apprenticed to the prominent Hayden family.[5] He assumed the paternal role in Eastport as the oldest son, advising Frank (who by 1846 preferred his middle name to Jonah) and caring for their mother as well as his youngest siblings, George Burton Dyer (1835–1913) and Adelaide Dyer (1839–1928). William Snow Dyer (1823–82) had moved after 1840 to Machias, not far to the southwest, where he ran a general store. William confessed some guilt that Charles "appears to have the charge of all the family and it is a heavy burden." He also joshed Frank, only recently apprenticed to a druggist, for "rolling out pills. I think you would look queer . . . *Dr. Franklin Dyer.*"[6]

In one of his rare undated letters, written before the Wilderness campaign, Surgeon Dyer regretted that he had not yet been able to buy a pony for his son, Frankie. "I mean that he shall have one some time, for I know how I wanted such things and couldn't have them, and for that reason I want him to."[7] This wish seems more the expression of a loving father than an accurate reflection of his own youth. Dozens of family letters from the 1840s indicate that his boyhood was of a middle status, neither rich nor poor. His mother took occasional trips to St. John, New Brunswick, to visit relatives. When she could find someone suitable, she had a servant girl to assist her in the house. Sometimes there were problems, though none of the scope endured by her Hopkins ancestor in Plymouth. When one of the maids burned her foot so badly with a pot of boiling water that she could not walk, Charles H. Dyer had to milk the family's "damned old cow" himself and complained that it made it hard for him to write. The letters show that the boys, at least, received formal education. George was learning Latin in the 1840s, and when Frank finally decided on medical school, William arranged to have his old Latin books sent to him.[8]

More important for the man who would endure three years of the Civil War, Frank's family was a warm and affectionate one. The bonds among the brothers were particularly strong. Frank corresponded frequently with Charles and William but less often with George and their widowed mother. The three oldest siblings loaned money to each other, even when hard pressed themselves. Frank benefited more than any from his family's generosity but was not the only child to do so. William thought highly of young George, for example, and would have liked to employ him in his store but thought it better that he stay in school.[9]

Hannah Snow Dyer (1793–1881) addressed her letters to Frank "Dear Child" and made it clear that she would like him at home for a few more years but that she would give her consent if he wanted to pursue any one of several different careers, even if it meant long separations.[10] Even sister Adelaide asked about him, saying she would write, except when the seven year old had the measles in August 1846 and was "as cross as a little bear."[11] All showed

Introduction

a real concern for Frank's present welfare and future prospects, giving advice but being careful of his feelings and offering constant encouragement and support, especially Charles and William.

By the time of his father's death, Frank was already the editor and publisher of a small weekly, the *Eastport Sentinel,* in partnership with Charles C. Tyler. Their close friend J. G. Blanchard remembered Frank at this time as "a humble typo."[12] In less than two years he was forced to abandon printing and the newspaper business because of unspecified health problems. William asked in 1846 whether he had given up cigar smoking for this reason, so the weakness may have related to his lungs.[13] Frank thought of moving to New York City, of going into the new and therefore risky practice of daguerreotyping (the cautious Charles called it "a rather uncertain business"), and of going to the frontier with William, who admitted, "I shall never be satisfied until I have been west."[14]

William went to Milwaukee in November 1847 and wrote from there, boasting of the prospects compared with opportunities in New England.[15] He returned in February 1848 and realized that he would be unable to borrow the money he would need to start a new business and compete with established firms in Milwaukee.[16] Instead he went into business with William B. Billings, the new son-in-law of Dr. Erastus Richardson, who had retired and sold his building to the two younger men and who would also help Frank get started in his medical career with letters of recommendation and supervision of his training. But William was not satisfied. In September 1849 he went to California with other forty-niners before returning east and graduating from medical school in Philadelphia, where the Dyers had cousins.[17]

As Charles struggled to establish himself in Eastport and William dreamed of the West, Frank decided to become an apothecary.[18] He apprenticed himself for three years to a druggist in South Berwick, Maine, upriver from Portsmouth along the Piscataqua near the New Hampshire border. The firm of Philbrick and Trafton also did business in Boston. Hannah Dyer and the family's physician, Dr. Richardson, who thought the profession would be the best of several options for his health, supported Frank's decision.[19] Frank returned from a trip to Boston in the summer of 1846 to work on a trial basis with Dr. Charles T. Trafton. The young man studied medicine under the doctor's supervision from August 1846 to February 1848 while working in the Trafton pharmacy.[20]

Charles Tyler advised him, "since you concluded to go into the apothecary business," that three years was too long to devote to the study of pharmacy. Tyler, with a Dr. Parsons whom they both knew, thought that only a few months' reading of medical books and a few more of rudimentary practice was all that was needed.[21] Fortunately for his Civil War comrades and other patients, Frank Dyer was intent on more advanced studies.

A visit in September 1847 with his employer to commencement ceremonies at Bowdoin, where young Augustus E. Trafton was graduating from the Medical School of Maine, probably convinced Dyer to seek a degree.[22] Despite a lack of money to pay for the course of lectures, but with the strong encouragement of his brothers and mother and their promise of aid, he began attending lectures at the Medical School of Maine in Brunswick in February 1848, the same month that Joshua L. Chamberlain entered Bowdoin College as an undergraduate. Charles provided substantial funds, but the biggest loan came from an old family friend that his mother contacted. When Charles agreed to sign the note as security, the arrangement was completed.[23]

Blanchard wrote from Eastport to congratulate him. "You are now then fairly committed as a disciple of Esculapius [*sic*], and have taken a seat at length in the consecrated halls of ["Brunswick" is crossed out] Bowdoin. . . . Well, go it; and see that you go it thoroughly. Be no superficial pretender; pause not till thoroughly informed in every branch of your anticipated profession."[24]

In July 1848 Frank was again working for Dr. Trafton between sessions of the medical school but was thinking once more of joining William if he went west again, though his brother now advised against the West for young doctors and lawyers, recommending New England or the South instead. Frank also studied medicine with Dr. Richardson back in Eastport from June 1848 until the beginning of his final session at Brunswick in February 1849.[25]

His financial troubles continued. Before the start of his last term, Frank asked that he be permitted to attend medical lectures on credit, but Prof. Nathan S. Cleaveland replied that such arrangements were allowed only in extreme cases. He advised Frank to borrow funds for the necessary tickets, recommended the best way

Introduction

to get a loan, and even suggested that he pay half of the fee in advance if he could not come up with the entire sum. But if the young man could not raise the money, he would not be barred from attending the lectures. Frank finished the last course of lectures in 1849, completed "A Thesis on Acute Hydrocephalus," and earned his M.D. with twelve other men.[26]

As a young physician Dyer continued his medical studies with Dr. Ephraim Marston in Boston from May 27 to August 14, 1849, when his degree was formally conferred. Charles wrote, "I feel very much pleased to think that you have succeeded in getting a situation and hope you may do well." Frank's diploma was sent to him by Professor Cleaveland in September. He stayed in practice with Marston until October 1850, when they dissolved their agreement. Dyer then moved to East Boston and continued to treat a few of his former partner's patients.[27]

Young Dr. Dyer found it hard to establish himself in Boston, with its large medical fraternity, despite William's early prediction that "your practice will increase." Frank decided to relocate to Annisquam, one of the villages in the town of Gloucester on the northwestern side of the Cape Anne Peninsula in Essex County. The little community may have lacked a resident physician; at any rate it was easier for Dyer to build a practice that would support him. The regular cash entries in his daybook resumed at that location in mid-July 1851. After earning his M.D., and following the short period in Boston, Dyer lived at and practiced medicine in Annisquam and Gloucester proper for the remaining twenty-seven years of his life, except for his time with the Army of the Potomac.[28]

Frank Dyer had a healthy interest in young women. Banter about the opposite sex, news of engagements and weddings, and kindly advice filled the letters from his brothers and other male friends. In July 1846, when Frank was thinking of various careers and a possible move to New York, Charles told him, "be a good boy and keep straight." That same fall William warned him about young women, especially "factory girls," meaning the workers at textile mills close to South Berwick. And the Boston druggist F. P. Philbrick wrote as Frank was nearing the end of his first term of medical school that women were "a failing of young men."[29]

Other letters bore news that was sad or funny, depending on

the circumstances. Charles Tyler told Frank of the sudden death of Lucy Hayden in Eastport in September 1846, commenting "strange isn't it how many young married women die." The following March his brother Charles wrote that William had given testimony in the trial of a man accused of murdering his wife, a customer to whom William had sold poison. Then he told of two young men whom they both knew. One asked the other how he had happened to meet a Miss Manning, who was now his wife. The new husband replied "that he got acquainted with her *Permiscuously*."[30]

Charles himself married in September 1847 and evidently found that it agreed with him, for he played the matchmaker for Frank in February 1848. Of the correspondence that his younger brother was carrying on with a local woman, Charles wrote, "I think you and she are doing a great business," but added, "look out for yourself that you do not get smashed with her pretty face." Frank's friend Blanchard was courting in person. According to Charles, he and a young woman stayed up with each other until one or two in the morning, never retiring before midnight. Other friends wrote him of women that wanted to meet him and described various social encounters. Frank responded to one of these letters, "God keep me from all such things."[31] His family and friends wanted him to be established in a career before committing himself to marriage and a family, and they hoped that he would find a wife from a similar background. Happily for all, Frank Dyer had the same priorities.

Less than two years after relocating to Annisquam, his practice was growing steadily, as reflected in the entries in his daybook, and he felt able to support a wife and family. On May 4, 1853, Dyer married Maria Haskell French in Boston. Like Frank, Maria was twenty-seven, but she had only a month to live. No death certificate has been found or other information about her other than her birth on February 17, 1826, and death on June 6, 1853. Dyer maintained good relations with her parents, Caleb French and Nancy Parmenter French, even when he remarried after the customary period of mourning.[32]

Frank Dyer married Maria Davis of Hancock, New Hampshire, the daughter of James Davis and Rebecca Symonds Davis, on September 7, 1854. She was twenty-six, two years younger than her husband, and met the "young, rising physician" on a visit to Gloucester. They stayed there briefly before moving to Annisquam, living first at the Partridge House at the head of Lobster Cove. They then rented, and eventually bought, a house on Leonard Street. One of his wartime letters mentions their first chance meeting in Annisquam and perhaps a stolen kiss in a railroad coach. "How I would like to spend September with you at the old house—but it can't be—and I can only imagine how splendid it would be. I think of it as some years ago when we met there on an occasion which accidentally brought you there, and when you came to live again, but not by accident. . . . That 'little episode' in the cars one morning was a very 'audacious' thing on my part, wasn't it?" It was the beginning of a romance that lasted until his death. Their first child, Franklin (Frankie in his letters), was born in Gloucester on August 29, 1856, and Dyer wrote a number of letters to him.[33]

It is to the second Maria (whose name the family pronounced with a long *i*) that Surgeon Dyer addressed virtually all of his surviving letters. As with most collections of soldiers' correspondence, none of her letters to him have been found. Unlike some famous Civil War wives, Maria was supportive. She became anxious and impatient for her husband to return only in 1864, when questions arose about his original muster date and the length of his obligated service.

Maria did not understand military bureaucracy and red tape, but few soldiers did. Nor could she comprehend why sick and wounded men were not given immediate care and the best of everything. At times she had difficulty understanding Frank's position and title in the Army of the Potomac, his true importance, and his very real responsibilities. He patiently explained to her, for example, that although he had been promoted, first to surgeon in chief of the Third Brigade, and then of the Second Division, of the II Army Corps, he had kept his commission in the Nineteenth Massachusetts. On September 9, 1863, for example, Frank explained to Maria that a Dr. Allen, a mutual acquaintance assigned to a Baton Rouge hospital, was only an assistant surgeon, not a brigade or division surgeon. Brigade surgeon was "a position which the senior surgeon in the brigade always holds, by right of the date of his commission—no appointment is made, but he is such simply by right of seniority. A surgeon in chief of a division is appointed by a general order and is generally the senior one in the division, unless he should not be a proper man. There was one senior to me, but he was not appointed. This is the case unless a 'Surgeon of Volunteers' commissioned by the President is appointed. In the first division, the surgeon in chief is one of these. In the second and third divisions, both are surgeons of regiments."

Maria also relayed the Gloucester news and gossip, some of it malicious, probably from Democratic neighbors. She kept him informed about home-front opinion, although the news irritated him to the point of anger, as occasionally seen in his correspondence to her. In a short letter written from near Harpers Ferry on July 16, 1863, Dyer said of the army at Gettysburg, "We have done all that men could do and now we want to have a rap at the Copperheads," a reference to the recent draft riots in New York and other Northern cities. Five days later he wrote: "One would think to read the Philadelphia papers, about the only ones we get, that Pennsylvania troops fought all the battles—when it is known that they always run away if anybody does. The Philadelphia Brigade in our own Division, is notoriously the most unreliable of any of our troops but at the Gettysburg fight their new General Webb kept them up pretty well. And the Pennsylvania troops at the attack on {the} Morris Island batteries failed to come up to support." The doctor often expressed his opinions about local men serving with him that he omitted from his journal. On July 21, 1863, he wrote Maria that William D. Knapp, a local doctor and assistant surgeon in the Nineteenth Massachusetts, "is not very well, and applied for a leave of absence. . . . He is no sicker than I have been a dozen times, but he don't like this campaigning . . . , he is a mere boy of no account whatever and nobody considers him anything more I find." On July 28 he continued: "I think Will Knapp had better resign—and I think he will. He finds it very uncomfortable I know. He is a timid boy, and they make sport of him." (Knapp failed to keep up with his regiment when it advanced after Gettysburg and was dismissed from the army in December 1863.) Frank told Maria about the war from his perspective. His concern for her and their marriage came across most clearly when he asked her to tell him about her doubts and fears, which were often caused by unpleasant things that she had heard, and not to believe rumors or gossip.[34]

Frank in turn asked about Frankie and Maria's health, which was generally good. When she was sick, he not only sympathized but often took practical steps too. On August 21, 1863, for example, Frank wrote that he thought her recent ailment was piles and that she should bathe with cold water and take the pills for which he sent a prescription. He also cared by mail for his father-in-law, writing him a prescription, enclosed with a letter dated July 17, 1863, for iodide of potassa (one teaspoonful three times daily) and telling Maria that her father should take twenty to twenty-five drops of laudanum at a time if he found it agreed with him. Frank also commented on his wife's exercise, especially when he thought she was overdoing it; her meals; and her financial situation. He did not want Maria taking in boarders in what was, after all, a rented house during the war. But he told her to hire a servant by all means. He felt that they could certainly afford help for her at home on his salary. They were members of the Congregational Church in Gloucester, but Maria may have been somewhat more liberal in her religious views. She frequently attended the Annisquam Village Universalist Church; it was certainly closer to their home. Once she wrote him that the sermon of a Universalist minister had upset her. Frank responded with a critical comment about the sect.[35]

The doctor even commented on Maria's reading and scolded her on one occasion for her juvenile taste in literature. On September 28, 1863, he encouraged her that she "could have a good photograph taken if you would sit in some natural position and not *try* so hard to get a good one. Take one reading, looking at something besides the 'machine' or any way you choose. It is not necessary to sit or stand bold upright, as these operators seem to think." The patriarchal yet loving attitude of a nineteenth-century husband is seen in his letter telling of a visit to Philadelphia relatives, who seeing her photograph thought that Maria was an author. He replied that his wife was not as strong-minded as she looked and wrote Maria of the conversation.[36] Finally, throughout his letters, Frank constantly reassured Maria of his health and well being, of his safe return home, and particularly after Gettysburg, of the certainty of Union victory.

Nowhere, perhaps, was Dyer's innate conservatism and adherence to military tradition more clearly expressed than in a letter after Gettysburg. Of women volunteers in the hospitals there, he repeated stories on August 23 told by Dr. Justin Dwinelle upon his return to the army from the battlefield:

Most of the women quarreled with each other, each whispering very quietly that they didn't want to associate with some others, on account of their reputation not being good. It is singular that each one was the only truly pious and virtuous one in the whole lot. A man wounded in the head wanted her to wash and fix him up a little, as the blood was dried on his face (of course the surgeons cannot go about washing men's faces, and if these women can do anything that is what they can do). "My dear friend," said she, "I will read you a chapter from the Bible and that will do just as well." Rather doubtful.

One night it rained very hard and only a part of the men had been brought under shelter. A lot of the Christian Commission got in one of the large tents and prayed very earnestly for some time that God would stop the rain, and made so much noise about it that the Doctor had to stop them. They could have brought all in in the time they were praying.

These outsiders may have good intentions, but they don't know how to do anything. The Sanitary Commission supply a good deal but the work that all these men and women do about the hospitals does not pay for the time necessarily spent in taking care of them and waiting upon them. They want ambulances to take them to and from their stopping places, men to wait upon them with all manner of things, and will insist that they are doing an immense deal of good. I have got a division hospital—it is neat, clean, well managed and all have enough to eat and drink and I would not have a woman about it for anything. I have heard that one has been threatening to come here, but I will not have her about. Very severe on the ladies I suppose, but I have had enough of them about field hospitals. I see that Miss {Clara} Barton, who was at the Lacy house last December {Fredericksburg} is down at Morris Island. I hope she will stay there, or not come here. She plagued me so that I had to get her out of the cook house and put one of my own men in charge.

Dr. Dyer served from July 1861 until August 28, 1864. He was mustered in on August 3, 1861, and began as the surgeon of the Nineteenth Regiment of Massachusetts Volunteer Infantry. At thirty-five, he was one of its oldest officers. The men came chiefly from Essex and Middlesex Counties, including the towns of Gloucester, Salem, Lowell, Lynn, Newbury, Medford, and Cambridge, as well as Boston, Worcester, and other locations. Dyer rose to become the Third Brigade's surgeon, surgeon in chief of the Second Division

Introduction

(December 3, 1862), and acting medical director of the II Corps. He was on the staff of Generals Oliver O. Howard, John Gibbon, and Winfield Scott Hancock.[37]

Two of Dyer's brothers also wore Union blue. Charles remained in Eastport with his mother and sister, but George enlisted in the Ninth Maine, was promoted to major, and mustered out in 1865 with brevets as a lieutenant colonel and colonel. Family tradition claims William as the regimental surgeon of the Seventh Missouri, serving at Benton Barracks in St. Louis, where he married in July 1861 and settled after the war, dying in Chicago in 1882. Frank's brother-in-law, Heber James Davis (d. 1918), was an officer in the Seventh New Hampshire. George Dyer and Heber Davis, whose units served together in South Carolina and were in Virginia by 1864, are mentioned frequently in Dr. Dyer's journal and letters. There are only occasional references to William, who wrote from Missouri.[38]

After joining the regiment in July 1861, Dyer went with it to Washington and experienced the Ball's Bluff disaster in October. He first began to win a reputation, according to the regimental history, not for his field surgery but in the far more mundane task of suppressing an epidemic of measles that broke out in the Seventh Michigan in the fall of 1861 at Camp Benton, Maryland. He was credited with preventing its spread throughout the brigade.[39]

Dr. Dyer's next major military experience was the Peninsula campaign and the Seven Days, followed by Maj. Gen. George B. McClellan's withdrawal from Richmond to Fort Monroe, where the Nineteenth Massachusetts went by steamship up the Chesapeake Bay and Potomac River to join Maj. Gen. John Pope. Dyer's response to Massachusetts treasurer Henry Kemble Oliver, who had asked the fate of Cpl. Horace Lakeman in the Nineteenth Massachusetts, is in appendix 1. His was one case among the thousands of sick and wounded men overseen by Dr. Dyer, and this is the only letter found written by him to a parent or friend of a soldier, though he mentioned others he had sent in his journal and in letters to Maria.

During the retreat after Second Bull Run, Dyer's assistant surgeon, Dr. John E. Hill of Charlestown, was mortally wounded at his side by friendly fire. Dyer particularly regretted his loss, for few of his assistants proved satisfactory, and most served only briefly.

xxv

The II Corps then marched with the rest of the army to Antietam, where Dyer "went into the fight with our regiment."[40] He watched from the Lacy house as the Seventh Michigan and Nineteenth Massachusetts crossed the Rappahannock to drive Confederate snipers out of Fredericksburg, clearing the way for Maj. Gen. Ambrose Burnside's pontoon-bridge builders in December 1862. Dyer got his first personal leave in January 1863 and visited Maria and Frankie in Hancock, New Hampshire, spending time in Boston as well, before returning to camp. That spring he had breakfast with Maj. Gen. Joseph Hooker and saw him off on his way to Chancellorsville.[41]

The Nineteenth Massachusetts and the Second Division played an important part in the efforts of the II Corps at Gettysburg. After Gen. Robert E. Lee's retreat, Dyer exulted in the victory at Bristoe Station but suffered like most Union soldiers through the extreme cold of the Mine Run campaign. Frank then managed to get his second leave, going home to Gloucester for a visit with Maria and Frankie. Shortly after his return to camp in early 1864, the Nineteenth Massachusetts was granted a regimental furlough for reenlisting, and Dyer went home yet again.[42]

Dr. Dyer returned to camp in time to watch Lt. Gen. Ulysses S. Grant take charge of the war in the East. The II Corps marched into the Wilderness; moved on to Spotsylvania, where Surgeon Dyer saw Hancock greet captured Confederate generals; and fought finally at Cold Harbor. Major Dyer crossed the James with the rest of the army, watched the explosion at the Crater, and bore the pain of hearing that most of his old regiment, fighting along the Weldon Railroad, had been "gobbled—gone to Richmond sure enough." He immediately wrote a letter that was published in Boston defending his veteran unit, arguing that its "gallant conduct . . . on so many battle-fields will more than balance this single disaster."[43] But his Petersburg letters to Maria reflect growing boredom, fatigue, disillusionment, and longings for home.

Dyer's journal and letters are important for several reasons. They are, first, a fine example of an unusual genre. More than a generation ago the editors of *Civil War Books* listed only a handful of published letters and diaries by Union and Confederate surgeons. Such works are still rare in the great body of Civil War accounts. About thirty have been published, most no longer in print, includ-

Introduction

ing such important titles as *John Shaw Billings: A Memoir,* with
details of service in major battles in the East (1862–64), as well
as the Washington medical bureaucracy. Other standard accounts
have been reprinted, such as the *Personal Memoirs of John H. Brinton,* who began with Grant in the West and finished with him in
Virginia, and *One Surgeon's Private War* by Dr. William W. Potter
of the Fifty-seventh New York. Two of the most recent new works
are *A Surgeon's Civil War: The Letters and Diary of Daniel M.
Holt, M.D.* and *Alexander Neil and the Last Shenandoah Valley
Campaign.* Holt was the assistant surgeon of the 121st New York
Volunteers and served from August 1862 to October 1864, when
he resigned because of the onset of tuberculosis. Neil served both
in the Shenandoah Valley and with the Army of the James. *The
Wounded River: The Civil War Letters of John Vance Lauderdale,
M.D.* describes that doctor's service in the West aboard hospital
ships. In his letters to Maria, Dr. Dyer mentioned Lt. John Gard-
ner Perry, surgeon of the Twentieth Massachusetts, several times.
Perry's own account, *Letters from a Surgeon of the Civil War,* is now
regarded as a classic. *Letters of a Civil War Surgeon* has excerpts
from ninety-one letters by Maj. William Watson, with the 105th
Pennsylvania Volunteers from September 1862 to May 1865.

Six Confederate examples include Spencer Glasgow Welch, *A
Confederate Surgeon's Letters to His Wife.* A slim volume like Perry
and Watson's accounts, it is revealing for what Welch saw as the
surgeon of the Thirteenth South Carolina Volunteers, McGowan's
brigade. Lengthier and better known because he rode with Nathan
Bedford Forrest is John Allan Wyeth, *With Sabre and Scalpel.* Other
accounts include *Confederate Surgeon: Civil War Record of Dr.
William L. Scaife,* who served with the Ninth Texas; *A Surgeon with
Stonewall Jackson: The Civil War Letters of Dr. Harvey Black*; and
Confederate Surgeon: The Personal Recollections of E. A. Craighill,
who fought under Jackson as a private and served with Hunter
Holmes McGuire as a hospital steward before being commissioned
as a surgeon. A similar recently published account is *Doctor to the
Front: The Recollections of Confederate Surgeon Thomas Fanning
Wood, 1861–1865.* Wood became interested in medicine while recovering from a fever in a Richmond hospital, and after eight months
of intense preparation he passed a medical exam and became an
assistant surgeon. These fourteen titles are among the best of their

kind and represent a significant fraction of the published accounts by Civil War surgeons.[44]

Even if surgeons' letters and journals were more common, Dyer's would still be valuable for their intrinsic qualities. His letters are lengthy and detailed, colorful and often filled with personal observations, and marked by their good humor and wit. The entries, whether excerpts from letters copied into his journal or the actual surviving letters, are seldom shorter than a page, often considerably longer, and are filled with factual details and Dr. Dyer's judgments and opinions.

And finally, Dyer was lucky as a soldier because he survived, twice escaping death or capture in his final days at Petersburg, not to mention the battles of the previous three years. He was equally fortunate in being attached to the II Corps, which was so often in the right place at the right time, where the fighting was hottest on fields whose names continue to reverberate through our history. Of the II Corps he wrote on October 22, 1863: "Since the Eleventh Corps left the Third is the worst. It might be expected of one commanded by such a man as Dan Sickles. . . . The Second and Sixth are the two corps of the army." His pride in John Gibbon's division is shown by the *New York Times* article after Gettysburg that he sent to Maria and later copied into his journal, reproduced here in appendix 3.

Dyer witnessed in action men still remembered for their courage and devotion to duty. He used his medical instruments as skillfully as they used their weapons, operating on famous generals and obscure privates, saving their lives when he could, though often at the cost of an amputated limb. In the finest medical tradition, he also tended to enemy wounded. At Fair Oaks a captured and unidentified Georgia surgeon assisted him. His comrades in the Nineteenth Massachusetts honored Dyer's memory because of his ability as a doctor and his personal qualities. Students of the Civil War will remember him for what he wrote about our greatest conflict.

Medical historians will be disappointed that there are few details of the operations Dyer performed, other than passing references to an amputation or a bullet removed, especially for generals; but readers familiar with this genre will not be surprised. The technical details of a number of his operations can be found in the *Medical and Surgical History of the Civil War* and are described below. Dyer based his journal on his letters to Maria, not on reports for his professional colleagues. His superior efficiency, intelligence, and ambition, as well as a knack for avoiding military squabbles, made him a fine medical administrator, which is why he rose in less than three years to be acting medical director of the II Corps. His roster of Second Division surgeons (appendix 4), and especially his reports as division surgeon in chief from Antietam to Petersburg, are examples of these qualities. Readers new to the war who peruse the casualty statistics may be staggered as men by the dozens, then hundreds, and finally thousands melt away. More kept coming. The order of regiments changes, a new brigade is added, old surgeons' names vanish, and new ones appear. It goes on and on, a ghastly procession of suffering and death, all recorded in Dyer's cool, precise hand.

Dr. Dyer chose to stay in the field with the II Corps and his old division rather than take a position at a large hospital in the rear. Despite his role as surgeon in chief of the Second Division, he continued to operate on his former comrades in the Nineteenth Massachusetts until the final months of his service, saving lives when possible, easing suffering when that was all he could do. On May 12–13, 1864, Dyer amputated the left leg of Cpl. Archibald Buchanan, Company K, Nineteenth Massachusetts, hit in the knee at Spotsylvania. Buchanan was twenty-eight, from Charlestown, Massachusetts, and enlisted on August 13, 1861, reenlisting on December 31, 1863, like so many of his comrades. He died of his wounds in a general hospital on May 20, 1864. Pvt. J. Kennelly, Company F, 170th New York, wounded at Deep Bottom, August 15, 1864, came to the Second Division's field hospital. Dyer reported a "Fracture of elbow joint. Resection of head of ulna by Surgeon F[rederick] Douglas, 170th New York." Kennelly died at Satterlee General Hospital, Philadelphia, on September 24, 1864.[45] It was the last case reported by Dyer found in the *Medical and Surgical History*. Ten days after writing it up, he left the army.

Frank Dyer was not a desk-bound Washington bureaucrat, but a physician with considerable administrative and some political skills. Yet for him, judging from both his letters and those portions he used in his journal, medicine and its routine procedures and arcane details were secondary to the larger goal of winning the war and saving the Union. That he possessed medical knowledge and ability well above the average is shown by his twenty-six case reports cited in the *Medical and Surgical History* on wounds and injuries of the spine, abdomen, and hip joint; the lower and upper extremities; the rectum; and atrophy of the testis. He described primary amputations at the shoulder, arm, and elbow and secondary amputations of the thigh. [46]

Dr. Dyer also wrote longer reports on scurvy, typhoid and "continued fevers," and chronic rheumatism. His report on scurvy was one of the earliest in the Army of the Potomac's Peninsula campaign and a brave act, for the disease's presence had been denied both at McClellan's headquarters by the surgeon Charles S. Tripler, medical director of the Army of the Potomac, and in Washington. The compilers of the *Medical and Surgical History* noted: "the majority of our volunteer medical officers had . . . at the beginning of the war no personal familiarity with the disease. . . . Surgeon J. F. Dyer, 19th Mass., furnished a report of the condition of his command, showing 18 cases of pronounced scurvy, 100 of the scorbutic taint, and many of diarrhoea which he attributed to the causes of scurvy, inasmuch as it was controlled when the patients had access to a free supply of vegetables." [47]

Following the "scurvy alarm" in the summer of 1862, obscure pains in the muscles, bones, or joints were often attributed to scurvy's onset rather than to chronic rheumatism. Dyer's report on the symptoms and causes of the latter ailment in his regiment was also cited in the *Medical and Surgical History*. His reports were also invaluable to military medical experts trying to distinguish between remittent and continued fevers, or typhoid. "If the practice of keeping clinical records of fever cases had been generally, instead of exceptionally followed," wrote the authors of the *Medical and Surgical History*, "there would have been ample proof that in a large class of cases the symptoms were not such as to indicate with certainty the specific typhoid or malarial origin of the febrile phenomena. Fortunately Surgeon J. F. Dyer, 19th Mass. Vols., has preserved in his regimental case-book a series of sixteen cases which illustrates the difficulty that was frequently experienced in making a diagnosis." They also cited Dyer's reports on the pains in feet and legs resulting from forms of typhoid fever. [48] In the judgment of the most authoritative medical historians of the Civil War, J. Franklin Dyer had proved himself to be a fine regimental surgeon, an excellent medical administrator, and a man with good scientific knowledge

aided by the experience gained from his civilian practice in Gloucester, his own powers of observation, and a healthy skepticism for
bureaucrats and brass.

Dyer's journal, which he completed before the fall of 1866, shows
remarkable restraint for an account based on wartime letters home,
with passages that he selected and transcribed while the conflict was
still fresh in his mind. The doctor omitted some of his criticisms of
various groups and individuals, but even in his letters he generally
displayed more rancor and bitterness against Copperheads and stay
at homes than toward his Confederate foes. He recognized Jackson's
merits as a man and what his loss might mean to the South in an
entry written shortly after Stonewall's death. Dyer thought that
Robert E. Lee was an intelligent and dangerous opponent. And he
gave full credit to the fighting abilities of Confederate infantry. Yet
this veteran of the Army of the Potomac doggedly defended Maj.
Gen. George Meade after Gettysburg and never quite lost hope. His
pride and confidence in his regiment, brigade, division, and corps
were honest and based on his own experience and observations.
Dyer had little regard for those who lacked such experience but
who spoke knowingly about the war. In his letter of November 24,
1863, he dismissed Edward Everett's Gettysburg oration as marred
by major errors, observing that "it takes years to get at the facts of
history and in ten or fifteen years from now the history of this war
will be written."

Of course, Dyer had served on the winning side. The Union
had been preserved. The frustrations, defeats, and some would say,
failure of Reconstruction were all still in the future. "Waving the
bloody shirt" was less common immediately after the war than it
would be later, and most veterans, like Frank Dyer, were too busy
resuming their normal lives to be consumed by bitterness.

Dr. Dyer ended his journal by quoting from the final sentence of
the Gettysburg Address. Before the earliest excerpts from his letters,
he began with a preface whose language is somewhat reminiscent
of the tone in Lincoln's Second Inaugural. Frank Dyer's journal is
an account by a Maine man and a Massachusetts doctor who tried
to do his duty in our Civil War.

Note on Editorial Method

Two volumes of J. Franklin Dyer's antebellum letters are known to have survived, those for the 1840s and the 1850s. All but a few of his wartime letters were taped into a third volume, a hardbound scrapbook. Four that he wrote to Maria (three of them from the Chesapeake Hospital in Hampton) on November 5, 6, 8, and 10, 1864, and one from her brother George (Morris Island, South Carolina, July 23, 1863), are loose, along with an envelope sent to her addressed in Frank's handwriting, bearing a penciled notation. Most of the war letters were written in ink, but a number are in pencil, and many of the latter are badly faded. The text of many is obscured or unreadable because of the masking tape used to secure the letters or overlapping paper from another letter or the scrapbook's signatures. In such cases, the obstruction was carefully pulled away so that the full text of the letter could be transcribed. The first of the letters was dated June 27, 1863, near Poolesville, Maryland, in the early days of the Gettysburg campaign. Dyer wrote the last of the bound letters to Maria from Reams Station, Weldon Railroad, on August 25, 1864.

This edition has only the text of the postwar journal that Dr. Dyer made based upon his letters to his wife. Dyer wrote it in a beautiful script, probably in the first seven months of 1866 as indicated by the misdated entry for December 5, 1862, which bears that year. The text fills 365 lined pages in a handsome, green, leather-bound volume. His letters of recommendation fill seven pages; his roster of medical officers, three; his casualty reports, eleven; and the *New York Times* article, eight. He wrote the journal entirely in ink. Dyer completed it soon after August 1866, around the time of the fall elections as shown by the final pages, which describe his abortive appointment as Gloucester's postmaster on the third of that month.[1] He related this bitter personal incident, one that reveals much about Massachusetts politics during Reconstruction, in the last pages of the journal, which is a kind of postwar afterword.

Dr. Dyer based his account almost entirely on extracts from his wartime letters, beginning in August 1861. His entries were pared not only of salutations and closings, of most personal and family references, but also of many details about the war, including the mundane routine of camp life and his own observations, particularly comments about generals as well as his fellow officers, both staff and field. This latter category includes some of the most interesting insights about the personalities of Union officers and events of the war. Wherever appropriate, particularly striking passages have been placed in the notes with appropriate references.

The appendixes include a letter Dyer wrote from the Peninsula to an important Massachusetts politician explaining his treatment of a wounded man, a widow's son, from a prominent Salem family. All of the Gettysburg material has been included, both the journal excerpts from his letters and in appendix 2 the original letters, for there are important differences in the two versions. Dyer was under terrific strain and pressure during and immediately after the battle and probably thought the Gettysburg letters were not as coherent or well written as his others. But they are especially vivid and like all the others contain material omitted from the journal, while the journal entries have details not included in the letters, which Dyer remembered as he wrote his memoir. Both make interesting reading for anyone who cares about the battle of July 1–3, 1863.

Also included in the journal entries are the relatively few occasions where the doctor inserted bracketed material as commentary on a letter he was transcribing. Such insertions are brief and usually of an explanatory nature. This additional later material is marked by the regular brackets that Dyer used as a modern editor would and appears in the text of the journal entries in the same place where he inserted the addition. For this reason, I have used {curved brackets} for my own rare editorial insertions, which I have kept to a minimum. No words written by Dyer in the journal have been omitted, and no language has been added except as noted above.

The journal required little editing, but it is not meant to be a facsimile edition. I have tried to make the journal into a smooth narrative accessible to any general reader interested in American history. Dyer very rarely crossed out or erased words or letters in his inked entries. The occasional omissions of punctuation have been supplied. A very few omissions of letters and articles, as well as spelling errors, have been silently corrected. To indicate his own omissions of material from his letters, I have used the less intrusive modern ellipsis in place of the "XXX" that Dyer used. The spelling and punctuation have been regularized. Capitalization follows modern lower-case style. (These changes also have been made to the letters in the appendixes.) Dyer wrote so well that little of the flavor of his prose has been lost by my few minor changes to the text of his journal.

CHAPTER 1

"A Blunder Has Been Made"

July 1861–March 21, 1862

Lincoln called for regiments of three-year volunteers early in May 1861, but it was more than two weeks before Massachusetts governor John A. Andrew received authorization to enlist six new regiments. The Commonwealth had furnished five regiments of three-month men, but they were insufficient to deal with the crisis. Andrew won permission to raise additional regiments in mid-June. The Nineteenth Massachusetts was one of ten new regiments recruited, the third group from the Bay State. [1]

Frank Dyer offered his services just before First Bull Run. His early army experience was typical of Union soldiers from the Northeast, especially those serving in what became the Army of the Potomac. After initial training at Camp Schouler in Lynnfield, the regiment went by train to Boston, then on to Fall River, where it caught a steamer for New York City. They continued by train via Philadelphia and Baltimore to Washington, camped briefly in the area, and marched to the vicinity of Rockville, Maryland. The regiment was in this area, as far west as Harpers Ferry, until the Peninsula campaign. Dr. Dyer's only real battle experience was the disaster at Ball's Bluff in October. He watched Rebel pickets, treated camp diseases, and suffered from a fever himself. He recorded changes in the officers and the reorganization of the brigade, made up of the Nineteenth and Twentieth Massachusetts, the Seventh Michigan, and the Forty-second New York.

July 1861

Obedient to the will of their political leaders, the South raised the standard of rebellion. The people of the North rose to overcome it. Whatever errors may have been committed in the beginning in

1

failing to appreciate the magnitude of the undertaking, they were alike shared by all, both North and South.

The three months' regiments had been sent forward, but it was soon discovered that they were insufficient, and a call was made for three years' troops. One or more regiments were to be raised in Essex County.[2] I considered this a just and righteous war on our part, and I should not be doing my duty if I did not take part in it.

On the seventeenth of July I called upon Dr. William J. Dale, surgeon general of Massachusetts, who received me cordially and assured me that he would call upon me when my services were needed in the capacity of surgeon.[3] In a few days I was appointed (after examination) acting surgeon of the Nineteenth Regiment.

Proceeding to Lynnfield on the twenty-fourth, I found a few companies which had not been inspected or mustered into the service.[4] The Seventeenth Regiment was encamped on the same ground, the whole under command of Colonel Dyke.[5] A few days after, assisted by Dr. William H. W. Hinds, who had been detailed as acting assistant surgeon, I commenced the examination of the men in camp, rejecting such as were found unfit.[6]

Going home occasionally to see my family, I took up my quarters in camp, sleeping in a large tent on the field, common to several officers, and messed with Colonel Dyke and others — a very pleasant company.

Colonel Hinks of the Eighth Regiment, Massachusetts Volunteer Militia, was appointed colonel, and A. F. Devereux, lieutenant colonel, Henry J. Howe of Haverhill having been appointed major, and John C. Chadwick of Salem, adjutant.[7] Levi Shaw of Rockport was also appointed quartermaster.[8] Some of the officers were on the ground, others recruiting.

Dr. J. N. Willard was transferred to the Nineteenth as assistant surgeon in place of Dr. Hinds, transferred to the Seventeenth.[9] Recruits gradually came in, and the business of drilling and preparation for service went briskly on.

Mrs. Dyer and Frank having gone to Hancock after a day's visit at Lynnfield, my home was thenceforth "in the field."[10] The following narrative is made up of extracts from letters.

Lynnfield
August 19, 1861
You will probably see an order in today's paper to have all regiments and parts of regiments ready to leave forthwith. So we are ordered to be ready to go on Thursday next. . . . The adjutant general has been down all day, and all the officers of the Seventeenth have been appointed. Colonel Hinks had been telegraphed to return immediately. Both regiments are filling up fast.

Lynnfield
August 23, 1861
Now about eleven o'clock at night. I sit down in our almost deserted quarters to tell you what we are doing. The Seventeenth has gone. It has been a very busy day. At two o'clock the tents were struck — the men had their haversacks filled, their knapsacks and equipments put on, and at five o'clock were brought into line. Prayers and speeches were made, rum was drunk (brought in by friends of the men), and numbers of them were drunk in an hour. Some had to be left behind. Our guard has picked up a number of stragglers and will keep them till we go. The Nineteenth cooked supper for the regiment, and they got off at about eight o'clock. The camp ground looks like a battlefield after a fight. The ground strewn with all sorts of "traps" which had accumulated there. [11]

At dress parade tonight the roster of officers was read.* A good many have been left out and others appointed. Colonel Hinks made a few remarks, and hoped we should get along pleasantly together. A chaplain will be elected tomorrow. Thousands have visited the field today — a perfect jam.

We are off tomorrow, Monday. Things are going on pretty well, and I hope we shall get off without the confusion that attended the departure of the Seventeenth.

* We received our commissions, dated August 22.

Meridian Hill, Washington
September 1, 1861
Arrived here last evening, in the city the night before. [12] We are in a beautiful place, overlooking the city, two miles from the Capitol. I wrote you a brief note this morning mentioning our arrival here. We

left Lynnfield Wednesday afternoon, came round through Salem and Lynn, and after a short stay on the Common in Boston, where we got nothing to eat, left for Fall River about eight o'clock in the evening. [13] Took the boat in the night and arrived in New York two o'clock Thursday P.M. [14] Had an excellent dinner in the park. That for the officers was particularly good—speeches, etc. Arrived in Amboy during the night—poor cars—no sleep, but in Philadelphia, where we arrived before daylight, a good breakfast awaited us near the depot, where they feed all the troops passing through. [15] Six regiments were fed in one night—all free. [16]

Leaving Philadelphia in the morning, we marched through Baltimore in the afternoon. [17] On entering the city there was considerable enthusiasm among the poorer classes, but in the better part of the city all was quiet. Saw but two flags and heard no cheers. A good many friends of the officers however came to the depot.

After some hours delay in landing, owing to the great number of troops arriving, we went to the barracks near the depot, and at two o'clock I laid down on the floor with the colonel and several other officers. Some slept out of doors. Next afternoon marched to the hill where we are now encamped.

September 2, 1861
Today getting our hospital in order. Visited the city to get blanks and to report to the surgeon general. Visited some regiments about us. On the other side of the river they have frequent skirmishes with the Rebel pickets. Our regiment is getting to work drilling. I find the officers generally well disposed.

September 4, 1861
A great stir about us last night. Regiments moving here and there, and reports of fighting abound. We are getting something better to eat. The men live well—if they do not it is their own fault. They have enough. [18]

September 8, 1861
Took a walk about a mile this afternoon—as far as we went the fields were dotted with tents. It is estimated that over one hundred thousand troops are encamped in and about the city.

September 13, 1861
Started yesterday for Poolesville, are now near Rockville, in General Lander's brigade. [19]

September 19, 1861
When I last wrote you, I was on the road. Since our arrival here I have not been well enough to write. Have kept my tent four days. Hope to be about soon.

September 21, 1861
This is the first day I have sat up. My intense headache never left me until this morning. Never suffered more in one week in my life [bilious remittent fever]. [20] Dr. Willard is sick also. Dr. Crosby, brigade surgeon, was over. [21] Dr. Bryant, formerly of the Twentieth, was over and reported himself brigade surgeon. [22] Had a good batch of letters from you today, which had a good deal to do toward my recovery.

Camp Benton near Poolesville
September 27, 1861
The health of our regiment is good—have nine in hospital, and six others off duty. [23] The Seventh Michigan, near us, have sixty in hospital. [24] Yesterday one of their captains died of typhoid fever. None of our Massachusetts regiments have suffered at this rate. Quite a stir in camp, on the arrival of Lieutenant Bishop with thirty-two recruits for the Zouaves and a band of twenty-four pieces. [25]

September 29, 1861
For the first time in a fortnight put on my uniform and appeared at Sunday morning inspection. [26] A cold night last night. With a couple of blankets and an overcoat could hardly keep warm. Have had letters from some officers of the Seventeenth requesting me to get exchanged into their regiment. I think I shall not do so. They will undoubtedly enjoy themselves in Baltimore, but I came out to see service and think they will not see much. [27]

October 4, 1861
More than half our men are down at the river. Some shells have been thrown back and forth. [28]

October 5, 1861
Woodchoppers are detailed from various regiments and it looks as though we were to stay a while.

Camp Benton
October 7, 1861
Went down to the river today to see some sick. Rebel pickets in sight, but no firing took place. Our men were talking across. They, the Rebels, say they wish the war was over. All they ask is to be "let alone." I think likely our troops will be put across the river in a few days. We have everything ready — cavalry, artillery, and infantry, probably 20,000 to 30,000 men within three hours call. What Generals Banks or Stone are waiting for I don't know.[29] If Lander had his way we should cross within twenty-four hours.

October 9, 1861
Last night General Lander ordered the companies remaining in camp to the river, as the Rebels had taken possession of Selden's Island and driven our pickets in.[30] We marched to Edwards Ferry and down the towpath about a mile, accompanied by Andrews Sharpshooters, armed with telescopic rifles.[31] Here we remained until morning, shivering with cold. Edwards Ferry is a village of two or three houses, a store, and toll house.

Camp Benton
October 11, 1861
Have had the band out today, drilling them in the use of the ambulances. These, with one man from each company, are employed as an ambulance corps, and I drill them an hour a day.

October 15, 1861
General Lander went to Washington several days since and has not yet returned. Went up the river yesterday. The enemy are moving one way or another all the time.

October 19, 1861
Was down to the river today. A movement is on foot. Our troops have crossed to the Virginia shore, without opposition. A brisk musketry fire was heard toward evening, but all is now quiet.

Camp Benton
October 24, 1861

I will tell you more fully about the affair at Ball's Bluff and Harrison's Island.[32] Our pickets have occupied the Maryland shore for several weeks and about ten days ago occupied the island, which is a stone's throw from the Virginia shore, on which rises a very steep hill covered with trees. At this point the crossing was made.

The Fifteenth Massachusetts crossed first, followed by the Twentieth, some of Baker's California regiment, and the Tammany regiment, with one of Vaughn's Rhode Island guns and two howitzers.[33] These guns were dragged up the hill and lost there. The fight lasted from 11:00 A.M. till 6:00 P.M., the enemy being most of the time concealed. After being terribly cut up our men retreated. The only means of crossing was by two scows, most of the time but one, and at last that was sunk and many drowned.[34] Others were drowned swimming the river. Many were taken prisoners. Some hundred or more wounded were brought across during the fight, and the bodies of some officers. The Nineteenth were about crossing when the retreat commenced. Nine companies were here — Co. K at Edwards Ferry with Major Howe. Two companies of the Twentieth did not cross, and two were at Edwards Ferry.

The half-naked and unarmed remnant of the Fifteenth and Twentieth were sent across to the Maryland shore, and all night the wounded and stragglers were going. Colonel Lee, Adjutant Revere, and Asst. Surgeon Revere of the Twentieth were made prisoners.[35] Colonel Hinks was ordered to hold the island at all hazards. The Tammany regiment crossed to the Maryland shore in spite of remonstrance. We had there about seven hundred men on the island with three of Captain Vaughn's guns. Lieutenant Dodge crossed with a flag of truce, and a party was permitted to cross and bury the dead.[36] Some of our wounded were also brought. Our only means of communication with the Virginia shore was a small skiff (the same one in which I crossed to the island the night before with orders from General Stone to Colonel Hinks).

The surgeons of the other regiments having left in the morning, I remained to attend to the wounded, which we were allowed to bring across. Colonel Burt of the Eighteenth Mississippi told Captain Vaughn that a surgeon would be permitted to cross and attend to the wounded still remaining.[37] On preparing to cross I was told by

Colonel Burt that I should be held as a prisoner, when I declined to cross. He was not well pleased and expressed a great desire to shoot me. He was unquestionably drunk.

The conditions of the truce were that all firing should cease and that no troops be permitted to cross to or from the Maryland shore. We threw up some entrenchments, which they objected to and threatened to shell us. [Captain Thurman, of the Twentieth Mississippi, captured at Fredericksburg in 1862, told me they would have fired on us from the captured pieces, but none of them understood the use of shell.[38] He stated also that their troops consisted of one brigade, under General Evans, and that they scarcely knew whether to attribute their good success to skill on their part or blundering on ours.[39]]

At dark, orders were received to evacuate the island. As soon as Captain Vaughn returned, we sent the artillery across. This was a difficult job. The banks were steep and muddy, and the night was dark. Three guns with caissons and thirty-six horses were transported in two or three hours. All property was removed, the dead buried, and the troops were all over about three o'clock in the morning, giving the Rebels a parting salute of four shells.

We reached our old camp before day, muddy, tired, and hungry. It had rained for more than twenty-four hours. In the meantime, skirmishing was going on at Edwards Ferry. Co. K and our sharp-shooters were there and did well. This morning all our troops have crossed, and *this* fight is over.

A blunder has been made, but who is to blame nobody appears to know. General Lander, who has hastened from Washington on learning of the movement, was wounded in the leg at Edwards Ferry and is now at his quarters near us.

In crossing to the island I left my horse on the Maryland shore in care of one of our men. After remaining there twenty-four hours I returned to find he had been taken away. (I afterward found him in possession of Lieutenant Young, quartermaster of Baker's California regiment, and recovered him.[40])

Camp Benton
October 29, 1861
The nights are very cold now. Most of the men have built furnaces in their tents, made by digging a trench in the ground under the tent,

covering it with stones, and making a chimney of a barrel. Many of the men are suffering from severe colds, contracted by exposure and want of thick underclothing.

November 8, 1861
As I expected, Colonel Hinks has made a disturbance by the publication of his report on the Ball's Bluff affair. General Stone censured him in a special order for reflecting on the Tammany regiment. But he told the truth.[41] Many do not hesitate to charge General Stone with something more than incompetence.

November 16, 1861
We have had a very severe storm of wind and rain. If our tent pins had not been frozen in we should have all been upset. We are making great preparations for Thanksgiving.

Camp Benton
November 23, 1861
Our Thanksgiving is over and we have got things about "cleaned up." Had a very good time. Had thirty from Baltimore, sixteen of them ladies. Had an excellent dinner—speeches by General Stone, Colonel Hinks, Colonel Devens, Lt. Colonel Devereux, Lt. Colonel Palfrey, Mr. Howard of the *N. Y. Times*, Mr. William D. Miller, and Colonel Bruce of Baltimore.[42] In the evening a ball to which a good many officers of neighboring regiments came, with some of the citizens. Turkeys and geese were procured, sufficient for the whole regiment.

November 28, 1861
The weather is bad, and there is a good deal of sickness in consequence, but the number of cases of fever does not increase. We have a large log hospital nearly completed, but so far fever cases do better in tents.

December 3, 1861
Our regiment is bound for the neighborhood of Darnestown tomorrow.[43] We are to picket the river between Great Falls and Seneca to build blockhouses on the river and remain for the winter.[44] We are having very cold weather.

Camp near Muddy Branch
December 7, 1861

Have again "set up housekeeping." Marched here from Camp Benton, about twelve miles, leaving two companies on the river as pickets. Getting here after dark there was no time for pitching tents, but no one appears to have suffered from sleeping out. We are on the ground occupied by Banks's division, which left for Frederick City the day before we came.

We are about two miles from Darnestown, a small place, from which so many dispatches all summer assured us that "all was quiet on the Potomac." The country "about yere" as the people say, is thinly settled. There has been a good deal of heavy firing in the direction of Dranesville.[45] I have located the hospital about a mile from camp, occupying a dwelling house and a schoolhouse near. One or both of us visit it every day, and I visit the stations on the river every two or three days. Dr. Willard and I have pitched our tents together and have a small stove. We mess, with the rest of the field and staff, in a small house near.

Muddy Branch
December 10, 1861

Rode to Poolesville yesterday, twelve miles, very warm. General Stone had a review of the Van Alen cavalry and Second Rhode Island Artillery.[46] Our band plays very well, and our morning and evening parades are quite pleasant. The regiment is very well drilled. Our new uniforms have come — no blankets or overcoats yet. Most of the men are now at work getting out timber for the blockhouses or on picket, so the "new clothes" will not be given out yet. The men look quite ragged.

January 2, 1862

Went to Rockville yesterday, where Co. A is stationed, quartered in the building on the agricultural fair grounds. Found one man sick with measles. Visited Judge Bowie's, a little out of the village, where Mrs. Hinks is stopping for a few days.[47] It was a splendid day — mercury 68 in the shade.

January 8, 1862

Went to Washington Sunday P.M. with men for discharge—returned next day—a cold ride—and next day a ride to Rockville to see some sick men.

January 15, 1862

Have had bad weather—snow, rain, ice, and snow again, with crust, and our encampment looks like a picture of Valley Forge. Six teams arrived tonight with blankets and clothing. Our men have something to grumble about, I acknowledge, but they are sometimes a little unreasonable. The ration of food is large, some companies making quite a saving. We have built a bakery and supply the regiment with soft bread.

Muddy Branch
January 28, 1862

The colonel's little boy died yesterday at Rockville. In the morning I took a ride there with the major and chaplain, but on our arrival found he had just died. [48]

February 2, 1862

Day by day we go through about the same routine. I rise at surgeon's call, which is at seven-thirty o'clock. This I always attend. Sunday morning inspection at eight o'clock, first of men and arms in line, and then inspection of quarters, which occupies us nearly all the forenoon. This inspection I make and report the condition of quarters to the colonel.

February 6, 1862

Today a snowstorm and Captain Wass had the "Tigers" out at skirmish drill. [49] Then dress parade—a dark line on the white snow. In the evening a concert in "the house" by members of Co. K.

February 10, 1862

Quite pleasant to stand in front of my tent this morning in the warm sunshine and witness "guard mounting." This is a very pretty performance, and our band, led by Rimback, plays very well. [50]

February 19, 1862

General Stone is placed in arrest.[51] No one seems surprised. Our new general, Sedgwick, will take command of the division today.[52] By order of General McClellan we are to use increased vigilance until next Sunday morning, and the impression is that as soon as the roads are in good condition the Army of the Potomac will move.

February 23, 1862

Our brigade is now reorganized, consisting of the Nineteenth and Twentieth Massachusetts, Seventh Michigan, and Forty-second New York, the Tammany regiment. Colonel Dana of the First Minnesota is appointed brigadier general and is to have command.[53] Surgeon Dougherty is to be brigade surgeon.[54]

February 26, 1862

Everybody and everything appears to be moving except our regiment. General Sedgwick has gone with General Gorman and the First Brigade, and General Dana is at Poolesville.[55] Most of the troops have gone to Harpers Ferry or thereabouts. Rode to Poolesville today with Colonel Hinks, Lt. Colonel Devereux, the chaplain, Winslow, Adjutant Chadwick, and Quartermaster Shaw. Dined with General Dana and staff. A new set of men here. Since Stone's arrest, his A.A.G., Capt. Charles Stewart (Lord Vane Tempest), has resigned.[56]

Muddy Branch
March 3, 1862

We hear tonight of General Lander's death. He was a man of great energy and activity. The inaction of the Army of the Potomac is making some officers restless. I don't think McClellan is as great a favorite as three months ago. Secretary Stanton's letters, one concerning Fort Donelson, and the other to Lander, seem a good deal like censure on someone.[57]

March 9, 1862

We shall leave here in a few days. Every preparation has been made. Leesburg is in our hands.[58]

Harpers Ferry
March 12, 1862
Our first great movement has taken place. The breaking up of a winter camp is quite an event. The mass of property of all kinds on hand, for which no transportation can be had, must be disposed of, the sick provided for, etc. At daylight I commenced my duties, sent some fifty sick to the river, with hospital property for transportation to Edwards Ferry by canal, where I left some by order and took others to a temporary hospital at old Camp Benton. Our regiment with others had gone to Harpers Ferry in canal boats, and at eleven o'clock at night, having been in the saddle all day, I started for Harpers Ferry with Dr. Willard. Our solitary ride of twenty-five miles was relieved only by the glare of the burning picket stations on the towpath, and at sunrise, tired and sleepy, we entered Harpers Ferry, where we found our regiment.

Bolivar Heights
March 21, 1862
Came up here on the twelfth, and soon after received orders to march to Winchester to Banks's assistance.[59] Went as far as Berryville and then returned, making a very uncomfortable trip of three days.[60] The people are strongly secesh hereabouts. As we marched through Charlestown, the scene of old John Brown's execution, a woman put her head out of the window and spitefully called out, "Who are you going to kill now, you devils?" But the bands played, and the men sung the John Brown chorus, and the secesh windows went down with a smash. This is a muddy, cheerless place—but one or two pleasant days since we came here—this morning it snows. Have had no mail for twelve days but get papers. We are impatient to be gone out of this.

CHAPTER 2

"We Have Been Obliged to Retreat"

March 26–August 27, 1862

The Peninsula campaign was Dr. Dyer's first major military experience. Here he began to display the administrative talents that served him and the Union so well. Dyer's brigade traveled from Harpers Ferry to Washington, then by steamer to Fort Monroe via the abandoned resort at Point Lookout, Maryland. The army advanced past the battlefield of Big Bethel to Yorktown. Dyer recorded with elation the occupation of the Rebel entrenchments in early May. He went up the York River to West Point by steamer and mentioned both the battle of Williamsburg and a "sharp fight" at Eltham's Landing. At West Point, Surgeon Dyer first began to care for large numbers of sick and wounded men, arranging their food, lodging, and transportation and making decisions about who would stay and who would be sent to hospitals in the North. By the time of Fair Oaks, he was treating thousands rather than dozens or hundreds of men. He also diagnosed the growing presence of scurvy in the ranks and had his first serious encounter with the military and medical bureaucracy at General McClellan's headquarters and in Washington. Summing up the Seven Days, he called McClellan's change of base to Harrison's Landing a "retreat." Dyer and much of the army marched back down the Peninsula. Arriving at Newport News, the army embarked on steamers for the voyage up the Potomac near the end of August.

Washington
March 26, 1862
Were ordered while at Bolivar to be ready to march at daylight on Monday; then to wait further orders.[1] Then to be ready at eight o'clock Monday morning to cross the bridge at Harpers Ferry—marched down, awaited further orders. Banks had had a

fight at Winchester and might need our help.[2] At eleven o'clock were marched to Sandy Hook to take the cars — cars had not come — stacked arms and remained until two o'clock in the morning — very dark. I varied the monotony by falling in a culvert and getting covered with mud from head to foot. Two or three others performed the same feat. But at last we got off, reaching Washington in the afternoon. Stopped that night in the large barracks near the depot — slept on the floor as a luxury. Next day marched to a field east of the Capitol and pitched tents — soon orders came to be ready to go on board transports.

Point Lookout
March 30, 1862
Same day marched to the river and embarked on steamer *North America*.[3] Next morning took two schooners in tow and headed downriver in company with a large fleet of transports containing men, horses, artillery, etc.; the Army of the Potomac bound for the Peninsula. When ten miles below Point Lookout, our heavily loaded old steamer came near foundering, so cast off the schooners and made the best of our way back to Point Lookout for shelter. Next forenoon, during a snowstorm, landed and took possession of the large unoccupied hotel, where we remained all night and had a very comfortable rest.[4] Music and ten pins varied the monotony. Now on board again.

Hampton, Va.
April 1, 1862
Landed at Fortress Monroe at ten o'clock. Marched to Hampton, where we bivouacked just beyond the ruins of the village.[5] The number encamped about here is very large — probably over 100,000 — an army large enough to go *anywhere* in this country. Saw the *Monitor*, keeping watch for the *Merrimac*.[6]

Camp near Yorktown
April 10, 1862
Leaving behind at Hampton all but the most necessary articles of baggage, and a few tents for the use of officers, we marched here on Friday. Halted in the woods near Little Bethel while Heintzelman's division passed us.[7] Here General McClellan came up with his

staff and a few cheers were given. Reached Great Bethel in the evening. Got some corn pone at a shanty near, and after a short sleep on the ground took up our line of march at five in the morning. Halted at Howard's Branch, where there are extensive earthworks and barracks abandoned the night before.[8] Amid rain and mud arrived on this ground Saturday. McClellan's headquarters near. The army is in three columns, General Porter on the right, General Sumner in the center, and General Keyes on the left.[9]

Monday morning, dull and cold, our regiment with the Twentieth and Andrews Sharpshooters ordered out on a reconnaissance, some three or four miles. When near the enemy's position deployed the regiment and advanced through the woods. When in sight the Rebs opened with shot and shell. Our men returned it and then retired, the Rebels yelling like devils. Then moved down some distance and came out in front of another battery, where we were engaged some time. One man killed, and some half dozen wounded. Rain began near dark, when we set out on our return, the men wading these dismal swamps knee deep in water, pitch dark, carrying wounded on stretchers. At camp, no shelter; rained all night and all next day. We have five tents, in which as many of the officers as possible crowd. The men have not yet received their shelter tents and are suffering for want of them. Large numbers of men are employed in building corduroy roads, on which to transport artillery. Our officers and men feel rather blue at their hard usage, but pleasant weather will put a more cheerful face on affairs.

We have bestowed unnecessary pity on the "poor Rebels" and think we can starve them out. This is one of the "fallacies of the age." Their barracks, about a mile below us, are fitted up very comfortably, much superior to those built by the Army of the Potomac last winter.

Camp near Yorktown
April 13, 1862
Our army lies in front of the enemy, their line of defense stretching from Warwick River across the Peninsula to somewhat above Ship Point, varying the direction to conform to the natural defenses of the country.[10] All along this line are batteries, some of them quite heavy. Our artillery, especially field, is much stronger than theirs. I think we might have gone into Yorktown a week ago much easier than now. We have been lying through a storm of more than a week without

tents, and the weather is quite cold. Tents were left behind in order to enable us to move with more rapidity, but I have seen no rapid movements yet. There does not seen to be as much enthusiasm in the Army as there was, and McClellan is by no means worshiped, except perhaps by some of the old regulars.

Today, Sunday, an inspection of our division ordered at eleven o'clock. It is now four and our turn has not come yet. The men have been in line for hours. "Little Mac's" piety is about "played out."

Camp near Yorktown
April 17, 1862
We have better weather now, and thousands are employed in road making. We moved forward about two miles today, and our men are employed building batteries. On the left, Brooks's Vermont Brigade met with a severe repulse. [11]

Camp near Yorktown
April 19, 1862
Under arms all night. Today our regiment supporting batteries. A desultory artillery fire is kept up on both sides. At night we withdraw our artillery to the rear of the batteries. After supper we lay down to sleep, soothed by the screaming of shell, cracking of rifles, buzzing of mosquitoes, and biting of wood ticks.

Camp near Yorktown
April 24, 1862
Have been out nearly every day and night in front with the regiment, but for the past two days have had a touch of remittent. [12] Better today. Our brigade now goes out on picket every other day and remains twenty-four hours, without fires, rain or shine, and it has rained more than half the days we have been out. Intervening days working parties are detailed to build roads and fortifications. Last Sunday called out and stood all day in the rain. Next day on picket, it rained again, and all night.

It does not appear to be General McClellan's object to push matters until General McDowell is farther advanced. [13] After it is all over perhaps I shall be satisfied that all is right. I don't see it now. Captain Bartlett of the Twentieth was hit in the knee by a minié ball—amputation necessary. [14]

Camp near Yorktown
April 26, 1862
Turned out last night on account of an alarm on the right. The Massachusetts First made a sortie and took some rifle pits, but had to abandon them; three killed and twenty-three wounded. Don't know who orders these smart things, but suppose they are a part of the "great plan" we hear so much about.[15] Nothing has yet been accomplished here and much time will have to be spent in preparation. Sharp firing takes place once in a while, but we are getting used to it.

Camp near Yorktown
May 2, 1862
Were turned out this morning at three o'clock. The whole army was under arms at the same time. At six o'clock ordered to take off equipments. Telegraph lines connect the whole army and all are ordered out at the same moment, then to stack arms, then to eat breakfast, then take off equipments, or march out, as the case may be, all doing the same thing at the same time. When General McClellan smokes the whole army is supposed to light their pipes.

Nine o'clock, May 3, on picket. Dr. Willard and I are stretched out under our little shelter tent in rear of the battery. The booming of cannon and whizzing of shell keep sleep away. During the intervals of firing I hear the Rebel bands playing "Dixie." Frogs, whippoorwills, and owls put in the filling.

Camp near Yorktown
May 4, 1862
Hurrah! We have been in the Rebel works. They evacuated them last night. Our regiment was in the first on the center.[16] I have been two miles back in their camps, found tents pitched, fires burning, and food cooking. We are back in camp, awaiting orders to march.

Yorktown
May 6, 1862
Marched yesterday morning, halted, marched again, halted in a field. At five o'clock marched again in the rain to the place of embarkation, about two miles. Went a mile, then halted in the mud

and rain and darkness five hours. Brigades and divisions went by, infantry, cavalry, and artillery. Then we moved forward, and when we laid down in the outer works, wet and supperless, it was three o'clock in the morning. At six o'clock marched to the beach.

This place, insignificant as a village, is great as a fortification, and large stores of artillery and ammunition were found.[17] But the cowards buried shell in the roads and fortifications, just beneath the ground, so that a step or the weight of a wheel would explode them. Some of them did explode, but dangerous places were discovered and marked.[18]

West Point

The Nineteenth and Twentieth went on board the *Vanderbilt*, and arrived at West Point in the evening.[19] Disembarked in the morning. The river full of steamers, vessels, and barges, and boats passing to and from the shore all day—a grand sight. We landed on a plain, bordered by woods, when our advance met the enemy in the woods, and a sharp fight ensued. I had a good view of the field, and afterward assisted in the care of the wounded, none of whom however belonged to our brigade.

Eltham, Pamunkey River
May 13, 1862

Have been here several days, a good landing on the Pamunkey River, a narrow but deep stream, now filled by steamers and vessels.[20] As we marched from West Point they were burying the dead in trenches. It was quite a sharp fight.[21] The engagement at Williamsburg was also severe. The papers do not state our loss correctly. I have reason to believe that we lost 2,400 in killed and wounded.[22] Our division ambulance train, which has been employed there, has just come up. Sick and wounded are as soon as possible transferred to general hospital, and as regimental surgeons are employed principally in the field, they rarely see their patients but a few times.

Bread, beef, and pork are plenty, of course, but everything else is very high. Butter 50 cents to $1.00. Hams $5.00 to $6.00 apiece. Shad (caught in the river) 75 cents. Cheese 40 cents.

Cumberland
May 17, 1862

Marched here, ten miles in a drenching rain, over the worst of roads, the mud knee deep.[23] Men fell out badly on the march. Halted near night in thick woods, where we now are, our teams twenty-four hours behind stuck in the mud. It is quite pleasant today. Have been down to the river with a number of sick whom I put on board the hospital boat. This business of moving is very perplexing. I have to decide who is sick and who not, who shall be conveyed and who shall march, and our means of transportation are very limited. General McClellan's headquarters fill twenty-six wagons.

The little shelter tents pitched in regular lines in the woods look pretty lighted up. I sit by the side of my little tent writing by the light of a lantern. Shall soon pull off my coat, creep under my blanket, read the *New York Herald*, which I got at the landing today, and then to sleep. At 4½ o'clock reveille sounds, then surgeon's call, which occupies me from one to two hours—then see that all personal and hospital property is properly packed and the hospital corps in good order, then breakfast. The "general" beats at 6:30, "fall in" at five minutes to seven, and "forward" at seven. This is the usual program.

Near New Kent Court House
May 20, 1862

Passed New Kent Court House on our way here, a small village of half a dozen houses. We are near Dr. Mayo's house, a fine place, very ordinary house.[24] The roads are horrible, new ones cut through the woods soon become mire.

Went up to White House landing yesterday on business.[25] The medical purveyor's boat is here, where we get our requisitions filled. Gunboats and shipping fill the river. The "White House" is a common two-story wooden house, with outbuildings and some very poor Negro quarters. A good plantation, low and level for miles.

May 21, 1862

Marched today about ten miles to a point two miles from Bottom's Bridge.[26] Men are fast giving out. I am up tonight getting off the sick of the brigade to go to White House by the teams going for rations. We send over fifty.

Camp near the Chickahominy
May 23, 1862

Came here today, encamped in a low, swampy field, where we get water a foot below the surface. Meadows and fields are filled with flowers. The climate has a debilitating effect, and a hard march melts away a good deal of patriotism. I am sorry to send so many to the rear, for they seldom get back to be of much service.

Near Beaver Dam Creek
May 30, 1862

Now in the midst of a fine thunder shower, but we have fortunately moved our camp to higher ground. A train of ambulances has just passed containing wounded from the fight day before yesterday at Hanover.[27] Several hundred prisoners passed yesterday. Went out a few miles on Wednesday morning to reinforce Porter. Order after order came, first to go back to camp, when a short distance on the way ordered back, and teams sent for three days more rations. At one o'clock men turned out to draw rations and be ready to march to Hanover at daylight. But daylight came, and we remained until near night, when we came back to camp.

The country about here is deserted by all except old men, women, and children. They come for guards for their houses, while they sell their bread and milk at exorbitant prices. The owner of the place on which we camped has four sons in the Rebel army. We handle the scoundrels tenderly.

The people about here all have a sallow look. We should too if obliged to live here one summer. The army would melt away by disease in one season. Not that many have died, but the men become so debilitated that they are unable to march with equipments and rations, and large numbers have to be sent to the rear. It is astonishing to see the amount of clothing thrown away on the march as warm weather comes on.

Fair Oaks
June 2, 1862

We are on the battle ground of the last two days.[28] Our regiment was on picket on the thirty-first, and did not participate in the fight on that day. We crossed Sumner's "grape vine bridge" at daylight yesterday morning, soon after which it was carried away by the freshet.[29] It seems that our division reached the front in the afternoon just as Casey's division had got the worst of it.[30] The New York Second and Thirty-fourth, Massachusetts Twentieth, and Seventh Michigan were in the fight. The Seventh lost about one hundred. The Twentieth had two or three killed. They drove the Rebels through the woods, leaving the ground strewn with their killed and wounded. This ended the fight that day.

After crossing we were left in a swamp some time, then moved up a mile. In the afternoon were ordered up to the front and were soon before the enemy, but before having a chance to fire, were ordered to right about, march, and back we went double quick. The Rebels had disappeared suddenly, and it was thought they intended to attack us in the rear. General McClellan personally gave the order. He was most of the time between the river and the front. At night ordered to the front again. Roused up once, skirmish, one man killed, four o'clock up again, an attack expected, but it was found some hours after that they had retired.

Today we are engaged in caring for the wounded and burying the dead, while the Rebels are throwing shell at us quite lively. We have a great many Rebel wounded on our hands. They are a miserable looking set in their mud-colored dress.

Fair Oaks
June 4, 1862

I have this evening returned from the hospital at the "Adams" house, a mile from here, where I was detailed yesterday with several others.[31] The house, barns, and other outbuildings were filled, besides the yard, with our own and Rebel wounded. Worked all day at the operating table and at night attended to those upon whom we had operated. Have sent off 250, all that were at that place, though other houses are as well filled. It has rained heavily, and after cattle sheds, horse stalls, and outhouses were filled, others were sheltered merely by a rubber blanket supported on four muskets. I operated mostly on Rebels, as we had many of them, assisted by a Rebel surgeon from Georgia, whom we had taken prisoner.

The loss in our corps is reported {as} 1,050.[32] We have already buried eight hundred Rebels, and many lie unburied in the woods. I send you a rose, picked near the grave where more than a hundred of our men lie buried together. Separate graves surround this trench, where personal friends {from} all regiments have buried their own dead. I can find nothing else to send you. All is of the most disgusting nature. Have not had much to eat for two or three days. We expect our wagons with personal effects and medical supplies to come up in a few days. All we had was what was carried in hospital knapsacks, and I carried my instruments strapped to my saddle. Though within five or six miles of Richmond, all is wilderness about us.

Fair Oaks
June 14, 1862

We are yet in the same neighborhood, very little going on except picket firing, and turning out nights, and an occasional spell of shelling, and a few men killed now and then. Reinforcements are constantly arriving. We moved down about a quarter of a mile in the woods, our brigade having been to the front so long, picketing, digging, and ditching. They needed rest. Several cases of scurvy have occurred in our brigade, a few in our regiment.[33] This is owing to the want of fresh vegetables. We have had potatoes issued as a ration but once since we came on the Peninsula, and even vinegar but seldom. We reported cases of scurvy sometime since, but its existence was denied at headquarters of the army. "The troops should not have scurvy. Their rations are plentiful and good. Therefore scurvy does not exist." Our brigade surgeon, Dr. Dougherty, went to headquarters and represented the state of affairs, and today a surgeon was sent down to see. He was obliged to acknowledge the existence of it. An order was immediately issued that the troops should be supplied with fresh vegetables. [This order was extensively published in the newspapers at home, but beyond satisfying the people that the army was well supplied, nothing came of it. We got no more potatoes for it.] Other corps are better supplied I think. It takes so long a time to bring a matter to notice at headquarters, and get action on it, that it is hardly worthwhile to attempt anything. Requisitions which I made three weeks since on the medical purveyor at White House are not yet filled.

The Rebels are in pretty strong force about here I think. A body of their cavalry captured a train near Tunstall's Station last night, burnt one car, and sixteen baggage wagons filled with grain. It was a bold thing.[34]

Gen. McClellan reviewed the army yesterday. Each regiment was drawn up in its own camp, and he rode along, followed by his staff, about as fast as they could get through the swamps. The most of the army seem to have confidence in him, but I have not yet witnessed the enthusiasm we read of.

Hundreds of men are at work felling trees in our front and will clear the ground ahead before making an advance. Our position is strong, our entrenchments reaching a great distance.

We are ordered to send no more sick home or to general hospitals. It is *supposed* we are to keep them to send home via Richmond, when we take it, which according to the admirers of General McClellan will be very soon. The surgeons who volunteered to come out for a short time have been of but little service.[35] They want to perform surgical operations, but a sick man stands a poor chance with them.

Fair Oaks
June 16, 1862
Our regiment has been drawn up in line for two hours and just now, sunrise, ordered to stack arms for breakfast. There was a good deal of firing toward morning, but all quiet now. [During our campaign on the Peninsula, we were turned out every morning at three o'clock, the men to stand in line half an hour, then lie down but not take their equipments off, and breakfast at sunrise. With all other officers I answered roll call, "armed and equipped." Just before dawn is a time usually chosen for making an attack, and this order was perhaps necessary, but such severe duty wore out the strength of our men and was productive of disease.]

Fair Oaks
June 21, 1862
There is considerable sickness in the army, owing to the want of fresh vegetables. Of course this is known at headquarters, but movements there are slow. Dr. Willard has been sick a week with remittent fever. I have a good deal to do and find it very tedious to spend four or five hours at surgeon's call, keep the books, etc., and as soon as my duties in camp are over I go in the trenches and stay till morning. Here we are roused up several times each night. The men stand to their arms until the alarm is over, then lie down to sleep again. Of

course we are all more or less disturbed, sleeping on the ground a few yards in rear of the breastwork. Our men have now been in the trenches several days, the invalids in camp.

Fair Oaks
June 26, 1862
We had quite an engagement today.[36] This morning our regiment was ordered to advance in front of the entrenchments, Sickles's brigade leading.[37] They broke, when the Rebels advanced upon us. Our regiment received them with three or four good volleys, standing their ground like a wall, then advancing with cheers {as} the Rebels gave way. The regiment moved off to the right, and being engaged with wounded, I did not become aware of it until the enemy were again upon us and was obliged to retire when our skirmishers came in. Soon got all our wounded inside the entrenchments, and after applying temporary dressings, had them removed to our hospital in the rear. Dr. Dougherty came over, and we performed all the operations before nine o'clock P.M. Our loss was 7 killed, 33 wounded, and 5 missing. All our wounded were brought to our hospital and treated there under my care, and no one has suffered for want of attention. Lieutenant Warner is among the killed, and Lieutenant Rice wounded.[38] Our regiment behaved well.[39]

Dr. Willard has been unable to sit up for a week. Our brigade surgeon is also sick. I am well and attend to the business of both. I shall go to look at the wounded once more, and then to sleep.

Harrison's Landing
July 2, 1862
You are probably aware of the series of engagements which have taken place during the last few days. The *fact* is, we have been obliged to *retreat* and have fought our way from our works in front of Richmond to this point.[40] The army is now near the river, protected by the gunboats and our own artillery. What is left of the grand Army of the Potomac is in good spirits (probably for the reason that we are in a safe position). We are now in the mud, scarcely a man having anything to shelter him. I will attempt to give you some account of the affair.

On Thursday, the day following our fight in front of our entrenchments, Porter's corps had a fight on the right and was obliged to retreat.[41] On Friday all was quiet, the awful stillness preceding the storm which was soon to burst upon us. It was feared that the Rebels would come round on our right, on account of superior numbers, and on Saturday we threw up new works and prepared for an attack.

At night all were ordered to be in readiness to march, and some of the artillery and the trains were sent ahead. After a long and anxious night in the trenches, we fell back at daylight under cover of a thick mist. Of course when our pickets were withdrawn, the enemy became aware of the evacuation. The left wing of the army was on its way before us, Sumner's corps being in the rear. Marched about a mile down the railroad to Orchard Station, and knowing the enemy would trouble our rear, General Sumner drew up his corps to offer them battle.[42] We established our hospital in the woods in rear, and the enemy soon came down upon us.

There was sharp work for a few minutes, and the wounded soon began to come in, and the shells too. While dressing the wounded, we were ordered to leave immediately. The troops were mostly gone when we left, taking our wounded off on litters. Moved down to Savage Station and formed on the south side of the railroad. Here we prepared for another fight, and the enemy gave it to us. They commenced shelling from the other side of the railroad, and then from the left, throwing in a perfect storm of shell. Our artillery soon replied, and the engagement became general toward night.

Many wounded were brought in and attended to as well as possible, but at about ten o'clock we were ordered to march again, which we did, leaving hundreds of sick and wounded at the house at Savage Station and the tents near it and on the field. A march of eight miles brought us on the other side of White Oak Swamp at daylight. Here we rested a few hours, a very few, and were ordered to move. Went about two miles and waited events. The rear of our column was at White Oak bridge, the head about two miles in advance. An artillery fight took place at the bridge, our brigade with others in reserve. Soon firing on our left begun and we were ordered up. The enemy were endeavoring to cut off our corps by advancing upon us near the Nelson house, or Glendale. Our brigade went into the fight, which was in the woods, and after losing heavily withdrew at dark.

Of our regiment Major Howe and Lieutenant Lee killed, Colonel Hinks, Captain Devereux, and Captain Wass wounded.[43] Our loss in the regiment is 187 killed, wounded, and missing. We labored under the greatest difficulties in taking care of our wounded. Our trains were in advance, and all the materials we had for hospital use were carried in hospital knapsacks by orderlies. Most of these orderlies were missing after the first day, but my two came through in good order and assisted me in the field, in hospital, and everywhere, wherever their services were needed. [44]

I performed amputations on the ground by the light of a single candle stuck in a bayonet, but had not sufficient time to perform all that were necessary, when we were ordered to move and leave our killed and wounded on the field and in hospital, with a detail of surgeons to remain with them. We brought off our wounded officers, some on horseback and some on litters. During the night our corps was got into line on the road and at daylight reached Malvern Hill, where the advance was drawn up. In the afternoon the Rebels attacked. The fight was principally artillery, our division being in support of batteries. Our regiment lost but one killed in this engagement.

At daylight another retreat, through mud and pelting rain, and here we are at Harrison's Landing, seven miles further, and the whole army is on the field of mud. The men we have lost, the amount of property, wagons and stores, abandoned and burnt, and our present position, under cover of gunboats, looks like a retreat to a place of safety. After a week's incessant fighting by day and marching by night we are pretty nearly used up. The last day was perfectly horrid, rain pouring in torrents, mud knee deep, and teams, artillery, infantry, and cavalry hurrying along, in some kind of order to be sure, but not much. General Sumner's management was very good under the circumstances, but we have lost a great many men and much materiel. What the result will be I cannot tell. I am tired. Without sleep for nearly a week and but little to eat, with plenty of work, has left me very tired to say the least.

Harrison's Landing
July 7, 1862
We are now about a mile from the river, a little out of the mud and alongside a small stream where the men can wash.

There has been too much talk at the North about what we were going to do, so that the hopes of the people were excited to an unreasonable degree. The truth is, there has been no enthusiasm among sensible men; they were not "spoiling for a fight" but were willing to fight when occasion called. I never could see the way clear to Richmond, and cannot now. We must have more men, and I am not sure but we shall have to have better generals.

It is thought that the enemy suffered more than we did on the retreat. [45] I do not know how that may be, but it was a terrible thing to leave our wounded in the enemy's hands, as we were obliged to do all along our retreat. Of the fight of the twenty-fifth, when we lost so many, General McClellan makes no mention in his report of Sedgwick's division being engaged and in his dispatch speaks of it as being in the afternoon. It was in the forenoon, finished before twelve o'clock. After the fight, McClellan and his staff rode through our entrenchments while we were removing the wounded, and without stopping to take notice of anything, went over to Hooker's, and there I suppose wrote his dispatch. The whole army would give more for one word from Abe Lincoln than all the speeches, or orders, or acts that all his generals can do or say. [46]

I have very little baggage to trouble me now. All the clothing I possess is on me except one extra shirt. My dress consists of flannel sack, pants, and shirt. Thinking it highly probable that our baggage train would be captured or destroyed on the retreat, I packed all my best articles of clothing in a bundle, which I strapped to my saddle, and which bundle I lost at Savage Station. So went all the "pride, pomp, and circumstance of glorious war" of which I was the owner. It is almost impossible to get anything to eat except beef and hard bread. Men are rotting with scurvy and have been for months, and no vegetables, and {the} government either cannot or will not furnish them. [I learned afterward on good authority that ten thousand bushels of potatoes were destroyed at White House on our retreat. Why were they not distributed to the suffering troops?]

I think we shall have to stay here several weeks unless we are driven out, for we are not strong enough to advance and could not stay here a day only for our gunboats. I can tell our Northern people that if they expect we have a Napoleon to lead us to victory next week, they had better change their minds. We have smart men, and a good many of them to fight against, and no "little Mac" or little anybody else is going to fight this out without going to work on a different plan.

29

Harrison's Landing
July 16, 1862

The weather is very warm, some days 102 in the shade. I have a new assistant, Dr. Hill of Charlestown.[47] (Dr. Willard went home sick immediately after the retreat.[48]) I feel somewhat relieved of a part of my duties. I have twenty-four in hospital and forty to fifty sick in quarters. We shall have soft bread for the hospital tomorrow, the first for four months.

Harrison's Landing
July 22, 1862

We often hear the remark by officers and men that the war is "played out." The truth is, the war is not played out, but the patriotism of the men is. I have never seen the time when I would resign, or go home on leave of absence, or get taken prisoner and paroled (without good reason). I consider that my place is with my regiment, and I have kept with it. I have seen some surgeons today who were taken prisoners unnecessarily, hoping to be paroled and sent home, there to receive their pay and do nothing for the service. They are put on duty, I am glad to say.

We had a review of our corps today, by General McClellan. A general order complimented the Nineteenth as the best regiment in the corps.[49] Our men feel justly proud. The Nineteenth is a good regiment, and I am not afraid to place it alongside of any other.

The weather is quite warm, nights as well as days, with a shower now and then. We have as many flies as they had in Egypt, but no mosquitoes. Lately we have had ice and lemons for the hospital; a very good thing. Everything remains pretty much as before. No reinforcements are sent up now. Dr. Hill has been sick with remittent fever several days but is getting better. I shall outlive and outwork a dozen of them yet, I expect.

Harrison's Landing
July 26, 1862

We have a new supply of tents within a few days, and I slept in my own tent last night, the first time for two months. We have four tents for officers, a space in the center covered by tent flies, where our mess table is placed. We have things pretty comfortable for warm weather and are living pretty well now. But the men do not get enough vegetables, notwithstanding the order that they "shall be supplied" with such and such things. The cause is far back of everything that we can control. It is necessary that something more than giving orders should be done.

You see in the papers lists of surgeons who it is said "voluntarily remained to attend the sick and wounded" and have been released on parole, etc. The facts are these. At every hospital on the route where wounded were left, surgeons were detailed by authority to remain, and others had no right to. But it seems that about fifty surgeons were made prisoners and released on parole. Two in our brigade remained without authority, and now when they have returned they are in difficulty, considered as having deserted their posts, which they certainly did. I saw them just before we left Nelson's Farm, and there was no necessity of their remaining. A sufficient number were detailed to remain and did so.

In my tent are the colors of the regiment. The state flag is in shreds, has several bullet holes, and is torn by going through woods and by long use. Three color bearers were shot while carrying this flag, and General Sumner says "don't mend it." The U.S. flag has one hole through it. [These colors are in the state house in Boston.]

You say I do not speak in very flattering terms of General McClellan. True, I do not have much enthusiasm for "little Mac." I know an error has been committed. Whose fault it is I know not. I think McClellan's friends have injured him by claiming too much for him.

Harrison's Landing
August 1, 1862

About eleven o'clock a brisk cannonade took place from the other side of the river. The Rebels threw shot and shell into our camps and transports for an hour. Not much damage was done. A few men were killed and some horses, and some steamers and vessels got a few shots. The gunboats were up the river, looking out for the Rebel "New Merrimac," which they were expecting every hour; but one of them came down and gave a few shots. We are completely surrounded by the Rebels, and though they cannot drive us out of the place until we choose to go, they can annoy us, and it will take a large fleet of gunboats to keep the river open. The scoundrels are smart, and if we had been half as smart as they we might have finished up this affair long ago. A party of about six hundred men went across the river this afternoon and destroyed a large quantity of grain and a house where Rebel pickets had been. [This house belonged to Colonel Ruffin, a son of the "Venerable Edmund Ruffin," who fired the first gun at Fort Sumter and after the close of the war committed suicide.[50] The colonel was wounded and taken prisoner by our division at Bristoe Station in 1863, and I think died in our hands.]

Went down to Westover this afternoon.[51] This is a splendid estate, or was before the war. A fine large old mansion of brick, stone ports and gateway, with two large stone eagles on each side, a fine garden, with roads and walks shaded by trees, large outbuildings and Negro quarters; one of the palaces of the F.F.V.s, sadly altered now. General Porter occupies the house now as his headquarters. Until we go into the enemy's country, and take and use all we can and destroy the rest, the war will never end. We have set guards over Rebel property, when afterward the Rebels came back, occupied the ground, and used the goods for their own benefit. I cannot remember with any satisfaction the time when, on our march through Charlestown and Berryville, our hungry men killed a few pigs belonging to a rebel and were obliged to pay twenty dollars to General Dana to pay the owner. Soon after, Jackson was about there and had the benefit of all that was left.[52]

Harrison's Landing
August 13, 1862

We have for three days been under marching orders, with tents struck and teams loaded and surplus baggage on board of transports. When we shall march, or where, is not known, at least to any of us. Lieutenant Hume arrived today from Richmond.[53] Before he left, prisoners were brought in from Banks's force.

The weather is very warm, in fact *hot*. An inkstand in the shade was uncomfortably hot, and iron felt as though it had been warmed in the fire. Some troops have gone down the river with a great deal of artillery. The sick were sent down on transports, our regiment alone sending one hundred.

Newport News
August 23, 1862

It must be peculiarly gratifying to all our friends to know that the grand Army of the Potomac is again "safe." Well, it is so, and we are here in a very pleasant place on the banks of James River.[54] The army was several days on the road, our corps in the rear. We left Harrison's Landing on Saturday morning, marched five or six miles that day, far enough to leave behind the swarms of flies which followed us at first. Here the trains and artillery passed us. Where there is but one road, and that not a very good one, it is slow work to get an army along. Through the open country, or even through woods, troops can march in three or four columns and pick their way, while the teams go in the roads, but crossing a stream or swamp causes a delay. There had been no rain for a long time, and the dust was suffocating. All were covered with it, mouth and nose were full of the "sacred soil," and sometimes we could not see ten steps ahead.

Sunday we went as far as Charles City Court House and bivouacked on a place belonging to John Tyler, a little beyond the "city," which consists of a brick building (the courthouse), a small building near it for records (which I am sorry to say our men did not respect at all), two houses, rather poor, and a small jail, all deserted, and the weeds around as high as a man's head.[55]

Tuesday made a march of eighteen miles to Barrett's Ferry, at the mouth of the Chickahominy.[56] Here a pontoon bridge was in place, with some gunboats lying near. Crossed in the morning, and after the road was sufficiently cleared ahead, we moved on. As we left, the engineers were engaged in taking up the bridge.

Marched to Williamsburg that day, halted a mile or two west of the town.[57] Afterward passed through to the other side, where we remained overnight. Williamsburg is a quiet old place, the seat of William and Mary's College.[58] A very fine insane asylum is located here.[59] In ancient times this was the capital of Virginia and a place of note, now sadly dilapidated. Everything wears an ancient look. Along the streets are chimneys of immense dimensions overgrown with ivy. I noticed nothing new in architecture. I should judge that the sound of a hammer had not been heard in the town for at least fifty years.

From Williamsburg to Yorktown the next day: and here we expected to remain a few days and to go on board transports. But there were not enough to take all, and so we were ordered to march next morning at daylight. Friday morning, reveille at three o'clock, march at four, and arrived here in the forenoon in the midst of a drenching rain. But it was soon over, and our men have enjoyed bathing and the cool breezes from the water. This march was a pleasant one to us for many reasons. None but able-bodied men started with us, all the disabled having been sent down by transports; and the pleasant incidents of a march tended greatly to fortify men against sickness, often the effect of despondency. Immense fields of corn on the route were stripped of their ears, much to the gratification and bodily improvement of men almost famishing for vegetable food.

You will see that the distance on the map is not great, but the roads are crooked, and it is fully sixty miles from Harrison's Landing to this place. We were a week on the march, but as officers were told to provide themselves with three days' rations, they found themselves rather short. The men got theirs, however.

Without Richmond, we might as well have nothing. We came on the Peninsula about five months ago. We have lost half our army by battle, wounds, and sickness; and thousands who have gone home will never return, sick or well. Whose fault it is I don't pretend to say. One thing I know, the Army of the Potomac has fought well and never retreated except by their general's command.

Potomac River
August 27, 1862
Embarked on the twenty-fifth on board steamer *Atlantic*, and toward night moved up Chesapeake Bay.[60] We have on board some two thousand troops: the Nineteenth and Twentieth Massachusetts, and Forty-second and Fifty-ninth New York.[61] While here off Aquia Creek, a good many transports are in the river, apparently discharged.[62] We are a good deal crowded, men have no means of cooking. Officers get their meals at the table of the steamer by agreement. The men of the "Tammany army," as the Forty-second New York is called, are not on amicable relations with others, and a good deal of disturbance is consequently the result.[63]

CHAPTER 3

"Into the Fight with Our Regiment"

August 31–November 10, 1862

After its return from the Peninsula, the army fought at Second Bull Run in late August 1862. Dyer says his brigade marched on a night that Fitz John Porter claimed was too dark to move. The surgeon again experienced Washington's red tape, which delayed getting his wounded into the capital's hospitals, including his assistant surgeon, who had been mortally wounded by friendly fire. Marching north, the doctor describes the fighting at South Mountain and at Antietam, where he handled thousands of casualties, including many of his fellow officers. He writes that the wounded were so scattered in an area about three miles long and two miles wide that it was impossible to group them for hospitals even by corps.

In the aftermath of that battle he complained that packages sent from home to officers were often pilfered, particularly of liquor. His comments on politicians, the press, civilians, and particularly Virginians in the town of Paris near Ashby's Gap are colorful and pithy. Dyer describes the reaction to McClellan's removal in some detail.

On the Road to Manassas
August 31, 1862

"There is no peace for the wicked, nor rest for the 'Sogers.'" We have marched more than forty miles since night before last, and the men are tired out. Our regiment, small at first, is smaller today, for many were obliged to fall out from fatigue and sickness, and not a few from want of shoes. There was not time to supply them at Alexandria, and time is of vast importance now. I think Jackson considered his chance to be before the Army of the Potomac got round here.

But Hooker and Kearny were here before us, via Aquia Creek,

35

and we bring up the rear.[1] Great numbers of new troops are in and about Washington and Alexandria, got up in the highest style of the art, with new uniform coats, large blue overcoats, full sets of Sibley tents, with board floors, etc.[2] Our boys march by with their fast and easy step, their shoes sometimes slung to their back, going barefoot in preference sometimes on account of chafed feet and ragged stockings, with flannel blouses instead of coats; and a rubber blanket or piece of shelter tent hung over their shoulders, they look like rather hard cases; but such men are worth five times their number of new troops, and tired as they are they cannot be spared at this time.

We now take no teams with us, and no tents, and march mostly by night. We were congratulating ourselves with the prospect of garrisoning forts; and in fact were ordered to Fort Ethan Allen, but the order was countermanded before we got into it, and our men, packing up their "traps" again, marched on, declaring with good humor that it was too dull business for them.[3]

The Fourteenth Massachusetts (First Massachusetts Heavy Artillery), 1,800 strong, after garrisoning forts nearly a year, were sent out for the first time the other day and came near being captured near Manassas. Were gone three days; had one man wounded, accidentally; and came back thoroughly used up. The regiment is a very fine one but entirely unused to field service.[4]

On the Road to Manassas
September 4, 1862
After finishing my last letter we halted by the roadside a while. Trains from the front began to come in, most of them having wounded. Soon the trains belonging to Pope's army began to come in, and for hours they passed on the double quick. It was evident that *we* were falling back. A long ambulance train also passed, made up in part of coaches from Washington pressed in the service, as our ambulance trains were not yet off the transports in the Potomac. At ten o'clock that night ordered to march. Went as far as Fairfax Court House, where we arrived just before daylight. [This was the night which Fitz John Porter considered too dark for marching.[5]]

At Fairfax Court House our regiment acted as provost guard, arresting stragglers and protecting property. Troops and artillery were passing back and forth all night the following night, apparently without any definite object. Some fighting was going on at Centreville and Germantown. The army all came in to Fairfax during the day, and was massed on the east of the town. One corps after another moved, and our regiment with the First Minnesota, Colonel Sully, were left as rear guard, with a squad of cavalry, and two pieces of artillery, all under command of General Howard.[6] Toward night we moved out on the road. As we did so the Rebels got two guns to bear upon us very accurately, and threw shell among us at a brisk rate, but beyond some slight wounds no serious damage was done. The general impression that the wind of a shell or ball will injure is erroneous. There is no injury without contact. A shell burst within reach of my hand without injury to me.

Moved on a short distance and got our guns in position across the road, we behind them. It was now dark. A squad of Rebel cavalry charged down the road, but the First Minnesota, who were immediately in the rear of our pieces, gave them a volley that sent them to the rear double quick. Then moved on to Vienna, where we overtook the division.

A few miles beyond this a terrible affair occurred. We had been marching in two columns and had halted, our column resting on each side of the road, when a squad of cavalry came through to the rear. A gun was accidentally discharged, a stampede of the cavalry began under the impression that it was an attack by Rebel cavalry, shots were fired here and there, and in a few moments an indiscriminate firing by infantry upon all mounted men. To get out of the stampede, I dashed into the woods with other mounted officers, the bullets flying about us like hail. But it was soon over, and I found Dr. Hill, my assistant, who was riding by my side, with his leg shattered just below the knee by a ball. Four men were killed and thirty wounded, some of whom were brought along, but no conveyance could be got for Dr. Hill and three others. Sent the chaplain in for an ambulance, but after waiting two hours I went in with the rear guard, leaving Dr. Hill in care of two of my men. (Memo: Did not see the chaplain again for several months. He did not stop till he reached Massachusetts.[7])

Obtained two or three ambulances and started the next morning with them, preceded by a party of cavalry pickets. Met the men whom I had left with Dr. Hill coming in, bringing him on a wagon which they had obtained. Got three others and brought them to the hospital at Georgetown.[8] Dr. Hill had preceded me and expressed himself as quite comfortable. They had, on consultation, thought best to amputate the leg. The officers could be admitted without a special permit, but having two enlisted men in my ambulances, I could not be permitted to leave them without a permit from the office of the surgeon general; and while the army was moving on, and my place was with my regiment, I was obliged to wait until my steward could ride into Washington and get a permit. Their wounds were not sufficient evidence of their right to be received in general hospital. Of course I did not fail to express my indignation, but their whole object seemed to be to obstruct my endeavor to facilitate business. "How not to do it" is the motto in some of these institutions.[9]

This took me nearly all day, and in the meantime the corps had moved across Chain Bridge to Tenleytown, where I joined them last night near Fort Gaines.[10] I left Dr. Willard at Alexandria with some sick and the remainder of our brigade. They are coming up tomorrow. We are detached from our brigade and are now in the first, under General Howard. He is a splendid man, lost an arm at Fair Oaks. General Kearney, with whom he was going to "buy gloves," was killed a few days ago.[11]

Near Rockville
September 7, 1862
Back again where we were a year ago, but under different circumstances. The enemy have crossed in large force above, several thousand of them at Edwards Ferry, and occupied Poolesville night before last. We are on picket at the forks of the road leading to Muddy Branch. Cavalry pickets ahead of us report no enemy in sight, though they have not been as far as Poolesville. What the result of this will be I cannot tell. Very little dependence can be placed in dispatches, when they read as Pope's.

Keedysville
September 18, 1862
We have had a great fight, killed and wounded numbered by thousands.[12] Colonel Hinks badly wounded. Captain Batchelder killed. Captain Hale, Lieutenants Thorndike, Hinks, and Reynolds wounded. Captain Rice also.[13]

Valley Mills, Antietam Creek
September 23, 1862

I will try to give you some idea of our doings for the last week or two, though I cannot very accurately give every day's movements. [14] We made short marches, following the enemy closely, sometimes skirmishing with them. Followed them through Frederick, where the people welcomed us as deliverers, and Hooker came up with them at South Mountain, where they had a large force posted in the pass on the turnpike. Our troops engaged them with artillery nearly all day, and near night having flanked their position, charged and drove them. While moving up in the evening met the wounded coming down with the body of General Reno. [15]

Monday followed through Boonsboro, a neat little town, which the enemy had just left, and were skirmishing with our cavalry. Churches and other buildings were filled with Rebel wounded, and we passed several hundred prisoners in squads in fields and barns. Hurried through town and came across the valley near Keedysville. Took position near Antietam Creek Monday night and remained there all of Tuesday. The Rebels threw shot and shell at us all day from their position on the other side of the creek. Ours did not reply very sharply. Went up on the hill in our front and had a good view of their lines, though in not a safe position by any means.

Next morning ordered to be ready at daylight, without knapsacks, and with eighty rounds cartridges. Our corps marched in three columns, our regiment leading one column. Dr. Willard and myself, with our attendants, as did most of the surgeons of our corps, went into the fight with our regiment. Forded the Antietam and advanced nearly a mile in the same order, through ploughed ground, cornfields, and woods. Then faced to the front, forming line of battle, and advanced over the same kind of ground nearly a mile toward the Rebel lines. All this distance we were under the fire of the Rebel batteries. A shell would plough through the ranks, a break would be seen, and as the line passed on, one or more men would be left lying on the ground.

Getting nearer we passed many wounded who had been lying there since the night before, both Rebels and our own. While occupied in dressing wounds in the rear of the regiment, just in the edge of the woods, the fire became pretty hot. Kirby's battery was ahead of us, a little to the left, about seventy yards distant. [16] The Rebels came

39

up in heavy masses to take it, pouring in an irregular but terrific fire. The battery was well worked and threw showers of canister among them. A regiment in support got up and fled past us through the woods.[17] The battery maintained its position, however, and drove off the assailants, after which, anticipating a more vigorous attack, it moved to the rear. The Rebel fire became so sharp, frequently hitting the horses of a battery halted near us, that we sheltered ourselves as well as possible, and when the fire slackened were obliged to move to the rear, our lines having fallen back; our regiment had been obliged to move to the right and rear, and our whole corps having been considerably shattered. Dr. Willard's horse was hit but not killed, and the whistling of bullets was livelier than anything I had ever heard before.

On retiring, met the medical director of the corps, who ordered me to go to the Hoffman house and take charge.[18] The wounded were fast coming in, and in an hour there were five hundred there. Remained there twenty-four hours, when Dr. Palmer, surgeon in chief of the division, having arrived, I got relieved to go and collect together some of the wounded of my own regiment who were at other places.[19] Colonel Hinks, with three other officers, was at Mr. Pry's, Valley Mills. Found him severely wounded, a ball having passed through the right forearm, shattering the radius, and passing through the abdomen, came out on the left of the spine. Surgeons who had examined his wound considered his case quite hopeless, and very little had been attempted for his relief. Fixed him up comfortably as possible and then hunted up and got together as many more as possible. They are so scattered however that it is impossible to have those of the same corps, even, together. Some have gone to Hagerstown, others to Frederick, and others leaving for more distant houses or hospitals as soon as they are able.

I cannot say how many thousand wounded are in this vicinity, but every house and barn for miles is filled with them. All the churches and schoolhouses in Sharpsburg are used as hospitals, also those in Keedysville and Boonsboro.[20] At Mr. Pry's house, where I now am, we have five of our wounded officers. Yesterday I got an order from the medical director to accompany some of our wounded Massachusetts officers home, but the colonel was not able to be moved, and I had to send the rest off and remain here. The colonel's wound is a bad one, and it is very difficult to handle him. How he escaped with life is almost a mystery.

Dr. Willard is sick here too, not able to take care of the few we now have here, and the army has moved on to Harpers Ferry. There are other wounded officers here; and in the mill barn and other outbuildings are now about one hundred fifty, many of them with amputated limbs. Some contract surgeons have been sent here, and we shall leave as soon as satisfactory arrangements are made.[21] I do not want to remain here long; the army will soon be on the move, and there is scarcely a medical officer in our brigade with his regiment.

It was early morning when we went into the fight, and it continued until night. The roar of musketry and artillery was terrific. At night the enemy held possession of a small part of the field, but we held most of it. Next day but little was done except to remove the wounded, and the night following the Rebels left. We got some prisoners, but as they could ford the river very well, all went over except the rear guard, who were taken. I went over the battlefield on Friday, and even then all the wounded had not been removed, many of them having been within the Rebel lines. The fight had raged over a space about three miles in length by two in width; and in places where our own or the Rebel line of battle was formed, a perfect row of dead was lying. In one place, behind a rail fence, the Rebel dead were lying as closely as if their line had laid down for shelter. In front of the place where Ricketts's (Kirby's) battery stood, the ground was covered with dead.

The wounded are being removed from hospitals near the field, as the odor is horrible. Hundreds of horses were killed. They were generally burnt. Citizens have been flocking in by hundreds, not generally to render assistance, but to go over the battlefield and pick up mementos, such as broken muskets, etc., and some to steal what they can find. But there is nothing about the poor ragged Rebels to covet. Many good-hearted men have, however, come from neighboring towns, brought supplies, and taken wounded to the hospitals at Frederick City and Hagerstown. Surgeons have come from Baltimore and other places, but I am sorry to say they do not care to stop and do the work.

Asst. Surgeon Revere of the Twentieth was killed. He was just on our left, next regiment. Dr. Hayward, surgeon of the Twentieth, was taken prisoner but released when the Rebels retreated. Dr. Kendall of the Twelfth was killed, and a Dr. White, of what regiment I do not know.[22]

Hoffman Hospital
October 1, 1862

I have been for three days in charge of this hospital, where I was ordered on the day of the battle. We have been removing the wounded as fast as possible, but have yet one hundred fifty here, all of them severe cases, amputations, fractures, etc. We have seven surgeons, of whom three or four each day are unfit for duty, on account of the severe labor of the past fortnight, but each one has his ward to attend, and each one is obliged to dress all the wounds in his ward, none of this being left with nurses. We would have been glad if those surgeons who visited the army soon after the battle had remained to assist us, but they did not seem willing to remain and dress stumps.

Many die of course, as the nature of their wounds is such that a large percentage of deaths is to be expected.[23] I hope that all will soon be removed, as the atmosphere of the whole neighborhood is tainted. Some are to be removed to Frederick, but the greater number will be collected together from the field hospitals and placed in one now being prepared about a mile from here called the Smoketown hospital.[24] The tents are now being put up. The wounded will be much better off in tents than in houses or barns.[25]

Baltimore
October 9, 1862

Came down yesterday with Colonel Hinks and Dr. Willard. The Hoffman Hospital is broken up, and all the patients removed to Smoketown. After getting a supply of clothing, which I need very much, I shall go to the regiment at Harpers Ferry tomorrow.

Bolivar Heights
October 12, 1862

Came up yesterday with Colonel Devereux, Captain Russell, Adjutant Chadwick, and Charles Mudge.[26] Left Colonel Hinks and Dr. Willard doing well. . . . It looks cheerless enough about here. All public property was destroyed by the Rebels, pontoon bridge, railroad bridge, and what few remaining buildings were left last spring, all but old John Brown's engine house. The heights around are being strongly fortified. . . . Found some very good friends in Baltimore, strong Union men too, though there is a majority of Rebel sympathizers, generally of the aristocratic classes, and foreigners, Germans, of whom there is a large number.

This war is now more than ever before a matter of principle. When I see such men as are to be found in our ranks, many of them leaving good homes and families to come out here and give their lives for their country, I cannot help feeling that there is a deeper feeling than mere fancy in it. When I had charge of the Hoffman Hospital, every day fathers and mothers, wives and brothers, came looking for their friends. Many of them learned for the first time of their death, but I never heard one of them in the bitterness of their grief reproach any one for influencing them to engage in the war.

On the battlefield I found a young man mortally wounded and stopped to assist him. He asked me to take his name and write to his mother in Philadelphia, who was a widow, to tell her that he died a brave boy, that she must remember while mourning for him that he died in a good cause, and that his mother and his country's flag were last in his thoughts. I know nothing more concerning him. We were driven from that position, and when we occupied it again I was in a hospital at the rear. I wrote today as he desired and shall probably know nothing more than I have written. But he was a hero, and there were thousands of such that fell that day.

Harpers Ferry
October 14, 1862
The Rebel cavalry made a raid completely around our army and crossed the river on their return with their booty.[27] It is a disgrace to the army that such things are allowed. We have cavalry enough to prevent it, but I am not alone in the belief that orders from headquarters come a little too late sometimes. When we left here last spring we stored a large quantity of hospital stores, clothing, etc., which the Rebels have appropriated to their own use.

Harpers Ferry
October 17, 1862
I expect in a day or two to get the boxes which have been on the way so long. But I have felt indignant at the treatment we have been

subjected to. All the boxes have been opened in Washington, and every bottle of liquor taken out, even from boxes of hospital stores. Packages for officers of all ranks were searched, and bottles of wine and choice liquors taken.[28] It is outrageous. If an officer is not fit to be trusted with such things, there is a remedy. He is accountable for his conduct to his superiors. These boxes are generally sent from home and contain the gifts of friends. They should be respected. Mr. Mudge, who went after the boxes, protested against this abuse of authority, and the chief of police gave him an order to recover the liquors, but it was all mixed with others, and there is no knowing what he got. [He got none of the wine or brandy which had been taken out.] How can it be expected that the people at home will contribute articles for the sick to have them overhauled by a set of irresponsible persons in Washington who have the *opportunity* of taking out whatever they choose, and they improve it sometimes.

I have not felt good-natured about this and several other things. For the last few months there has been a continual issuing of orders at Washington tending to make the position of an officer humiliating. They have cut down our pay and taxed the remainder; have denied the privilege of leave of absence except on account of wounds, and refuse to accept resignations except on account of disability. There is too much despotism about it. I see it is said in the papers that officers do not wish to end the war; that they want to keep their places and obtain promotion. But I don't see it in that light. I know that a great proportion of them would resign if they could be permitted to. Well, I have had my say, and now I shall hold on to the end of the war if I am able to.

Upperville
November 4, 1862

We were unexpectedly ordered away from Harpers Ferry and are now making our way along Loudoun Valley and occupying the gaps. Our advance is skirmishing with the enemy every day and drove them across the Shenandoah yesterday. We have got along on the march so far very well. The roads are good and no rain. This is a fine country about here, and there is no trouble about living well.

Rectortown

November 7, 1862

Passed by Snicker's Gap, leaving a force there, who had a little skirmish afterward. Arrived at Ashby's Gap on the fourth. The enemy had just passed through, skirmishing with our cavalry. They could be seen from the mountains, making their way across the Shenandoah, but we did not follow. Had business elsewhere.

Remained the next day at Paris, a little town of a dozen houses, at the Gap. [29] Took our meals at the house of a Mr. Orear, who had a wife and two daughters. [30] The ladies were the most rabid secessionists I have met with. One daughter is married, and she had been up on the mountain the day we came, to see her husband, who belonged to Stuart's cavalry. The younger, unmarried, is the most severe on us miserable Yankees. The mother does the bargaining and "prefers" to take Rebel shinplasters for pay, but if we have got a little sugar and coffee which we would be glad to get rid of they would take it. [31] Also, would be very glad to send a "servant" to pick up salt emptied from our pork barrels.

The father voted against secession (I never saw a Virginian who did not), but he was a states' rights man, and "when his state went out it was his duty to go with it." He believed that slavery was ordained of God and that they were in duty bound to keep and provide for their slaves; and yet he believed that it had impoverished the state. He knew it had made him poor, and if the president's proclamation for the abolition of slavery in the Rebel states could be enforced, it would be a blessed thing. His mind seemed to be just emerging from the darkness which the spirit of slavery had thrown around it but not yet sufficiently enlightened to comprehend the principle that God created all men free. He seemed to be an honest man and a Christian, and he deeply deplored the condition of his state, but he had sat under the preaching of the gospel of slavery until he could see in it only a divine command to enslave the black man.

Marched yesterday six or eight miles over these miserable mountain roads, very cold and the wind raw. Not a very good night to bivouac on the bleak hillside, but I managed to sleep very comfortably when I *did* sleep, but it is unpleasant to sit up in the cold, and I can't sleep all these long nights, so I have to lie awake part of the time.

Today we remained here. It has been snowing, blowing, and freezing. The men have their little shelter tents, which keep the snow and wind off some. I got my tent up this afternoon, as did some of the other officers, and a little sheet-iron stove and have been quite comfortable. Have had a good deal of writing to do and have been engaged all the afternoon and evening. Being surgeon in chief of the brigade I have to transmit orders and make reports, and circulars and orders have come in pretty fast, this being the first time we have pitched tents for several days.[32] I have no accommodations for a clerk. My seat is the ground and my desk my knees. We little know how few things are necessary in this world until we find out by experience. It is about as cold as at any time last winter. Icicles hang from the tents, and the air is keen and cutting.

I dreamed last night of being home. There was nothing very homelike about my resting place, for I was sleeping on a bare hillside, one blanket over and one under me, and my coat cape over my head. Quite a number of Rebel prisoners have been taken about here. I should think they would freeze to death with their miserable clothing. The weather is severe for the season.

Near Warrenton
November 8, 1862
Marched to this locality, about eleven miles, this morning. It has been cold, and tonight a little snow is falling. This morning while on the march General McClellan and staff passed us. We did not know at that time that he was relieved of his command. He was looking well. Some are very much disappointed and feel very sore about it, condemning the administration severely. I feel rather sorry to have him go now, as he has done some things very well, but I am not going to find fault until I know all the circumstances. Soon after General McClellan passed, General Sumner came up, his first appearance since his return from Massachusetts. The men cheered him well, for they all like Sumner. General Howard also returned yesterday and is in command of the division today. He is one of our best generals, I think, though not a great man yet, and the men have the greatest confidence in him. I don't know of one of our generals that I like better as a man than General Howard.

Passed through the little town of Salem today, like all other Southern towns, two or three pretty good houses, the others log and clay principally. The citizens about here don't like the result of Stuart's raid in Pennsylvania, for now our army takes their horses for artillery and cavalry service wherever found. They say they expected it when they heard of Stuart's doings. Some fifty prisoners came by, the worst looking set I ever saw. What must an army of them look like! And yet they will fight.

Warrenton
November 10, 1862

This morning the army was ordered out to bid McClellan goodbye. He passed along the road with a long retinue. Troops were drawn up in line, and three batteries fired salutes as he passed along. Cheers were loud and long. A good many regret McClellan's departure, and some are more violent about it, not hesitating to wish that he would take the reins of government in his own hands and march to Washington and all such nonsense. A little wholesome discipline would do these traitors good. They may like him as a man, for aught I care, but when it comes to preferring George B. McClellan to the country and everything else, I say it is time to have a change, and I am satisfied that no change can be made for the worse. Time is passing. The country has furnished men and means, and the people are impatient to have something done; and if Mac won't do it we must have somebody who will. The Union will not hold together a year at this rate, and I am not willing for one to see this great army waste away without accomplishing something. There has been "strategy" enough, and "organizing," and "perfecting details," and "saving the army." We must beat the enemy or abandon the contest, and such work as we have been having for a year will never do it. If we are to be whipped it is time we knew it, and if we are to beat it is time we were about it.

McClellan has done some good things perhaps, but who is to be responsible for the thousands who perished in the swamps of the Chickahominy except him, for if he is to have the credit of successes he must bear the responsibility of reverses. I have nothing against him; he has been unsuccessful; and there are men, a dozen of them I have faith to believe, who can fill his place. If I thought we had no man in our country but McClellan fit to lead our armies, I would pack up and leave; for a country with but one man fit to command is a poor concern. The Rebels about here have a high opinion of

McClellan. They never fail to speak well of him, and McDowell they admire. But they have no good word to speak of Hooker, Sumner, or Burnside.

It is a very pleasant country about here, but while we were among the mountains it was very cold. The tops of the Blue Ridge are covered with snow. I hope to get home again and live like a reasonable being once more. Not that I am "played out" or any thing of the kind, for I have been at my post at all times and have done my duty, but there is a craving for home and society. If there were not we might as well live like the wandering Arabs.

You read sometimes of bands playing and drums beating, to cheer the men, and how much better they feel and fight for the music. This is all in the fancy of those who write from "afar off." Not a note is sounded, not even the tap of a drum. Columns move along day after day, over the roads, and into the fight, and the voice is the only means used to communicate orders. On the march each regiment has a bugler, who sounds the "forward" and "halt." In camp the music comes in, and then it is very refreshing.

CHAPTER 4

"Such a Row in Washington"

November 12, 1862–January 23, 1863

Dr. Dyer continued to comment frequently on the controversy following McClellan's second removal by Lincoln as army commander. During the Fredericksburg campaign that followed, he was appointed surgeon in chief of the Second Division, II Corps, serving on the staff of O. O. Howard.[1] From that vantage point he commented on various officers, life at division headquarters, the loss of yet another of his assistant surgeons, and the shortages of food, tobacco, and warm clothing suffered by the men.

The battle and its aftermath were the subject of extensive comments, including many problems in caring for the wounded and criticism of the treatment given them from various quarters. Among the thousands of casualties were a number of regimental surgeons. Included in this chapter, because they date from this period, are various complimentary letters from Surgeon General Dale in Boston and other individuals, which Dyer placed at the end of his journal. The chapter ends with Maj. Gen. Ambrose Burnside's "Mud March" and the approval of Dyer's furlough to go home for a visit.

Warrenton
November 12, 1862
The excitement created by McClellan's removal is very great, and some officers have sent in their resignations, but Burnside will permit no such nonsense. Our regiment is small, and we have few sick, having left them at Harpers Ferry, so instead of having one hundred fifty at sick call in the morning (as I have had in times past), I have about a dozen, and held my levee this morning in my tent while eating my breakfast, with an instrument case for a table.

This breakfast is not an elegant repast by any means, a piece of beef, a hard cracker, and mug of coffee is the maximum.

I see now more and more the propriety of McClellan's removal. We shall see whether he is the only living man who can lead an army. The esteem and regard which many have felt for him has been almost completely extinguished by the injudicious course of his friends. No loyal man could hesitate which to prefer, when McClellan was placed in one scale and the country in the other.

We are encamped just outside the town. It looks as though it might have been quite a respectable place but is now deserted to a great extent. There is very little attractive about these Virginia towns.

Two miles from Fredericksburg
November 18, 1862
A march of three days brought us here, where we rested for the night. Nothing unusual occurred on the march. General Sumner is here in command of the right wing of the army, comprising his old corps and Franklin's.[2]

The McClellan feeling is not as strong as it was, but the out and out Mac men are in a terrible rage and would say much more than they now do; but from warnings they have had they begin to be a little more cautious of their treasonable expressions. It has not been unpleasant on this march, very little rain, and the weather not as cold as a week ago. . . . I am sitting by a fire of rails (rails are a great institution) while some dozen or more "lame ducks" are about me (as surgeon's call has just sounded), wanting permits to fall out of the ranks or ride in ambulances, but most of them are new recruits, 300-dollar men, and the poorest set of beings ever enlisted.[3] It is too bad to send such men out here. They enlist knowing they will be unfit for duty, many of them having before {been} discharged for disability; and on their arrival they immediately set themselves to work to get another discharge. I have no sympathy for them.

Near Fredericksburg
November 23, 1862
Have been lying here quietly for some days with an understanding that during some negotiations for the surrender of Fredericksburg

there shall be no movement of troops on either side. We have a good many troops in and about the village of Falmouth, and artillery posted on the hills, while the rebels picket the opposite bank of the river, but no firing. At the farther end of a broken bridge, two or three rebels sat cooking their dinner unmolested. I have a new assistant, Dr. Stone.[4]

Falmouth
November 28, 1862

I will tell you how we passed Thanksgiving. Some few of us thought we would like to have a dinner worthy of the day but did not see much chance of it. However, each one got what he could, and we had quite a good dinner, to which Colonel Hall, commanding brigade, and staff were invited, ten of us in all.[5] We had chicken soup, roast duck, potatoes ($3.00 per bushel), turnips, butter ($1.25), pickles, tea and coffee, and an Indian pudding. All these things are very difficult to get, and we have to go four or five miles sometimes for a few vegetables. The butter we got of a Negro woman whose mistress had sworn five minutes before that there was not an ounce in the house.

The men had rather a poor dinner, hard bread and pork; these are all the rations they have had since coming here, except fresh beef twice a week—no beans, rice, vegetables, or molasses. With all the talk about the bountiful provision for the army, it is well known that this army, at any rate our division, have had potatoes but six times since last February; and if the men had not, in spite of orders, stolen all the vegetables they could get (from the ground) not one would have escaped scurvy. Some of McClellan's favorites, Fitz John Porter's corps, and others fared very well, while others starved.

The want of tobacco is very severely felt by the men. When short of provisions it is a great comfort to have tobacco. What little there is here is sold at exorbitant prices. We tried to buy some yesterday for distribution among the men, but it was not to be had; while opposite, in Fredericksburg, they burnt $100,000 worth of it for fear we should capture the place and get it. But there seems to be no prospect of that just now, for each army is looking across the river at the other and throwing up earthworks, neither molesting the other.

Falmouth
December 3, 1862
Today I was appointed surgeon in chief of the division, on General Howard's staff. I still have my quarters with my regiment, have my tent well fitted up, and shall remain here until we make a move. Besides, my assistant is not very well posted up, and I am obliged to render a good deal of assistance. As long as I can make it convenient, I wish to attend personally to the affairs of my regiment.[6] While brigade surgeon, I attended to my regiment in addition to my other duties. I think the plan of our advance is not abandoned. We shall probably move soon if the weather permits.

Falmouth
December 5, 1862
Today it began to rain and ended in snow, and we now have two inches of snow on the ground; not very comfortable moving about.

Lacy House, Falmouth
December 18, 1862
Since the battle on the eleventh and twelfth I have been very busy and have not yet got through my work. . . . The fight began on Thursday morning. Our regiment, with the Twentieth Massachusetts and Seventh Michigan, or rather detachments from them, crossed in boats before the bridge was laid.[7] This was a perilous undertaking and was well performed. Lt. Colonel Baxter of the Seventh Michigan was in command of the forlorn hope and was one of the first wounded.[8] Captain Weymouth of the Nineteenth was also wounded.[9]

A thick fog hung over the city when the bombardment commenced, and nothing could be seen but a steeple here and there. One hundred and forty pieces of cannon threw shot and shell into the city, making wrecks of the houses and burning a few. The roar of artillery was incessant. I was down on the bank during the first of the shelling but afterward established a hospital under the shelter of a hill about half a mile from the river and attended to the wounded as fast as we {the surgeons} came in. The next day the Lacy house began to be filled, and I came here, where I have been ever since.[10] We have about two hundred here now and have had all the time, some coming over the bridges, and some going all the time. We retain the more severely wounded. Part of them are in tents.

The room in which I write, and in which all our surgeons sleep, is used as an operating room, and for six days the tables have been occupied from morning until late at night. I have charge of the hospital and perform what operations I can find time to, but I find my time much occupied in superintending affairs and providing the patients with means for their comfort. Considering all things I think they have been as comfortable as could be expected; more so than in some other hospitals. The weather is very cold, and we have great difficulty in keeping the wounded warm, especially those in tents, as we have no stoves. A congressional committee has been here, and the surgeon general, Dr. Hammond, and inspectors, but as far as any benefit arising from their presence, they might as well be in their pleasant offices in Washington. [11]

I was over in the city during the fight on Saturday. It was not at all comfortable, as the rebels were shelling the city continually, their batteries enfilading the streets leading up from the river. Found Dr. Haven, surgeon of the Fifteenth Massachusetts, in the courthouse, badly wounded. [12] He died in a few hours. Finding the wounded were being sent over the bridge as fast as possible, we were soon ordered to return, and I have been here ever since. The upper bridge was but a few rods above the Lacy house, and the shelling about us was very brisk, several men being killed while on their way down to the bridge. I ordered a red blanket to be hung out as a hospital flag, which I think they respected to some extent, though a shell was thrown on Monday into the entry next the operating room, knocking the bricks about quite lively.

The house is a fine large brick mansion on the river bank, within sight of the fighting. The river is narrow, and we can easily speak across. We expected a lively shelling in the morning, but the enemy did not discover our movements until our army was nearly all across. The bridges were swung round about sunrise; pickets were taken across in pontoon boats. Stragglers hurried through the streets down to the bank, and wading out were taken in the boats, but a good many were gobbled up by the rebel pickets, who followed closely.

Yesterday four or five hundred prisoners were exchanged, and the wounded who were unavoidably left in the town were brought over. We received thirty-three of them here, all severely wounded. Flags of truce have been over every day with parties to bury the dead, and all firing is prohibited. Both armies are back in their old camps, and we have lost at least ten thousand men.[13] The Nineteenth lost 107 in killed and wounded. It is now only a good-sized company.

In a field opposite is the unfinished monument to Mary, the mother of Washington, whose house was in Fredericksburg, and who died there.[14] The monument is considerably battered by shot and shell.

Lieutenant Newcomb of the Nineteenth lies upstairs dying of a severe wound in both legs.[15] Captains Mahoney, Dodge, Palmer, and others have gone home.[16] Captain Weymouth, with a wound of the knee, lies on an old sofa in the operating room, preferring to see the work of blood going on rather than go in the crowded rooms.

Being in an exposed and isolated position during the battle and the evacuation, and thinking the enemy might open a lively fire upon us when our design was discovered, I felt it due to the wounded under my care, as well as to myself, that I should have explicit orders in regard to the removal of wounded. I had received orders of a contradictory nature, and so during the evacuation on the night of the fifteenth I sent a note to Dr. Dougherty, medical director of the Right Grand Division, as follows: "I do not understand from your note that I am to remove the wounded from the Lacy house. Am I right?" to which I received the following answer: "I think your wounded will be taken after the town is emptied. But of course, if the enemy gets to shelling, you will commence moving your wounded to the hospitals in the rear. I would not have you put up any more hospital tents at present. Yours, etc. A. N. D."[17]

At 10½ P.M. received the following: "Headquarters, Right Grand Division, Dec. 15, 1862. Dr. Dyer: General Sumner recommends that the wounded in your hospital (the Lacy house) be left there for the present, unless the enemy begin to shell it. I would have the ambulances ready in case they should be needed, horses ready to be put to, and impress the men in the camps near you as stretcher bearers, etc. Yours Respectfully, A. N. Dougherty, Surgeon, U.S.V., Medical Director, R.G.D."

Sent a dispatch again saying that the men in the camp near us had been ordered away and that an orderly whom I had sent to find the division ambulance train had been unable to do so, I requested that in case it was considered necessary to remove the wounded, the ambulance train should be sent to report to me. At one o'clock A.M. the following reply came. "Surgeon Dougherty says it will be attended to. F. Beardslee, Capt."[18] It is always best for medical officers to act under orders, when possible. Commanding officers have but little time, even if they have the inclination, to see that the wounded are properly taken care of. The medical officers must see to that; and yet the commander may censure him for neglect or what he may consider an error of judgment. I give these specimens of orders only to show the circumstances in which we are sometimes placed.

I am somewhat tired; have not had a night's rest for a week. They promise to take the wounded off tomorrow; hardly think they will. I have the house full, men lie on the floors as close as they can be stowed, a little straw here and there; the best we can do for them. Back of the house I have six hospital tents, ten in each tent, with no fire, and the weather is cold. We cover the ground with pine boughs and give them as many blankets as possible. The Sanitary Commission have a depot near, and I have drawn upon them nearly every day for clothing.[19] We try to send our wounded away looking as clean and tidy as possible.

Lacy House, Falmouth
December 20, 1862
It may be asked why were the wounded not better provided for. The distance from Washington is short; the battle was resolved upon; the surgeon general was here during or immediately after. Yet the surgeons were provided with no facilities beyond those furnished afar from all bases of supplies. There was a lack of administrative ability or willful neglect. I had a conversation with Hon. Henry Wilson, who visited the hospital, and who was astonished to find the meagerness of the supplies at our command.[20] Stoves might have been provided in a few hours from Washington, yet only today, the twentieth, after a considerable number of our wounded had been removed to Washington, I received the following from the medical director. "Dec. 20. Dr. Dyer: There are stoves at the depot. Send for some at once, as many as you think you require, and make the men comfortable. Yours, A. N. Dougherty." Sent a note to Dr. Dwinelle in charge of the hospital near the depot to draw enough

for himself and me at the same time.[21] He wrote in reply: "Doctor. I undertook to get some stoves from the depot this morning on Dougherty's order, but they would not issue them except on a triplicate requisition, approved by Dr. Letterman [medical director, Army of the Potomac].[22] I immediately referred the matter to Dr. Dougherty, but he had gone off and would not return for several hours. If I succeed in getting what I have asked for in time I will send you some of them. Justin Dwinelle." The next day, when the requisitions were approved and teams sent for the stoves, it was found that no pipes had been sent. Having sent away so many {patients}, we can do without them now.

Camp near Falmouth
December 23, 1862
Came back to camp on the twenty-first, having removed all but thirty wounded from the Lacy house and nearly all out of the corps hospital in the rear.

A great deal has transpired since we left our old camp on that dismal, cold, and smoky morning of the eleventh, amid the roar of cannon, and marched down into the fight. Coming back, all looked deserted, desolate, cold, and cheerless. I think none of our commanders expected to come back here, but the thing didn't succeed; and here we are back again, and the people of Petersburg {he meant Fredericksburg, but Petersburg was still fresh in his mind} are back again in their battered and plundered houses. All is quiet on the river; hundreds of rebels are walking about within a stone's throw of the Lacy house, near which flags of truce are passing back and forth. Great numbers of the rebels are dressed in blue, the clothing taken from our dead and wounded. Unfortunate as this affair was, I am glad Burnside is man enough to assume the responsibility, and not whine like a child, saying "you made me do it," as some others have done.[23]

I suppose the repulse at Fredericksburg will cause such a row in Washington that we shall have to wait a long time before everybody is satisfied who is to blame. Meantime the army does nothing. The little success we have had in North Carolina does not amount to much, come to look at it in reality; and I am afraid Banks will not accomplish much on account of his old, leaky vessels.[24] Things look rather blue, but a few days or weeks may see a great change.

{Letters copied into the journal}

Commonwealth of Massachusetts
Office of Surgeon General
Boston, Dec. 23, 1862

Doctor,

I have the honor to forward you a copy of a letter addressed to Colonel Hinks, commanding Nineteenth Massachusetts Volunteers, by J. Mason Warren, M.D., an eminent surgeon and patriotic citizen. It gives me pleasure to convey to you the pleasing information that Dr. Warren has decided that the old Nineteenth is one of the regiments whose noble daring in the field, and yourself one of the surgeons whose faithfulness and devotion toward its men, justly entitle that regiment to the distinction indicated in Dr. Warren's letter. The knapsack is now in my possession, and awaits the order of the regimental surgeon, under whose care it will be placed for the use of the regiment.

I remain, very respectfully your obedient servant,
William J. Dale, Surgeon General

Surgeon Dyer, Nineteenth Massachusetts Volunteers
Surgeon in Chief, Second Division, Second Army Corps.
Boston, Dec. 20, 1862

Dear Sir,

Mr. Turner Sargent of Boston, now in Paris, has sent out two French surgical knapsacks, similar to those used by the French and Italian armies in their two last campaigns, as presents to our Army, placing them at my disposition.

In consultation with my friend Dr. Dale, Surgeon General of Massachusetts, we have decided to give them to regiments that have particularly distinguished themselves.

I take much pleasure therefore in sending one to your regiment, which has borne so active and honorable a part in the contest. I am doubly induced to do so from knowing that it will be duly appreciated by your energetic surgeon, Dr. Dyer, who has done so much to sustain the honor of the medical profession of Massachusetts at the seat of war.

Wishing your regiment continued success, I am, with much respect,

Your obedient servant,

J. Mason Warren

Colonel Hinks, Nineteenth Regiment, M.V.
Boston, Jan. 1, 1863

J. Mason Warren, M.D.,

Dear Sir, Your letter of the twentieth ultimo, informing me that in consultation with Surgeon General Dale you have determined to award one of the two French surgical knapsacks recently placed at your disposal to my regiment for having particularly distinguished itself in the field, and as a mark of your appreciation of the energy and skill of its surgeon, Dr. J. Franklin Dyer, has just been received under cover of another from Surgeon General Dale.

You will please accept the expression of my thanks for this kind acknowledgment and recognition of the excellent behavior and gallant bearing which have ever characterized the officers and men of the regiment entrusted to my command in whatever service it has been called upon to perform.

And permit me to add to yours my own testimony of the superior skill, constant exertion, and great success of our most excellent surgeon, Dr. Dyer, and to thank you for your kindly remembrance of him.

I am very respectfully,

Your obedient servant,

Edward W. Hinks,

Colonel, Nineteenth Massachusetts Volunteers

Camp near Falmouth
January 3, 1863
I am having my tent put up at General Howard's headquarters today and shall move over there tomorrow. They have got a new mess kit and some supplies, and I shall get something fit to eat. You have no idea how we have been pinched. Nothing a great part of the time but bread and meat. No potatoes, no butter, or anything that one would like to eat. For the first time now they have permitted sutlers to come up. I think the old regiments have a good deal to complain

of. They have to do the greater part of the fighting and the hardest work and never have any favors shown them.

McClellan's friends are making a great outcry over Burnside's defeat, and many of them would be willing to have the army again defeated if they could by that means bring back their "darling little Mac" to the command of the army again. But I hope we shall do something to shut their mouths.

Headquarters, Second Division, Second Corps, Falmouth
January 6, 1863
Moved up here with General Howard yesterday. We have a good cook, and we all live better than we have since we came out.[25] Our quarters are on a hill, sheltered from the wind by woods, which the general is very particular not to have cut off. Spent the evening in the general's tent, talking over old times and mutual acquaintances.[26] He was in Bowdoin College while I was attending medical lectures there. He has prayer every evening in his tent, generally assisted by Captain Whittlesey, assistant adjutant general, formerly professor in Bowdoin College; and by Lieutenant Howard, brother of the general.[27] A. D. Richardson, correspondent of the *New York Tribune*, is with us and keeps us posted up in rebel news.[28] He gets the *Richmond Enquirer* every day.[29]

January 13, 1863
All quiet here now, but we are expected to be always ready, and we may start on an expedition before long. Although we have had a victory at Murfreesboro, it has cost us about as much as it is worth, and I see but little encouragement just now.[30] Galveston is gone again, and we lose generally about as fast as we gain.[31]

Falmouth
January 19, 1863
After being kept in a state of preparation for several days, we have about made up our minds that we shall not move at present, though it seems to be the intention to do something this winter. A battle during the cold weather such as we have had for a few days would be very bad for the wounded; but we must run some risks in war, of freezing as well as everything else. You speak very strongly about Burnside. His plan was a good one after all.[32] If he had succeeded

he would have been the best general we have had. As it is, he is considered by many a failure.

We had a review of the Second Corps yesterday. I was out with General Howard, very cold day. Generals Burnside, Sumner, and Couch, with their staffs, were present.[33] We rode through the lines at a rapid pace, that the men might not be kept in line very long. Very few cheers were given for Burnside, but that was owing as much to the uncomfortable state of the men as anything else. Sometimes men will cheer anybody, and sometimes they will not.

General Howard had a meeting in his tent last evening (Sunday). Mr. Alvord, who has a tent at our headquarters, Rev. Dr. Childs, and others were there.[34] Had a good meeting and afterward a sing.

If every officer and man belonging to the army had been in his place, we should have driven the rebels into the Gulf ere this. But the people at home seem to be trying to keep men away from their posts and encouraging desertion. We get no men out of all who are recruited for us, only one now and then. More than ninety recruits were in camp at home for the Nineteenth; had received their bounty, pay, clothing, and rations; and all we got was *four*. The rest deserted before leaving the state and probably enlisted again, to repeat the same process. The Twentieth Massachusetts had sixty-one, and only one came out. He was a poor old fellow, probably too feeble to desert.

General Howard read me a short sketch of his life, which he had prepared for a friend. He is thirty-two years of age, born in Leeds, Maine, near Augusta; entered Bowdoin College at fifteen, graduated at nineteen; immediately entered West Point, and graduated at twenty-three. Went to Watervliet Arsenal as ordnance officer, afterward to Florida in the same capacity, then to West Point as assistant instructor in mathematics. Was first lieutenant when the war broke out and resigned to take command of the Third Maine. Was at the first Bull Run battle; promoted brigadier general in September 1861. Lost an arm at Fair Oaks, etc. Has a wife and three children.

The general is unlike most military men, especially West Pointers. His piety is a prominent trait, and in common life his gentleness is almost girlish, but he is severe when occasion calls and is one of our best fighting generals, always in his place, and he considers his place to be where the fighting is.

Falmouth
January 21, 1863
Raining all night and all day today, and our troops moving all the time. Yesterday and today Hooker's and Franklin's corps have been moving to the right, intending it appears to cross six or eight miles above. The Second Corps has not started yet. It is hard for the men to be out in such weather, marching and camping in the mud. I am in hopes the move will be a successful one, but I wish it had taken place a week earlier.

There is a great deal of dissatisfaction in the army. The men will fight, but they seem to have no confidence in anybody. It has been drilled into their minds by many of their officers, and by such papers as the *New York Herald*, that they are "fighting for the niggers" until they really believe it, or a good many of them do.[35] And they have not been paid for so long a time that they are less enthusiastic.[36]

It is an uncomfortable night to be out in. I have been out at such times too often not to feel a good deal of sympathy for the men. In my department, everything is prepared for a move, and everything provided for the care of the wounded as far as we are able. Each brigade has its medicine and supply wagons well filled; each regimental hospital wagon has its supplies and hospital tent, with a stove for each {of the} two tents. (The tents are so made that they can be joined together.)

I had an opportunity yesterday to go to Aquia Creek to take charge of the corps hospital but declined and had another detailed. Had a letter from Dr. Dale yesterday. He says: "A good many surgeons are at home now. Why don't you get a leave for a time?" That is the very reason why I don't. There are so many loafers about home that we have to stay and do the work. [The army returned to its old camp without having accomplished anything. This is known as "Burnside's Mud Campaign."[37] The elements seem to be against Burnside.]

Falmouth
January 23, 1863
I applied yesterday for leave of absence for twenty days. [This was disapproved, and I immediately applied for fifteen days, which was granted, and I left for home on a very cold morning, Jan. {left blank}.

61

By rail to Aquia Creek, standing on a platform car, a detention some hours there to get a pass; a leave of absence duly signed and sealed is not a pass. Then up the Potomac in a miserable old steamer on which we could scarcely keep from freezing. Another detention in Washington to get another pass, and in four days from camp I arrived in Hancock, New Hampshire, where my wife and Frank then were. After nine days at home, spent in Hancock, Boston, and Gloucester, left for camp again, February {blank}. I had made an application for an extension of time, ten days, but even the intercession of my friend and predecessor in office, Dr. Sherman, Medical Corps, from New York was unsuccessful.[38]

CHAPTER 5

"A Far Better State of Things"

February 20–April 23, 1863

After returning from his leave, Dr. Dyer describes in detail the conditions and events of the army's winter encampment before the onset of the Chancellorsville campaign and the changes made by Joseph Hooker, including the introduction of corps badges with divisions marked by different colors. The reviews, receptions, horse races, and festivities of all kinds were numerous and elaborate, particularly the events held on St. Patrick's Day. Dyer also records his impressions of President and Mrs. Lincoln when they visited the army at Fredericksburg.

Headquarters, Second Division, Second Corps, Falmouth
February 20, 1863

Back again in the old place, and it seems like home compared with such places as Washington, Aquia Creek, and all along the miserable route that we have to take to get here. The mud is perfectly dreadful. I hardly see how it is possible for the teams to draw enough subsistence over the ground. But the weather today is very pleasant, and I write with the front of my tent open. All well here. General Howard is going as far as Philadelphia in a few days. He is going to get an artificial arm.

March 4, 1863

I think the army is in much better condition than when Hooker first took command. Deserters are being brought back by hundreds, and any officer or man staying away beyond his time is instantly brought up on his return, and if he cannot give a reasonable excuse, is recommended for dismissal if an officer or other punishment if an enlisted man. This tends to bring them back on time. I am impatient to hear of success south or west. We want a good victory to encourage

63

the country. Things have looked blue about long enough. It is time for the tide to turn. I do not think the army opposed to us is large.

Falmouth
March 8, 1863
General Howard returned yesterday. General Hooker reviewed the Second Corps on Thursday, a pleasant day but cool. The troops looked well, and all passed smoothly. No cheering, as it was ordered that commanders should not call for cheers. The army is in first rate condition and on hand for anything. Generals Couch and Howard being absent, General Hancock commanded the corps, and General Owen the division.[1] Went through the review with General Owen. Reviews are not altogether for display, as some imagine. Men see and know their officers, and as each regiment is expected to look its best, the men are kept in good condition. The daily, weekly, and monthly inspections keep up the efficiency of an army. Several regiments were necessarily absent from the review, on picket, and yet there were 15,000 men in line.

General Hooker rode a white horse and looked well, hair almost white and clean-shaven face, with an eye as keen as an eagle's.[2] I do not think he is addicted to drinking as much as is generally believed. Those who have seen Hooker and "little Mac" drink whiskey, think the "little Napoleon" can hold his own with Joe. General Owen, just promoted, likes to make a good show. But General Meagher and staff are the most "gay and festive" set you would wish to see.[3] Their style is peculiarly their own, the most marked feature being a profusion of gold lace.

The hospital at Aquia Creek has been broken up, and we now have division hospitals. Ours is placed just below the hill on which our headquarters are, and we are beginning to put the patients in. There is a far better state of things since Hooker took command. If the army does not have fresh bread at least four days in the week and vegetables at least five, he will have some good reason from the commissaries.[4]

Falmouth
March 10, 1863
The members of our staff presented General Howard a silver pitcher on the occasion of his promotion to major general.[5] It is an elegant thing, cost $120. He sent us the following in reply:

Headquarters, Second Division, Second Corps
Near Falmouth, Va. March 9, 1863.

Messrs. of the Staff—

I do accept your beautiful present, and most heartily thank you for this additional expression of affectionate regard. We shall never be likely to forget our association in this trying season in the history of our country; but it will be indeed pleasant to look back upon these scenes fraught with so much interest and danger from the quiet of home after the war shall be over, and it will then as now ever fill me with thankfulness to the Giver of all perfect gifts, that he permitted me to have so noble, able, and generous staff to help me on. Asking for you his blessing and protection, I am,

Affectionately yours,

O. O. Howard, Maj. Gen.

To Dr. J. F. Dyer, Surgeon of Division.

March 14, 1863

My newly appointed assistant, Taft, has resigned and leaves for home tomorrow.[6] Stone will I hope follow his example. We cannot get suitable men to fill the position of assistant surgeon. No one at home seems willing to leave their comfortable firesides to enter the service, while they cry out at the inefficiency of the surgeons. It would be truly an inefficient service if we were obliged to depend on the patriotism of the profession at home. Most of the surgeons first appointed still remain, and we have to depend almost entirely on them. I shall send home these inefficient ones as fast as they are sent out.

Falmouth
March 15, 1863

Our cold and disagreeable weather still continues. This evening we have had rain, hail, and snow, and the ground is now covered with the mixture. I have been out visiting hospitals today, a part of my duty, visited eleven and left four to inspect tomorrow.

Falmouth
March 17, 1863

Today *has been* St. Patrick's Day, and General Meagher and the Irish Brigade have celebrated it, or probably will have done so when the night is finished. At ten o'clock General Howard, with the rest of us, went over to the place where the races were to take place. Thousands were already there. A high platform was built of the plank and boards of the pontoon train and another stand for the band. Flags were flying, and hundreds of officers were riding here and there over the field and about the stand. General Meagher, dressed in an English hunting suit (white hat, black cutaway coat, drab knee breeches, red top boots, and a long whip) with six or eight officers in jockey dress, were keeping the ground clear. It was to be a "hurdle race." First, a fence three or four feet high of long poles, soon a ditch eight-feet wide, then another hurdle and a ditch, eight of them in the course a mile round.

The bugle sounds, away go six, one swerves to the right, refuses to go over, and keeps on outside; another balks, but after urging goes over; another clears it but throws his rider. Two go over fairly; but the sixth throws his rider against the post at the left of the hurdle, and I thought he had broken his neck; but they are all up again and after the leaders; and there is only one tumble before they reach the stand, no one far behind. Captain Gosson, General Meagher's adjutant, leading on a little gray mare.[7] Gosson is dressed in white tights, yellow top boots, red and blue shirt, and a white and red cap. He is the best rider by far and a good hunter from the old country.

Again the bugle calls attention; horsemen urge the crowd back to widen the course, and the second heat begins. All clear the pole handsomely except one, and Gosson comes in ahead. Three cheers, the band plays, and some champagne corks are popped on the platform. All this time the mud is splashing. The ground was frozen, with a light covering of snow. The sun coming out thaws it into mud, and it flies from the horses' feet in a shower. As the riders go round the course, the crowd of horsemen, probably a thousand, rush across the field to see them cross the ditches on the opposite side, and the rush and hurry and splash of mud is terrible; but the excitement is up, and away we go.

After a rest, the lists open again. General Caldwell announces that the next race will be open to all officers of the army.[8] Entrance fee five dollars, for stakes, and a liberal donation by the gentlemen on the platform, which General Caldwell says will be placed in General Meagher's white hat. General Meagher calls upon all desiring to come and enter the lists. General Hooker passes some money.

"Gen. Hooker gives fifty dollars." Cheers. Then Generals Hancock, Howard, Berry, and others, and the sum is $135.[9] "Enough," says General Meagher, "for anyone to break his neck for." (These amounts are somewhat fabulous, fifty sometimes means ten, etc.) Six horses enter this race, all clear the hurdles, all go round; one artillery officer on a little sorrel leads. The track is cleared again, and again they go round. The sorrel leads again. He has the first prize, two-thirds of the amount. He is Count Blucher, a grandson of him of Waterloo.[10] A grandson of Blucher wins a horse race on St. Patrick's Day in America.

General Caldwell then announces that there will be a recess of half an hour, and those who have been specially invited by General Meagher will accompany him to his quarters. "He regrets that his accommodations are not as large as his heart." They ate and drank punch. A second race followed. Three horses were killed. Cannonading was heard to our right and rear, and by request the assembled thousands dispersed to their commands.

March 23, 1863

We are gradually getting things in order for active operations, first reducing baggage. We shall all send our trunks to Washington (I have carried a small one) and each take a valise; the general no more than the rest of us. By a recent order, each corps is to be designated by a badge, which men are to wear on their caps.[11] The First Corps a circle, Second a trefoil, etc., the divisions to be designated by colors, red, white, and blue.

Falmouth
March 28, 1863

"April showers bring forth" *mud*, and so do March showers. We have a shower about every day now, and water and clay make mud. Yesterday was very fine, and General Birney had a race and other amusements at his headquarters.[12] It was a very well got up affair; the ground was fine, everything was got up on a grand scale. A long platform of pontoon boats and planks, two bands played, and two or three regiments kept the course clear. The course was more than a mile round and none but mounted officers allowed inside. Others had good places outside, and there was not so much crowding as at Meagher's race. Many of the horses and riders were the same.

Colonel Von Schack rode his own horse and came in ahead.[13] Count Blucher got thrown in the mud and considerably bruised, as did Prince Salm Salm, who got thrown in a ditch and came near breaking his neck, while Mrs. Salm Salm was looking on, attended by General Sickles.[14] After the races, a greased pole, a revolving drum, a foot race, a race in sacks, and a Negro concert, at which General Hooker, other officers, and ladies were present.

March 31, 1863

General Howard is assigned to the command of the Eleventh Corps, formerly Sigel's, and goes tomorrow, taking his two aides, Lieutenants Howard and Stinson.[15] We all regret his leaving very much and fear that the Eleventh Corps may not enhance his reputation. General Gibbon comes here.[16] I have a new assistant, Knapp.[17] We will see whether he will share the fate of the rest. Stone departed some days since.

Headquarters, Second Division, II Corps
April 2, 1863

General Howard left yesterday, with Charles and Stinson. General Gibbon came soon after, with his aides, Lieutenants Haskell and Moale.[18] I think we shall like him very well. He is a regular army officer, a captain before the war, and was in command of a battery of light artillery in the Utah Expedition.[19] Although the general is a North Carolinian and has two or three brothers in the Rebel service, he remained faithful to the country.

I am to have a drill of the ambulances belonging to the division this afternoon, about forty-five, for the purpose of instructing the men in their duties. The ambulance department of a division is organized in this wise. One first lieutenant is in charge, and two second lieutenants, with one sergeant, for each regiment. The surgeon in chief of division must inspect and instruct, and order when necessary.

Falmouth
April 5, 1863

After a few pleasant days, and the flying of dust on the hills, we were treated to a snowstorm last night. Yesterday morning I was awakened by the sentry to find my tent on fire. My boy Curtis had made a fire and left me asleep, and the fire caught round the stovepipe. [20] A pailful of water put it out, but the tent is rather airy now. Yesterday General Gibbon reviewed the First Brigade, when Governor Ramsey of Minnesota presented the First Minnesota with a new flag, made a speech, etc. [21] Another of General Gibbon's aides came, Lieutenant Hildreth of New Hampshire, and his adjutant general, Captain Wood, is to come soon. [22] Major Whittlesey is to go with General Howard.

I hope they will soon commence the draft, as this month and next quite a number of nine months' regiments go out and thirty-eight two years' regiments from New York. We have just begun to carry on the war systematically. I am satisfied that no material resistance will be made to the draft. [23]

Falmouth
April 7, 1863

There was a review of the cavalry of the army yesterday, attended by the President and Mrs. Lincoln. I was not able to go. Dr. Dougherty is away on leave of absence, and I am acting medical director of the corps. About 16,000 cavalry were on the ground. Everybody came back splashed with mud, and the review of infantry announced for today was postponed on account of the mud.

I suppose Uncle Abe and Hooker have been talking over matters and have probably decided what to do next. We shall know when we *do* it and not before. I have been reading the report of the Committee on the Conduct of the War. [24] It is a plain exposition of the weakness of McClellan, and all the laborious reports he may make will never change the opinions of the great mass of the people.

April 10, 1863

Day before yesterday went to the grand review of four corps and the reserve artillery. The president was there with General Hooker and staff, and Mrs. Lincoln and a lady friend were in a covered wagon. [25] The day was chilly. Mrs. Lincoln is a fat-faced, comfortable-looking woman. Their little boy, about eight years of age, rode a pony. [26] The president looked thin. About 70,000 men were present at this review. General Howard's corps is to be reviewed today by the president as soon as this is concluded.

Falmouth
April 13, 1863
Have been engaged two days in making preparations for removing the sick of the corps, an order having been issued to that effect. Dr. Dougherty is still absent, and I am still acting medical director of the corps. There are indications of a move.[27] *Evening.* Thirteen thousand cavalry moved somewhere today, and this evening we are under orders to march with eight days' rations, the men to carry rations in their haversacks and knapsacks, leaving their clothes out. This indicates a rapid march. This will give some of the nine months' men a chance to fight before they go out. A good many must be killed and wounded, both friend and foe. When will the Rebels learn that we will never give up the contest until they lay down their arms.

Falmouth
April 16, 1863
Have removed our division hospitals below Potomac Creek, on the line of the railroad to Aquia Creek.[28] Dr. Dougherty returned in the afternoon. At night troops were moving (fourteenth) but at twelve o'clock a heavy rain came on and continued until last night. All the little streams were rivers, and the land was flowing with water.[29] All movements were stopped, but it is clear today, and everything is going on again. This is understood to be a grand movement of the whole army, say 140,000 men, besides about 30,000 at Manassas under Heintzelman.[30] No doubt a great fight will take place within a week. The army will not have to wait for trains to come up with rations, but if operations are favorable can go right along.

Seventeenth. Nothing new yet, but a report that a brigade of General Howard's corps were out and lost a battery.[31] I was quite interested in watching a regiment of Rebels drilling across the river yesterday. We are in full sight of the drill grounds of each other, though their camps are mostly in the woods back of the town.[32]

Dr. Hurley, an assistant surgeon in Hancock's division, was killed yesterday by his horse falling upon him.[33] Dr. Ware, surgeon of the Forty-fourth Massachusetts, died recently in Washington, North Carolina.[34]

Falmouth
April 20, 1863

No movement yet. Has been raining all day and bids fair to rain tomorrow. Shall send two hundred fifty sick and disabled from our division hospital to Potomac Creek tomorrow. The cavalry are out and have had a skirmish. Newspaper correspondents are forbidden to publish anything relating to intended movements. Denyse, correspondent of the *New York Herald*, was sentenced by court-martial to hard labor on the public works for sending such an article for publication.[35]

Our staff is pretty nearly all changed now. We have but three of the old members. We have now Major Baird, 82nd N.Y., inspector; Captain Wood, assistant adjutant general; Captain Embler, commissary of musters; Captain Owen, quartermaster; Captain Crombargar, commissary; Lieutenant Steele, ordnance officer; and Lieutenants Haskell, Moale, and Hildreth, aides.[36] I am the senior in rank as well as the oldest in service on the staff.

Lieutenant Garland, ambulance officer of the division, was dismissed {from} the service for traitorous language and conduct.[37] He is a native of Fredericksburg and belongs to the Forty-second New York. Some time since he wrote to a friend in Shanghai, and the letter not being prepaid was sent to the dead letter office and opened, when the treasonable language was discovered. He was fortunate in having no worse punishment.

So some of our Copperheads at home think I am not exposed a great deal.[38] To be sure I have not been as much as some men in the front line and shall endeavor to keep out of extreme danger as much as is consistent with my duty, but shot and shell reach a great distance and are no respecters of persons. If advancing for half a mile in the face of a heavy artillery fire, and then under musketry, until the line breaks is a safe and pleasant amusement, then I have been quite amused. I would like nothing better than to lead in half a dozen of these Copperheads with a rope round their necks into just such places as I have been. [It is hardly worthwhile to pursue this subject. These remarks, and others stronger, were drawn forth by unkind and ungenerous remarks by those who, if they did not see fit to go themselves, should have sustained and encouraged those who did.]

71

We have a new set of tents (two staff officers are to occupy each tent) and have sent away our stoves. Some of these nights are cool and damp. I sometimes sit with General Gibbon and smoke evenings, and we pitch quoits for amusement.

April 23, 1863

Wet and cold weather. Can form no idea of when or in what direction our movement is to be made. Called on General Caldwell, commanding a brigade in the First Division, and took tea. Had a pleasant time talking of mutual acquaintances. The general was principal of the academy at East Machias, Maine, before the war.[39] I do not go visiting much. This is the first time I have called on General Caldwell. General Gibbon is very quiet. Sits in his tent playing solitaire. Found him this evening writing letters to his two "babies" as he calls them, whose photographs he has on his table.[40] I read myself to sleep today and dreamed among other things that in conversation with a Rebel, I told him that if we could not whip them in two years we would acknowledge their independence, but can't say that I acknowledge that when awake.

CHAPTER 6

"Those Dutchmen Would Not Fight"

April 27–June 11, 1863

The Chancellorsville campaign did not begin well. Brig. Gen. Alfred Sully proved to be unable to deal with a mutiny by the men of the Thirty-fourth New York, who differed with the army over the date of the expiration of their enlistment. Sully was removed from command of the First Brigade, Second Division, by the division's new leader, John Gibbon. Dyer had breakfast with Joe Hooker before he rode off for the first day of the battle. Victory seemed at hand with the surprisingly easy crossing of the Rappahannock and capture of Fredericksburg, but it was not to be. In defeat, General Hooker praised the army for its efforts. Dyer also comments on the death of Stonewall Jackson, the welcome arrival of spring, and the horde of women visitors to the camp.

Headquarters, Second Division, II Corps, Falmouth
April 27, 1863

We now have fine weather. The fields across the river are green, and wherever grass can find a place it springs up. Movements are going on today.[1] I was down to General Howard's today and dined with him. I think the general is a little too good-natured. He allows too many newspaper correspondents about his quarters, not because he wants them either. His corps, the XI, is to move today toward Kelly's Ford.[2] The XII Corps, General Slocum, is also on the move.[3] It looks as though we were to remain and hold this place. A new and beautiful railroad bridge has been built over Potomac Creek and fortifications erected to guard it.[4] Below are the hospitals. Now a body of cavalry is passing with wagons and pack mules. All is activity. But at our little headquarters all is quiet. General Hancock calls, or an officer comes up, or an orderly with dispatches, and as yet all is quiet.

April 28, 1863
The First and Third Divisions of our corps move this morning.[5] We are to be last. Shall have to picket the river and hold the lines at present. Expect lively times in a few days. If our division is kept out of the fight I shall not complain. We have had a good share.

Falmouth
April 29, 1863
This morning a division of Sedgwick's corps (VI) crossed below in boats and have completed their bridge.[6] It appears to be the intention to cross above and below.[7] A deserter just brought in reports short rations, but his appearance belies his report.[8] Yesterday three corps were across at Kelly's Ford, and one division of Sedgwick's is across below.[9] Last night troops were moving to the right, and this morning a pontoon train went up. We are ordered to be in readiness.

The Thirty-fourth New York, a two years' regiment, refused duty today, maintaining that their time was out.[10] General Sully, in command of the brigade, reported that he was unable to bring them to duty.[11] General Gibbon went over and had the mutineers drawn up in line, made them a little speech, ordered the Fifteenth Massachusetts to load, and gave them five minutes to return to their colors, which they did to a man in about four minutes.[12] General Gibbon has relieved General Sully of his command, though an intimate friend.

All the afternoon heavy firing has been going on at the right, at Chancellorsville. Some one hundred fifty prisoners brought in today.

Headquarters, Second Division, II Corps, Falmouth
May 2, 1863
Fighting commenced on the right this morning about seven o'clock. On the left it began about the same time. The First Corps passed here for Banks' Ford about noon, and one brigade of our division has gone up there.[13] So we have but two brigades now here. We hear nothing reliable from the right except that the main body of the army is at Chancellorsville. General Hooker stopped on his way

this morning and breakfasted with us. He seems in good spirits. Tomorrow I think a big fight will take place.

Falmouth
May 3, 1863

Another day of battle has passed. I only know what has been done in our front. Last evening about ten o'clock, we were ordered to proceed to the Lacy house and cross to Fredericksburg. We came down (the general and staff) about one o'clock, before the troops arrived. The engineers were here with pontoons and after unloading them began to run them down to the water. The enemy opened fire upon us from the houses and rifle pits, and we scampered up the bank, only one man wounded. The two brigades came down and waited for daylight. Then volunteers from the Third Brigade (our old brigade that always volunteers) went over in boats and commenced laying the bridge. [14] At the same time, Sedgwick's men, who had been fighting all the morning on the left, came hurrying through the town, and we soon had possession of their first line of rifle pits. Our brigades crossed and formed to the right, engaging the batteries there. Brisk shelling threw shrapnel among our men lively. Captains Holmes and Murphy of the Twentieth wounded. [15] After some hours of this fighting on our line, Sedgwick sent a column against their works on Marye's Hill. I saw them go up the steep hillsides and pour into the Rebel works, and it was such a charge as one does not often see. From the balcony of the Lacy house, which I am using again as a hospital, I had a fair view. All held their breath as we watched their ascent, but a stunning cheer broke forth when the Stars and Stripes were planted on the enemy's battery. I went over in the town. The dead were lying about in the streets, and pools of blood where men had fallen. The town has a desolate appearance, houses torn by shot, streets filled with rubbish, rifle pits across streets and through gardens and fields. Our division now holds Fredericksburg. I have somewhat over a hundred wounded at the Lacy house.

Sedgwick went on and is some distance in advance, but firing was heard near him, and he must have an enemy opposing him. [16] But I know one thing for sure, the heights of Fredericksburg have been taken, after it was proved to the satisfaction of all that they could not be.

Falmouth
May 6, 1863

Here we are all back again on the left, and the whole army is on its way back again to its old position. I wrote my last on the evening of the third. All looked well then on the left. During the night Longstreet arrived from Richmond with reinforcements and came up in Sedgwick's rear.[17] In the morning the Rebels regained the heights. Sedgwick fell back to Banks' Ford. Our third brigade occupied the town all day. Pickets were out, but the enemy nearly surrounded the town, and I felt afraid they would capture the whole brigade. In the morning a thick fog came up, the brigade crossed without loss, and the bridge was taken up. The enemy occupied the town immediately. Sedgwick and Couch crossed at Banks' Ford same night and came down yesterday. The whole army is now crossing at United States Ford and will probably get over without trouble.[18]

I had orders in the morning to remove the wounded from the Lacy house and got them all off, two hundred twenty-five of them. Our two brigades lost about fifty killed and wounded. Battery G, First Rhode Island Artillery, with us, lost thirty killed and wounded. Lieutenant Kelley killed, and the two other officers wounded.[19] Our wounded at this place, most of them men of the VI Corps, have been well attended to, and I left the Lacy house about noon. Am now at division headquarters, near the ruins of the Phillips house.[20] There has been a very heavy rain, part of the railroad {"bridge" partially crossed out} is washed away, and Potomac Creek is not fordable. Stoneman's cavalry is back again. They have been to the rear of the enemy but have not done much.[21]

General Howard's corps is reported to have behaved badly. Those Dutchmen would not fight.[22] The general I hear feels very badly about it, but of course nobody can blame him. He worked hard to make them fight. The fact is, the battle has not been fought. This was nothing but a "fizzle." I am sorry. I hoped better things of Hooker. The revulsion of feeling will be the worst feature in the case. We are in as good condition as ever to fight, but I am afraid there will be lack of confidence. The men are not yet back in their old camps, and many are out in this cold rain tonight without fires. General Berry was killed, also Captain Dessauer of General Howard's staff.[23]

Falmouth
May 9, 1863

Back again at our old place on the hill, where we spent the winter, and where we hoped we should not stay any more. All is cleared up, the tents pitched, and the general and others are having a game of quoits. The sun came out today, the first time since the storm. A lot of wounded came over today, by flag of truce, and were taken to the cars. We all feel a good deal disappointed at the termination of this affair, and it is certainly difficult to see what necessity there was for pulling back so hurriedly. A small part only of the army fought. Hooker withdrew without taking time to get his army in shape to fight them again. I am disappointed in him. It is useless to say (as the papers do) that the army has unbounded confidence in him still. They do not. I am afraid it is too late to take advantage of Stoneman's success.[24] The enemy will have time to repair all the damage he has done before we move. Why Peck could not come up from Suffolk and strike at Richmond I cannot tell.[25] This Army of the Potomac seems to be fated to always fight and never win.

It is undoubtedly true that the XI Corps misbehaved, and General Howard will of course have to bear a share of the reproach.[26] I have even heard Sedgwick blamed for not holding his position, when he fought greatly superior numbers and brought his men off in good shape, losing nearly as many in killed and wounded as all the rest of the army, but not in prisoners.[27] I saw his corps fight, and they fought well.

The president and General Halleck were down day before yesterday. I have heard that they were not at all pleased with the appearance of things.[28] I have heard that Hooker intended to cross the river again below, but they objected, and again that the army was to cross in three days. There is no reason though why we should not fight next week as well as next month. If we do not fight next week, my opinion is that we shall not for three months. [We did not until the enemy invaded Pennsylvania.]

Headquarters, Second Division, II Corps, Falmouth
May 13, 1863

Still here, hard and fast, and no signs of a move yet. General Hooker has issued a general order congratulating the army on its achievements, which is all very well, only we didn't achieve what we attempted. Hooker's course is severely criticized. I am disappointed that we do not move again soon, but I think there is not a perfect agreement between the generals. General Couch has felt dissatisfied for some time, and I have heard that he has resigned.[29] I think this will finally result in General Hooker's being relieved of his command.[30] I think I should be willing to have Hooker try it again.

The Rebels have lost one of their best generals. Stonewall Jackson died after the amputation of his arm at the shoulder.[31] I have heard Jackson highly spoken of as a man. The army is as impatient to "do something" as any at home, and it is hardly proper for the latter to hurry up the army in the field. Every man knows when he goes into a fight that he stands a good chance of being hit, and officers are no better off than privates. They suffer more in proportion, and they don't want to fight merely for the fun of it.

Falmouth
May 14, 1863
It is said that every corps commander, except Sickles, the poorest of all, recommended Hooker to remain and renew the fight, but he refused.[32] You notice the papers say that our wounded are doing well and are being brought in from the field. They neglect to say that they are in the hands of the enemy; but they have allowed us to remove them, and a long train brought in many today.

Falmouth
May 17, 1863
Was down to the XI Corps today. General Howard was very pleasant and doesn't seem to be entirely cast down by the censures of the *New York Herald* and other papers. He managed his troops as well as they could be managed. They were driven and panic stricken. Nothing would stop them.

Two ladies were present. Mrs. Barlow, wife of General Barlow, is a large, smart woman; believes her husband, next to General Howard, is the greatest man living; and talked military a good deal, a little too much of a general.[33] The other little woman was very smart and discussed matters of which she knew nothing, but the general is very pleasant and doesn't disagree with anybody if he can help it. We dined very pleasantly. Officers' wives are very fond of getting compliments for their husbands, but personal bravery is not so uncommon as to be considered remarkable.

Many are going away on leave for a few days, none more than ten days. General Gibbon has gone for five.

Falmouth
May 20, 1863

The warm spring days come and go, and all is quiet on the Rappahannock. Along the river the pickets stand or walk about, sometimes bathing and fishing together, but they are not allowed to go too near, as the Rebels have a strong tendency to get over on our side, and one does occasionally.[34] They catch a good many shad, by seines, but we never interfere with them. The hills over the river look beautifully green, and hundreds of horses are grazing about the fields. Drills and reviews are held in sight of each other daily. Only a small number however are in and about the city. The bulk of our army, as of theirs, is farther down the river. Most of our troops have moved to new ground, as the old camps get filthy after long occupation. The army now is remarkably healthy, very few sick are in camp, the principal number in division hospital at Potomac Creek. Very few deaths take place among the sick and wounded. In our division hospital but one death has taken place for a fortnight among four hundred patients, over one hundred forty of whom are wounded.

General Owen, being temporarily in command of the division, had us out on drill yesterday. Rather a small show. Our division numbers now only as many as one of our brigades last summer. Was down to the Lacy house yesterday. Mrs. Harris still remains there, with sanitary stores, and the pickets on the river quarter there.[35] General Gibbon was here last summer, with McDowell, and describes it as an elegant place. But it is sadly changed, and so has Fredericksburg and all the country about here. Virginia has paid dearly for her secession. Some of the old families hold on here, while their sons and brothers are in the Rebel army. The Washingtons live just back of us.[36] General Birney has his headquarters near his house, a very common wooden house, but the garden must have been very fine. The old man is shabby, two daughters are with him, and one son in the Rebel service. So with all the families about here. Duff Green of Falmouth has sons and sons-in-law in the Rebel army, while all the daughters and daughters-in-law are here under our protection.[37]

A number of females have been sent away from the army, some of them suspected of being spies, and I think they are very apt to engage in that business. One lady who was very efficient about the Lacy house hospital has been ordered to Alexandria by the provost marshal. She was from South Carolina and seemed to be acquainted with a good many of our wounded prisoners. Some women who came over from Fredericksburg to offer their sympathy for the Rebel wounded were not permitted to return but compelled to throw themselves on the hospitality of their friends on this side.

When business is over our principal occupation is pitching quoits. We have iron quoits, one set two and one-half pounds each and one of three and one-half pounds each, and pitch about eighteen yards. Very pretty amusement while waiting for orders to move.

May 23, 1863

General Gibbon returned the twenty-first. Leaves of absence are pretty freely granted where they can be spared by corps commanders, but applications from surgeons have to go to headquarters of the army, and Dr. Letterman generally disapproves them. Drills, and reviews, and policing the grounds is the principal occupation now. Every precaution is used to prevent disease.

I did feel in hopes that the army would move out of this place soon, but we are likely to remain here for an indefinite time. Oh! that somebody would do something to break the monotony. If Lee would attack us, or go somewhere else, fall back to Richmond, or elsewhere, we should *appear* to be doing something. But there is no such appearance now.

Headquarters, Second Division, II Corps, Falmouth
May 24, 1863

General Gibbon came from headquarters of the army this afternoon and reported Vicksburg ours.[38] It was a bold thing and well done, and will have a good effect. It will be asked why we have not done the same. A good many reasons why. The army opposed to us is the largest and best army the Rebels have, and their best generals are in command, and they fight too.[39] No such fighting has been done as by the Army of the Potomac, but the two armies are so nearly equal that neither gets much advantage.

General Couch is absent and will not come back to the corps. General Hancock, now in command of the First Division, will have it. It is very well to keep up appearance of confidence in our commanders, but I know that General Hooker has not the confidence of a corps commander in the army except Sickles. Most of the generals are really opposed to him, and others are only willing to fight under him *because* he is in command.

As warm weather comes, millions of insects of all kinds come with it. As I write at least fifty kinds, large and small, are running over the paper and into the candle. Whippoorwills and mockingbirds sing, and snakes, lizards, and flying squirrels are plenty. We have the only trees in the neighborhood. For miles around all is cleared and nothing is planted in the fields. All is desolation.

Falmouth
May 26, 1863
Visited the hospital at Potomac Creek today and called on General Howard. Some ladies were there. I think home is the best place for them now. A party of singers and players serenaded us last night. This evening have just come from a review of the third brigade. We are to remove our headquarters tomorrow. A line is selected for defense, in case the enemy should think proper to come over and attack us, reaching from Falmouth across to Potomac Creek bridge, four or five miles. I hardly think they will attempt it.

Falmouth
May 28, 1863
This morning went with General Gibbon to the review of General Caldwell's division, formerly Hancock's, General Hancock being present as reviewing officer. Very warm and dusty. After review went to General Hancock's headquarters at the Washington house. When about to start on our visit to the hospitals at Potomac Creek, some ladies, one a daughter of Secretary Cameron, came, and a delay of an hour or two was the consequence.[40] Leaving them with General Caldwell, we went on. Dined with Dr. Dwinelle and then went through the hospital. General Hancock took care to speak to every wounded man and make some pleasant remark. It has a good

effect. There are over one thousand men in the division hospitals of the II Corps, many of them from the Chancellorsville fight. The other corps have their hospitals in the neighborhood.

Did not get back in time to see a race run by Lt. Col. Jo Smith, corps commissary, and Lieutenant Steele, $40 stakes.[41] Steele broke a stirrup and got thrown and bruised, and also lost the stakes. He has gone to bed (he tents with me) feeling sore in body and in mind, as he considers his reputation somewhat impaired. There must be something for excitement.

There are reports tonight that numbers of the enemy are moving up river, and Griffin's division have gone up to Banks' Ford.[42] The Richmond papers are urging an attack. So we have not got Vicksburg yet. I am afraid if Grant does not take it soon, the Rebel army will be largely reinforced.

Headquarters, Second Division, II Corps, Falmouth
June 1, 1863

Almost buried in dust for three or four days. The wind has been blowing a gale, and it was almost impossible to write or do anything else. Went to review of General Howard's old brigade, in the First Division.[43] He was present, with Generals Hancock, Gibbon, Caldwell, Barlow, with their respective staffs. It was the anniversary of the battle of Fair Oaks, the second day, when he lost his arm. After the review the general made a speech, referring to their battles, their thinned ranks, the great number who had fallen on the field, and encouraged them still to fight on till the work is done. Had refreshments at Colonel Cross's, now in command of the brigade.[44] Reviews and drills are the order of the day. Our division was reviewed on Friday, and tomorrow a division drill takes place. On Friday the nineteenth was called up to headquarters after the review, and Generals Hancock, Sykes, and others who were present, pronounced their drill as fine as anything they had ever seen.[45]

Yesterday the Rebs were notified to stop fishing in the river. They have been carrying it on with seines, but there is too much mixing up of pickets, and perhaps communication might be carried on between them and some of their friends on this side. Thinking they might possibly resist, batteries were placed in position, and things made ready for them, but they desisted. It is quite amusing to sit and watch them with a glass at their work and amusements.

Falmouth
June 5, 1863
Have had orders to be ready to march for two days. Yesterday the V Corps moved up, and today others are moving. This morning not a Rebel encampment is to be seen opposite, perhaps only changing camp, but they are up to something.

More racing. The prospect of a race seems to be more exciting to many than the prospect of a battle. Fights are common, but a good race doesn't come off every week. A splendid serenade last night. General Hancock was over and stayed till a late hour. This morning had orders to be ready to move. Sedgwick moved down toward the river and about three o'clock this afternoon commenced laying a bridge, where they crossed before. Our artillery opened a heavy fire on their pickets. Two brigades then crossed and drove the Rebels out of their second line of rifle pits. While the fight was going on two miles below, at Falmouth and opposite, pickets were walking about with the utmost unconcern, as though it were none of their business. Men have learned not to waste powder and trouble each other when no advantage can be gained, but when they are ordered to attack, they go at it in earnest. During the fight, a horse race was going on about a mile off, and regiments were out on their usual dress parade.

I do not think it is the intention to cross and fight here again. This is a movement probably to get the enemy back again, supposing they were moving up country toward Maryland. I do not think they have gone yet but are massed back of the hills, in readiness.

Falmouth
June 7, 1863
Went down to Sedgwick's crossing this afternoon. One division is across, with some artillery. Their front is a semicircle fronting on the Bowling Green road. [46] Some six hundred or eight hundred yards in front of this is a range of hills occupied by the enemy. I am pretty sure we shall not fight there. General Sedgwick was stopping in a tent on this side of the river, not having moved his headquarters. He had an old felt hat on, with two old sack coats and a blue shirt. He is never more uncomfortable than when in full dress, but when occasion calls can and does look quite smart. "Uncle John" as we all call him is a good fighter and a pleasant old man, though a bachelor.

Since the crossing, there have been about eight killed and twenty wounded, as General Sedgwick told me. These are generally picked off by sharpshooters. Our sharpshooters have gone down, and since then they have not been so venturesome. It seems that Banks has had a bad time at Port Hudson.[47] I am afraid that neither he nor Grant have a fine prospect, and there is nothing very encouraging here.[48] There may be a change in some of these departments before long. If not, we shall have to begin over again.

Falmouth
June 11, 1863
An expedition went out several days since under General Pleasonton composed of five thousand cavalry and two or three thousand infantry, with artillery, with the intention of going to Culpeper to break up Stuart's cavalry rendezvous.[49] They came back yesterday, and a telegram from headquarters of the army announces that they met the enemy, twelve thousand strong, fought him and took one hundred prisoners, and then recrossed the river, having crippled him so that he could not pursue. The facts as I hear them are that we did not get far; had a fight; lost a good many in killed and wounded, several hundred prisoners, and two pieces of artillery; and came back pretty quick.[50] Colonel Davis of the cavalry was killed.[51] I don't think the expedition gained anything.

General Couch is finally relieved and ordered to the Department of the Susquehanna, with headquarters at Chambersburg.[52] His staff leave today to join him. I am very sorry to have General Couch go. He is one of the best officers in the army. Hancock is a smart man, but unlike Couch. I heard that Hancock had been offered command of Stoneman's cavalry corps.[53] Stoneman is ordered to Washington. Hooker is not satisfied with him.[54]

Was down to the division hospital yesterday; all going on well. Only two deaths have occurred in our division for a month (excepting two who were killed). Last year at this time one a day would not cover the loss.

CHAPTER 7

"My Heart Almost Failed Me"

June 17–July 6, 1863

On June 17 the army began its march from the Occoquan River to Gettysburg. Once again Dyer records crossing old campsites and battlefields. On the way into Pennsylvania in pursuit of Lee's army, Hooker was relieved of command. Dyer got the news about June 28. Meade continued the march through western Maryland into southern Pennsylvania. The three-day battle that followed at Gettysburg was the greatest test the Army of the Potomac ever faced, and probably the high point of Dyer's army service.

His account of the battle is particularly detailed. He writes about it at length in the earliest of his letters to survive, all of which are in appendix 1 and can be compared with the journal version in this chapter. Surgeon Dyer provides numerous details about the battle, the casualties, their treatment, the establishment of hospitals, and the suffering caused by the lack of medical supplies in wagons that were kept from the front. Dyer also transcribed a long excerpt from an account of the battle that he believed was written by a member of the Second Division, II Corps, which appeared in the Baltimore American. *Well known to Gettysburg scholars, it was actually from the pen of John H. B. Latrobe of Baltimore, based on what John Gibbon told him of the battle while recovering at his house from a wound.*

Wolf Run Shoals, Occoquan River
June 17, 1863
Since I wrote last, a good many movements have taken place, and we, the rear guard of the army, are here. On Saturday night Sedgwick recrossed the river and marched Sunday. We were ready to march then, but the roads were not clear of troops and teams, so we did

not leave until after sunrise on Monday morning. The Rebels did not follow us, at least not in force. Our first day's march to Aquia was terrible. The heat was oppressive. Many were sunstruck, three or four men in the corps died from heat, and there were crowds of stragglers. Passed through Stafford Court House. There is a small courthouse, a jail (which was on fire as we passed), and three other buildings. Yesterday marched to Wolf Run Shoals, a place of splendid scenery, fortified by earthworks. This was another terrible march. Being in anticipation of an attack on the flank or rear, all broken down teams, ammunition, etc., was destroyed as soon as it was found impossible to bring it on. A good deal of property was burnt up. The whole corps, myself included, had a good bath in the Occoquan, and our staff slept in the front yard of a house. Generals Hancock and Gibbon slept on the floor in the front entry.

Sangster's Station
June 17, 1863
Came on here today and shall probably wait for further developments.[1] Had papers today, the first time since we marched. All surplus baggage is to be sent off in the morning, and the sick will also be sent. Our ambulance train was loaded with sick and "played out" men and had to be sent out a second time to bring them in.

General Gibbon went home today to attend the funeral of his little boy.[2] General Harrow, a western man, is in command temporarily.[3] I am writing on my cot for the last time this evening. We shall make a bonfire of all these things in the morning. We are in for another campaign, and somebody has got to suffer. The future is uncertain. We must whip these Rebels before we can do anything else.

Thoroughfare Gap
June 21, 1863
Arrived here last evening, having marched since last Monday morning about seventy miles. Left Sangster's Station on Friday and marched to Centreville, a splendid position as approached from Washington, the range of heights being fortified strongly. The works were thrown up by the Rebels in 1861–62 and afterward strengthened on the other side by us. They are now occupied by General Abercrombie with the troops who were surrendered last fall at Harpers Ferry.[4] They are living very comfortably there. Centre-

ville is a little village about half destroyed, dilapidated houses with immense stone chimneys on each end, outside, sometimes two.

Heavy rain, a cool night, and next afternoon marched to Thoroughfare Gap, the last six miles in the dark. Forded the Bull Run and some smaller streams and finally got in position and occupied the Gap at half past ten o'clock. General Gibbon joined us yesterday, and I rode with him over the old battlefield of Bull Run as the troops were moving along the roads. Very little of the effects of the first battle are to be seen, except ruins of buildings here and there. But of the battles of the twenty-eighth and twenty-ninth of August last, evidence enough is seen, both there and at Gainesville, where General Gibbon's brigade fought on the twenty-eighth, the Second Wisconsin losing about four hundred, seventy of them killed within a few minutes.[5] They were buried where they fell, that is, some days after a little earth was thrown over them as they lay, but now the bleached bones are sticking out of the ground, bare skulls, some with bullet holes in them, and the ground covered with the debris of the battlefield, everything except arms, which the Rebels were careful to collect after the battle.

The country is almost deserted, only a few poor whites and some Negroes occupy the few miserable houses left. In the dooryard of a house occupied by a white man and his family were the partly uncovered skeletons of two men, who were probably buried where they fell. When I asked the old scoundrel why he didn't cover them up, he said he had "buried a heap of them, but the rain had washed the dirt off," but he had not probably thrown a shovelful of earth on them. The country for miles is one vast graveyard, and rank weeds and grass growing in gardens where houses have been burnt. I picked a rose in a garden where a house had been burnt and a woman killed in the first Bull Run battle.[6] The first and second Bull Run battles were fought on nearly the same ground. Gainesville is a small village of three buildings where the railroad crosses the turnpike. A few miles beyond, Haymarket was quite a large village, now entirely destroyed. Immense stone chimneys are standing about here and there. This is a fine country, and with a good population would be elegant.

Fighting has been going on nearly all day within a few miles between Pleasonton's and the enemy's cavalry, and at one point our pickets were driven in, but all is quiet now.[7] We gave our tents up and business going on. No other corps are about here but are probably stretching across the country as far as Leesburg. Dr. Perry, assistant surgeon of the Twentieth, broke his leg on our first day's march from Falmouth, and after riding in an ambulance for two or three days, went home from Fairfax Station.[8]

Thoroughfare Gap
June 24, 1863

We are still here in a delightful little spot in this Gap in the Bull Run Mountains, no other corps near us, and our lines quite circumscribed. Went out through the pass as far as our pickets but have concluded that I won't do that again, as one is apt to get into trouble. General Gibbon has placed General Owen in arrest for going out beyond our pickets and for giving passes to some of his men to go beyond the pickets to forage.[9] The best thing one can do is to go to sleep, and then he will be sure of getting into no difficulty.

From what I hear today I think we shall march tomorrow, or very soon. By dispatches to headquarters of the corps this evening it is reported that the Rebels are moving into Pennsylvania in force, and that fifteen thousand crossed at Shepherdstown yesterday.[10] That is near the old field of Antietam. I have an idea that they will go into Pennsylvania, but after destroying property there, they may find it necessary to go back and will arrange themselves for battle near the old field. There is no danger of their getting to Washington or Baltimore, for we can march to Leesburg and cross at Edwards Ferry in a very short time. A thousand rumors are afloat in the papers, of course the greater part without foundation. Armies do not rise up and disappear in a moment, and they do not move without the knowledge of somebody.

I cannot think Hooker is a fool, and I will wait and see what comes of it before I blame anybody. Great games are being played on the chessboard, and Lee is a smart man; but the game is not finished yet. And I have not lost my faith in the administration. No man ever had such a weight of responsibility on him as the president, and no one ever such a set of scoundrels to oppose him at home. It is almost too much to fight an enemy at home and abroad too, but he will come out right yet. The Copperheads do not want the war finished now. They would rather sacrifice half a million more lives than not have their way. I could tell you of a great many things that keep an army from victory; but all these things will be known in due time. I hope to see the end of it all soon. I shall be nearer you in a week, somewhere in Maryland or Pennsylvania. We are living rather shabbily now and shall for some time, but I shall be willing to do anything to finish up this war and "lick out" these Copperheads.

Near Poolesville
June 27, 1863

Back again near old Camp Benton. Left Thoroughfare Gap day before yesterday and crossed the Potomac at Edwards Ferry last night. Had a small skirmish at Haymarket; one killed and eight wounded.[11] The VI Corps cross today. We are under orders to march again today, go toward Pennsylvania. I am well and hope we shall do the right thing by the Rebs.

Monocacy Bridge near Frederick City
June 28, 1863

We have had a tiresome march up here, arrived this afternoon at four o'clock. From Camp Benton to Barnesville, just under Sugarloaf Mountain, our march was through mud and rain. Arrived there at 10:30 P.M. Got something to eat and slept till six. Ordered to march. The baggage and supply trains impeded our march very much. Passed through the neat little village of Urbana, about which time a report came that General Hooker was relieved of his command, and General Meade is now commander of the Army of the Potomac. I can really say that no one felt aggrieved or disappointed, and I have heard of no resignations being tendered in consequence. General Meade is said to be a good officer and was in command of the V Corps. General Gibbon is intimate with him and has gone to Frederick this evening to see him with General Hancock.[12]

We have got a big piece of work on hand, but where the fight will take place no one can tell. The Rebels are well into Pennsylvania, and we shall have to head them off and fight them somewhere. We are to march in the morning at six o'clock toward New Market in the direction of Baltimore. We shall not go over South Mountain probably. Yet no one can tell from one hour to another what is to be done, and we have not the sources of information that they have at headquarters of the army, yet I generally keep posted up pretty well.

Major Webb, formerly chief of staff for General Meade, an officer of the regular army, has been appointed brigadier general and ordered to report for duty to General Gibbon today. He will command the Second Brigade, General Owen's Philadelphia brigade. [13] Owen is now under arrest for irregular conduct. He had a very good brigade, but his discipline has been so loose that they have become notorious stragglers.

My position during this march has been no sinecure. The superintendence of the medical department of the division requires much labor, and besides General Gibbon requires everyone on his staff to use his utmost endeavor to prevent straggling.

Uniontown
June 30, 1863

We started on our march again yesterday morning, passing east of Frederick City through Johnsville, Liberty, Union Bridge, and Uniontown, where we arrived just before dark, the troops coming in till ten or eleven o'clock pretty well tired out, having marched from twenty-five to thirty miles that day, a very long march. [14] The men kept up well too, especially in our division. A new brigade that joined us the other day straggled so that but few were left at night. [15] We are following pretty close upon the Rebels. [16] Their scouts have been here and taken a good many cattle, horses, and mules. The Rebel pickets were within two miles of us last night, but I think they are gone today. We shall probably remain here today until the position of things is better known. The Rebs are at Harrisburg, but many are yet threatening Baltimore and Washington. [17]

There are many good Union people about here and some violent secesh. Some shut themselves up in their houses or scowl at the windows, while others freely give what they have. One poor old lady stood at the door of her little shanty as the troops came by, handing out slices of nice soft bread to the soldiers. When it was almost gone she looked down the road, and seeing the countless multitude still coming, exclaimed in despair, "dear me, there ain't half enough to go round!" Her will was good and in striking contrast to the behavior of some others.

Some threw bouquets, and a pretty young lady at Union Mills showed her good taste by throwing me a fine one. This is a splendid country, and the wheat fields are magnificent. The prospect from the hills is splendid.

Near Gettysburg
July 2, 1863

On our march to this place yesterday we met wounded from the fight. Our advance had been driven through Gettysburg, a good deal broken up. Reynolds killed and Howard had taken another position on Cemetery Hill. General Hancock was ordered by General Meade to hasten forward and take command of the right wing, I and XI Corps, leaving General Gibbon in command of the corps. We marched this morning from our bivouac, about four miles, and took position. Skirmishing and artillery firing occupied nearly all day until we found their position, and the fight began about four o'clock in earnest. From that time until after eight the roar of battle was terrific. They came down on our left (III Corps) in heavy force and at first overpowered us. We then threw in more troops (V Corps), they put in more, column after column poured into the gap, which they tried to force. About dark Sedgwick came up and they were forced back. Several times my heart almost failed me as our men fell back. The III Corps seemed completely broken up, and men, horses, guns, and caissons rushed through the orchard, which we were using for hospital, but when I saw "Uncle John Sedgwick's" flag advancing, I knew we would check them or the VI Corps would not survive.[18]

We were nearly driven out of our hospital but held on and were relieved of our anxiety when they were driven back.[19] I was too busy to indulge my curiosity to any great extent, but from the position I occupied I could see some of the most important movements. The fighting was severe. Hour after hour the volleys poured incessantly. Some of the regiments of our division lost heavily. The First Minnesota had colonel, lieutenant colonel, major, and three captains wounded.[20] Colonel Revere of the Twentieth Massachusetts will die.[21] Colonel Ward of the Fifteenth will lose his other leg.[22] (He lost one at Ball's Bluff and died of this wound.) Colonel Huston and three captains of the Eighty-second New York killed.[23] Captain Dodge and Lieutenant Stone of the Nineteenth wounded. I cannot remember all at this moment. I have sat down in the little kitchen of the house near which we have our hospital to write a few words.[24] The family have fled, and well they might. All in the neighborhood took their children and fled in terror. I have here about five hundred or six hundred wounded in the house, barn, and under the apple trees.

The fight will probably be renewed in the morning. It is now one o'clock. I hope we shall be able to hold our position if nothing more. I must get a little sleep and be up at daylight. God help us and give us the victory! Our army has fought well and will fight tomorrow. I think so far there has been no blundering, we have done the best we could, and if we fail it is because we have not men enough, or God is not on our side.

July 3, 12 meridian
There has been fighting this morning, but all is quiet now. A grand attack is to be made this afternoon by us, if not by the Rebels. They have so far been repulsed. They are desperate however, and will try to cut their way through. The hospital was rather close yesterday, and we are now about moving back to be more out of the way. Reinforcements are coming. Couch is on the way. [We were led to expect some help from the militia under Couch, but the Pennsylvania militia was a myth. I have never seen it and have not yet seen the man who has enjoyed that sight.] Hoping for a joyful Fourth, I send a note by Captain Patten, who goes home wounded.[25]

Gettysburg
July 4, 1863
Just after Captain Patten left, about one o'clock, the enemy opened his artillery, and ours soon replied. Along the whole line there was a perfect roar. All seemed blended in one continuous roar. For about two hours it continued without cessation. Batteries fired till all their men were disabled, and men from the infantry were detailed to take their places. Gun carriages and caissons were knocked to pieces, wheels replaced, and knocked to pieces again. Guns fired till they were heated and taken off to cool, while new batteries were put in their places. Horses killed by the hundred. Then the enemy came up in line to the assault, moving steadily on. The engagement was fierce in front of our division, and at one point the enemy forced our lines back, where our Second Brigade was posted. Our old Third Brigade faced round and poured such a fire into them that they were forced to yield. Here twenty-one Rebel colors were taken. The Nineteenth took four.[26] Hundreds, some say thousands, of prisoners, remained in our hands. This finished the fight in a manner, though they made some feeble attempts last night and this morning to force our lines.

Today they are not in sight, except skirmishers. We are victorious. For three days they have attempted to force our lines, and each attack has been repulsed. The last assault was a desperate one. Never in the history of the war has been known such a fiercely contested fight, or such slaughter. It seemed as much impossible for one man to escape as it would be for one man to escape a drop of rain in a shower.

Generals Hancock and Gibbon wounded, General Zook of Third Division, and other general officers.[27] Colonels Revere and Ward are dead. Major Macy lost a hand.[28] The Second Corps has lost upward of 3,000 in killed and wounded, the Nineteenth Massachusetts at least sixty, the Nineteenth Maine, 212.[29] They did finely.

We have about six hundred fifty of our wounded, and two hundred Rebels in our hospital here, besides some two or three hundred in the hospital nearer the field, and all are not brought in yet, but are cared for at temporary hospitals near the scene of the fight.[30] This would be a joyful Fourth of July only for the dreadful scenes about us. I am now sitting in a little shelter tent which one of the men has put up, while the rain is pouring down in torrents on thousands of wounded gathered together. Our corps and some others have no tents, no houses or barns. Some of the men are sheltered by the shelter tents which their comrades have put up for them. Our hospital trains were left behind at Westminster, with all other baggage, as the road was to be left unencumbered for the passage of the VI Corps and also to be secure in case of a retreat. Even after the battle was decided, the stupid quartermasters would not allow our hospital trains to come up without special orders from the quartermaster of the army. That comes of having the medical department interfered with by others. We shall have them up tomorrow.[31]

It will be impossible to work fast enough to perform all the necessary operations for two or three days. I am waiting for the rain to hold up a little to go to work. I have had a good deal to do in superintending the bringing up of wounded to the hospital and providing for them when here. Was up all night last night, our ambulances being at work continually, but we could not operate as the rain was falling in torrents and candles would not burn. All have been fed with soup and tea, and whiskey when necessary.

These hurried notes, written at odd moments of leisure, give but a meager idea of the great battle. Such accounts can be found elsewhere. Of the part our division bore in the fight, I found at the time a very good description in the *Baltimore American*, written by a member of the division, from which I make some extracts:[32]

Of the fight of the second, Thursday, I have little to say. I was not there. I only know it was a touch and go affair, in consequence, as they told me, of Sickles swinging his corps forward until it occupied a position nearly at right angles with the left arm of the horse shoe (the shape of our line of battle), whereas he ought to have kept his place on the outline of the crest. But tempted by what he thought was a better position, he brought his left so that the Rebels enfiladed his line, and drove it back in confusion. The enemy at one time gained a position inside our lines, but reinforcements coming up, checked what came very near being a defeat for us.

Of Friday's fight I know more. Lee's attack on this day was on what is called the left center, the position held principally by the Second Corps; the Second Brigade of the Second Division of which, under Gen. Webb, was on the right, looking over the valley and down upon the Emmitsburg road. Next to it on its left was the Third Brigade (Hall's). The First Brigade being still farther on the left, the three brigades forming the Second Division being thus in line on the crest. Just in front of Hall's brigade, and a little way down the slope towards the valley, was a stone wall, and to the left, and somewhat in advance of the stone wall, was a rail fence in front of Hall's brigade. This wall and fence, and the clump of trees were features in the case, let me tell you. Away to the left was the Third Corps, and to the right, facing Gettysburg, the Eleventh Corps. . . .

The morning of the 3d passed quietly. . . . About one o'clock a single gun on the opposite side of the valley went "bang"—and there was the whir of a shot. Presently another bang, and then bang, bang, until it was impossible to count the shots; and along with these reports came every kind of bustle, whirr, whistle and shriek that man has heard or can imagine; the most terrific of all proceeding from some elongated missile, which ceasing to revolve around its axis, dashed "promiscuously" through the air, becoming visible on such event. The 12-pound shot were also to be seen as they came, and the worst of it was that every shot seemed to be coming straight to hit you between the eyes. Horses were the greatest sufferers here, for the men laid down and escaped somewhat, but the poor brutes had to take it standing. Gen. Gibbon had sent two regiments to the house on the Emmitsburg road, from which we inferred that he expected an attack in that direction, and began to brace up for what was coming.[33]

By this time, after an hour and a half of such firing as I have described, we could see, from where we stood, the enemy moving up in three lines from out of the woods. They would come out, marching by flank, till they reached the desired ground, when they would face to the front. Their second line was about a hundred yards in rear of the first, and on the edge of the woods, across the valley, was a third line. It was a splendid sight to see them. No one looked at their uniforms or no uniforms, their hats or caps or bare heads. Everybody looked at the beautiful way in which they arrayed themselves in order of attack, regardless of the shot and shell which we threw into their ranks. The soldiers on our side again and again praised, while they waited the approach of the enemy. Nor did they wait long. When about within two hundred yards of us, a part of our division, I think it was Hall's brigade, opened fire, and we could see men fall and others go to the rear. Still on they came, crowding a little in front, but as steady as rocks. Just then an officer rode by and said the Vermont regiment on the left was worrying the enemy. But they did not mind that either—on they came.

When they got within a hundred yards, more of our regiments opened fire; but it did not stop them. Some regiments reserved their fire until they got within fifty yards, and then the enemy fell fast, but still on they came, and we could see their faces and hear their officers. It was almost too much for human nature to stand, and a portion of the Second Brigade, which was behind the stone fence, began to leave cover—not because the enemy were upon it, but because it seemed impossible to stay. Not a man *ran*, or seemed to feel like running but they fell back slowly, loading as they did so, and firing, while the flags of the enemy, which are small red affairs, with a white cross diagonal on them, got up to the stone wall, and some crossed the line of rail fence, perhaps a hundred or so, led, as I heard by General Armistead. [General Armistead was wounded here and died in our hands.] They were able to do this because the Second Brigade did not stand up to the line of the stone wall and rail fence, so that the Division was bent back, in the center, as it were, the ends at the right and left standing fast.

95

This was the pinch, and the officers knew it. Gen. Gibbon had just been hit, some one said, and almost at the same time Gen. Hancock was badly wounded, and both were taken off the field to the rear. But I recollect seeing Gibbon's aide try to rally the men, and do it manfully, too [Haskell]. He did a man's part in steadying the line. So did Webb, who was on foot in the midst of the men. Entreaty, command, expostulation, encouragement, were employed. At this time the enemy were crowding over the stone fence near the clump of trees, and their red flags were waving, it seemed to me, in triumph already; though Hall was all right, and his men were steady on our left. Presently some one near me said the enemy were massing their men in front of Webb, opposite the clump of trees, and we began to wish for Hall's help.

By this time the officers had stopped the falling back, and were driving stragglers to the front, though we did not go forward to the stone wall, yet, but all were facing the enemy and firing heavily — not in ranks — for every one seemed going it pretty much on his own hook — but cheerfully, which was a good sign. We had wished for Hall, so he came as we wished, and his right marched by the flank to our left and got mixed with our men. As the Third Brigade (Hall's) came up, by the flank, there was a disposition, under the heavy fire to which it was exposed, to edge away from the stone wall, but the officers overcame this, and soon a compact body of men was formed, who delivered a heavy and well directed fire upon the enemy, as they came over the wall and rail fence towards us. Just then Gibbon's aide, Haskell, came over with some regiments from the First Brigade (Harrow's) on our left, and reported that the extreme right of the enemy was breaking badly, and that the men were running to the rear. This greatly encouraged us, and we cheered and went about our work with a will.

We now advanced, and as we did so, could see that the battle was raging in front of the Third Division. We delivered a steady volley from the crest, at short range, which cleared the wall, to which we then rushed, flags waving and men shouting. The wall was gained and crossed, and the work of taking prisoners commenced. Hundreds, who threw down their arms and rushed towards us, were sent to the rear. Here and there was a struggle for flags, but the battle was ended on this part of the field. Lee's great assault had failed. . . . One thing struck me much. It was the intelligence of the men. For a good part of the time, and in the heaviest of the fight, the ranks were lost and there was no organization. The officers were in our midst everywhere; but still we kept together, and seemed to understand without orders what to do, and to feel that the quicker we fired the sooner the thing would be over. After the assault on our division was repulsed, there was another made on the left of us, a good way off (near Round Top) but it failed, and by six o'clock the fight was done everywhere.[34]

It has generally happened that during our greatest battles and immediately afterward, I have been too much engaged to write particulars. In the early part of the battle of Gettysburg, I was engaged in locating and preparing the hospital, after which I went to work attending to wounded, but frequently had occasion to go to the front, to see that all in my department was going on right—that those surgeons who were ordered to examine wounded and dispatch them to the rear were at their posts and that the ambulance officers were doing their duty. The ambulance horses were worked night and day, and many broke down. Mules were sometimes substituted.

The road just in rear of our lines, where I had occasion to pass frequently, was within range of the enemy's artillery and at one time of musketry fire. I noticed a group of men sitting down quietly, playing poker, while shells were bursting frequently and unpleasantly near. They sought mental occupation to divert their attention from more serious subjects. General Meade's headquarters were at a small house near the road, and as many as seventeen horses of officers and orderlies were killed while standing there. General Gibbon's orderly, John, was killed by a shell while holding horses at the rear.

While going up I met Generals Hancock and Gibbon, and Major (afterward Brevet Major General) Macy coming wounded from the field. I accompanied them to the hospital, where Dr. Dougherty dressed General Hancock's wound, Dr. Hayward Major Macy's, while I attended to General Gibbon. Lieutenant Haskell, who was slightly wounded, soon came down and reported the attack entirely repulsed.[35] General Gibbon, who sat on the step of an ambulance while I dressed the wound in his shoulder, was feeling rather faint, but on this announcement was so elated that he got up and walked to General Hancock's ambulance to shake hands with him and congratulate him on the victory. After taking some refreshment they kept on to Westminster to take the cars for home.

On the same day, while going up to the front, I met Major Rice of the Nineteenth walking down with a flesh wound of the thigh, which he called a "good joke," and carrying three Rebel flags.[36] There were none of us who did not fully appreciate the magnitude and importance of this engagement. Men fought with desperation, and each seemed to feel that here on the soil of the North was to be decided the great contest between freedom and slavery. A Confederate officer remarked that when they came into the state the whole population seemed to rise in arms — a great mistake, however. He did not know that the old Army of the Potomac was all they had to contend with and seemed surprised when told that no other troops had been engaged in the fight. Their officers encouraged the men by telling them there was nothing but Pennsylvania militia before them, but they found to their cost that their old adversaries were there instead.

On the morning of the fourth I looked over the field, where the dead lay unburied. Our men were carefully collecting the remains of their comrades and marking headboards for their graves. The enemy still maintained his old position, and a bullet from one of their sharpshooters warned me to dismount if I wished to remain.

We were still expecting an attack and rather courting it. Regiments were sending in to headquarters the captured flags and obtaining receipts for them. Lieutenant Barrows, formerly my hospital steward, aide on the staff of Colonel Hall, commanding brigade, had then about a dozen.[37] Our division captured twenty-one I believe.[38]

Of the number of men in our division and losses, I have not preserved a copy of my report made at the time, but to the best of my recollection we had fifteen regiments, numbering 3,600 men.[39] Our killed, wounded, and missing numbered between 1,700 and 1,800 men, according to field returns on the fifth, reduced to perhaps 1,600 in a few days by more correct reports and collecting of stragglers.[40] On the fifth we had in our division hospital some seven hundred to eight hundred and three hundred Rebel wounded. Many slightly wounded had walked or obtained conveyance to the nearest station and made their way home. The First and Third Division hospitals adjoined ours, and their numbers were about the same — the First a little less. During the fight on the second, the First Division was driven back with the III Corps and suffered considerably. They rallied in the rear of our hospital.

I collected the names of such officers as wished to go home, and leave to such was granted in general orders. Eight hundred Rebel dead were buried in front of our division. One could not ask for stronger proof of the fierceness of the attack and obstinacy of the defense. Riding over a part of the field on the sixth with Lieutenant Haskell, we noted some of the marks of the combat.[41] Toward the right on Culp's Hill, where the XII Corps was attacked on the night of the second, the trees were completely cut to pieces by bullets; withered leaves and branches strewed the ground. In an ordinary-sized tree we counted one hundred fifty bullets within eight feet of the ground. Passing to the left, the broken and battered monuments of the cemetery told of the severe cannonade of the third; and to the left of that, on the line of the II Corps, the dead horses of the batteries covered the ground; where Cushing, wounded, fought until he fell in death and every officer but one of our two Rhode Island batteries was hit.[42]

Gettysburg
July 6, 1863

Where the Second Division fought so well, the rows of graves were long, and the little "clump of trees" so often spoken of was torn and stripped by the storm of shot. The few rails and stones hastily gathered and the little earth scraped up by sticks served but a poor purpose for protection, and these were mostly thrown up after the battle in anticipation of another attack.[43] Indeed this part of the line was more open and easy of approach by the nature of the ground than other parts, and although the attack was intended to be on the whole length of our line, on this side of the "horseshoe," it centered on this point, and the breach at one time seemed to be complete.

General Meade was on the spot immediately after the attack, and when informed by Lieutenant Haskell that the attack was repulsed, he asked again if it was "entirely repulsed," and when informed that it was so, a fervent "Thank God" broke from his lips, and then in his prompt business way {he} gave directions for placing reinforcements, which he had ordered up but which were now unnecessary.

Hancock and Gibbon were away, Webb was slightly wounded but on duty, every inch a hero, and the division was under command of General Harrow, a man of no military ability, and in the opinion of some, of doubtful courage. [44] Hall, Devereux, and Mallon were with us, but Ward and Revere were gone, and our little division seemed sadly cut up, though covered with glory. [45]

Working at the amputating table and attending to other duties, my time was fully occupied. The small amount of surgical dressings, chloroform, etc., in one of our medicine and one supply wagon was sufficient for immediate use, though we were without shelter and cooking apparatus of a proper kind—only a few camp kettles. On the evening of the fifth our hospital trains arrived and at the same time the wagons of the Sanitary Commission—also our commissaries; and henceforth supplies were sufficient. Tents had to be put up and straw obtained to protect the wounded from the dampness of the ground, ground policed, and preparations for a long stay completed. In this I was employed until the evening of the sixth. Details of surgeons were made to remain in hospital—the others to go on with the army. My duty and orders required me to move on, and leaving the hospital on the seventh, I joined the division already on its way.

Surgeons Dwinelle, Hayward, and Burmeister, with four others, were detailed to remain at Gettysburg, leaving less than one medical officer to each regiment with the army. [46]

CHAPTER 8

"I Have Faith in Meade"

July 7–September 28, 1863

After Gettysburg the Army of the Potomac pursued the Army of Northern Virginia into Maryland and Virginia, as quickly as possible in Frank Dyer's view. His comments are a bit defensive but closer to the assessment of historian Edwin Coddington than to the many critics of George Meade, starting with President Lincoln, who have felt that a more vigorous pursuit was not only possible but also essential and that Lee could have been caught and his army destroyed. Dyer describes the casualties and gives an overly optimistic picture of the treatment that would be provided for the wounded in Gettysburg. He argues that an army on the move, in pursuit of a weakened but still dangerous foe, needs most of its surgeons and that the required minimum of doctors had been kept at the battlefield. His criticism of war correspondents continues. Civilians in Virginia were untrustworthy because provost guards left behind to protect their houses from the Union army were apt to be taken prisoner by Confederate cavalry or guerrillas. The poor quality of the substitutes sent to the army became even more apparent, and the number of desertions continued to increase, as did the frequency of executions for deserters and bounty jumpers. Meade and Lee maneuvered for favorable position into the fall. Dyer also comments on the Union cavalry, especially Brigadier Generals Judson Kilpatrick and George Custer, and describes rural Virginia and various towns in some detail.

Taneytown, Md.

July 7, 1863

Marched today from the neighborhood of the battlefield and are encamped just outside the town. Most of the troops have preceded us. We have taken large numbers of prisoners. Our wounded will

101

do very well now, but no thanks to the people in the neighborhood. They are very mean—charged $1.00 a quart for milk and 50 cents for a loaf of bread.[1] One man charged $3.00 for making a crutch for a wounded man, who with others slightly wounded were allowed to make their way to the nearest depot to go to {the} general hospital at Baltimore.

In this neighborhood the people are much more liberal and will sell everything they have at a fair price. You would be pleased to hear the exclamations of satisfaction from the men when we crossed the Maryland border. "We are in the United States again." Our supply train failed to come up last night, and the men had but little breakfast this morning, the first time I ever knew the commissaries to fail in issuing hard bread and coffee at least; but they had cattle and bought all the supplies in town, and the train arrived before night, so nobody was hurt.

We are following Lee and hope to trouble him yet. I could tell you all day of deeds of heroism performed by our men. Neither Mac nor Hooker, nor any other man but Meade, ever fought a battle with such skill as that. The Army of the Potomac is immortal! And our little division, numbering less than three full regiments, is ready if necessary to fight another such battle. The Nineteenth has but few left. They lost about seventy killed and wounded and have but a little more than a company left.[2] The sun has not been out full and free since we left Thoroughfare Gap. It is now raining, and I am writing in an ambulance.

Near Hagerstown
July 13, 1863

Here we are gradually creeping up to the enemy, who has retired before us until now he has thrown up entrenchments not far from us, where he is in strong force. I do not know whether it is the intention of General Meade to attack or not, but I know we have got to be careful. They have an army as large as ours now and will fight desperately.[3] We have lost many of our best officers and a good many men, and the stories you hear of reinforcements are not true. The troops under General Couch are few and good for nothing, and are not within fifty miles of us, and never will be nearer.[4] They cannot be depended on.

The papers say such and such troops have "gone to the front," that is, anywhere within a hundred miles of it. The New York Seventh was in Frederick City when we passed through, acting as a provost guard; looking very trim in their "secesh gray" uniforms. They are the only new troops I have seen, and they will not be brought to the front. I have heard through the papers of reinforcements from North Carolina; but no one here knows anything of them. The old Army of the Potomac, after fighting as no other army has fought, has now to fight again without help. It has been allowed to dwindle down to half the number it had last winter, and the government has made no effort to reinforce us. It seems as though it were intended to wipe us out entirely.

But the salvation of the North depends on this army, small as it is. I do not think we have more than 60,000 men, and the enemy have probably more. They have supplies too, having gathered up large quantities about the country. The idea of starving them out is as foolish as ever. We must *fight* them out, and we shall do it. But people talk about "crushing" them, driving them into the river, etc., without knowing exactly what they mean. We have not lost a moment. Have marched 270 miles in a month, and our men are worn out with fatigue and want of sleep. They never have a whole night's rest and very seldom have a chance to get their clothes dry. It has rained nearly all the time since we left Thoroughfare Gap. Hay and grain are spoiling for sun. Immense fields of wheat are destroyed by the march of the army.

Hagerstown
July 13, 1863

On our way I called to see our friends at Pry's Mills, Antietam. The Rebels had made them a visit, and taken some flour from the mill. They had levied contributions on the inhabitants—one man had five hundred barrels taken from him.

I expect the people at the North are now beginning to ask "why the Army of the Potomac don't move?"[5] Our men are busy throwing up entrenchments; we shall find as much as we want to do to hold this line if we are attacked.

Hagerstown
July 14, 1863

I hear that some of Keyes's men from the Peninsula are on their way here. Hope it is true. With 40,000 additional troops we might capture or destroy Lee's army entirely. I hope something will be done to fill up our old regiments by conscription. It is too bad to have them die out.[6] Our division is now very small, not much over 2,000 men present for duty. The general and division staff are pretty much all changed. From such men as Howard and Gibbon, gentlemen and soldiers, we have Harrow, appropriately named. He is a rough western man, no soldier, and generally has one or more brigade commanders with him when anything is going on.

It rained yesterday and today. If rain is any damage to the Rebels they have enough of it, but I do not imagine it makes much difference. The next battle will be more decisive in its results than Gettysburg. If we whip the Rebels again they are "gone up." If they whip us, goodbye Washington, Baltimore, and whatever they choose. So I think if the government does not send all the troops it can, it intends to commit suicide. I have faith however in Meade and don't think he will make a poor move.

I should have mentioned that after leaving Taneytown, we marched to Frederick City, stopped a little to the east of it, and then on through the city next day, through Jefferson, Burkettsville, and some other places, and through Crampton's Gap in South Mountain.

Newspaper correspondents are a nuisance as a general thing.[7] (There are some honorable exceptions.) Two-thirds of their stories are untrue. As for drunkenness, it is not so common as they represent. The Rebels drink all they can get, and they fight well. It is the want of brains in our generals that we have had to contend with.[8]

We advanced upon the Rebel lines on the morning of the fifteenth to find them gone, and following on to Williamsport, succeeded in capturing their rear guard of a few hundred men. They had escaped across the river.

Sandy Hook, near Harpers Ferry
July 17, 1863

Made a long march day before yesterday from Williamsport to Maryland Heights, camping on the tow path and on the hills, and yesterday came down here. The men are pretty well tired out, of course, but I think we shall keep on the march and shall probably start tomorrow. We shall have reinforcements, and if Meade moves at all it will be swiftly.[9] We have not McClellan now, who crept along six miles a day and lost more men by lying idle than Meade does by marching and fighting. It seems rather hard and almost cruel to start the army again so soon, but when division surgeons were called upon for a report on the condition of the army this morning and their capacity to make long and rapid marches, I expressed an opinion that two days' rest, with new clothes and shoes, would put them in better condition than weeks of rest. If we wait, we shall have sickness as we did last fall, and by waiting, all the advantages of a campaign now would be lost.

We have had almost incessant rains, yesterday the sun came out a little while and we got our clothes dry for once, but everything is damp and moldy, and now raining again. The mud is terrible, and I hope never to be obliged to come near Harpers Ferry again. It is a miserable hole, whatever it was before the war. [10]

A nominal list of wounded in our division hospital at Gettysburg gave 875 of our men and 145 Rebels. [11] As these were all lying about on the ground, or walking about, or under little shelter tents; it was a difficult thing to make correct lists. I had one surgeon and a clerk at work at it, and by comparing notes they got nearly all. There were probably some whose names were not taken.

War is a terrible thing at best; and all the horrible things you read of it are inseparable from it. There probably never was a better organized ambulance and surgical corps in the world than we have, but there must be sufferings after all. As a military necessity our trains were twenty-five miles in the rear, and all the inhabitants who could get away had left and taken what they could with them. Two hundred thousand men fighting over a country make everything scatter.

You ask about my personal attention to the wounded. I cannot see or attend to all of course. I try to see all the worst cases and attend to all that I can, but during and after the fight I had a good many things to attend to, principally to keep others at work and see that they worked according to orders, to see that the ambulance corps did their duty, and to obtain something for the multitude to eat. And then we had to move our hospital in the midst of the fight, no small thing to do. On the fifth I worked at the operating table all day.

Surgeons must go about their business in a business like way and not run about for the sake of seeing and talking with everybody. We left seven of our surgeons behind but had to take enough with us to attend to the troops on the march (which duty is not small) and to establish another hospital in case of action with a sufficient number of surgeons. [12] Volunteer surgeons do but very little, they are not willing to do the dirty work, they want waiting upon, and only wish to perform operations. Even those from the hospitals in Washington and elsewhere are not in their element at all. They are unused to the manner of life and find it impossible to work to advantage with the limited facilities we are obliged to content ourselves with. A lot of them came up from Washington the other day when we were expecting a battle. Two of them were assigned to me, and I have been troubled to get them along. One has gone home today, and the other will go soon I hope. They are gentlemen of ability but unused to the field. They came to me in distress night before last, no supper, and no place to sleep except the ambulances (a very good place). I slept on the ground in wet clothes, and having no blanket could offer them none. I had a smoke for dinner and another for supper, and my unsubstantial diet would not suffice for them, but it gives a wonderful appetite for breakfast. [13] We got our tents up yesterday the first time for two or three weeks and find living quite luxurious.

The ball is rolling on—Vicksburg and Port Hudson, and I hope for Charleston soon. After this campaign is over, I shall try to get leave for a visit home. I want to stay now, for my position is quite important, and I think I can do some good here. Dr. Dougherty would not consent to my going now. Some of the older surgeons must remain to fill these places. Dr. Hayward is at Gettysburg yet, as operating surgeon. I hope he and the rest will get back before we move. We may have work for all our medical staff before long.

Camp near Snicker's Gap
July 21, 1863
We left Harper's Ferry on the seventeenth and have been making short marches through Loudoun Valley. We cannot move very fast, as the roads are poor and our supply trains have to go along with us. [14] We are expecting to have a military execution today. Captain McMahon of the Seventy-first Pennsylvania shot Captain McManus of the Sixty-ninth Pennsylvania at Falmouth, was tried, and sentenced to be shot today between twelve and four o'clock. [15] It is now 6:30 in the morning. No reprieve has come yet. His coffin is here, ready for

him. It is a very unpleasant duty, but one which must be performed if ordered, and every one considers the sentence just. [A reprieve came about ten o'clock, and the prisoner was subsequently pardoned in consideration of having gone into the fight at Gettysburg with the provost guard, who had him in charge. He was requested to resign, which he did.]

This is a fine country, but the "first families" are contented with very insignificant houses. Everything looks old. No new buildings are to be seen for miles. Blackberries are very abundant. Everyone can have enough without leaving camp. Every day stragglers are picked up by guerrillas who come down from the mountains, and yet it is very difficult to keep men from straggling. It is the great sin of our army; and men will run the risk of capture any day for the sake of a few eggs or a chicken or what they can steal.

Near Warrenton Junction
July 27, 1863

Since I wrote you last we have been on the move continually. Left Bloomfield for Ashby's Gap twenty-fourth, stopped there one night, near Paris. Next day to Manassas Gap, through Upperville, Markham Station, Farrowsville, and Linden. These are all in and about the gap. Hills are all around and villages lie in the valleys. I went up on the mountain and saw our troops advance into Front Royal. The cavalry made a dash through the town, and after a little skirmish scattered them. The main body of the Rebels could be seen across the Shenandoah making their way south. We came through the pass and offered them battle, but they didn't feel like stopping.[16]

The view from the mountains down into the Shenandoah Valley is beautiful. We left the gap on the twenty-fifth and marched to White Plains, eighteen miles. Remained one night and started again for Warrenton, passing just the other side of Thoroughfare Gap from where we passed a month ago. Came to Warrenton at twelve, and at one pushed on to the junction, six miles; a march of twenty miles in a hot day. A good many dropped from heat, and one man died of sunstroke. It is strange how much men can undergo. Nobody will now ask why the Army of the Potomac doesn't move.[17] We should push on today, but the men cannot march, and they need shoes and clothes. One thing after another wears out, and some men were marching in drawers yesterday, some with a blouse and no shirt, some with a shirt and no blouse, and some barefooted. Recruiting parties are going home today, Colonel Devereux with them.

The country is full of guerrillas and bushwhackers. Men wandering fifty yards from the column in the woods have been nabbed. The inhabitants are concerned in it. Yesterday a few miles out of Warrenton two young ladies came out of a house and asked General Hays for a guard.[18] He sent two men, and General Harrow ordered Major Hooper of the Fifteenth (our inspector general) to go to the house and remain until the column had passed.[19] He did so and has not yet returned. We all congratulated the major on the fine time he would have, a nice house, and three or four ladies about, and thought likely he would get a good dinner. It is hard to write sometimes. After being on the road all day I feel tired, and we generally march at four o'clock in the morning.

Warrenton Junction
July 28, 1863
Three commissary officers and six men were ordered home to bring out conscripts and to recruit. I am afraid they will not get many, as too many will be willing to pay $300, and some will run away from the draft. Those who cried out with horror when Negro soldiers were talked of now cry out, "Why don't you send the Negroes to fight?" Very well. I would rather have a good hearty Negro than twenty Copperheads who lack courage either to fight for their country or openly against it. I have some respect for a good soldier if he *is* a Rebel, who is willing to fight for what he calls his rights, but none for a sneaking traitor who dares do neither one thing nor another.

Our campaign is not yet ended, but we cannot get on so fast now. One-third of our men are without shoes or stockings, or both. We have marched 420 miles in 42 days, averaging ten miles a day, with picket duty, fighting, &c., making one of the most active campaigns on record. But the people of the North are not satisfied, already they grumble that Meade has not "bagged" Lee. What would they have? Before the fight, if they could have been assured of the safety of Baltimore, Washington, and Philadelphia, they would have been satisfied. Now they demand that we capture an army larger than our own.

I have seen no list of killed and wounded at Charleston. Whether our brothers are among the number or not, I feel that they are doing their duty, and that is better than to run away.[20] "How those poor wives must have felt to know that their husbands ran away, and were killed afterwards," was the remark of one whose husband fell in the front rank.

I have been selecting sick to go to general hospital and arranging matters as far as possible for another move. Wagons and ambulances break and wear out, supplies have to be replenished, and a very limited time is allowed to get things ready. If you had seen the roads, fields, swamps, rocks, and hills we have had to go over, you would not think it possible to get our army along. Major Bull, provost marshal of the corps, got in last night, and reported that as he came along in rear of the corps with six mounted men, a party of fifty guerrillas came upon them (Major Hooper had joined them).[21] The Rebs nearly surrounded them near a stone wall. They abandoned their horses and took to the woods. Major Bull and two men got in. Major Hooper was probably captured. He was to go on recruiting service next day.

Our friends say we should march as fast as the Rebels.[22] Rebel officers that we took at Gettysburg were astonished to find our army there. They knew of our being at Thoroughfare Gap on a certain day and counted upon a certain number of days our utmost. When told that we marched thirty miles one day they were incredulous. I heard a North Carolina colonel say they never marched more than eighteen miles a day.

On the March
July 31, 1863
While waiting by the roadside for another division to pass, I will indulge in a short *growl*. About four o'clock yesterday we got orders to march and came seven or eight miles in the direction of Falmouth. Clothing has been received, but there has been no time to issue it. Men are yet going barefooted. The shoes are miserable. Some will not wear a fortnight, and for all the destruction of shoes and clothing the soldiers have to pay; no allowance is made for it. Those who loaf about cities and do the ornamental get the money, and the old veterans, who have marched and fought two years, get nothing but orders to march farther. No four hundred dollars bounty for them, or rest, or easy duty. And the reason given is, "we can't trust these

new men," and so the old troops must go on till they are all killed. I do not see the justice of it. If they cannot trust them now, make them fight and learn.

Morrisville
August 1, 1863

Weather excessively warm. Our march from Warrenton Junction on the twenty-eighth was very severe. We are six miles from Kelly's Ford on the Rappahannock. One division of the XII Corps is across, with some cavalry, skirmishing. Reports that sutlers on the way up have been captured. We need their goods now. Trains cannot go very well without escort. This is a poor country about here.

Gen. William Hays is in command of the corps, a very easy man, and business is not pushed at corps headquarters.[23] We should have vegetables, or men will have scurvy soon.

August 7, 1863

Papers professing to support the government attempt to dictate to the president what he shall do; that he shall order the army "onward to Richmond." What do they think men are made of? The men are worn out with fatigue, and as for marching, when the weather is so hot that one hundred men die of sunstroke in New York in one day, how can men be expected to march here, where it is still hotter.

Morrisville
August 13, 1863

We have a new corps commander, General Warren; said to be a good officer.[24] Was chief of staff for General Meade and has been nominated for major general. No rations of vegetables for the men yet, but we have managed to get some potatoes, corn, &c, and buy a sheep once in a while. I do not care so much for the mere gratification of the men, but scurvy is making its appearance in many cases, and without vegetables we can do but little toward its cure.

We have a fine division hospital, fourteen tents, two together, an arbor in front and rear, about two hundred feet long, and beds built up of poles, on which are ticks filled with straw, and it looks really nice. We have everything we want except vegetables. Have an ice house and all conveniences. Tents, poles, straw, and a few such articles make a better hospital than brick, stone, or wood, for the treatment of fever and wounds, and I would rather take my chance in a tent with typhoid fever than in the best house ever made.

Morrisville
August 16, 1863

I do not mean to say that it is by anybody's neglect that these extra rations are not brought. The army must be subsisted by means of this railroad, and it is taxed to its utmost to bring supplies and ammunition absolutely necessary. The army is very healthy, our division has not lost a man by disease since coming here. The papers do not mention it, but the army is much depleted until it is now quite small. One division of the XI Corps has gone, one division of the V Corps has gone to New York, and the other has gone somewhere on transports. At least one brigade from every corps in the army has left. Yesterday, the First Minnesota and Seventh Michigan left for Alexandria. The division turned out to see these two old regiments off. The Seventh has fought in the old Third Brigade ever since it was formed, crossed twice at Fredericksburg, and fought Barksdale's Mississippians through the whole war, until they buried him at Gettysburg. If Seymour goes to making trouble we can depend on these men. [25]

While our army is so small, Lee may make an attack at any time, and we may be obliged to move. About four hundred conscripts, or rather substitutes, came on, half for the Fifteenth and half for the Nineteenth. There is but one drafted man among them. They are a hard set and will desert the first opportunity. [26]

Harrow has gone on leave, and General Webb is now in command of the division. He is a gentleman and a soldier, will have everything in order, or know why. This is as I like it. One likes to have his efforts appreciated, and if all is not as it should be a slight reprimand is a good thing. General Caldwell has gone—will not probably return. [He was assigned to duty in Washington.]

Morrisville
August 21, 1863

Our substitutes desert every chance they get. There is to be an execution in our division in about two hours—a man of the Seventy-first Pennsylvania who deserted nearly two years ago. I must prepare to go out with the general and staff to attend the ceremony.

Evening. The execution of the sentence on Mayberry, Seventy-first Pennsylvania, was carried into effect at three P.M.[27] The division was ordered out, a hollow square formed, the open grave in the center. The procession came on, the provost marshal of the division leading—fourteen men with loaded rifles, then four men carrying the coffin. The prisoner followed with a firm step, walking with the chaplain of the Seventy-second Pennsylvania, the band playing a slow march. The coffin was placed near the grave, the prisoner sitting on it, while the chaplain most inappropriately consumed a long time in reading remarks and prayer (for if such suspense is terrible to the lookers on, what must it be to the condemned, who had known of it and prepared himself). He then took off his blouse, while the provost marshal bandaged his eyes. Sitting on his coffin he extended his right hand, the officer commanded ready—aim—fire! and he fell with seven bullets through his chest. Some little signs of life remaining, the reserves, two men, were ordered up—fired, and all was still. The troops marched past, and all went on as before. About the time of this execution, two conscripts deserted from the Fifteenth. The old soldiers do not desert, only those who make bounty jumping a business. One of the Andrews Sharpshooters deserted last winter and after reenlisting and deserting several times was sent out here and found himself unexpectedly among his old comrades, was recognized, arrested, tried, and will be shot.

Morrisville
August 27, 1863

Yesterday went to Warrenton with a number of officers on the occasion of the presentation of a horse, saddle, and equipments to General Sedgwick by field and staff officers of the old Second Division, which he had commanded. The horse, an elegant black owned by Colonel Batchelder, our corps quartermaster, cost $400.[28] The sword is a splendid one, several diamonds in the scabbard, and a large amethyst in the hilt, cost $900. The whole cost $1500. Went in the cars and were joined near Rappahannock Station by General Meade and staff. The day was cool. General Sedgwick's headquarters are in the front yard of a house, where several ladies were looking on, enjoying it as much as Rebels can. A fine band of the First New Jersey played. Captain Corkhill, brigade commissary, made the presentation speech.[29] "Uncle John" was very much affected and could scarcely read the reply he had written. Tears came to his eyes as he spoke of those who had gone to their graves from the old Second Division. The names of the subscribers will be engraved on parchment, to be presented to the general. After a fine collation, returned home; probably the festivities were kept up till a late hour.

Tomorrow the Pennsylvania Reserves present a sword to General Meade. General Webb and staff invited. We have a more solemn duty to perform. Two men of our division are to be shot for desertion. Three were condemned, but one was reprieved on account of his youth and other circumstances. I would rather not see it, but it is my duty to be present, and I shall be, though I cannot help hoping something may occur to prevent it. Yet I suppose this is not right. Desertion is an evil that must be stopped, and too much leniency has lost us much.

Morrisville
August 29, 1863
Still our cold spell continues. Yesterday the execution took place. It is my duty to be present and to state to the provost marshal that life is extinct when that is the case. I cannot look upon this with the horror that one unaccustomed to such things might, and yet I would not have witnessed it if it had not been my duty. But when I know that thousands of brave men have met their death manfully at their posts, I cannot have so much pity for these abject cowards and scoundrels who have not only deserted but offered themselves again and again as substitutes, only to desert again.

We have changed our headquarters to pleasanter ground, and a special messenger sent to Washington for supplies has returned, bringing some luxuries, principally fruit, and we have had quite a feast. Generals Warren, Hays, and Caldwell (who has returned for a time) happened along (perhaps smelling the peaches and things "afar off").

Our men are well fed and our hospital well supplied by purchases with the hospital fund. I have considerable pride in my division hospital; some say it is the best in the Army of the Potomac. We have accommodations for 100, now 75.[30]

Banks' Ford, Rappahannock
September 1, 1863
On Sunday evening an order came to prepare to move in the morning at daylight. Harrow is back. Webb is in command by order of General Warren. Harrow was a good deal "exercised" and made remarks more forcible than elegant, punished a considerable amount of whiskey, and went to bed near morning. We rose at two o'clock, came down by Grove Church and Hartwood Church to the ford, and are now within five miles of our old campground at Falmouth. The object of this movement is to accomplish a piece of "strategy" — the recapture of two small gunboats in the river.[31]

Saw Kilpatrick yesterday at his quarters near Hartwood Church.[32] He may be a smart man, at any rate is a smart talker. General Custer, who has a brigade of cavalry near, is a gorgeous-looking young man — smart though — his dress a black velvet jacket and pants, double knot of lace on sleeves, and two gold stripes on the legs, and light flaxen hair falling in curls on his shoulders.[33] Some men can dress like circus riders without making themselves ridiculous.

Morrisville
September 4, 1863
Back again in camp. Got the order at five o'clock and marched back last night, eighteen miles. Nothing accomplished.

Morrisville
September 7, 1863
Substitutes continue to desert even after the shooting. They are desperate fellows and don't mind running great risks for the sake of further bounties.[34] I suppose you saw the glowing account of Kilpatrick's expedition. It was a *failure,* but you see what can be done by keeping a correspondent along.[35] The II Corps has now no correspondent within its limits and therefore is spoken of seldom. Doubleday is relieved. When Mr. Lincoln heard of it he said: "What, Doubleday sent in? Well, take his halter off and turn him out to grass."[36] [I believe he has been grazing ever since.]

The society about here is not elegant, though I believe the people consider themselves a little extra. One thing is certain, they consider themselves above work, for they never do any and are so prejudiced that they never *have* any done. We have been encamped alongside of a house a month and eat in an old summer house in the yard, but I have never been in the house. The two females are not disposed to be communicative, and it doesn't seem to me that they could contribute to my pleasure or enlightenment.

I see that Surgeon General Hammond is to be displaced. I cannot say that I regret it, for I do not think he is a man of sufficient ability for the position.[37] General Harrow is with us, and General Webb back to the Second Brigade. Harrow has not been twenty rods from his tent since he came here and has never been in the camp of the division. Webb was always up before sunrise and through the camps, seeing that the troops were out at their morning drills.

Morrisville
September 9, 1863

There seems to be some apprehension of trouble with France. I think however it will blow over. Louis Napoleon is getting on a little too fast, a fault of the family.[38] If Charleston falls we shall have things in a fair way, and the French and English will be glad to keep quiet. Just at this moment a telegram was received from headquarters of the army saying the *Richmond Enquirer* of the seventh had been received, announcing the evacuation of Forts Wagner and Gregg and the whole of Morris Island. Things are progressing.

I have been engaged all day on a board examining substitutes and shall be tomorrow. All have been examined here once in their regiments, but we give some of the doubtful ones a more thorough examination. Quite a number of unsuitable men have been sent out, some of whom have been previously discharged for disability.

Culpeper Court House
September 13, 1863

When I wrote last all was quiet and had every appearance of remaining so. But night before last we got the order to march at ten o'clock next day. So we broke camp, packed up, sent off some of our sick, and marched by way of Bealton to Rappahannock Station. The day was very hot, and the march, though not long, was severe on account of the heat. At night rained and was cold.

Started this morning across the Rappahannock, the cavalry ahead, with horse artillery, in three columns, Gregg right, Buford center, Kilpatrick left.[39] They encountered the Rebels before reaching Brandy Station but continued driving them all the way. By noon they had driven them beyond Culpeper, and I think across the Rapidan. One brigade of our division occupies the town, the rest of us on the east of it. It is thought the Rebel cavalry did not stand well. Ours took three pieces of artillery, with the men attached to them and a hundred or so besides. It was cavalry against cavalry, no infantry, some three or four killed and twelve wounded of ours. We have more of the enemy's. We are probably out here to feel and see what they have, as there are reports that part of their army has gone to Tennessee. [40]

September 15, 1863

No more troops up here besides the II Corps. It is now so small that it is quite handy. Went into the town yesterday. It looks as though war had been through it, but dirt is common in all Southern towns that I have seen. As usual the ladies are dressed in mourning and affect great contempt for the Yankees. There is nothing in town for sale but tobacco. [41] The cars come up now with supplies. The country looks beautifully, very few fields are cultivated, but everything looks green, and the Blue Ridge shows some of its highest points near.

Somerville Ford, on Rapidan
September 18, 1863

Came down here yesterday to picket the river in place of the cavalry, who have gone on some other business. [42] The enemy are in strong force on the other side of the little stream and keep up a pretty smart firing. The line of our corps extends from Cedar Mountain, where Banks fought, to Raccoon Ford, about ten miles from Culpeper. [43]

This is a Godforsaken country. What little there was growing has been destroyed by the passage of troops; the inhabitants gone except the poorest and a few old Negroes and children. We had no tents with us and use for headquarters a house which is partly empty. An overseer, a conscript now, lived here, and his wife with four little children, the youngest but a fortnight old, now occupy the house. A Negro woman of seventy and a man older were here, but they could do very little, and they were nearly starved. They have nothing to eat except what we give them. The cavalry had taken everything eatable from the premises. This is the first time we have had our headquarters in a house, and I hope we shall not have occasion to do so again. Ten of us sleep in a room on the floor, with doors and windows open. For two days it has been pretty tedious. Feeding these little ragged children with sugar, reading the papers, and a game of whist once in a while occupies the time. It is a very uncomfortable place for the men. Pickets have to be relieved in the night, as they have range of all our approaches to the river and open as soon as our men appear.

Somerville Ford
September 21, 1863
This country is thinly settled but must have been very productive before the war. Plantations were large and a great many slaves owned. [44] All the able-bodied ones are gone, either ran away or taken south. Went over to Cedar Mountain yesterday, about four miles. But little indications of the fight are to be seen now. The country is uncultivated, except here and there a small patch of corn, not enough to keep the few people from starving next winter. A poor old crooked-legged Negro gave us an interesting account of his position in the fight, which he demonstrated by crawling about on the ground and showing us how terrified he was at the bursting of a shell over his head. He was a specimen of the "Uncle Ned" genus, and he and another old man had been living in "Missus' house" for more than a year, picking up what they could get to eat. They seemed to feel grieved that "Missis wouldn't take em along wid her." She took all the young and able-bodied.

September 22, 1863
News from Tennessee not very encouraging. I am afraid Rosecrans has got the worst of it. A little too much "Bragg" about there. Saw a Richmond newspaper of yesterday. Nothing in it about the fight in Tennessee. But our signal corps, who have the key to the Rebel signals, read a message from their station that Bragg had captured 2,500 prisoners and seventeen guns. [45]

Somerville Ford
September 26, 1863
All kinds of rumors prevail, but we quietly wait for something to turn up. I suppose it is true that the XI and XII Corps have gone west. [46] The other day General Meade made preparations for a

move. Rations and ammunition were distributed. He then went to Washington, and when he returned all settled down again still. This afternoon General Warren called at our headquarters and left maps of the country south of us with the general. These maps are very minute—give every road, stream, house, and piece of woods, and the commanders of divisions are generally furnished with them previous to a movement.

Our substitutes desert frequently, the executions not appearing to intimidate them. [47] Many go over to the enemy—their safest way. Today three deserted from the Nineteenth while on picket. The Rebel pickets told our men so. Said they were miserable scoundrels and wished they would come and get them. They couldn't see the case clear enough to go however.

Buford and Kilpatrick have been having a bout with the Rebel cavalry, in which they gave and took about alike. I heard the sound of their guns near Madison Court House. [48]

Rockwood, assistant surgeon of the Fifteenth Massachusetts, was tried by court-martial and dismissed the service for "conduct unbecoming an officer and a gentleman" for associating and messing with the privates, and what was still worse, not paying his mess bill. [49]

September 28, 1863

I can readily account for Rosecrans's defeat. He had to fight against Longstreet's men from the Army of the Potomac [sic]. They find them very different from those who fought at Stones River and must have different men to oppose them. The II Corps has lost in one action more than Grant's army lost in the siege of Vicksburg. Both armies here are stubborn and will not yield until one or the other is pretty badly used up. [50]

Saw two deserters from the enemy yesterday. They say they have between 40,000 and 50,000 in and about Gordonsville. That is as many as we have, and they are in a good position. If our idle army about the coast of North Carolina were put to use it might be of some benefit to us. Foster's army has done nothing, and from present appearances never will. However there is no doubt about the result now. One or two victories on either side will not end it, but the result will be all right.

CHAPTER 9

"Certain Death Awaited So Many Brave Men"

October 2–December 11, 1863

The fight at Bristoe Station and the abortive assault and bitter cold at Mine Run are the most important topics, but Dyer describes a variety of events in this chapter. A captain in the Twentieth Massachusetts was murdered by one of his men, and the assailant escaped detection. There is more discussion of the feeling for McClellan in the army. Lincoln, opposed by Copperheads, called for 300,000 additional men. While condemning them as traitors, preferring an honest Confederate foe, Dyer has sympathetic words for the Virginia unionist John Minor Botts, exiled from his Richmond home and visited by Union officers. The surgeon describes the Rebel dead at Bristoe and A. P. Hill's responsibility for that debacle, as well as the bitter exchange between Major Generals George Sykes and Gouverneur Warren when the latter needed help. There were frequent cavalry clashes as Meade and Lee continued to feel each other out. In mid-December Dyer received another leave to go home.

On the Rapidan
October 2, 1863
We are having the first rain for several days, and when it rains here the whole country is flooded. The soil, being red clay, does not absorb the water, and small rivers are running in every direction. Was at General Warren's headquarters yesterday. The occasion was the presentation of a sword by citizens of his native place, Cold Spring, New York. General Meade was present and in conversation said it was not his intention to fight the Rebels there unless they obliged him to. The papers are crying out, "on to Richmond." The *New York Herald* thinks we ought to go or send forty or fifty thousand

men to reinforce Rosecrans.[1] All remaining after that might get on board one boat, a small one at that.

I hear the "Rogue's March" in the Third Brigade. The interesting ceremony of drumming out is being performed on a deserter who was tried a few days since. As it was not a clear case of desertion, owing to some mitigating circumstances, he was not sentenced to be shot but to be marked with the letter D on his right hip, with India ink; have his head shaved; and after being drummed through the entire brigade, to be drummed out of camp. Two conscripts deserted last night across the river.

We are yet in the same quarters. The poor, sad-voiced, pale woman still mourns and whines, the ragged children run about. We do what business we have to and wait for the mail at five o'clock. It is very monotonous here. A court-martial is in session every day in the next tent, whose two or three cases a day are disposed of, but twenty or more are awaiting trial. We always have more or less on hand, and they are accumulating now.

October 4, 1863

Dined this afternoon in company with the general and some dozen or more officers with Lieutenant Sproat, commissary of First Brigade.[2] Ex-Governor Kidder, one of the two commissioners from Minnesota, to receive the vote for governor.[3] He said he had so far recorded but two Copperhead votes among all the Minnesota men. These commissioners say nothing to influence voters. By law it is an offense.

I hear today of the death of Lt. William C. Meade, a volunteer aide on General Webb's staff. He was taken with fever after we came down here, and we sent him to Washington, where he died. He was a fine young man, a lawyer from New York.[4]

Culpeper
October 6, 1863

Marched from our camp on the Rapidan to this place, two miles north of Culpeper Court House today, a very cool, pleasant day to march. The VI Corps relieved us. When the Rebels from their signal station on the mountain opposite saw through the openings in the woods the long lines of troops marching down, they were no doubt considerably "exercised," for their signal flags were at work all day telegraphing, sometimes two or three at a time. Their system of telegraphing is like ours, by means of flags waved by hand. Our signal officers understand their code of signals, but as soon as they think we are acquainted with it they will change for another code. They read "The enemy is advancing in force, now crossing Kirk's farm," etc.

We are in our tents again. The day has been chilly, and the night more so—a good fire in front of the tent is very comfortable. I have a semicircle of bricks built up in front of my tent for a fire place, and having the tent open it warms it very well.

A sad affair took place last night in camp. Captain McKay of the Twentieth Massachusetts, being brigade officer of the day and hearing some noise about the camp, went to quiet it, when someone in the party shot him.[5] He never spoke and died in ten minutes. The murderer has not been discovered. The officers and men of the regiment have offered a reward of $1,000 for his detection. I wonder officers are not murdered more frequently. They are obliged sometimes to be very severe, and many of the men are the worst characters in the world.

Our headquarters are on a rising ground in an enclosure where a fine house appears to have stood some years ago. Trees in double rows are standing about the square, and several buildings, barns, Negro quarters, etc., but every board is stripped from them. An unoccupied house or barn dissolves in an hour. One after another takes a board, and it is soon gone. Occupied houses are not troubled. There is not a rail fence for miles, and the little crop of corn has vanished in a twinkling. Such is war. The Rebs had better end it.

Bealeton Station
October 11, 1863
Back again within three miles of our old camp at Morrisville. Saturday morning got orders to move. Went through Culpeper and took the road toward Sperryville, going about two miles and forming line of battle. Prince's division of the III Corps was out in front, and Kilpatrick's cavalry in front of them. One regiment of Prince's division was "gobbled" by the enemy, and Prince reported them too strong for him.[6]

Remained in line in the woods until two o'clock this morning, when we were ordered to march. Had breakfast, sent trains and artillery on another road, and took a path through the woods about four miles, coming out near our camp of the day before. It was a blind march too. You could scarcely see a horse before you, and when an interval was left between the men, they were very apt to lose the path. We got out of the woods about daylight. Everything is broken up at Culpeper — stores and hospitals moved — the whole army has fallen back this side of the Rappahannock. We crossed the river about twelve o'clock today — two columns of troops and three or four columns of trains and artillery at the same time coming along toward Bealton. Everything was orderly and complete — nothing destroyed or left behind. Four trains of cars left Culpeper about noon bringing away everything. On top of the cars were numbers of contrabands and several white refugees with a few necessary household goods.

This movement is in consequence of one made by the enemy, who is moving between us and the Blue Ridge, and if we do not meet him here we may at Warrenton or on the old Bull Run ground. If we do I think we can whip him.

Near Culpeper we passed the residence of John Minor Botts, a prominent politician before the war.[7] He has been imprisoned at Richmond since the beginning of the war until about two months ago. I saw him at General Warren's headquarters. His property at Gordonsville was confiscated, but he has a place of several hundred acres here. General Warren told me of a conversation he had with Botts. He was in prison in Richmond when our army reached the Chickahominy. The Rebels had concluded to fall back, and orders were issued to evacuate Richmond and all Virginia. The Rebel congress packed up and went, and all was ready. But Mac dallied about and did not advance. The Rebels took courage, their congress came together, passed a conscription act for 200,000 new troops, armed and equipped 100,000 of them, put them in front of us as we lay idly in front of them, and then drove us off the Peninsula.[8] That is some of Mac's strategy.

Webb tells some tales of the inefficiency of the headquarters of the army. Mac with his staff of seventy-six officers, and only a few efficient ones, and Mac totally inefficient. The unwritten history of war is sometimes more important than the written, which is often by favorites of officers concerned. The McClellan feeling, which we read of, in the army does not exist, it is artificial. The late attempt to get up a subscription was a miserable affair. Some officers were willing to pay the whole amount assessed on their men, but the men had no heart in it. It is now stopped.

General Warren left yesterday on five days' leave. He had no sooner reached home than a telegram called him back, and he arrived at noon today. General Harrow's resignation has been accepted, and he left for home yesterday. General Webb now commands the division. [Harrow was subsequently reappointed.[9]]

A proposition was made that regiments reenlisting would be allowed to go home and recruit, giving them the full bounty as veterans.[10] The Nineteenth has voted to go home but will not be allowed to leave quite yet. We may have another fight before long.

Centreville
October 15, 1863
After a week of marching and fighting, the II Corps is now in bivouac in front of Centreville on Bull Run, which we passed over at about four o'clock this morning. When I wrote last we were at Bealeton. Next morning marched back toward Culpeper, where our cavalry had a fight.[11] Again left Brandy Station at 10 P.M., marched all night, across the Rappahannock, up to Bealeton, and in the morning arrived at Fayetteville. The cavalry had a skirmish there. The First Maine Cavalry got cut off but came in next day. Marched in all directions next day and stopped at night near the house of Colonel Murray (an inspector general of Lee's army) between Warrenton {"Manassas" penciled in} and the junction.[12] Made our headquarters at the house of Colonel Murray. Mrs. Murray was an acquaintance of Generals Warren and Webb. Leaving in the morning our rear fought some. The Third Division lost twenty-five and took two guns.[13]

Making our way along slowly by the railroad in the afternoon, a column of the enemy appeared on our left flank (A. P. Hill's corps). We immediately formed line of battle and met them.[14] Our division captured five pieces of artillery, two battle flags, and 443 prisoners, besides killing and wounding as many more, with a loss of less than two hundred. Two of our staff were wounded, and the orderly carrying the division flag killed. The officers wounded were Captain Smith, 7th Mich., inspector; and Captain Wessels, 106th Penn., judge advocate; Colonel Mallon, 42d New York, commanding Third Brigade, killed.[15] Many staff officers were slightly wounded. The action was at closer quarters than usual and was a grand sight to see.

The enemy appeared to be endeavoring to cut us off from the rest of the army, so after dark we moved on and joined the other corps near Centreville. Afterward they appeared to be advancing in force, and we formed line of battle. Batteries were planted on all the hills around, and there was a smart artillery fight for a while. They tried to pass round our right but found the III Corps at Union Mills, and that checked them. For the last five or six days Lee and Meade have been practicing grand tactics, and so far Lee has the worst of it. We are pretty tired out of course. The Rebels too, so prisoners say. I have had but little sleep for four or five days and in the saddle two-thirds of the time. It is difficult to describe how tired and sleepy we all are.

Centreville
October 16, 1863
With regard to McClellan's popularity, I have only to say look at his electioneering letter and then to the vote in Pennsylvania of soldiers and citizens.[16] I know the opinion of the army with regard to such men as Vallandigham, Woodward, Seymour, and their supporters. They would hang them as soon as they got hold of them; and even George B. Mc. would not be safe here upholding such men. It will not do for stay-at-home cowards to impugn the motives of men who stand up and fight for their country, and the long list each battle of killed and wounded officers and men give the lie to all such imputations of interested motives. Well, I pity the men who are on the side of traitors.

October 17, 1863
Preparations are being made for another advance. The impression seems to be that Lee is trying to get round our right, but a deserter just in says they are falling back and burning the bridges. Stuart's cavalry did a smart thing the other day—captured seven hundred horses coming up from Alexandria.[17] I cannot conceive why an escort was not sent with them. The fault is at Washington. I see the president's proclamation calling out 300,000 additional troops.[18] Good, when we get them.

Auburn
October 21, 1863

Back again near our camp of the morning of the fourteenth. Left Centreville on the nineteenth at daylight; across Bull Run; past Manassas and the junction, where the Rebels had been a short time before; and soon came to Bristoe Station, the scene of our battle of the fourteenth. Here was a picture of wreck and ruin of a railroad. The bridges over Broad Run and Kettle Run were burnt, and the rails torn up and ties burned. The ties are piled up, "cob-house" fashion, and the rails placed on top — a fire is built under — the ties burn, heat the rails, which bend and are useless. A train was up with timber and rails repairing. The road will have to be entirely rebuilt. They blew up the abutments of the bridges and even shoveled out the road bed so that it has to be graded anew.[19]

I went over the battlefield, and there was abundant evidence of the severe loss on their side. Their dead were buried in trenches, and part of them were marked, but most of them were not. Within four yards of where their battery stood, seventeen dead horses lay, and they were scattered through the woods and fields. We found earthworks they had thrown up during the night, and the evidence of their whole army being encamped near. We whipped them badly.

Citizens here estimate their loss in killed and wounded at upwards of 1,000. They lost heavily in officers. It was a splendid thing for the II Corps, and its consequences are very gratifying. The cause of this whole movement was one made by Lee on our right to reach Centreville first and cut off our trains. It then became a race for Centreville, but the whole scheme was thwarted. Hill was next day placed in arrest by Lee. The Rebel officers blame Hill for the failure and say that if Ewell had been there it would not have happened.[20]

Our wagons have come up, and we have had something to eat — the first meal for twenty-four hours. We all slept last night by the fire. The only luxury I had was my saddle for a pillow — my overcoat my only covering. It is quite chilly toward morning, and about that time the fire gets low, and the chill creeps in. However, there is nothing like getting used to it, and I only speak of it to say that it is not so bad as many think, especially when a fire can be had. We have made some hard marches lately. Yesterday morning left Bristoe Station for Gainesville, when within a mile of it were turned off again toward Warrenton. Marched sixteen miles through mud and water, forded Broad Run three times — quite a river — over knee deep, and quite broad, and Cedar Run once, a stream quite as broad, besides many small streams. It was a very hard march.

The country bears marks of fighting all over it — dead slightly buried — and near our headquarters a man's hand sticks out of the ground. We are all in line across the country and not in the defenses of Washington, as the papers have it. The ridiculous statements of correspondents are really disgusting. I was amused to hear that Lee is counting on the demoralization of our army. All we lack is numbers. I see that Rosecrans is superseded.[21] From what I have heard of him by acquaintances I think it is time.

Captain Wood called at Mrs. Murray's today. Her husband the colonel was home the other day, sick, and left with the army. She said we had not left there twenty minutes when Stuart's cavalry came in and captured two of our provost guard who were left as safeguards. She scolded Stuart and sent a note to General Lee, who said the men should be returned via Norfolk. She said also that when we marched along here a column of Rebels was on each side of us. I think our escape and repulse of them at Bristoe was miraculous. Seventeen wagons were sent by Colonel Murray to remove his goods and furniture, but Mrs. Murray refused to go.

During the fight at Bristoe, General Warren sent to General Sykes of the V Corps, who was but a mile or two ahead, to come back. Sykes sent back a note saying, "If the enemy is not in force you can take care of him. If he is in force two corps are but little better than one against the whole army. General Meade has ordered the army to concentrate at Centreville. I shall move on," or words to that effect. Warren was terribly enraged. "Tell him to go to h——. We don't want him, but this day will either make the 2d Corps or kill Sykes." This is a specimen of the unwritten history of the war.[22]

Cedar Run
October 22, 1863

We are going to move camp tomorrow two miles forward, to be near the Warrenton Branch railroad, for protection.[23] It appears to be the intention to occupy this part of the country, and I hardly think Mr. R. E. Lee will come to fight us here. Two men drummed out today — one branded — one reprieved who was to be shot. One was shot in the First Division at Centreville. While at Centreville some miscreant stole a sash from my saddlebags in the night.[24] Well, *all* soldiers are not Christians.

Two miles from Warrenton
October 25, 1863

General Meade has been to Washington, and the papers say the president ordered him to move at any rate. The papers know nothing about it. It would be of no advantage to us to be nearer Richmond. Guerrillas capture trains, tear up railroads, and chased one of our Sanitary Commission wagons almost into Washington the other day. If every mile of railroad is not guarded, it is in danger of being torn up.

Near Warrenton
October 27, 1863

We have something to eat now, quite good. The people to whom we furnish safeguards are willing to sell us provisions such as they have, at a good price, but they still feel privileged to abuse our soldiers with their tongues. A guard from the Nineteenth Maine asked to be relieved from duty at a house where he could not endure their talk. Of course he could not retaliate. The common people here are wretchedly poor, and many of them depend entirely on our army for food and clothing. As officers are forbidden to sell or exchange provisions for other articles, the only way is to give them outright, and many a one is indebted to the charity of our mess for the first tea, coffee, and sugar they have had for months.

Went to Warrenton yesterday, called at General Sedgwick's, and at headquarters of the army, which are a little out of town and do not look quite as comfortable as our little camp at division headquarters. General Williams, adjutant general of the army, is favorable to the idea of sending the reenlisted regiments home.[25]

There was quite a sharp fight yesterday within hearing at Bealeton between our cavalry and that of the enemy.[26] They fight all day though without result. When I returned from Warrenton, found orders to be ready to move, teams hitched up, etc. Every day or two we are ready to move; but neither army is willing to fight unless they have the advantage of position. All quiet and peaceful this evening. The bright moon looking down on camps dotting the hillsides, and nestling in the edges of the wood, and the little campfires glistening in the cool, frosty air look like fireflies in the distance.

Near Warrenton
October 30, 1863
Some of our men, the First Minnesota particularly, have built the finest little huts I ever saw, about ten feet by six, and three or four feet high, covered with shelter tents, sides of split logs, with fireplaces, bunks, etc. Very neat indeed. Some very good bands cheer us with their music. The Fourteenth Connecticut have a very good one and last night played some fine airs. The railroad is now finished, and cars are running today. It was finished in a very short time, considering its condition.

People talk of the Army of the Potomac being kept here only to protect Washington. It is to protect the whole North. As long as there is a Rebel army in Virginia, there must be a Federal one. If the Rebels would be kind enough to agree not to go into Maryland or Pennsylvania and only go straight at Washington, we might withdraw a great part of our army. Perhaps some of our peace friends might propose this.

We had a new dish yesterday. Beef's head roasted in the ground. A pit is dug, fire built in it, then the head, wrapped in its skin and a wet sack, put in, covered up and a fire kept on it twenty-four hours. When taken out it is "done to a turn." General Warren was over to eat some, and it generally draws company.

November 3, 1863
We shall undoubtedly move soon. The men have eight days' rations, with seven days more in the teams. Our sick are to be sent to the rear tomorrow morning, and all preparations for a general movement are made. The weather is threatening.

Brandy Station
November 9, 1863
At daylight on the morning of the seventh we left our camp near Warrenton, reached Kelly's Ford, eighteen miles, in the afternoon. The III Corps were before us and surprised some Rebels on the north side of the river, capturing 250 prisoners. The pontoon bridges were laid before night, and we crossed in the morning. The III Corps

went off to the right. We sent out skirmishers and picked up a few prisoners and came soon upon the deserted camps, which they had left in a hurry. Their army had made preparations for a winter's stay, having good huts and some tents, which they left standing.

The V and VI Corps went by the way of Rappahannock Station, where the VI took four cannon and 1,100 prisoners. They came down to Kelly's Ford afterward. We felt our way cautiously, skirmishers in front and on flanks, but met no enemy and now are near Brandy Station, the VI Corps on the right, and Kilpatrick's cavalry at Stevensburg.

Stevensburg
November 10, 1863
Moved a few miles today, and one brigade of our division is occupying the very nice huts the Rebels left in such haste. It has been very cold. The summits of the Blue Ridge are covered with snow. We are trying to fit up our tents comfortably.

Stevensburg
November 12, 1863
Two young Englishmen have been spending three or four days with us. One Hon. J. Yorke, lieutenant of Royal Artillery, son of the Earl of Hardwicke, and Mr. Atkinson, holding a civil office at Prince Edward's Island.[27] We found them very agreeable acquaintances, after some false notions of theirs had been corrected, and went away much pleased with their visit, and congratulating themselves on having seen a bit of a skirmish. Many English visitors are with us, coming with introductions from the secretary of war and being entertained at the various headquarters of corps and divisions.

Stevensburg
November 15, 1863
I see that the Richmond papers are raving about the defeats they have met with lately. It appears to me that their cause must be getting more desperate when their papers coolly propose to starve prisoners to death as the only means of revenge left to them.

We are near Berry Hill, a fine place it was, owned by Col. John Thom, who died in 1855, now owned by a Mrs. Taylor. A son of his is a surgeon in the Rebel army.[28] They appear to have lived in some style. All scattered now.

A new order is out reducing transportation still further. It makes but little difference, for we have generally kept ours within limits. The amount of baggage is much less than when we first came out. One regiment then had as much as a division now. On the Peninsula our train numbered 7,000 wagons and was 70 miles long. We now have about 2,000. The men then carried but three days rations and had their tents carried for them. They now carry eight days rations, their tents, and 60 rounds of ammunition, and the pioneers {engineers} their tools besides. The trains have seven days rations, and the beef is driven along. These of course are not full rations—all the extras left out which men get in camp about Washington.

Stevensburg
November 17, 1863
It is sickening to hear men, Northern men at home too, talk of the honor and chivalry of the South. We know, for we see returned prisoners every day. I told you of two of our men who were taken prisoner while safeguards at the house of Colonel Murray, and that General Lee promised Mrs. Murray they should be released. Lieutenant Harmon had a letter from one of them the other day, through the flag of truce mail, dated at Belle Isle, where he and his comrade are with the rest of our prisoners.[29] He says he hopes measures will be taken to exchange the prisoners there, as they are suffering very much. This of course is all he dares write. This looks like chivalry; and this very case was spoken of in the papers as one in which the Rebel commander had acted in a very magnanimous manner. So he did, in *promises* only. This is a small matter, of course, only two men concerned, but it serves as an illustration.

The day being fine, the First and Second Divisions had a drill yesterday, at which some English officers were present. They expressed themselves much pleased and thought our men excelled in drill and in physical endurance.

November 21, 1863
Orders to be in readiness to move. Examined sick and made out passes for general hospital, but a steady rain had set in. We are

living very comfortably now but shall soon bid goodbye to our snug little quarters.

Stevensburg
November 23, 1863
Went up to Brandy Station yesterday to see our sick men off—seventy-four from our division. More than 1,000 sick were sent away on that train. When sick are to be sent to general hospital, a list is called for, and the surgeons in chief of brigades make up their lists and forward them to the surgeons in chief of divisions, who, if the number or nature of disease appears to be such as to require further examination, visits the regiments and examines personally those selected for removal. The list is generally large, and it is necessary in almost every instance to revise it. Men are anxious to be sent to the rear, and regimental surgeons are naturally disposed to get rid of troublesome cases. After the list has been revised, the surgeon in chief of division signs passes to general hospital for each man, a book in the form of a check book being provided, the duplicate to be kept in the book.

The business done at Brandy Station is immense. All supplies for the army are brought here, and hundreds of teams are employed in carrying supplies to the different corps. The contemplated movement is to be on a grand scale.[30]

Stevensburg
November 24, 1863
You probably saw it announced in the papers that we moved yesterday and were well on our way to Richmond. But we did not. But last night orders came to move at daylight. We were accordingly up at 3 ½ o'clock, struck tents, had breakfast, and the troops were on the march before daylight. We moved across the fields and were waiting for the First and Third Divisions to get out of the way, as they preceded us, when orders came to return to our old camp. It may be on account of the rain, for ammunition wagons were stuck in the mud; and it may be that our newspaper reporters have made the enemy acquainted with our movements. These newspaper reporters should not be allowed in the army if they abuse their privileges. They generally follow in the wake of those generals who wish to get up a newspaper reputation and are willing to pay for it.[31]

Stevensburg

December 3, 1863

Back again in our old camp after six days of the most exciting adventure. Since Thursday (Thanksgiving) morning, we have had hard marching and hard fare. Got orders on Wednesday evening to march at daylight next morning. Up at half past three, broke camp, ate breakfast by moonlight, and moved at daylight in the direction of Germanna Ford on the Rapidan. About sunrise, while halting, General Webb read the dispatch to the troops announcing the success of Grant.[32] Arrived at the ford at eleven o'clock—awaited news from the other columns (it was a movement of the whole army in three columns.) The III Corps was behind time—got off the road, had quite a fight, and we did not cross until near night. The enemy had abandoned their works on the Rapidan. Advanced about three miles on the plank road leading to Orange Court House and bivouacked in the open field that night. Had supper by moonlight and breakfast by the same luminary. It was very cold.

Moved at daylight across the country to the turnpike, which leads from Fredericksburg to Orange Court House. Met the enemy's skirmishers soon after coming on this road and pushed on to Robertson's Tavern. Here a strong line of skirmishers appeared to contest the ground, and our division sent forward a line also. A sharp fight took place here, the Second Division losing forty killed and wounded. Lt. Colonel Hesser of the Seventy-second Pennsylvania was killed, and Lt. Colonel Joslin of the Fifteenth Massachusetts taken prisoner.[33] Provided well for our wounded and established our line, making it quite strong.

The country along here is covered with wood, only a clearing here and there, and is called the Wilderness, about eight miles from Chancellorsville. Saturday morning advanced about a mile when the enemy appeared in force in our front in line of battle, having some works thrown up. The little village here, a few houses in a valley, is called Old Verdierville. This was their line. Our artillery was moved up and in the afternoon fired pretty smartly, the enemy replying but little. On a slope about eight hundred yards distant two lines of battle of about eight thousand men remained in position all day. In the afternoon they built breastworks.

After the wounded were provided for, I went to the front again.

It rained at intervals all day, and the flinty turnpike, so hard before, was quite muddy at night. We slept in the woods, in which our lines were posted, on mud and leaves, and having blankets made ourselves comfortable. We have on these occasions generally two meals a day, have our mess wagons brought up at night, have supper, and send it to the rear in the morning. If the position is too much exposed, we send to the wagon for something. Did not sleep much. Teams driving through the woods, bringing rations, and making a good deal of noise about it, more than usual it appeared to me. Then ordered to move at daylight again. This was on a new enterprise. The II Corps, and a division of the VI, with Prince's division of the III, were placed under General Warren to make a sudden movement to the left and carry that point. Gregg's cavalry were now our left. Marched across the country from Robertson's Tavern to the plank road, coming out near New Hope Chapel, a small house with a few dwellings near it. While going through a low pine growth, we were obliged to dismount and lead our horses. Scratched ourselves and tore our clothes.

On nearing their left on the plank road, General Caldwell's division with our Third Brigade was sent as skirmishers and drove the enemy's pickets into their rifle pits. Here the golden moment was lost. If we had had an hour more of daylight we should have whipped them. Our picket line was established here, and during the night the order came to get the troops in position to assault at eight o'clock in the morning. They were marched down and placed in position with a good deal of difficulty owing to the nature of the ground. After an hour's cannonade on the right the whole line was to advance. The men when in position were mostly out of sight, under the hill and behind woods, about eight hundred yards in front of the enemy's works, which they had strengthened fearfully during the night—a continuous line of breastworks with eighteen pieces of artillery in that part opposite the II Corps.

I went down on the line at half past seven—the assault was to be made at eight—and felt sad to think how certain death awaited so many brave men. General Webb went along in front of the line saying words of encouragement. They were firm as a rock and waited the order to advance. I went back to an eminence 1,000 yards from the line of the enemy, and as I saw it before me with its frowning guns

133

and swarming with men, I felt that of four thousand men who were to advance at that point, not more than one thousand could reach it alive, and they only to be taken or killed.

The firing on the right slackened, then ceased, and I began to think General Warren had taken a sensible view of it and countermanded it. He had sent for General Meade to view the ground, which he did, and the assault was not made. All day the men waited, nearly perished with cold, until night, when the line was moved back into the woods and fires built. Cattle were killed, and all had supper.

The night was very cold, everything froze up. Breakfast by candlelight. Moved back a few rods, in a corn field. An old log barn was soon used up for fuel. Remained there all day and at night prepared ourselves for sleep, with a good fire at our feet, when orders came to move. The movement to commence at nine — different divisions to come in on specified roads at specified times — pickets to be kept out as usual, until three A.M. when they were all to be withdrawn at once — men to be left to keep up the campfires until that time. The cavalry to leave at daylight and join us at Culpeper Ford. It was done, but I cannot tell in a single letter the long story, how the night was bitter cold; how from some obstacle ahead we of the Second Division, who were in rear, were halted frequently in the bleak wind; how I dismounted and led my horse to keep warm and awake and suffered more from cold and sleepiness than I ever did before from the same causes. The whole country was lit up by our campfires. Gregg's whole division was scattered about, every horse saddled and every man equipped, stamping their feet to keep warm. The roaring fires lighted up the woods, the wind roared through it, and the fire in the dry leaves on the ground crept along in regular lines.

Soon after sunrise, reached the river and crossed on pontoon bridges — were not followed by the Rebels to any extent. After a halt of two hours, marched again for our camp of a week before and arrived here at six o'clock, having made a march of thirty miles since nine o'clock last evening.

Our campaign was short but fatiguing. It will be discussed in the papers sufficiently. My opinion is that General Meade managed it judiciously and skillfully.

December 6, 1863

On our return we used Milton's Mill, an old grist mill on Mountain Run, for a hospital, and after proper operations and dressing, sent them (the wounded) next day to Washington. This failure of General Meade's, as they call it, is making a great disturbance, and in Washington they are calling for his removal. Better let him stay. He has done better than anyone else. A good many find fault with Warren, and though I have no regard for him personally, I think he did perfectly right in not rushing his men up to be annihilated. Well, we cannot campaign much longer, and then I will try to go home.

Stevensburg
December 8, 1863

I made application yesterday for twenty days leave of absence. Ten only are granted to Massachusetts officers, but I made mine to headquarters of the army, and as they deduct half pay during absence (except on sick leave), they need not be so particular, for nothing can be done now for a while. The weather is very cold. We are having chimneys built for our tents. General Hancock is in Washington and will be here soon.

December 11, 1863

So far I have heard nothing from my application. In the meantime Dr. Dougherty has put in one, got his leave, and gone. General Webb has also got ten days and gone, taking Lieutenant Simms, his aide, with him.[34] Several of our staff are now absent.

[Received my leave the same evening and next morning started for home. Remained at home, most of the time in Boston, until the latter part of January, having had my leave extended in expectation of the arrival of the Nineteenth Regiment on furlough. So many delays took place that I became discouraged and returned. The various reenlisted regiments were allowed to go home, and their officers who were on detached service usually accompanied them. Nothing of importance occurred for several days.]

CHAPTER 10

"Hancock and Myself Run This Machine"

January 31–May 3, 1864

Frank Dyer returned from Massachusetts to camp at the end of January 1864 and within days went home again with the Nineteenth Massachusetts to recruit. The entries resumed on March 21, shortly before Dyer was named acting medical director of the II Corps. The Army of the Potomac was consolidated into three corps that spring, the II, V, and VI, under Major Generals Winfield S. Hancock, Gouverneur Warren, and John Sedgwick; the I and III Corps were broken up. General Meade was still the titular head of the army, but Lt. Gen. U. S. Grant was clearly in command. There were also changes in the cavalry. Maj. Gen. Phil Sheridan arrived, while Generals Alfred Pleasonton, Judson Kilpatrick, and others were sent west.

Surgeon Dyer comments in several entries on Grant's appearance, manner, and how he was regarded by the men. With almost two and one-half years of service, the doctor was now a veteran of the Army of the Potomac. His general attitude toward Grant was not hostile but cool, showing more than a bit of New England reserve for this westerner. Dyer took pains to debunk a number of popular stories about Grant. Perhaps he was determined not to put his faith in an unworthy commanding general as he might have done earlier.

Stevensburg
January 31, 1864
Have had a wet, foggy day and a wet and dark night. The sick are all to be sent to Washington (except the smallpox patients) tomorrow morning at daylight, so they will have to leave here at three o'clock. Rather bad, but they can't get the train through before night unless they start early. This does not indicate a movement but is done by order of the secretary of war, who has a notion probably that they

can be treated better there than here. I am perfectly willing to send them all away, but we have spent a good deal of time and labor in preparing hospitals here.

This morning went with the general on a ride through the camps of the division for inspection. They look well generally, but it requires the efforts of everyone concerned to keep an encampment in perfect order. The weather is now pleasant, but we have had some very cold nights, and several men have been frostbitten.

Stevensburg
February 1, 1864
Have been to a concert this evening at Second Brigade headquarters. It was well got up and had a very good audience. General Webb and staff, General Kilpatrick and aide, General Hays and wife, and several other officers and their wives. General Webb had a message from General Sedgwick (now commanding the army) saying that the Nineteenth would probably go home within ten days, and I have made up my mind to go with them.

[A few days after this the order came, and the Nineteenth took the cars at Brandy Station for home. Had a reception in Boston at Faneuil Hall, speeches &c.; then come on to Salem, where another reception awaited us, with speeches, refreshments, etc. Here the regiment was dismissed by Colonel Devereux, to assemble at Wenham in thirty days. On or about the sixteenth of March, took the cars at the Providence Depot in Boston for the front. Major Rice returned in command of the regiment, Colonel Devereux having resigned, and Lt. Colonel Wass having been detailed on recruiting service, from which he did not return to do further duty with his regiment.]

Headquarters, Second Division, II Corps, Stevensburg
March 21, 1864
Arrived here this afternoon, having spent one night in Washington and one with Dr. Willard at Fort Whipple. Visited several of the forts south of the city and called at Arlington House, where General DeRussy is stationed.[1] The house stands in a splendid position, commanding a fine prospect of Washington, the river, and the country for miles around; but the building is a magnificent failure. The plan of the establishment hangs in the hall, made in 1807, but a

small part only has been built. The drawing room was very fine, the walls hung with picture frames, from which the paintings had been removed by Lee when he left. Some execrable daubs hang in the hall, painted by some promising member of the family—battle pieces—a number of men fighting, with a figure supposed to be General Washington on a white horse in the center.

The ladies have left our headquarters—met Mrs. Webb in Washington—and all visitors will soon take their departure. General Grant is expected here in a few days. Burnside is gathering a large number of men at Annapolis, and I think we shall make a move in a few weeks.

Stevensburg
March 23, 1864
Snugly quartered in a neat little house, or hut, with three rooms, which the general had built during my absence, for his family, and which I now occupy with him. A furious snowstorm is raging, snow six inches deep and drifting. One after another comes back. Captain Gale came tonight, and Steele is the only one of our staff now absent.[2] Regiments are returning from furlough, and Generals Hancock and Gibbon will be here soon. I have been absent during the "gay season." Balls, lectures, and concerts have been the order of the day, and those who have been obliged to remain in camp have enjoyed themselves to the best of their ability and have been quite successful.

March 24, 1864
Our sick will be sent off to Washington tomorrow. We are obliged to empty our hospitals every few weeks as the sick accumulate. General Hancock is at General Meade's headquarters. Dr. Dougherty left this morning on leave of absence, and I am acting medical director of the corps until his return.

Stevensburg
March 25, 1864
The army is to be consolidated into three corps, the II, V, and VI, the I and III to be broken up. General Hancock is to have the II, as before; General Warren the V, and General Sedgwick the VI. General Grant has given General Meade authority to reorganize

the army and will hold him responsible for his appointments. He has appointed his corps commanders, and they in return appoint their division and brigade commanders. Our cavalry commanders do not stand very high at headquarters, and some changes will be made. One division of the III Corps reported to the II Corps today. I have in my department some sixty regiments from whom I receive reports. Many staff officers are on the anxious seats today, wondering what is to become of them in this process of reorganization. General Caldwell left this evening, having been relieved, and General Barlow is to take command.

Stevensburg
March 27, 1864
The order has been issued assigning regiments to the different corps. The II Corps now contains over eighty regiments of infantry, besides artillery, and some cavalry. The artillery consists of eight batteries—forty-eight guns. It would not be proper to say how many men this corps numbers, but you can make up your mind there are "right smart of men," and General Hancock and myself and a few others "run this machine."

The corps is divided in four divisions: Generals Barlow, Gibbon, Birney, and Carr are to command them, and in the Second Division, Generals Webb, and Owen, and Colonel Carroll, are to command brigades.[3] General Webb has the largest brigade, some nine regiments, General Owen the smallest, four.

Stevensburg
March 30, 1864
Yesterday the II Corps was to have been reviewed by General Grant, but rain began to fall in the morning and continued twenty-four hours. The low lands are flooded, small streams are rivers, and if it were not that we have a corduroy road the whole distance to Brandy Station, it would be impossible to get there. Some of the troops from about Washington are ordered here and will have a taste of field service.[4]

I made up the roster of the medical staff of the corps yesterday to forward to headquarters of the army that they might be announced from there (Special Orders No. 97, Headquarters, Army of Potomac, April 12, 1864). I retain my place as surgeon in chief of

Second Division. There is but one "surgeon of volunteers" in the corps, Surgeon Dougherty, and one "asst. surgeon U.S.A.," Dr. Calhoun.[5] I consider it quite complimentary to the surgeons of the corps that no new appointments are made to the corps to take rank over us. But I think some of those who are serving in hospitals should be sent to the field for a time.

My boy Curtis has symptoms of varioloid, and I have sent him to the hospital for a few days.[6] We still have some smallpox.

April 3, 1864
Several regiments from garrison have just come out and are obliged to sit down in the mud and rain. General Gibbon came today, looking not quite as well as last summer.

April 5, 1864
Rain, and more rain, the country is flooded. It is very fortunate our lady visitors have left camp. It has stormed ever since. We have a new adjutant general on our staff, Major Norvell, in place of Captain Wood, who died during my absence.[7]

April 7, 1864
General Sheridan has come to take command of the cavalry. Pleasonton, Kilpatrick and others are to be sent out west.[8] General Grant will make the Army of the Potomac his grand army and will have only the best. The weather is pleasant now, and the mud will begin to dry up. The work of preparation will now go on.

Stevensburg
April 9, 1864
Yesterday was pleasant, and General Grant ordered a review of the II Corps today, but about twelve last night the rain began to fall and has kept on ever since. Sutlers and surplus baggage to be sent to the rear by the sixteenth. All leaves of absence are refused now, except in case of sickness, where an officer's life is in danger from disease, not bullets. Quite a number of resignations are coming in now from officers who have been holding on all winter and now suddenly discover that from wounds or sickness they are unable to go through another campaign.

The wind blew the smoke down {the} chimney so that we could hardly stay in our little house, and now the rain has put the fire out. I shall go to bed and read.

April 10, 1864

The rain having ceased for a while I went with Dr. Lawrence, an English army surgeon, to visit our division hospital, but after riding for an hour or two through mud and water for a chance to cross Mountain Run, found that all the bridges were carried away.[9] There was no communication with the other side for some time. Men were at work rebuilding the bridges and will have all right tomorrow. Bull Run bridge on the railroad was also carried away.

Stevensburg
April 12, 1864

In the medical department measures are being taken to have everything in good condition for a movement. Although but a limited amount of transportation will be allowed for hospitals, the material will be well selected, and we shall be well provided with everything necessary. I am now engaged every day on a board of examination of applicants for discharge.

April 15, 1864

Our division was reviewed today.[10] Generals Meade, Sedgwick, and a dozen other generals were present. The division looked well and got a good deal of commendation. After a lunch at our headquarters, the Nineteenth and Twentieth Massachusetts were called out to drill before the assembled wisdom. They did finely and were highly complimented by Generals Hancock and Meade. During the review I was inspecting the ambulance train. After this the ambulance train was reviewed by the generals.

Stevensburg
April 17, 1864

Yesterday at Birney's division on a board of examination. A board of the surgeons in chief of divisions examine all officers and men of the ambulance corps with regard to their physical and mental qualifications. A meeting of the surgeons in chief was held this afternoon at the medical director's (Dr. Dougherty having returned) to get up a plan for our field hospitals for the campaign. We shall keep the sick with the ambulance train, pitch tents, and take care of them by divisions instead of by regiments. We did so to some extent last summer but had not perfected the system. We have twenty-two regiments in our division and shall have to provide not only for the sick on the march but for wounded in case of action. As our division is allowed but thirteen wagons for this purpose, and in these are to be carried twenty-two hospital tents, medicine chests, all articles necessary for cooking, a supply of medicines and surgical appliances, blankets, food for hospital, etc., for the whole division on the march and in action, it is important to make a good selection of articles. We have made arrangements which I think will work well.[11]

Stevensburg
April 20, 1864

The work of preparation is going on in every department. Boards of examination, inspections, and making of reports occupy all my time. More reports can be called for in five minutes than can be made in three days. The medical director calls for a report on the state of supplies. The general for a report of names and numbers of hospital men in the division, and whether more or less than allowed, of ambulance men, how many drivers, stretcher carriers, &c, and whether more or less than allowed, etc., and all these must be prepared.

Visited our hospital near Brandy Station today, with Generals Hancock, Gibbon, and Barlow. Most of the sick had been sent to Washington, but everything was in complete order.

I heard General Meade make a remark to General Gibbon yesterday that I thought worth remembering. After speaking of Hooker's report, which General Grant has spoken of in no very complimentary terms, he said it took some a long time to write a report—"for instance, Gen. McClellan has taken a long time to make his report, and yet it is very inaccurate in many instances" and mentioned some, about the movements of troops and particular engagements, where he was entirely mistaken. This was said in a friendly spirit, but it shows that his report is far from being an accurate one.

"Hancock and Myself Run This Machine"

Stevensburg
April 22, 1864

Last night a good deal of riding of orderlies back and forth, so I made up my mind "something was up." A review of the II Corps was ordered for today. At ten o'clock this morning went out with General Gibbon and the rest of the staff, and at eleven o'clock the whole corps was on the ground. Then the artillery and cavalry came on, and various corps and division commanders with their staffs from other corps; then General Grant and his escort appeared and took their stand, and soon after the troops began to move. He did not ride along the line as the reviewing officer does when a smaller body of men is reviewed.

The infantry came first, division front—then the artillery in columns of batteries, that is, six guns abreast and six caissons abreast, and yet the line was more than an hour in passing. The infantry and artillery were in splendid condition. I never saw troops march so well and look so well. Knapsacks, overcoats, blankets, etc., packed with such neatness and uniformity; clothes clean and tidy, though some worn and weather-stained; and there was a good, soldierly appearance about them. Then came the cavalry, Kilpatrick's old division, and I was really ashamed of their appearance compared with the infantry. They were dirty and slovenly with coats, blouses, jackets, buttoned and unbuttoned, hats and caps, long hair and short hair, and everything showing total neglect of discipline on the part of their commanders. There was no excuse for this, for the nature of the service they have been engaged in has not been more severe, or more destructive to clothing than that of the infantry.[12]

There were upwards of 20,000 infantry, besides cavalry and artillery, and although I have seen more men together, I never saw such fine, soldierly looking men throughout. Then all the transportation of the corps was reviewed, supply trains, ambulances, &c., and afterward all general and staff officers adjourned to corps headquarters, stopping on the way at our division headquarters to see the Nineteenth and Twentieth Massachusetts drill. I shall remember this as the finest review I have ever seen.[13]

There is nothing very remarkable in General Grant's appearance. He is a common-sized man, looks tough and healthy, but you would not pick him out of a crowd of officers as a remarkable man.[14] But then our "magnificent" men are not always the best soldiers.

I think Hancock is an exception. He is a fine-looking man and a good soldier. Grant rides a fine bay horse, with a very handsome embroidered saddle cloth, and was well dressed. The gossip about his extreme simplicity is nonsense. He dresses as becomes his position, no more, no less. When other officers are obliged to appear in proper dress, it is proper that their superiors should. Many would be glad to be relieved from the expense of dressing suitably, as the pay of officers is very small. It rests with Congress to do justice to them, but that is scarcely to be expected.

Well, no matter, I think I have patriotism enough to go through this campaign even without pay. When it is over I will go home with the satisfaction of having done my duty. But the people need not be alarmed about their money invested in government stocks. The government will triumph. Men may be corrupt, and officials and contractors may try to draw the very lifeblood out of the nation, but still the cause is progressing, and all will come out bright at last.

April 24, 1864
A man was hung yesterday for a crime committed last autumn at Morrisville. He was a fine-looking man, had been a soldier in the Crimea, and wore two medals won there. The details are uninteresting.

Stevensburg
April 27, 1864
The army is in good condition. All are expecting hard fighting and have coolly made up their minds for it. They don't cheer and shout as they did two years ago (not a cheer greeted General Grant in the review), but they are all the better soldiers for it and have confidence that they have a general, who, though not superhuman, has a strong will, good sense, and power to do as he thinks best. I think he is more than satisfied with this army, and he knows they will fight. He has issued no new orders, reducing transportation, etc., since taking command, as the papers have it.

April 30, 1864
Sent off more sick this morning. Sat up late signing passes for them and was at the station with them this morning. Burnside's corps relieved the V Corps along the railroad, and they moved up today.

The people at home are impatient and think that all we have to do is just to move on. But an army going into such a fight, or series of fights, must be prepared in every possible way.

May 1, 1864

Rode to Culpeper and beyond yesterday. Saw but few people in town, few ladies, and all of them dressed in mourning. Almost every unoccupied house in the vicinity of Culpeper has been torn down. The Rebels destroyed a good many, and our men finished them. Our division is ordered out of their huts tomorrow to form new camps, without fireplaces, etc., in order to get ready to move with more ease. Officers who visited our signal station on Stony Mountain report the Rebels very vigilant, with new lookouts and stronger pickets. They are looking for a movement.

May 3, 1864

Evening. We have orders to march tonight at 11½ o'clock and are now packing up for the movement. Tents will not be struck till after dark so that nothing can be seen by the Rebs from their lookout. A cold north wind is blowing today. The whole army moves simultaneously, it is understood. The column will not be embarrassed with useless trains. We shall have a long night march and probably cross the Rapidan near Germanna Ford at daylight. Although I am no fire-eater, I am glad to see a movement. This suspense is very trying. I can write only by private hands. A sutler going down will take this. When I write again I hope to tell you of a victory.

CHAPTER 11

"We Shall Hammer at Them"

May 4-30, 1864

Near the start of the Wilderness campaign, Dr. Dyer found himself back at the ruins of the Chancellor house and the scene of Hooker's defeat a year earlier. Soon there were one thousand wounded in his division hospital. He mentions a number of the officers who were casualties, the most prominent being John Sedgwick, hit in the eye by a sharpshooter. Next came Spotsylvania, the climactic fighting at the Angle, and an elated Winfield Scott Hancock demanding a pencil with which to write his official report. The numbers of killed and wounded were enormous, and the army needed reinforcements, but Dyer scoffs at all talk of new men as unfounded rumors. He mentions yet another deserter's execution, and the newspaper correspondents are again the subject of the doctor's scathing criticism. He also describes Virginia civilians, including black children, in some detail.

Chancellorsville
May 4, 1864
Crossed the Rapidan this morning, and I write you from the long to be remembered battlefield of Chancellorsville, where just one year ago took place the final of the series of battles which ended in our defeat. I sit by a stump, near the ruins of the Chancellor house, a large building standing at the time of the battle, the headquarters of General Hooker, and burnt by the Rebels, with many wounded unable to escape. All around we see the marks of the desperate conflict, mounds of earth where horses, and others where men, are buried; pieces of clothing, equipments, everything reminding us of a battlefield. The country for miles is intersected by rifle pits running in every direction. There is one small wooden house about half a mile from here, but this is the town. It is on the plank road to

Fredericksburg, distant about twelve miles. We have met no enemy yet—probably shall soon. We are having a lunch, the first since last evening—now two P.M. All are quite tired today.

Wilderness
May 7, 1864

We are again in the midst of a great battle, and I sit down for a few minutes in the shanty of a "first family," on whose ground we are, to write a note. We have been fighting two days and part of another and are not yet done; have about 1,000 wounded here in our division hospital. We left Chancellorsville on the morning of the fifth, marched to Todd's Tavern in the forenoon, then marched back on the Brock road toward the plank road, where the V Corps and Getty's division of our corps had been in and were driven back, when the Second went in and held the line. The fighting ceased then, and we rested quietly that night. We had established our hospitals by this time and had quite a number in. I went up and spent the night with the general and came down in the morning.

Hearing considerable fighting about noon went up again. The Rebels had been trying along our whole line and at one time drove us; at another we drove them. It is all thick wood, and nothing can be seen by either side a great way. Very little artillery has been used, as there is no chance to put it in, and it is impossible to see where to fire. The enemy made an attack on the part of our line held by our corps in the afternoon and drove us in nearly to our breastworks. Part of the IX Corps had joined us here, but they made no better stand than the rest—in fact they gave way very readily. But we checked them there and held the road. The Rebels had meanwhile set fire to the woods, and probably a great many wounded were burnt. They then appeared on our left, and men were mowed down, but they made no attack, or a very faint one. General Gibbon had command of the left of the line and made every preparation to receive them.

At this time men, regiments, brigades, and divisions were a good deal mixed up, they having been in and out of the woods, forward and back, but the lines of breastworks were held pretty well. I rode along the line of burning breastworks (they were built of logs) in the evening. The smoke was stifling. Our men were back in the woods to be out of the smoke, and only a line of fire was between me and the Rebels, but this they could not cross.

I remained at the front during the night and came down again this morning. I have to divide my time between the field and the hospital. Most of the operations have been performed. This is sooner than we have ever done before. The clerks taking the lists of wounded have now got the names of 929 and have not finished yet. The Nineteenth has had but few wounded (they were skirmishers). The Twentieth has suffered severely, nearly all their officers hit.[1] Major Abbott dead, and one or two others.[2] Colonel Connor of the Nineteenth Maine, fractured thigh.[3] Simms, of General Webb's staff, wounded in the head (ball imbedded in the petrous portion of the temporal bone. I removed it. He has since recovered). Capt Brownson of General Hancock's staff badly wounded.[4]

They are pounding away with artillery today on some part of the line, not very fiercely. We shall have to have another hard fight before the thing is settled. Yesterday it looked badly, today better, and tomorrow I am in hopes we shall whip them. Grant is here, but he gives few orders. Meade is the ruling spirit and is managing well. Grant's army never fought as ours has here, and all he can do is keep quiet and see what the old Army of the Potomac can do.[5]

Two P.M. An order has just been received to have the wounded in readiness to go to Washington. They are to be sent to Rappahannock Station, part to walk, part in army wagons, and part in ambulances. Distance to Rappahannock Station about seventeen miles. We shall send about 4,000 from the II Corps. It is the intention of the army to advance, and the wounded must be got out of the way.

[As sufficient transportation could not be furnished for all the wounded, a part were left at the field hospital. I extract from my report of the seventeenth the following. "Received in hospital of Second Division, on the fifth, sixth, and seventh, 996 wounded. Of these, 696 were removed in ambulances and army wagons on the eighth, and 300 left behind in charge of Surgeons Aiken and Monroe, and Asst. Surgeon Sawyer."[6] This hospital was visited, but the wounded not disturbed, by Rebel guerrillas, with the exception of robbing them of their sugar and coffee and a few useful articles of clothing; and in about a fortnight were removed to Fredericksburg. The route by the way of Rappahannock Station having been rendered unsafe by guerrillas, the trains were turned toward Fredericksburg, and hospitals organized there for the reception of the wounded. Moved from our position at night, and next day,

moving parallel with the Rebel army, took up a new position near
Spotsylvania Court House.]

Spotsylvania
May 9, 1864

Yesterday riding with General Gibbon, went down with General
Grant and staff to the lines to reconnoiter. There was considerable
skirmishing, and bullets flying "right smart." A brigade or two of the
VI Corps went in, terrific firing for a while, a good deal of yelling and
shouting, and some prisoners taken; but no substantial advantage
gained.

May 10, 1864

After riding about the country five hours to select a place for a
hospital, I ordered the teams up and then came down to the front
with General Gibbon. General Meade and staff were there and talked
some time. General Sedgwick was killed yesterday while standing
where we were with General Grant the day before. A bullet pierced
his eye, and he never spoke or breathed again. We have lost one of
our best generals at a time when we could ill afford to spare him. In
the afternoon crossed the Po, the First Division above and Second
below. Remained there overnight and recrossed in the morning; our
division, with the Third and Fourth went into position for assault,
which was made with little gain, our division losing 500—had 400
in hospital.[7] The First Division was driven across the Po, losing
many and leaving 500 behind, wounded. The VI Corps had a
terrible fight on their part of the line after the II Corps, with what
success I know not, only I know we are not driven back. We have
excellent facilities for taking care of our wounded, good surgeons
in every department. I have six operating tables where six sets of
surgeons work constantly, so we get rid of the cases pretty fast. We
shall probably send them to Fredericksburg tomorrow.

Today we received news from the West and that Smith was advancing on Richmond from Petersburg.[8] I was over the river today
when General Grant received the dispatch. It was copied and read
to the troops whenever opportunity offered. Grant, Meade, and all
the rest of the "U.S.A." were there (over the river) but even their
presence doesn't make the Rebel army fight less stubbornly.

Dr. Dougherty got a wound today, which would have been a

severe one but for his pocket book. I am all right, only tired; have been in the saddle half the time for the past week, have worked a good deal in hospital besides. I have not taken my clothes off since we started and have not seen my valise. The dust is so thick on the ground and in the air that we can scarcely see at times, and the heat has been oppressive—a little rain would be good now. Sleeping out of doors with only a flannel sack on is not bad now. We have rations for ten days longer, but our horses have only five pounds of oats a day and take the rest in leaves and fence rails. We shall hammer at them as long as they stand, so you may conclude we have not done fighting yet. The ambulance trains are still coming in with wounded tonight. We shall have another battle tomorrow. The armies seem to be pretty well matched, but Yankee endurance will count in the end.

Spotsylvania
May 12, 1864

Today has been one of the most eventful of any in the eight days continuous fighting. Yesterday we had been engaged during the day pretty smartly; the II and V Corps had assaulted the Rebel works three times unsuccessfully. I left the division hospital (from which we had been sending about 500 wounded to Fredericksburg) about ten o'clock in the evening and went down to division headquarters in front. I had heard that orders were expected, and in about an hour the order came to move. It was raining, and we were until daylight getting into position to assault on the left. The Rebels seemed to have an intimation of something going on, for they sent several shell directly over our heads when we were about moving. At daylight the lines of the II Corps were in position and then the ball opened.[9]

The first line went in quietly without firing until quite near, and although their skirmishers always give notice of an advance, as ours do, by frequent firing, still it was so sudden and overwhelming that each line followed the other over their breastworks, fighting sharply, until they had carried an important part of their main line of works and taken three thousand prisoners and twenty pieces of artillery. We were obliged to send so many back with prisoners and with captured guns, and they became so scattered, that there was danger of demoralization of the men. But Hancock was there, and by the provost guards of the divisions and corps the prisoners were "herded" together, where they remained very quietly, and I think some of them cheered. They were taken so quickly and hurried to the rear that I felt almost alarmed when I saw them coming over the breastworks, for in the gray of the morning we could not tell whether they were armed or not. Our artillerymen were sent in with their horses to bring out the guns, and streams of Rebels came in, many of them carrying our wounded with them into our lines, where the ambulances soon arrived.

There is a house on our line (the Landrum house) where we had artillery before, around which and through which shells were flying pretty fast and where General Hancock made his headquarters. There I found General Webb, who was wounded in the head, but not fatally, and several other officers. Hancock was sometimes on foot and sometimes on horseback, directing the movements and keeping his staff pretty well employed. He was nervous, as usual, never still a moment, but his head was clear enough. It was an intensely exciting time and a glorious hour for him. I had just dressed General Webb's wound and sent him off in an ambulance when General Hancock impatiently called for a pencil.[10] I lent him mine with which he wrote a dispatch to General Meade, one of the proudest things he has done during the war, saying he had taken 3,000 prisoners, thirty to forty pieces of artillery, and held three lines of their rifle pits. As soon as they were driven back there they commenced a furious attack on the right, on the VI Corps, and for five hours there was the most furious cannonade and musketry that I have heard on this campaign. It was Gettysburg over again.

About ten o'clock A.M. the enemy made an attempt to retake their works, and a Mississippi brigade (Battle's) came up to close quarters.[11] The rifle pits and ditches are filled with their dead where they fell; they are literally piled on each other. Two colonels were lying there with their men within six yards of the breastwork. This was a salient angle of their line and considered an important position. Our men suffered as much as they. We still hold all the captured positions.

This afternoon I am at the hospital. We have four hundred to five hundred here, and fighting is still going on. The whistling of shots can be heard, and the band of the Fourteenth Connecticut is playing between the First Division Hospital and ours. Of the Nineteenth, Major Rice is missing, Lieutenant Ferris killed, Lieutenant

Thompson missing. Sergeant Brown has just died, and I amputated the leg of another. They have lost 12 killed, and we have already 30 of their wounded. The Twentieth has suffered more, and the First Brigade was last night commanded by Major Hooper of the Fifteenth.[12] Our army is tired out; eight days continued fighting without sleep for days and nights will wear men out, but we shall give the Rebels no rest as long as we can stand. Hope for the best and pray God to save the Union.

Spotsylvania, May 13, 1864
The reinforcements that we heard of as coming are like the Pennsylvania Militia last summer, not near enough for use. Burnside's corps came along with us, but none of Augur's 20,000 men that were said to be at Fredericksburg day before yesterday.[13]

May 14, 1864
All day yesterday sharpshooters were at work, and wounded were coming in all day. Colonel Carroll took some rifle pits and received another wound.[14] Last night and early this morning we sent away five hundred wounded from our hospital, all the wagons being collected for the purpose. I left the hospital early this morning and came down to the front. An assault was to have been made by the II and V Corps at five o'clock but for some reason failed. Sat down near an old house a while. Hancock, Gibbon, and others there—raining. Lots of wounded Rebels lying in and about the house, mud knee deep. Some men buried where we sat, and a fire built on top, not however by design. Then came over where General Gibbon has a tent pitched. General Hancock is lying here asleep. General Burnside has been here, and they are trying to get up some kind of a forward movement. Reinforcements not up yet.

Spotsylvania
May 15, 1864
General Meade says we captured 8,000 prisoners altogether, and eighteen cannon is all we can claim. After lying in the captured works all day yesterday with but little fighting except skirmishing and taking two guns, which were between the lines, we withdrew this morning to a hill about a mile in the rear near headquarters of the army—a large estate called Beverly.[15]

Here we have been lying about two hours, the troops massed on the field and making coffee. Generals Gibbon and Hancock just come from army headquarters, and we are all lying on the ground, most of the staff asleep. It has just ceased raining, and the ground is not turf, so you may imagine it is not very clean. General Grant's headquarters are within a few hundred yards. His staff is composed of four or five officers. He has not much for a staff to do. He has two large hospital tents and ten wall tents in a row besides a great number for clerks, servants, &c, in the rear. All very well, but not exactly the popular idea of General Grant's simplicity — a shirt and toothbrush. General Meade has a larger headquarters camp, but he has three times the staff and ten times the work to do.

I got my valise yesterday, the first time since we started, and was much refreshed by clean clothes. Near me is a telegraph wagon in which I hear the clicking of the magnet. The poles are carried in a wagon, and the wire reeled on the back of a mule so that it can be put up and taken down very quickly. About two hundred of the enemy's cavalry came into the V Corps hospital in the rear yesterday but did no damage except taking a few stragglers and some of our wounded who could walk. A surgeon was afterward shot by one of our men who mistook him for a Rebel. All now very quiet.

May 16, 1864

We have had some shelter for the last two days, a tent and two flies, which serve to keep the rain off at night. On the whole we have not suffered for food, but it has been a pretty rough campaign. It is now the twelfth day of fighting, and yesterday was the only day on which our division was not engaged in some of it. Colonel Wass is not here.[16] He has been ordered out, and others who started at the same time have arrived. Colonel Macy of the Twentieth, with but one hand, returned on the fifth, was wounded, and went home on the sixth. Our pioneers have destroyed several thousand stand of small arms, captured.

Spotsylvania
May 17, 1864

Five o'clock A.M. Standing by the fire (would sit if I had anything to sit on). Major Norvell up, but the others don't stir yet, though all have been called. It does not look promising for a fair day. We have had a great deal of rain, and the roads are in a miserable plight.

Yesterday afternoon our division made a very successful expedition. Some six hundred wounded had been left in the II and V Corps hospitals who could not be brought away for want of teams when we left that part of the line. So we were ordered out to remove them. The enemy's cavalry had been there. We took two brigades, with artillery, 150 ambulances, and a lot of wagons; loaded all up, Rebel wounded and all; and got in by nine o'clock in the evening. The poor fellows were glad enough to see us come. The Rebels had not injured our wounded but took all their sugar and coffee. In a house where twenty-nine of their wounded lay, they took three of our men prisoners who were taking care of them, and they left none in their places.

I have been reading the *N. Y. Times* of the fourteenth. The "News from the Army" is perfectly ridiculous. There is scarcely a truth in the whole. The Rebel army is still in our front, it is not broken up nor demoralized. The old Army of the Potomac is still fighting Lee, and Lee is not given to running away. He has not lost more than we have, and we have a good deal of heavy fighting to do yet or else we must entrench ourselves and stay here. The reinforcements that are "rushing to the front" are not equal to our losses by straggling. Our men have suffered severely, our division has already lost about 2,500; the whole corps 8,000 in killed and wounded besides stragglers, some of them prisoners, and some yet skulking in the woods. There are hosts of cowards always.

May 19, 1864

After writing the above, all was quiet till evening. Part of our corps was withdrawn, when the enemy's skirmishers drove ours in. Other troops were brought down, and an attack was planned for morning on their works near where we attacked on the twelfth. Troops were moving by us all night. Went up with the general to the Landrum House, where the troops were massing. The Corcoran Legion joined our division in the night, and about 8,000 heavy artillery from Washington came up. [17]

The assault was made but was unsuccessful, and we remained in our old position. The loss of the corps was five hundred. We had 153 in division hospital. [18] Sent our wounded to the rear in the afternoon.

At nine o'clock ordered to pack up hospital. At ten o'clock the division appeared, going to the left. Joined the general, and we are now lying on a flat by the Ni below the Anderson house.[19] Got some sleep, the first for a long time. The Thirty-sixth Wisconsin, Colonel Haskell (formerly on our staff), joined us yesterday.[20]

Spotsylvania
May 20, 1864

Up since four o'clock, expecting to move, but no order yet. A man of the Nineteenth, Starbird, is to be shot at seven o'clock.[21] In the first place he deserted from the Peninsula and reenlisted and deserted a number of times afterward. Was tried at Fort Warren and sentenced to be shot but pardoned through Senator Wilson's exertions and sent back to his regiment. He deserted his colors on two occasions during this campaign and was tried yesterday and sentenced to be shot this morning.

We lay pretty quiet yesterday till afternoon, when sharp firing was heard on the right, and the corps was ordered up. Ewell's corps had made an attack on our trains, but by the time we were well underway, they were repulsed. Came back after dark and about eleven o'clock started on a march, but as soon as we got fairly started the order was countermanded, and we laid down again.

Four P.M. The man was shot at precisely seven o'clock and died in a moment. Afterward went up to the hospital of the brigade of heavy artillery, which was engaged last night. The First Massachusetts lost three hundred, the First Maine a number; altogether about six hundred in the brigade. They had no medical supplies, so we were ordered to send up some, and our surgeons went to work with them. We are now expecting to move tonight.

I saw papers of the nineteenth today and am surprised at the amount of lying, particularly about the wounded at Fredericksburg. They speak of the great work of the civil surgeons, and of the Sanitary and Christian Commissions, and the destitution of supplies. The truth is, we sent our surgeons down with the wounded and sufficient attendants and rations. They have kept our surgeons there and placed them in charge of hospitals and will not let us have them back. They keep our nurses and everyone necessary for the care of the wounded. We need our surgeons and wish they would send them back. They have plenty of supplies at Fredericksburg, for we send there and get what we want.

Milford Station
May 21, 1864

After twenty-four hours as hard work as we often see, we are here near Milford on the Fredericksburg and Richmond Railroad.[22] About eleven o'clock last night took up our line of march, and all night, and until afternoon of today. Passed through Bowling Green to Milford Station, Torbert's cavalry in advance, and are now occupying a line about two miles across the river and fortifying it by entrenchments. The last of our column has not been up long, and the V Corps was to move today to join us.

Heavy firing is now going on at the right. The movement so far has been successful, and we may get some advantage from it. But it was a terrible march, not only all night, which is very well, but all through the hot and dusty day. I was entirely exhausted, having had no sleep and nothing to eat for twenty-four hours. But now since sundown it is cooler, and I feel refreshed but must have some sleep before I shall be fit for duty. I don't see how the men stand it. They are now at work building breastworks miles long. The enemy are now shelling us, inconveniently near.

May 22, 1864

Six A.M. The shelling soon ceased, and I went to sleep and slept well until five o'clock. There is some skirmishing, and General Gibbon and most of the staff are out on the line. It is very tedious riding with the general at all times and places but no harder than for others, and some of our staff work very hard. Staff officers generally have an easy time in camp but on a campaign are the hardest worked of any, and those who are the most intelligent and reliable are worked harder than others. Two or three of ours do nearly all the work.

Bowling Green is quite a little village, some good buildings, the courthouse and jail quite prominent features, houses more than half verandah. Roses, seringas, and locusts in bloom.[23] The town is nearly deserted, very few men, but great numbers of women and children, black and white, the whites principally of the *poor* quality, yellow, miserable things. One young gentleman of four or five was dressed in the picturesque costume of a waist and a piece of shirt as low as the waist.

P.M. We have very strong works here. I was surprised to see the formidable breastworks all along our lines. The men, though terribly tired, have been at work constantly night and day. But I don't think we shall have use for them here. A reconnaissance which went out today found no enemy except some cavalry. We are twenty-six miles from Fredericksburg and forty-four from Richmond. I think we shall go on soon toward Hanover Junction. Our trains are at Bowling Green, and we shall have a base on the Rappahannock, at Port Royal, sixteen miles from Bowling Green.

North Anna River
May 23, 1864
Left Milford yesterday morning and marched to North Anna River, which we reached in the afternoon. We are on the line of the railroad a few miles from Hanover Junction. The Rebels had formed a line on the other side of the river and fortified strongly. Some pretty smart fighting took place, and Birney's division charged and took some rifle pits on this side of the river.

May 24, 1864
The enemy kept up a skirmish fire all night, the balls singing about our headquarters once in a while, and this morning they threw over some shells but are now quiet. We have had but few wounded in the division for a few days past. Some killed and wounded by shell yesterday. They were running their cars off from Hanover Junction last night, but they are so well fortified that we could not trouble them. They will probably make a stand a few miles from here.

May 26, 1864
All quiet at six o'clock on this dull and foggy morning, while we lie on the south side of the North Anna River between it and the junction. Day before yesterday we crossed and drove the Rebels out of their line of works near the river to about a mile beyond. The II Corps was on the extreme left, the V and VI on the right, and the IX in the center. The II, V, and part of the VI crossed, but Burnside did not cross until we had cleared everything from his front and then he crossed on our bridges. He got a sharp message from Grant

and was ordered to report to General Meade. He has heretofore had command of his corps independent of General Meade, taking orders from General Grant. His Negroes are not at the front and have not been. They are behind with the trains.

Our division lost over one hundred in taking some rifle pits on this side of the river.[24] We shipped them off in army wagons to Port Royal yesterday. It is pretty hard for the wounded now. We get them in our hospitals and take care of them, perform all necessary operations, &c., but they are sometimes obliged to ride in wagons thirty miles or more, and many die during the trip. It is impossible to take them with us, and they cannot be left in the enemy's country to starve. It is one of the miseries of war. If we left hospitals and depots of supplies on the route, it would take half our army to guard them.

The fact is, we are halfway through a heavy job, and we must fight right along every day or all we have gained will be lost. The campaign is not half over. We have only begun to fight. A part of the VI Corps went off the other day to the right, which may result in some good. Sheridan's cavalry is about here. I think their destruction of railroads was not very complete. The cars are running from the junction all the time, and I don't think there is much of a break in the road. We are now destroying the railroad for several miles, burning bridges, etc., which seems to indicate that we are not to use this route for supplies but probably to keep on to the left and make the next base at White House.

We have very strong works here, and everywhere we go we dig. We are now on the premises of Major Doswell, a celebrated sporting character and the owner of "Planet" and other fast horses.[25] He has a plantation of 1,500 acres and everything very fine but got up and left the morning we came. By the time the army passes through a place, with teamsters and followers, it is pretty well stripped of all eatable things.

Across the Pamunkey, Totopotomoy Creek
May 28, 1864
On the evening of the twenty-sixth, after advancing our pickets with a smart skirmish, we withdrew across the North Anna and got out on the road to the Pamunkey, the rear divisions holding the ground nearly all day on the north side of the river. Got our wounded in

that night about one o'clock and shipped off about eighty in army wagons to Port Royal. There was some shelling as we left, and we suffered by it. The Thirty-sixth Wisconsin lost several by shell wounds. Got no sleep that night.

Next day while halted slept an hour. Owing to a delay by mistake of one of the brigade commanders, we did not reach our destination until after dark. That was on the other side of the river about five miles. This morning hurried up at 5½ o'clock and marched to the river. The VI Corps crossed first, and we followed. The cavalry was ahead and had quite a fight. We are now in position, about two miles from the river, awaiting an attack. I hardly think they will favor us.

Now near dark, I sit on a bucket turned up for a seat; have had my supper, the first meal since 5½ this morning; and feel comparatively happy in the prospect of sleep tonight. We have some luxuries. The general has for two days had a tent, and we also have a tent fly. I don't care much now what I sleep on or under now. When I am tired I can sleep wherever I am. We are getting down near our old ground on the Peninsula, now about sixteen miles from White House. We have a shower about every day. All is now quiet. Our corps is well entrenched, and everything appears well. Gregg's division of cavalry had a fight today, and, I hear, lost a good many.

May 29, 1864

All remarkably quiet this morning. Rose at four. The general and staff went out at that time along the lines to be prepared for an attack if one should happen to be made. All being quiet, took another nap. All seems just now like our old quiet times in camp. Bands playing, men cleaning up, sleeping, resting, cooking, eating, etc. Roses and magnolias are in bloom—picked strawberries yesterday. We are near Hanovertown, which is on the Pamunkey. A fine house, Dr. Pollard's, is near.

I hear that General Smith, with 20,000 men, is at White House and our cavalry all between here and Richmond. Sheridan pushes them about with great energy.

Totopotomoy Creek
May 30, 1864

Advanced our lines two or three miles yesterday and are now lying in front of the enemy's breastworks. Considerable fighting took place

yesterday but not a general engagement. We have large reinforcements now, and the II Corps is as large now as it was when we
started. The Eighth New York Heavy Artillery (all heavy artillery
regiments act as infantry) and the "Corcoran Legion" of four regiments, under General Tyler, have joined our division with two other
full regiments. Our division now numbers twenty-nine regiments.
I hear that General Gibbon has been appointed major general. I
am sorry Butler has been whipped so.[26] It disturbs our plans very
much.

We are now thirteen miles from Richmond, only a few miles from
the place where the battle of Fair Oaks was fought two years ago
tomorrow. I slept at the hospital last night, expecting a large number
of wounded in as an assault was to have been made. The assault
was only partial, and only a few were brought in.

Official portrait of J. Franklin Dyer, third mayor of Gloucester, Massachusetts, by Albion Harris Bicknell (1837–1915). Courtesy David Stotzer, Cape Ann Photography, and City of Gloucester.

Map of the Virginia theater. From E. B. Long, *The Civil War Day by Day*
(Garden City, N.Y.: Doubleday, 1971). Courtesy Random House.

Detail of *Island of Mercy* by Keith Rocco, depicting the Pry Mill hospital
at Antietam (called the "Valley Mills hospital" by Dyer). Courtesy
National Museum of Civil War Medicine.

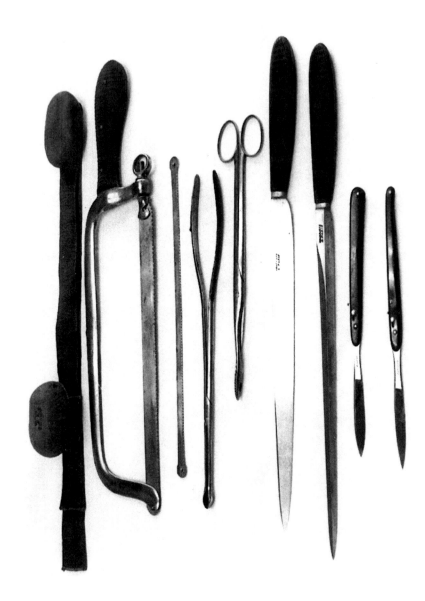

Left: Instruments from the French surgical knapsack made by the firm
Charriere, including several scalpels, knives, scissors, forceps, and
saws. Courtesy Mrs. Nancy Dyer Witmer.

Above: The large, standard boxed set of instruments made by
G. Tiemann and Company in New York City. A regular medical kit of
the type used by Civil War surgeons in field and general hospitals, it
has dozens of items set in both halves of the box and its filled
trays. Courtesy Mrs. Nancy Dyer Witmer.

J. Franklin Dyer's house at 54 Leonard Street in Annisquam,
one of the villages in Gloucester on the Cape Ann Peninsula. Courtesy
David Stotzer, Cape Ann Photography.

CHAPTER 12

"Very Few Wounded Were Brought In"

May 31–June 15, 1864

Dyer's description of camp life at Cold Harbor is almost surreal. Men were being killed and wounded every minute, while staff officers worked, slept, or lounged about; loafers congregated at headquarters and the division hospital; and servants attended to their chores. Dr. Dyer also mentions the wounded, mostly Union, caught between the lines, without appearing to assign blame for their fate. John Gibbon became a major general, and President Lincoln was renominated. General Hancock gave another display of his mercurial temperament. Dyer comments once again on the Virginians, especially the planter class and their current way of life. Grant moved south to the James and over the river to Petersburg.

May 31, 1864
Within a few minutes a sharp fight has sprung up. I shall go out to see what is going on. These things get so common that we take them very quietly. First sharp skirmishing, then two or three shell, then a volley and a yell, a hurrah, rapid firing, two or three more shell in as many seconds, then slack up, only a shot in a second or two, then the same thing over again. That is the way they are fighting now, but it is not a general engagement.

Totopotomoy Creek
June 1, 1864
There was sharp skirmishing all day yesterday and some charges.[1] Our division took some rifle pits in front of them but suffered a good deal from sharpshooters. A large proportion of officers were killed and wounded. Captain Mumford of the Nineteenth killed, and several other officers.[2] We received over thirty wounded and at

night sent off eighty sick and wounded to White House.[3] After they were loaded, I went up to division headquarters at Washington Jones's house and slept.[4] There was a constant skirmish fire all night, and a good many orders received and sent out. But I got a number of the *Atlantic Monthly* from General Tyler and read an article on doing housework, a very quiet sort of reading for such times, continually interrupted by sharp firing, or the whistle of a stray bullet.[5]

General Gibbon spoke this morning of the strange and dissimilar scenes about us.[6] We had finished breakfast, one was reading a paper, another writing, others talking. I was enjoying the fragrance of a bouquet of roses; the band of the Eighth New York was playing. The Negroes about the house were gaping and listening to the music, while three hundred yards in front there was pieces of artillery firing and farther in front a sharp skirmish going on, every moment someone being hit—orderlies coming and going—business going on as usual—boys washing dishes and blacking boots, everybody minding his own business. The general had been ordered to do what he thought best—he was ordered to keep up the skirmishing; the ambulances near, and the stretcher bearers in their proper places, ready to carry off wounded; the hospital ready to receive them. After going out to the line and seeing that the surgeons detailed to the front were in their proper places, I came to the hospital. A few wounded came in. We are expecting more. We are now on the extreme right and expecting the enemy to attack us there. If they do we are ready to pack up our hospital and move in a very short time.

Loafers and malingerers gather about the hospital on the plea of sickness and trouble us very much. We have daily examinations and order back those who are fit for duty. We have examined ours this afternoon and find forty-eight able to go on duty. I have sent for a detachment of the provost guard to escort them to their regiments, for it is useless to send them except under guard. There are hundreds of men straggling in the woods—"coffee boilers" who drop out on the march when they get a chance. They steal whenever they can and never fight. The provost guard pick up all they can find, but many escape detection.

Cold Harbor

June 3, 1864

Moved on the night of the first and arrived here yesterday. General Smith arrived here the afternoon before and had a fight.[7] Our corps has had a heavy fight today, and our division suffered badly. We have one thousand now in division hospital. Lieutenant Thompson of the Nineteenth killed. Captain Hinks badly wounded. Captain Hale also.[8] George is here, with Gen. "Baldy" Smith's corps.[9]

June 4, 1864

I wrote you a hurried note yesterday by Captain Hale. Heber is wounded I hear, but you probably know about it.[10] We are still in the fight, our lines near together, and every few hours an assault is made on some part of the line by one side or the other. I wrote you from near Hanovertown. That night we made an assault, which was not successful. Got our wounded, and the corps took up their march that night. It was a severe one, everybody was so tired and sleepy. We met here the XVIII and part of the X Corps, and while I slept George came and found me.[11] He is well but looks as though he had had rough times lately. They took about six hundred prisoners. Our corps had some fighting that day, but yesterday we made an assault on their works and lost over one thousand men in our division. Sent away three hundred yesterday and now are loading up as many more. We send them to White House.

We are close up to their lines all along, and they are hard pressed, but we can't get much advantage so far. They made an assault last night but were repulsed. Lee has a large army, his lines are as long as ours, but beyond this I know nothing. I suppose General Grant does, and I think both armies will concentrate here for a grand contest, and the siege of Richmond will be a part of the program.[12] For a month we have been fighting steadily. Not a day has passed that the II Corps has not been engaged more or less, and I think the next month may pass pretty much the same. We shall come out right though, no doubt of it, only keep hammering at them.

June 5, 1864

We are about sending off the remainder of our wounded, about four hundred. I have not been to headquarters for thirty-six hours.

When we got our wounded away I shall go up. We have a large army here, and there will be a good deal of fighting and digging.

Cold Harbor
June 8, 1864

"All quiet along the lines," the first time in forty days. Yesterday afternoon a flag of truce was sent out, some wounded brought in, and the dead buried between the lines. Until late this morning no firing had taken place, and a considerable time has been occupied in interchange of civilities between officers and men of the opposing armies. Very few wounded have been brought in, not so many as we expected. [13]

Those who were out in front tell me the Rebel lines are very strong and that we shall not be able to take them by assault but must continue to flank them until we can do so no longer, when regular siege operations will begin. The railroad is nearly completed to this point—within two miles—where we were two years ago. We are now at the house of Dr. Tyler, two miles from the Chickahominy. [14]

This time of inactivity is not a time of rest. Our men are not relieved from duty at the front and cannot have a chance to wash or get anything clean to put on and, on many parts of the line, cannot go to the rear without getting hit. Cooks and officers' servants going back and forth get picked off, and we have generally between twenty and forty each day wounded in this way by sharpshooters, besides those killed.

Colonel Wass has not been with his regiment for some days. Has not been in any engagement yet. Came to the hospital sick the other day, and when we moved day before yesterday he went to the wagon train in the rear. It is a very unfortunate thing for an officer's reputation to be sick at such a time. He had better keep with his command as long as he can stand—do anything but go to the rear. I know officers and men now with their commands who are suffering from slight wounds, and sickness besides, who will not go to the rear, while others go on the slightest excuse if permission can be obtained. Every day we send large numbers of men back to the front under guard, convalescents and loafers who accumulate about the hospitals. Officers who are considered fit for duty are ordered to report to their regiments and a list of their names forwarded to headquarters of the division.

166

Squads of men whose term of service has expired are going off every day, but their number is not large enough to make much difference in the army. When a regiment is mustered out it takes only the original members who have not reenlisted, sometimes not more than fifty or a hundred.

June 10, 1864

There is a little firing along the lines, which are very close together in some places, and men have to be very careful, for at such close quarters they kill nearly every one they hit, and our men do the same. They have breastworks with logs on top, making little portholes to fire through. This will not last long. A movement will soon take place, and before forty-eight hours we shall perhaps be twenty miles from here.

June 11, 1864

We were ordered to have our hospital ready to move at any moment. We have now but sixty sick and fifteen wounded, having sent off seventy-five yesterday. [15] After dinner went over to see George (XVIII Corps). They were pretty well situated in heavy entrenchments. Line officers are obliged to live roughly now, and unless the men get vegetables soon I think there will be a great deal of sickness. I noticed along the line of three corps strong entrenchments were being thrown up inside of the others. Our trains moved down some miles on the White House road last night. I see that General Gibbon is confirmed as major general and am glad to hear that Mr. Lincoln is nominated again for the presidency. [16]

Cold Harbor
June 12, 1864

Sent George a bag of good things today. The orderly found them about moving, toward the White House they thought, and probably back to the other side of the James. George and Captain Gray were messing together on ham, hard tack, and coffee, and a supply of luxuries was very welcome. [17] We shall move soon, tonight perhaps. I have great hopes of success.

James River, opposite Windmill Point
June 14, 1864

You will know before this reaches you, that the "Army of the Potomac is safe under cover of the gunboats near Harrison's Landing,"[18] but we are here under very different circumstances from those which existed two years since.[19] I wrote you on the twelfth, the day we were preparing to move. At four o'clock all the sick and wounded were sent off to White House, the hospitals broken up, and teams sent forward. I went up and joined the troops, and after dark the withdrawal commenced. The strong interior entrenchments which had been built were only to be used in case the enemy followed.

The different columns were put in motion, and by eleven o'clock all were moving on different roads, all centering near Long Bridge on the Chickahominy, which our division reached at seven o'clock in the morning. Here was a pontoon bridge (Long Bridge no longer exists).[20] The V Corps had crossed. We crossed at eleven o'clock, leaving one brigade as a rear guard, which did not leave until the bridge was taken up. (They arrived here this morning.) We came in last night. It was a long and weary march, about twenty-seven miles by the road we came. The men were very tired, and it was two hours after some of the brigades got in before they were put in position, owing to somebody not deciding where they were to go. A good many provoking things take place at such times. Staff officers misunderstand, or lose the road, or can't find the troops, or anything else may happen that affects the comfort of the men. Of course every one is out of humor, and a good deal of grumbling and no little swearing is the consequence.

Our headquarters are in front of a deserted house, a very comfortable place; the prettiest thing about it being a splendid bush of variegated roses. I have one bunch before me having five or six of different shades. From Dr. Wilcox's house near here, I can see the James River, Windmill Point opposite, and some troops camped there.[21] We are eight miles from Harrison's Landing and twelve or fourteen from Bermuda Hundred. The XVIII Corps took transports at White House and have gone back perhaps to where they came from.

I suppose this movement will create an intense excitement at the North, and gold will go up still higher. People will not understand it, and the Rebels will claim it as a victory. It is simply a movement to go to another base, without a battle. We remained at Cold Harbor ten days and could accomplish nothing there; in fact I do not think General Grant intended to begin a siege there, for he did not bring anything to do it with. We all regard it as a continuation of the flank movement which began when we started on the campaign.

General Hancock's headquarters are near ours. He was just round here, bareheaded and in his shirt sleeves. He is a curious man, will fret and scold and swear he "has not a staff officer who will carry an order properly, and *return*, though all are supposed to be intelligent and educated gentlemen." Everybody listens to this talk with the most careless indifference, but when he gives an order of course it is obeyed.

South Side James, Windmill Point
June 15, 1864
Soon after I closed my letter of yesterday, we were ordered to embark and cross the river but did not get across till about dark. The scenery here is beautiful; the James winds round a point, the river is full of steamers; some with troops from below, the XVIII Corps on their way up to Bermuda Hundred, our corps, with the V, VI, and IX crossing in steamers. A pontoon bridge is being laid across the river below.[22] This estate, on which we are encamped, is a very large one, owned by Mrs. Wilcox (a common name about here on both sides of the river). The house is pleasantly situated on a rising ground about half a mile from the river, surrounded by trees; the grounds finely laid out, and though the house in itself is nothing remarkable, the surroundings give it an imposing appearance. Trees and flowers grow here luxuriantly, box borders eighteen inches high, and box trees standing alone three or four feet high and as large as my arm.

Mrs. Wilcox has two sons in the Rebel army.[23] There are very few Negroes about the place now except the very young and very old. An old "dark" said they went away two years ago when the gunboats came up. There are 2,000 acres in this plantation, but I should think not more than 30 are cultivated. The gardens are running wild. The general has orders to put guards at all houses on the line of march. Aside from the uselessness of destroying and stealing the private property of women and children, the moment a soldier is allowed to leave the ranks to plunder he is demoralized and is fit for nothing. Of course public property and large quantities of provisions should be destroyed or appropriated, and wheat fields do generally get grazed down by horses and cattle, but robbing "poor old niggers" of their meat and corn does not help "crush the rebellion."[24]

The day is splendid. Birney's division is on the march. We follow next toward Petersburg. This is a splendid country, and compared with the other side of the river is a perfect paradise.

CHAPTER 13

"A Mass of Earth Rose in the Air"

June 17–July 31, 1864

Dyer saw the early days of the Petersburg campaign, ending in the battle of the Crater. White soldiers increasingly approved of black troops, and he began to accept them himself. New men from the Washington forts were less effective. Those in both armies were reluctant to charge earthworks unless there was a fair chance of success. Confederates were using boys, some of whom had been found dead in trenches occupied by Union forces, while the Union drummer boys were useless. Dyer describes the logistics of cooking in the division hospital, while commenting on the work of the Christian and Sanitary Commissions and scurvy's reappearance. He was mortified when the remnant of his old regiment, the Nineteenth Massachusetts, was captured along with several other veteran units. Meade joshed Hancock about his misfortune. It was not the same army that had entered the Wilderness.

In the Union lines that summer, the heat, dust, and lack of water were pervasive. Despite his two stars, John Gibbon, whose popularity in the army had plummeted, was a bitter critic of the government, and still defending McClellan. Sheridan and Brig. Gen. James H. Wilson did some damage on raids but had trouble getting back. Maj. Gen. David Hunter failed in the Shenandoah Valley, like Nathaniel Banks, Benjamin Butler, and other generals elsewhere who were not a part of the Army of the Potomac. Union gunboats on the James impressed Dyer by firing 15-inch shells.

Before Petersburg
June 17, 1864

We moved from the James River on the afternoon of the fifteenth and after a rapid march came to the position before Petersburg in the evening. Telegrams had reached us in the afternoon that Smith had carried the outer line of works. We found on our arrival that three or four redoubts had been taken, partly by the black troops, Hinks's division. While our troops were coming into position, I found General Hinks about one o'clock in the morning and got something to eat. He was enthusiastic in his praise of his darkies, and in fact they did very well, though it appears the works were manned by raw troops, who ran away with very little fighting. Men were taken from the streets and put in the works, hands from the factories, schoolboys, anybody.[1]

But during the night they poured in great numbers of old troops, and in the morning it was a very different affair. We had a good deal of artillery practice during the day and some loss, but in the evening an assault was made by the II Corps, continued till nine or ten. The firing was fearful, and our loss in the corps was about 2,000.[2] We have now about four hundred wounded in division hospital. We gained some ground but no important works, only put things in better shape. In the morning Burnside went in and was quite successful, capturing six guns and some prisoners. The XVIII Corps, with Hinks's division, captured some guns, some say ten.

June 18, 1864

Ten o'clock A.M. Still fighting, and gradually advancing. There was fighting last evening, and at four o'clock this morning a general advance was made, resulting in a success I think. I was down a mile in front of where our headquarters were yesterday, but they begun shelling us very smartly, and I retired. The works are detached, the ground hilly, and the line very irregular; so that while some parts are far advanced, in other parts a battery will break out almost in our rear. Still we take one position after another and have not been obliged to abandon anything we have taken. Constant shelling and sharp skirmishing are going on now; houses on the line here and there are burning, set on fire sometimes by one and sometimes by another.

We have positions now I think but little more than a mile from the city, and I am in hopes we shall get possession of the railroads.[3] A good deal of hard fighting has got to be done first, however. Wounded are coming in gradually, ambulances on their way back and forth, and business going on quite regularly. At the hospital there is a good deal to do, and I have been down this morning for more surgeons, as a good many are sick and off duty.

As I write I stop every few minutes to watch our skirmishers and the Rebels. On one part of the line our men appear to chase the Rebs, but on another part I can see some of ours putting themselves across a cornfield "right smart" to the rear. So they go, first one way and then the other. Saw George yesterday. Last night his corps moved down the river a short distance. They have begun to throw shell in here, and I will close my letter. I came here to write because it was quiet.

Hospital
June 19, 1864

Yesterday's attempt was not a successful one. We gained something but lost a good many good men, and the Third Division suffered very much. The First Maine and First Massachusetts Heavy Artillery suffered most. They are large regiments that have been in the forts about Washington for three years but are now serving as infantry. Our men are not deficient in courage, but they have become tired of making these charges against breastworks well defended unless there is a pretty good chance to go in. I think likely some other movements are going on that will render it unnecessary to butt against these entrenchments. When I was down this morning I noticed that our batteries were still further to the front and that we gain gradually on them. But whether they have as good or better ground in the rear I do not know. If they have they can afford to fall back, but not more than two miles without breaking railroad connection with the South.

I have faith to believe we have generals who know what they are about—otherwise I should despair. Our division lost about two hundred yesterday. We sent away about six hundred wounded this morning to City Point, but they have kept coming in all day, so that we have perhaps one hundred now. [4]

Our cooking department is an institution. We fed yesterday about seven hundred sick and wounded. To do this we have only camp kettles in limited numbers and tin dippers. But we gave them coffee and hard bread for breakfast, soup with vegetables (the first vegetables we have had) for dinner, and meat for supper, with bread and coffee. This morning we had sufficient tomatoes from the Sanitary

Commission to give each man as much as could be put on two hard biscuits. Today applesauce in the same way. This you see is not much of a variety, but it is more than we have had since the campaign opened. We are promised soft bread and vegetables in a day or two.

You will see that with the large numbers we have to feed, a system has been adopted that will ensure all getting their food, and that there is no Sanitary or Christian Commission that ever did or ever could do what many suppose, in our field hospitals. But they have large numbers and full supplies at City Point and do a great deal toward feeding and clothing the wounded. It is a mistake however to suppose that they go to the battlefield, bring off wounded, or do anything but the most insignificant share of work. They do a great deal of work afterward though.

We have had no rain for some time. The thousands of men and teams passing over the roads and fields raise clouds of dust. One can scarcely see sometimes, and everybody and everything is covered with it. It is a peculiar dust, fine and sticky, and lies on the ground an impalpable powder about two inches deep.

I find the colored troops are getting into favor among all. They appear to be very soldierly looking and feel that they are quite elevated by being made soldiers. About their brutality I think the less said the better after the heroic deeds of the "Chivalry" at Fort Pillow. I saw some fine-looking colored soldiers bring in a miserable wretch of a Rebel on a stretcher, and I thought at the time they were the better men. They could easily have saved themselves the trouble by putting a bayonet through him, but they brought a good many in.[5]

The Rebels put old men and boys in the works here, boys who were at school in the morning. An officer told me he saw one little boy, fourteen or fifteen years old, lying dead, neatly dressed, with white shirt and collar, and scarcely large enough to carry the large cartridge box strapped on him. It seems cruel to make such children fight.[6]

Speaking of children, we have a great many small boys, drummers, and they are a perfect nuisance. They are enlisted to "fill quotas"—do not drum, not one-quarter of them can. They don't go into battle or get very near; and when they are ordered to the hospital, it is necessary to put a guard over them to make them work.

We had three hundred of them camped near the hospital and under my orders, but sometimes it was difficult to get ten of them to work. They go off in the woods, out of sight and out of danger, and stay till they are out of rations. The ideal "drummer boy" is not met with in the army.

All is quiet again except skirmishing, which is continual through day and night.[7] On the part of the line within hearing, musket shots average about one a second, sometimes more, or less. This is very common and is tolerably quiet. Three or four times as fast is sharp skirmishing, but nothing more, and this is generally mixed up with artillery every five or ten seconds. Then in an attack there is a perfect roar, like the pouring of corn out of a bag on the floor.

June 22, 1864

I am sitting tonight at the window of a house where we have located our hospital, some five miles from Petersburg. We came out here yesterday on a flank movement, but I think we have rather got flanked ourselves. I am afraid the old Nineteenth has "gone up." The Third Division was on our left. We had entrenchments. The Third gave way on an attack. The Second Brigade of our division (the Pennsylvania Brigade) retired without fighting and lost the Twelfth New York Battery they were in support of. No warning was given to the First Brigade, and they being in a thicket, the first they knew the Rebels were coming in on their flank and rear, and before they had time to fire a gun they were gobbled—the Fifteenth and Nineteenth Massachusetts, the Fifty-ninth and Eighty-second New York, and what I most regret, our colors.[8] The regiments were very small, not three hundred men present all told. But the morale of the brigade is lost. In the room with me are Colonel Wass, sick, and Major Hooper, who escaped, wounded in the arm—five or six men with him.[9] We have about two hundred wounded about here in tents—all quiet now except an occasional groan. The firing is distinct in the still night air.

In this house—Westbrook's—is one man and a family of one old man, daughter, and two grand-daughters who fled here for safety.[10] Neat gardens in front, with magnolia trees and pleasant shades, but blood and carnage all around. I will go to sleep in a house, the first time in this campaign.

June 23, 1864

General Hancock has been off duty but is now about again.[11] The II Corps must do something pretty soon to redeem itself. The First Massachusetts and First Maine Artillery of the Third Division are pretty much used up. If Grant is going to do anything brilliant I wish he would do it soon. There is need enough of it. But I think we shall have them all right by and by. Hot weather, no rain, plenty of dust, and plenty of fighting.

Petersburg

June 28, 1864

I am this morning in one of the most comfortable places I have seen for two months. Yesterday the division was moved, stretching out over a good deal of ground, picketing in the rear of the army as a guard against cavalry, etc. Our line is about six miles long, and our headquarters are somewhere near the middle and rear of the line at a deserted house out of the way of the dust and noise. I slept here at headquarters the first time for many nights.

I am in hopes the hard musketry fighting is about over for a time and that more artillery will be used and the means we have in such abundance be brought up and put where it will do some good. During this entire campaign but little has been done by artillery. Our men have charged time after time against formidable breastworks, been mowed down by thousands, and then thrown on them again until they will do so no more unless they see a chance of making something. Neither will the Rebels. They cannot get a line of theirs to advance against us in that way.

The men will feel better for resting a day or two and the cool breeze that we are having. I never knew hotter weather than we have had for a week or two past. There is but little water in this country now, and the ground is parched like ashes. But it is a splendid country to live in, and with very little labor one might live here like a prince.

I would not wonder if the men were a good deal demoralized when many of the highest officers speak as they do of the government and conduct of the war. Gibbon has got his two stars, but I think he is more bitter against the administration than ever. He has got all the government can give him and would now probably like to go out of the field and live in some soft place. Not disloyal but fault-finding—nobody right but McClellan—and from being one of the most popular commanders in the army when we started, he is now decidedly unpopular in his division among officers and men. However, all is coming out right; and when I hear men talk of being discouraged, I feel more the justice of the cause and more willing to help fight it out.

Petersburg
June 29, 1864
You speak of promotion and having our services recognized. Our services will not be recognized at all, and all the satisfaction regimental surgeons get in being mustered out of service is an offer of $100 per month to remain at City Point, which none of them will do.

Our division moved again today to take the ground left by the VI Corps, who have gone out to the relief of Wilson's cavalry, who were down on the Weldon Railroad tearing up. They were attacked and scattered, lost their trains and three batteries with a good many men. Hancock has issued an order censuring officers of his corps for the affair the other day and promising that regimental commanders will be court-martialed. Two brigade commanders are in arrest now. Gibbon does not appear to be a favorite with Hancock now.

Our quarters are now in the woods. The tall, straight, Southern pines, running up fifty feet without a limb, the oaks, chestnut, and gum trees make a pleasant shade. We are about fifteen miles from City Point and six from Petersburg on the Jerusalem plank road. Wass as I told you had gone home sick. It is bad for an officer's reputation if he is not *very* sick, and many officers are away on one pretext or another. I have known cases lately where not a single field officer remained in a brigade and a major had to be taken from another brigade to command it. The best officers are killed and wounded. It is awful to think how many we have lost.

Petersburg
July 1, 1864
On this eventful day we are very quiet. One year ago we were marching toward Gettysburg, meeting the wounded coming from the field, and at night were drawn up in line of battle for the fight on the morrow. Two years ago today the battle of Malvern Hill was fought, at night we withdrew, and all the next day the army was dragging along, scattered and weary, to Harrison's Landing. Today I hardly know

what to say of our position. We are here before Petersburg, with a large army perhaps, but our original army with which we left Brandy Station lost. Not the individual men, perhaps, but in numbers, and losses and additions have so changed it that it is scarcely to be recognized as the same army.[12] We have met with reverses and at the same time have inflicted serious injury on the enemy. We hear of siege guns being placed in position before Petersburg, but as yet there is only the usual amount of cannonading and nothing like a vigorous attack on our part. I suppose however it is all right, as the whole wisdom of the army and navy is about here.

Sheridan's cavalry have done some damage but have had a hard time getting back. Wilson lost his guns, etc., and 4,000 of his men are straggling about, only a part of whom will get in. Hunter is probably whipped and driven off. It seems, looking at it in this light, as though we were getting the worst of it, but we will wait and see.

July 4, 1864

This has been one of the quietest "Fourths" that I ever knew. Scarcely the usual amount of firing has been heard. Our men have generally been at rest; and the only thing going on to indicate life is the music of the bands. They have been uncommonly lively, and last night, all day, and this evening, they have been playing far and near. Our division has three bands, in good order, and the First Division has a splendid one. We have been treated to the finest airs from the best operas in profusion. Everything is settling down quietly this evening; only the booming of a gun away at the right disturbs the stillness.

Men are getting sick very fast; scurvy is making its appearance. The Commissary Department seems to be slow in getting vegetables. The Sanitary Commission has furnished us with some but of course not a full supply. Yesterday Mr. Johnson, the superintendent, told me they had furnished eight hundred barrels to be issued today.[13] This seems to be a good deal, but it will give only about a pound apiece to the whole army.

The intense heat, like blasts from a furnace, and clouds of dust, covering everybody and everything, are not well calculated to make one feel very well. I take as good care of myself as possible, don't ride in the sun more than absolutely necessary, wear a straw hat and linen coat, and hope to keep myself in good condition till I get home, which will be in time to enjoy a bit of summer.

I have read in the *Journal* some remarkable stories about the capture of the Fifteenth and Nineteenth and the terrible fighting of the Twentieth.[14] The Fifteenth and Nineteenth went off without much fighting, and the Twentieth did not know they had gone for two hours, though they were nearby.

I read in the *N. Y. Herald* of the second how much refreshed the troops were by the rest and *rain,* that Gibbon's division took the place of the VI Corps, and that "the countermarching of the troops was a splendid sight."[15] Now if toiling along in the hot sun, everybody and everything enveloped in clouds of dust so that no one ten yards off could tell whether he saw a drove of cattle or a column of troops, is a splendid sight, I don't know what a miserable sight is. I mention these things as specimens of newspaper correspondence.

July 8, 1864

Still in the same place and keeping up the same round of duties but making no attacks. There seems to be some excitement about a raid into Maryland by Ewell. A division of the VI Corps has gone to see about it.[16] An order by the Secretary of War says that those surgeons whose term expires may be retained in service as Acting Staff Surgeons. That is a little better than the former offer, which was an insult.

Day before yesterday we had roast beef head, and Generals Meade, Hancock, Birney, and Burnside were over to partake. Meade said to Hancock, speaking of the affair of last week, "Well, 'tis time you had something of the kind. You have had everything your own way until now."

The sky is just as brassy, the sun as hot, the clouds of dust as high as ever, but the men are resting, in a measure. They are not marching. They are camped in the woods, or fix up shelters of green boughs, dig wells, and have a chance to keep clean, besides they get a better variety of rations.

July 10, 1864

Went over to the X Corps the other day to see George and took tea with him and Colonel Bell. They (the Rebels) treated us to a little shelling while at tea, pieces falling within a few feet, but these things, like lightning, seldom hit anyone. The whole of the VI Corps has gone to Maryland.

July 15, 1864

Our division is now in camp in rear of the V Corps and furnish men for the siege works, details of five hundred to one thousand men at a time. Sheridan started off on a raid day before yesterday and will probably go across the Danville road, destroying it more efficiently than Wilson did.

July 16, 1864

We had a splendid rain yesterday, the first for several weeks. George has been with me a few days. He is not well. I see that the president has called for half a million men—wish we had them long ago. [17] Grant has a large job on his hands.

July 22, 1864

Went down to City Point with George early yesterday morning; stopped at the hospital to lunch and then went to the landing. A good deal of business is carried on there, vessels and barges unloading, cars loading, depot buildings being put up, the river full of vessels and steamers, all the business of a city going on. We came back in the evening.

Our division was out yesterday on fatigue duty and returned in the evening. At four o'clock this morning were ordered out again to take the place of Ferrero's division, which was going off on some other duty. [18]

July 24, 1864

Our division is now occupying a line in rear of the army, with our headquarters at the Southall house, where we were several weeks ago. [19] All night long the axes were ringing in the woods. Men were putting up breastworks and "slashing the timber" in front. Trees are cut about three feet from the ground and felled outward so that it is almost impossible for an enemy to get through five or six hundred yards of this. At any rate he could not make a sudden rush. Siege works are progressing vigorously. General Gibbon returned last night from leave of absence.

July 25, 1864

We are again living in "summer bowers" with our tents and walks carpeted with red cedar and pine boughs. But it is dull. I ride over to the hospital and stay a while, then to corps headquarters, then back again, attend to official papers, etc., and then read or write. I should judge by orders we have this evening that we were going to make an attack or something of the kind about day after tomorrow.

Deep Bottom
July 28, 1864

Over the James again. I wrote you the other day that something was "up." We left our quarters at four P.M., marched all night, and crossing the pontoon bridge at Point of Rocks, crossed Bermuda Hundred and another pontoon bridge at Jones' Neck, and we are here again, with the cavalry. On our first advance we found quite a number of Rebs and a battery of four twenty-pound Parrotts, which we took after some little fighting. Our men straggled badly, and I think not more than two-thirds of the corps were in line of battle. This is bad for the II Corps, but a long night march is terribly fatiguing.

The cavalry went out this morning and we too. The Rebels have a line of battle of any required length. I believe if we should go to Nova Zembla we should find them in line of battle, throwing up earthworks.[20] They had about ten thousand men here yesterday, and this morning another division came. They have railroads and we have not. A part of their line is in sight, and the gunboats in the river keep throwing at them. While I write, sitting on the edge of the river, the gunboat *Mendota,* a hundred yards off, is throwing hundred-pound shells at them by signals from on shore and from the mast head, as they cannot see from the deck, and they make some pretty good shots at about three miles.[21] To ride through the woods where they have been shelling it looks as though no living thing could have stayed there. Another gunboat farther up the river is throwing shell, but the great distance makes them very uncertain in their effects. I do not think we shall do much here—they are too strong for us.

July 29, 1864

All quiet all down by the river. Under the shade of an enormous oak, where we have stuck up our headquarters flag, I will write. About two hundred yards in front of us on a rising ground, our division is digging and throwing up rifle pits. Lee has a large part of his army here, and we have a good many, but I think we shall not advance from here.

Toward night Grant, Meade, Hancock, Sheridan, and several other generals were here—talked about things generally and then went off—that is, Grant and Meade. We have been expecting the enemy to attack us, but I hardly think they will. Some of our troops are going back and others coming. They appear to be mixing things up generally, playing at strategy.

These gunboats are great things to have with us, and their fifteen-inch shells have a great moral effect. Today it is very still, only a little skirmishing going on, the gunboats quiet and a lull in the storm. I was at the bridge waiting for the column of cavalry to cross in order to go the other way, and you can have an idea what an immense body two divisions of cavalry make. They had been passing for about two hours, and after waiting nearly two hours more I gave it up and came back. The river here is very narrow, the gunboats look large for so small a stream, but the water is deep.

General Barlow's wife died in Washington of typho-malarial fever. She had been to the army and about the hospitals a good deal, and I suppose contracted the disease there. At first General Grant would not let him go but has now given him fifteen days.[22] He would not have done so, I think, only by earnest request of General Hancock.

General Hancock comes back from the line feeling better, I think, for as he passes he speaks to me very politely. He is one of the most singular men I ever saw, one moment swearing like a trooper at some unfortunate fellow who has incurred his displeasure, the next as affable and polite as though he had been brought up exclusively in a drawing room. I thought Grant looked a little troubled yesterday, but he has a hard, rough-looking face that doesn't show much feeling one way or another. Well, I am "only a passenger" and am glad I have not got the management of this thing.

Petersburg
July 31, 1864
Back again to our old camp at Southall's house after some pretty hard marching and fighting, though we have had more of the marching than fighting this time. Started from Deep Bottom at dark on the twenty-ninth, and after a hard march on which many straggled, and reached our works in front of Petersburg at daylight, and got into position ready for the grand explosion and bombardment which was to take place.[23]

After waiting anxiously nearly half an hour, the great mine exploded, a mass of earth, dust, and smoke rose in the air with a dull, heavy sound, and at the same instant a perfect hurricane of shell poured into the town and works. It was terrific. For two hours this continued without cessation, and then something of a lull, but for four hours it was kept up on both sides, batteries opening at every point. The mine was sprung opposite the IX Corps, but others participated in the assault. Went over to see George, who was in the assault and was entirely exhausted. The result was a failure. The work was blown up, with four guns and perhaps two hundred men buried under the ruins with some Rebels also in a mine they were at work in. We also took some prisoners. But they retook the ground, and we lost a good many men, perhaps more than the Rebels.[24]

Our corps remained massed, where we were shelled all day, then got an order to go into the trenches and relieve the XVIII Corps. Then another to be ready with five days' rations for a march. Then another order to come back to our old camp, for the reason I suppose that the men were found to be so exhausted that they could not march. The day was terribly hot, and I suffered everything with the heat and want of sleep.

This afternoon again we have received orders to mass the division in a place convenient for marching out and shall probably go tomorrow, I have no idea where.

CHAPTER 14

"The Prospect of Quarters in Libby"

August 2–29, 1864

J. Franklin Dyer decided to be mustered out under a War Department policy giving an officer that option after three years' service in the same grade. He was still a major, with no chance of being promoted. The army's demoralization, military politics, and the investigation of the failed Mine Assault all depressed him. As he prepared to end his service, Dyer notes in his journal the huge explosion at City Point, the target of which was U. S. Grant.

Maj. Gen. Gouverneur Warren's command was attacked on the Weldon Railroad and the II Corps went to his relief. At Reams' Station on August 25, the Rebels attacked repeatedly in overwhelming force, breaking the Union lines. Many officers were killed or wounded, and most of the men captured. Dyer escaped under fire with General Gibbon and a few others. The next day he began work on the papers for his successor as surgeon in chief of the Second Division and for his own departure from the army. There were farewell dinners as well as a letter of commendation from the medical director of the II Corps. As he was leaving on August 27, the doctor tried to find his brother George, with the XVIII Corps in a different part of the lines. Straying into no man's land on horseback, he narrowly escaped being killed or wounded for the second time in three days. He then went to City Point and took a steamer to Fort Monroe. A Boston paper printed a tribute from the officers of the Nineteenth Massachusetts soon after his return home.

Petersburg
August 2, 1864
Today Captain Brownson got a decision from the War Department, by which he can muster out officers who demand it after three years

185

service in one grade, so that I shall go out on the twenty-seventh instant, which is not far off. General Gibbon has gone home on sick leave. He had considerable trouble to get off, although he is a major general.

The result of the explosion and attack the other day was a most shameful failure, and the more shameful when it might have been successful if it had been properly managed. I don't know who is most in fault, but a court of inquiry is now in session at General Hancock's, and somebody will be made to suffer. Burnside was in charge of the whole affair and is of course responsible.[1] It is discouraging, and I see nothing that looks cheerful.

The II Corps made a rapid march, crossed the James River, and drew off a large force from the Rebel lines here; then came back rapidly and gave the army a good chance to go in here.[2] But you see the result, and I think according to appearances the siege will be abandoned for something else. Heavy guns will be taken away, and a good many troops have gone for the protection of Maryland and Pennsylvania. Grant, Butler, and the president met at Fortress Monroe yesterday.[3]

We are under orders to be ready to march but have not been ordered out yet. The news from Pennsylvania is anything but encouraging. The people do not lift a hand to defend themselves.[4] But what is more discouraging than all is the rejoicing of the people of the North over what they term the brilliant victory of Grant at Petersburg; and I cannot help thinking that if this is the kind of success we are having in other parts of the country, we have little to hope for.[5]

General Grant announced that the siege of Petersburg would be commenced, and some batteries were erected. The engineers talked of mining but said the fort that *was* mined could *not* be mined. The Forty-eighth Pennsylvania regiment, most of whom were coal miners, thought it could be, and the lieutenant colonel commanding undertook it without the help of the engineers, who are so profound in their skill that they know very well "how not to do it."[6] The mine was dug and exploded, and all was well so far; but Burnside did not advance because Warren did not, and Warren did not because Burnside did not, and the whole thing was a magnificent failure. The newspaper accounts are all untrue. We do not hold one foot of ground taken from the enemy in this fight.

Let us hope for better things on the principle that it is always darkest just before day.

Some of the officers of our regiment who were at home on leave and on recruiting service have been mustered out. I regard it as a shameful abandonment of their comrades in the field, as their term of service had not expired, and I find that it was obtained of the War Department by false representations.

August 3, 1864

Went down to City Point yesterday with Surgeons Dougherty and Evarts on business at the hospital.[7] Had some good things to eat, enjoyed the breeze from the river, and came back in the evening. Am sometimes tempted to get ordered to hospital, as I might be, but always after deliberation conclude to serve out my time in the field.

Petersburg
August 4, 1864

Night before last we were under arms some time before daylight, awaiting the explosion of a Rebel mine which was discovered, but no explosion or attack took place. They are mining under "Fort Hell" in front of the V Corps, but knowing the fact I suppose measures have been taken to prevent damage.[8]

It seems strange where all the drafted men and recruits go. We get but few of them here.

Today is fast day, and we are going to have some chaplains here at headquarters and some preaching. It is ordered that no work be done, but the work that is necessary to be done will be.

Evening. Had four or five chaplains, preaching, music, etc., then went to corps headquarters on business. I wish I could be for a while out of the reach of "orders." We have had a band playing some very fine pieces this evening, and a dozen or twenty officers sitting about under the arbors or lying on the soft pine carpeting that covers the ground. We have singing now, a variety, "Old Hundred," "Kathleen Mavourneen," now a French and now a German song, next "Haggerty's Breeches," followed by "No One to Love," etc.[9]

General Gibbon has not returned from his last leave of absence. Colonel Smyth of the First Delaware, a good-natured and gallant Irishman, is now commanding.[10] We have not brigadier generals to command divisions, much less brigades. This has been a terrible campaign, and many officers who had good reputations to start with have become terribly demoralized. The number is not confined to line and field officers, but generals have showed the white feather, and more than one has been mustered out of service for that reason.

August 7, 1864

Day before yesterday the Rebels attempted a great thing, which proved a mortifying failure. They exploded a mine, which they had been at work on for some time, in front of the XVIII Corps, but about forty yards in front, where it merely blew up the dirt without doing any harm.

Petersburg
August 8, 1864

Went over to the IX Corps hospital yesterday with Colonel Rice. Saw Colonel Gould of the Fifty-ninth, whose leg had been amputated.[11] (He afterward died.) Lt. Colonel Hodges of the Fifty-ninth, one of our old captains, was killed in the assault.[12] Everything quiet here. General Grant has gone to Washington—things need looking after there. He has a good many irons in the fire and must look sharp or some of them will get cool. We have been unfortunate here. Men that he depended on a good deal have failed him. Another court was in session today at General Hancock's. The papers falsify everything. They lie a great deal more than the Rebel papers. It is now past eleven o'clock, and the pickets are popping away quite lively, with sometimes a little volley. What shall I do when I can no longer be "lulled to sleep" by the popping of musketry and booming of big guns?

August 10, 1864

Yesterday there was a terrible explosion at City Point of a barge loaded with ordnance stores.[13] I was down at the hospital, within four miles of City Point, when it took place. A prolonged explosion was heard and a cloud of smoke arose, showing that something serious had happened. I have not heard the number killed, but many were blown to pieces and parts of their bodies carried nearly a mile. Everything is very quiet as far as the movements of troops is concerned, but working parties are out day and night. Night before last our division had several wounded while at work in the trenches. Today we have one thousand men on fatigue duty cutting timber for use in the fortifications.

The weather continues very warm and no rain. It is rather an idle time about our headquarters. The usual business goes on, but the duty now is not arduous. A medical board meets occasionally. A court-martial is in session in the half-torn-down house in front of which our tents are pitched. We lie down and read a good part of the time, some of the younger members of the staff amusing themselves once in a while by pulling each other off their beds or such other boyish freaks that would be considered very silly anywhere else—but it is awfully tiresome to stay about one place all the time or only to ride through the division, or to corps headquarters, or to the hospital. See the same ones and say about the same things. No one can go very far without business, for orders come at very unexpected times, so we have to keep within proper distance, and an order to move is sometimes a relief from what gets to be very irksome. I think now the time would pass much more quickly if we were actively engaged, and yet the weather is so warm and uncomfortable that I don't care to move. Well, we have very little to say about it one way or another, go where we are ordered and stay where we are told to.

August 11, 1864

I expect an order tomorrow to report to the secretary of war to go north on duty for the remainder of my term. My name, with Dr. Hayward's, was sent up by Dr. Dougherty to go from this division. This duty will be I suppose to visit hospitals and examine men to be returned to the army.

City Point
August 13, 1864

I wrote you night before last thinking I might get an order to go north, but yesterday we got an order to move to City Point, and we are expected to embark today for I don't know where, and the medical director has decided that no medical officers can be spared from the corps at present. So I shall wait until my time is out, which will be in a fortnight, and I shall be discharged wherever I am, as I shall not be remustered to remain in the field. I am a little disappointed, but I shall be home in a short time, and in the meantime we may have a fight and give the Rebels a good whipping.

Deep Bottom
August 16, 1864

I wrote you a note on the day we started not knowing where we were to go. The next day we embarked on transports and went down the river a few miles, lying until ten o'clock, when we all started upriver for Deep Bottom, the place we left a fortnight since.[14] It was intended as a *ruse*, but whether or not it effected its object I cannot tell. We landed in the morning, and the X Corps, which had crossed over from Bermuda Hundred, attacked the enemy at the same time we did, taking some guns. Our division got more roughly received than some others, having about two hundred killed and wounded. The rest of the day not much was done. Grant was over here a good deal, but nothing of importance was attempted, except that the X Corps crossed over and took position on our right for an attack, which did not take place.

Colonel Macy of the Twentieth, who had just returned, was badly injured by being thrown from his horse, which was shot.[15] This afternoon another attack took place, our right being at White's Tavern, nearly in their rear, and another being made at Dutch Gap, up the river, by Butler. Some movements are in progress, which I hope will be successful. The Rebels will have to bring back the troops they have sent north to assist Early or be pushed pretty close up to Richmond. Our skirmish line advanced today and took two or three hundred prisoners. Major Patten of the Twentieth has a fractured thigh (afterward amputated).[16]

August 18, 1864

Still here at Deep Bottom. Yesterday during a thundershower the lightning struck our hospital, killing one man and injuring two. Last night a very heavy cannonade took place in the direction of Petersburg and continued two hours. A monitor a little way up the river at Dutch Gap kept booming away all night, her immense guns waking the echoes in the still night air. We had a flag of truce yesterday to bury the dead. We have a very long line, stretching from Malvern Hill to and beyond Petersburg. It is very quiet all along the lines, the pickets talking with each other and no firing.

Miles's brigade went within four and a half miles of Richmond the other day but met a large force there and had to fall back, losing some men.[17] But we have done very well, taken some guns and several hundred prisoners, one brigadier general, and killed another.[18] Everything is so nearly equal on both sides that it will be necessary to maneuver a good deal before one can get the better of the other.

Deep Bottom
August 20, 1864

In the woods, raining. Went on board the *Hunchback* yesterday, afterward went out to the X Corps, found George, and stayed there an hour or two until after dark.[19] It was very dark and rainy when I started for division headquarters, and I had a very long ride through the woods getting to it. My orderly, Sgt. Meahan, was about as much puzzled as myself, but we reached it about nine o'clock.[20] Here all was wet and cheerless, and nothing to eat.

Soon after, Colonel Smyth came from corps headquarters with orders to make a charge at daylight, so all laid down to sleep, as we were to move at one o'clock. But at twelve o'clock an order came countermanding the former one. The charge would not be made, as the rain had swollen a small stream in our front so that it would be impossible to ford it.

This morning all quiet, rain nearly over, and after breakfast shall go down to the river.

Petersburg
August 21, 1864

We have had some pretty hard marching during the last twenty-hours, and from the extreme right of the army at dark last night, at Deep Bottom, we are now on the extreme left, south of Petersburg. While we were across the James, Warren made a strike for the Weldon Railroad and got a pretty severe handling but finally held his position, losing a good many men in killed and wounded and 3,000 in prisoners.[21]

Last night after dark we withdrew from over the James and marched for our old camp, through mud and rain, which we reached about five o'clock this morning, about fifteen miles. Then after breakfast had orders to be in readiness to move and this afternoon moved out three or four miles toward Warren's position, where the IX Corps also is.

This morning, soon after we arrived at our old campground near the Southall house, we heard a heavy cannonade in the direction of Warren.[22] He repulsed the enemy twice, injuring him pretty severely. There is a gap between our left and the XVIII Corps, and our line is thin, but so is theirs also, and they cannot make an assault on our lines. It is rather uncomfortable, however, and we have to do without our cooking and sleeping fixtures tonight.

After marching all night some of us got an hour's sleep this morning, but I have been in the saddle twenty hours out of the twenty-four and feel tired as well as sleepy and hungry. It was a miserable night's march. Just before daylight we arrived opposite Petersburg near the XVIII Corps and close to a battery of thirty-two pound rifled guns. While waiting for the division to close up, we watched a pretty smart artillery fight for about half an hour. They generally fire before daylight and stop soon after. Whether this does much damage to them or not I can't say. It does none to us. I heard some dozen or twenty Whitworth bolts strike about the fort near which we were, but they did no harm. It seems a waste of ammunition to fire in the night. General Gibbon arrived at City Point last night and took command of the division this morning.

Reams' Station, Weldon Railroad
August 25, 1864
Came out here yesterday morning early and have been with the First Division and the cavalry engaged in destroying the railroad.[23] There is a good deal of labor in it. We pile up the ties and burn them with the rails on top, which bend with the heat. Wilson's cavalry did not injure the road much, merely threw the rails about. Gregg's cavalry were here before us, and I have met Colonel Smith and his regiment (the First Maine Cavalry). He is now commanding a brigade. We were to have moved out on the railroad this morning, but the order was countermanded, and the troops are now waiting orders.

Reams' Station, Weldon Railroad
August 25, 1864
Here cease extracts from letters.[24] During the forenoon of the twenty-fifth we fortified our position on the railroad, our works

being somewhat in the form of a horseshoe and very limited, as our force consisted only of the First and Second Divisions of the II Corps and Gregg's division of cavalry, the whole numbering not over five or six thousand men. The Rebels first attacked us on the right, then left, and being repulsed both times brought a large force and attacked us on all sides with great impetuosity. This last charge was very obstinate, and the enemy's fire from one side of our position reaching across to the other, a part of our line had a fire both in front and rear.

Our lines finally gave way, losing Sleeper's battery and a part of the Twelfth New York Battery with some three or four hundred prisoners.[25] Among the killed was Captain Brownson and with the prisoners Colonel Walker, A.A.G., both of General Hancock's staff.[26] Most of the Twentieth were also taken.[27] Asst. Surgeon Jewett of the Fourteenth Connecticut was severely wounded.[28] I remained a few yards in the rear of the lines during the first and second attack and hoped the third might be repulsed, but finding the lines broken and the enemy coming over our works, I got the ambulance train started ahead and soon followed with several other medical officers.

There being but one road to pass over, and the Rebels having directed their fire toward that quarter, it became quite dangerous to pass that way; but the hope of going home in two or three days, on the one hand, and the prospect of quarters in Libby prison, on the other, being duly weighed, I concluded to run the gauntlet, the shot and shell from our captured batteries following us pretty fast, and the last one, a round shot, throwing the dirt in our faces as we rode along, congratulating ourselves on being "out of range."[29]

At dark we were on the road and before morning back near our old camp on the plank road. I stopped, with General Gibbon, alongside the road, and one contributing a rubber coat and the other a cape, we slept under a tree some two or three hours. Next day picked up our stragglers, established our hospital and took care of our wounded, and began to reckon up our losses and gains, the latter very small, the former rather large.[30]

August 26, 1864

This day I devoted to business and got my affairs in proper condition for my successor, Surgeon Maull, of the First Delaware Volunteers.[31] Captain Embler prepared my muster out papers, and my discharge paper was nearly covered by the autographs of officers present.[32] A goodbye to those with whom I had been so long associated, and I severed my connection with the old division.

My orderly accompanying me, I called at the division hospital, where I was entertained with a lunch by Drs. Hayward, Chaddock, and Aiken; and Dr. Aiken, in charge of the hospital, ordered out the band of the Twelfth New Jersey in my honor.[33] With many flattering speeches and mutual good wishes, I proceeded on my journey to City Point and was kindly entertained by Dr. Burmeister in charge of the II Corps hospital.[34]

Headquarters, Second Army Corps
Medical Director's Office, Aug. 26, 1864

Doctor:

We have been associated together, now nearly three years; a period certainly long enough to entitle a man to claim to know something of another's character. It gives me pleasure to be able, as our relation is on the point of dissolution, to state that I have always found you faithful, laborious, and capable in the discharge of your duties as Surgeon in Chief of the Second Division, and that I consider it a real misfortune to the service that you are about to leave it. I trust that your affairs will permit you to return to it, and in the mean time you have my best wishes for your health and prosperity.

Cordially yours,
A. N. Dougherty, Surgeon, U.S.V.
& Medical Director 2d Corps

to Dr. Dyer, 19th Massachusetts Volunteers
Surgeon in Chief, Second Division

City Point
August 27, 1864

My troubles were not yet over. Wishing to see my brother George, who was in the XVIII Corps, I started in the morning for Bermuda Hundred, but learning that the corps was crossing over and exchanging places with another corps near Petersburg, I followed the road from City Point up toward the city. But few men had arrived to take the places of those that had left, and the lines in some parts were unoccupied except by pickets. There was silence along all the line: the roads and fields through which we passed were quiet and unoccupied, and the pleasant morning sun shone down on a scene of perfect rest. The remains of our formidable batteries used at the time of the explosion of the mine were washed and seamed by the recent heavy rain.

While urging my horse to jump a gully in the road, "zip" came a bullet just before my eyes, and in a second another at my orderly. Others followed in quick succession but generally too high. Finding ourselves unnecessarily exposed, we dismounted and found we were very near the enemy's lines, but some of our men who were near, concealed in "gopher holes," and who had escaped our observation before, replied to the enemy's fire, while we walked across the field, leading our horses. A sharp fire all along the line, with artillery accompaniment, was the consequence of our "reconnaissance"; and Sergeant Meahan remarked that we had "raised the devil along the whole line—guess the Johnnies thought it was General Grant." I concluded that as I was out of the service I would mind my own affairs and go home while I had a head on my shoulders.

City Point
August 29, 1864
Spent the night at City Point with Dr. Burmeister, and bidding adieu to all, I embarked on the steamer for Fortress Monroe, a tugboat going ahead to search for torpedoes said to have been planted in the river by the Rebels the night before.[35] Found none, however, and arrived safely and reached home on the first day of September.

The feeling of freedom that I had not experienced for three years I found very pleasant, and home never seemed more attractive. A serenade in the evening and a cordial welcome from all my neighbors gave me great pleasure.

(From the *Boston Transcript,* September 16, 1864)

Headquarters, Nineteenth Massachusetts Volunteers
In the Field, before Petersburg, Va.
11th September 1864

The undersigned, officers of the Nineteenth Regiment of Massachusetts Volunteer Infantry, take this method of tendering their thanks publicly to their late Surgeon, J. Franklin Dyer, of Gloucester.

During his official connection with the Regiment, extending over a period of three years, his unvarying kindness and attention to their truest interests, have won for him a feeling of respect and affection in the hearts of his late comrades, which will terminate only with their lives. A skillful physician and surgeon, a Christian patriot and gentleman, a true and steady friend, a large hearted and brave man, he bears with him in his retirement the respect and affection of the entire command. It will be our greatest pleasure to learn of Dr. Dyer's prosperity and success in civil life; our deepest regret that we are deprived of his skillful attention and genial companionship.

Edmund Rice, Lt. Col.,
Commanding 19th Massachusetts Volunteers

Isaac H. Boyd, Capt.

William L. Palmer, Capt. & Ordnance Officer, Second Division

William A. Hill, Capt.

William F. Rice, Capt., A.A.A.G., First Brigade

Thomas F. Winthrop, First Lt. & Regimental Quartermaster

Charles S. Palmer, First Lt. & Acting Adjutant

Gustavus P. Pratt, Assistant Surgeon

William E. Barrows, First Lt.

William A. Stone, First Lt.

Joseph Libby, First Lt.

CHAPTER 15

"This Government of the People"

November 1864–December 1866

J. Franklin Dyer was home in a matter of days after leaving the Petersburg trenches. If Gloucester seemed strange after three years in the Army of the Potomac, his boyhood home of Eastport, Maine, which he soon visited, must have seemed on another planet. Within weeks he was back in Virginia, giving his individual attention to Maria's brother, who had been badly wounded and was in a Hampton hospital. While there, he also visited his old friends at Petersburg.

After going back home, he moved from Annisquam into downtown Gloucester, presumably because it increased both the number of his potential patients and his chances of finding a political appointment, which he sought to supplement his income while resuming his medical practice. He copied some of his letters of recommendation into his journal as evidence of what others thought of him and perhaps to bolster his own confidence. Major Dyer naively assumed that as a Union veteran, he would receive some preference for a political job. But veteran politicians had kept their fences mended while he was away in the army. The last lines of his journal describe his appointment as postmaster of Gloucester (on merit, he thought) by President Andrew Johnson's faction of the Republican Party and his abrupt removal when he would not support the approved slate of candidates. Yet this soldier and surgeon clung to his belief in the Union and in democracy.

Hampton, Va.
November 1864
After spending a fortnight at home, we went to Eastport on a visit. Soon after our return I received a note from Lt. Heber J. Davis, Mrs. Dyer's brother, aide to General Hawley, who was badly wounded

near Richmond and was then at Chesapeake Hospital, Hampton.[1] Started immediately for Fortress Monroe and remained three weeks at the hospital, taking a bed alongside his where I could attend him when necessary.

Finding considerable improvement in his condition then, I went to the front to see my old friends. Found George near Fort Burnham, north side James River—remained two nights and then visited the II Corps near Petersburg.[2] Found everything about as when I left. Headquarters, Second Division, at the Friend House near the "Petersburg Express" battery.[3] Grant's railroad over the hills had been built and in one part exposed to the fire of the enemy's batteries, an embankment high enough to protect the train, and half a mile long, had been thrown up.[4]

Returned to Hampton after an absence of six days; Heber still improving—left for home again, arriving in time for Thanksgiving.

Gloucester
December 7, 1864

Moved to Gloucester Harbor and took rooms at the Webster House.[5] Thinking my services in the army might give me some claim to an appointment under government, if changes were made, I mentioned the subject to some friends. Spoke also to B. H. S., who told me nothing had been done in the matter of application for appointments, but the subject had been under discussion, and when a movement was to be made he would let me know.[6] Learned in ten minutes afterward that he had a petition in his pocket for the appointment of another individual for collector and that he himself wished and expected the appointment of surveyor.

Was advised by friends to apply for the collectorship and did so. Called on Hon. John B. Alley, who said that Mr. Pew had claims on the *party*.[7] Also that Mr. S. had. That military service, except in very particular cases, constituted no claim to public appointment and discouraged my application. Discovered that he was pledged to Mr. Pew. Forwarded my application to him however and with it several documents, of which the following are copies of the most important:

Commonwealth of Massachusetts
Executive Department
Boston, January 21, 1865

To Hon. William Pitt Fessenden,
Secretary of Treasury, Washington, D.C.

Sir: Among the applicants for the office of Collector of District of Gloucester, Massachusetts, is J. Franklin Dyer, late Surgeon of the 19th Massachusetts Volunteers, honorably discharged by reason of expiration of his term of service (three years). Dr. Dyer left a lucrative practice for the service of his country. No man better sustained the credit of the State in the discharge of his duties. Further, he is a man of general information, unsullied integrity of character, good business qualifications, and a loyal, popular, and estimable citizen.

I am informed that his appointment would give general satisfaction to the people of Gloucester, by whom he is greatly respected; and it seems to me when men have sacrificed their pecuniary interests, and their personal comfort in the call of their country, that their services should not be forgotten.

I am your most obedient servant,
J. A. Andrew

Commonwealth of Massachusetts
Office of Surgeon General, Boston, January 22, 1865

To Hon. William Pitt Fessenden,
Secretary of Treasury:

Sir: I have the honor of cordially endorsing the recommendation of his Excellency Gov. Andrew in favor of J. Franklin Dyer, late Surgeon 19th Massachusetts Volunteers, for the Collectorship of the Port of Gloucester, Massachusetts.

Having been a resident of that place, with opportunities of knowing the feelings of the business portion of that community, I honestly believe that if the appointment of this meritorious and faithful officer should be made, that it would be an honorable and satisfactory recognition of the service he has rendered his country. I further endorse his integrity, capability, respectability as a man, and his loyalty as a citizen.

Very respectfully your obedient Servant,
William J. Dale,
Surgeon General of Massachusetts

"This Government of the People"

Headquarters First Corps, Medical Director's office,
Washington, D.C. January 24, 1865

Hon. William P. Fessenden, Secretary of Treasury:
  Sir: Dr. J. F. Dyer, late Surgeon of the 19th Massachusetts Volunteers, and Surgeon in Chief of the Second Division, Second
Corps, having made application for the Collectorship of the Port
of Gloucester, Massachusetts, where he lives, it gives me pleasure
to recommend him to you, as a man who for three years, under my
observation, did his duty with signal ability and fidelity.
  I considered that the service met with a severe loss when he left it;
and would particularly call your attention to his methodical business
habits and capacity (unfortunately too rare in our profession), which
particularly fit him for the place he seeks. I think a man of his
administrative ability, who has suffered loss by leaving his private
practice, in order to devote his talents to the service of his country,
in the army, for three years, deserves special consideration, and
should so far as practicable, be put by the authorities in the way to
live, while reestablishing himself.
  I have the honor to be,
  Very Respectfully, your obedient servant,
  Alexander N. Dougherty, Surgeon
  Brevet Lt. Col. U.S. Volunteers
  Medical Director, First Corps

The remarks of Colonel Dougherty I can endorse, and do so with
pleasure. Dr. Dyer served under my command for a long time, and
is well known to me.[8]
  Winfield S. Hancock
  Maj. Gen. U.S. Volunteers
  Commanding First Corps

Washington, December 25, 1865

Headquarters Army of Potomac
January 19, 1865

Surgeon J. Franklin Dyer,
  Gloucester, Mass: Dr. Knowing you as well as I do, I am delighted
to hear that some of your friends contemplate procuring a good

civil position for you. I stand ready to congratulate any community securing your services.

Since I have been in daily communication with you for more than a year, call upon me, if you desire it, for a testimonial to your honesty, efficiency, and zeal. My letter shall be strong, for you certainly deserve all I can write.

Believe me, my dear Dr.

Very sincerely, yours &c.

Alexander S. Webb, Bvt. Maj. Gen.

Chief of Staff, Army of Potomac

The letter promised, with one from Gen. Hinks, besides others from gentlemen in the district are on file in the Treasury Department at Washington. I have not preserved copies of all of them. It is perhaps unnecessary to say that I did not receive the appointment and that Mr. Pew did.

On my return from the army in September 1864, I was assured that I should have the appointment in a short time of acting assistant surgeon at the fort on Eastern Point. I went east, and on my return was told that if I would call on Dr. H., then occupying the post, and announce my intention of applying for it, that I should receive my appointment.[9] I did so, much against my will, and *did not* receive the appointment. Was then requested to petition for the post but declined. In May, however, a short time before the disbandment of the troops, I received the appointment, which I held two months and a half.

I had given up all thoughts of government appointments when on the third day of August 1866, Mr. Haskell, postmaster, congratulated me on my appointment as postmaster of Gloucester, which was announced in the papers of that date.[10] In a few days I received my appointment in due form with blank bond, which was duly executed and forwarded to the department at Washington.

This appointment, I was assured by Generals Butler and Hinks, who procured it for me without my knowledge, was not a political appointment but made by the president on purely military recommendations, and that I should be justified in accepting it. I did so with this understanding. Was then requested by gentlemen holding office and supporting Mr. Johnson to attend the Faneuil Hall Convention, to join the Johnson Club in Gloucester, {and} to contribute money to the Johnson Committee in Washington to carry on the fall elections, to each and every one of which invitations I returned a decided refusal. Afterward learned from a friend in Washington that my appointment was suspended. It seemed evident to the minds of the president and others concerned that I was not a friend of "the policy" and that the appointment had not converted me.

At the date of writing, December 1866, I have not received the promised commission. I have cast my ballot for the Republican candidates, and I pray that this "Government of the people, for the people, and by the people, shall not perish from the earth."

Epilogue

A Great Surgeon

Feeling that he had done his part in the struggle to save the Union, frustrated by the army's policy of not promoting surgeons above his current rank of major, and unable even to get a pay increase, Dr. Dyer had declined reenlistment, instead accepting a discharge after serving three years.[1] The veteran surgeon slowly rebuilt his medical practice in Gloucester, locating in the town center, but acceded to the wishes of his former patients on the north shore by returning to Annisquam in June 1871. He bought the house at 54 Leonard Street from John Pierce in September, and it remained the home of Frank and Maria for the rest of their lives.[2]

Seeking some means of making a living while recovering the practice he had lost during his absence, Dyer sought various political appointments. He was a loyal Republican as well as a veteran, and on the strength of his military letters of recommendation, he was appointed Gloucester postmaster in August 1866. Pres. Andrew Johnson's policies were not ones that Dyer could endorse, however, and when he refused to support them and candidates for election from that faction, he lost the appointment before it became official. Eventually, he won a brief tenure as the surgeon at the Eastern Point fort. Writing to Maj. Gen. O. O. Howard in 1867, Dyer expressed strong support for Republican policies during Reconstruction, which he had followed "with intense interest" while reading a report of the Committee on Reconstruction (probably the report released June 20, 1866). The doctor assured General Howard, "I do not regret my loss of position or business (for I have lost both—Massachusetts is not in peace as in war) but I watch for the time when our victories will be secured—you know best how." He had visited his brother William in Missouri and was glad to see that ex-Rebels in that state were leaving, hoping to find a friendlier political climate farther south. "I rejoice in the state of things there." Maria wanted to meet the general because her husband had talked about him so much.[3]

Dr. Dyer represented his district for the 1869 term in the Massachusetts General Court, but his most significant civic contributions after the Civil War were at the local level. He served seven years on the Gloucester School Committee, was appointed coroner in 1871 and then medical examiner, and served on the board of health and as the town physician and medical examiner for his part of Essex County until a few weeks before his death. Active in Gloucester's incorporation as a city, Dyer served four years as an alderman and was elected its third mayor in 1878, beating his Democratic opponent with less than 52 percent of the votes cast. Major Dyer was also the president of a mutual fire insurance company.[4]

Dyer's postwar career was an active one, politically, professionally, and socially, but it was both relatively brief and marked by great joy and terrible sorrow. Maria presented him with a second son, Edward James Dyer, on October 29, 1869. His first son, Franklin, prepared for college at Exeter Academy and enrolled at Bowdoin in the class of 1878. But Franklin died of consumption at the Annisquam house on July 27, 1875, a month short of his nineteenth birthday, before he could begin his sophomore year at the college in Brunswick.[5]

Like many of the veterans on both sides, including physicians, the war had permanently damaged Dr. Dyer's health. He returned to Gloucester "a broken-down man," his constitution "shattered . . . [by] intermittent fever." The winds on the north side of Cape Ann also sapped his strength, and at times he could not work. His lungs were affected, and after an attack of pneumonia in early June 1878, he developed active symptoms of tuberculosis.[6] His health had been a concern since adolescence, as the family letters make clear, yet he rarely mentioned it in wartime. He did so explicitly when he wrote to his old friend General Howard in August 1867. Dyer told Howard, who was then the embattled head of the Freedmen's Bureau, that "the campaign through the Wilderness . . . nearly exhausted my physical powers." He regretted not being at the surrender of Gen. Robert E. Lee's army, "but I was not physically able to continue in the field."[7]

J. Franklin Dyer died at his Annisquam home on February 9, 1879, two months short of his fifty-third birthday. His funeral was at Gloucester's Middle-Street Congregational Church, and he was buried in the city's Oak Grove Cemetery. A large crowd of mourners attended the ceremonies, including his old advocate, Massachusetts surgeon general William J. Dale, ex-Adjutant General James A. Cunningham, members of the Grand Army of the Republic Post 45, and a delegation from the Military Order of the Loyal Legion of the United States, to which Dyer had been elected in 1869.[8]

The mayor and aldermen of Gloucester, at a meeting on February 11, 1879, unanimously adopted resolutions, which read in part: "We bear witness to [J. Franklin Dyer's] public spirit, to his strong convictions of right, to his loyalty to duty, and to the self-abnegation with which he devoted himself to the public service, even when the hand of mortal disease was laid heavily upon him."[9] The board then adjourned and attended the former mayor's funeral. But of all the tributes paid to Frank Dyer at the time of his death, none are as moving as the two written by his comrades in the Nineteenth Massachusetts. The first had appeared in the *Boston Transcript* after his return home and was signed by Lt. Col. Edmund Rice, commanding the regiment, and ten other officers, including Dr. Gustavus P. Pratt, the Cohasset physician who succeeded Dyer as surgeon. He copied it into his journal.

When the regiment's history was finally published in 1906, the survivors of the Nineteenth Massachusetts still remembered their surgeon, J. Franklin Dyer, more than forty years after he left the army. In the opening pages of the volume, his comrades described him as "one of the most skillful physicians in the Army . . . , a man of gentle temperament, but thorough in every detail of his position." They testified that Dyer came to be as highly regarded in the First Brigade, the Second Division, and the II Corps as he was in his old regiment. More than a quarter century after his passing, these elderly veterans called Frank Dyer "a great surgeon."[10]

Maria Dyer raised young Ned with the aid of relatives and friends and her pension as a veteran's widow. She recorded both her expenditures and money sent by Frank's brothers, George and Charles (William died in Chicago in 1882), in a cash book for the years 1881–84. In 1886 she and Edward visited California, by ship on the way out, returning overland. The visit was at least in part because of his health, which she comments on in various entries Maria made during the trip in a diary that has apparently been lost, though notes from it survive. [11]

When women won the vote, Maria Dyer, a fervent Republican, registered at the village hall in Annisquam. She continued throughout her long life to be active in sewing and reading clubs and was regarded as Gloucester's leading expert on rare flowers. Dr. Dyer's premature death and her extended widowhood were yet additional costs of the Civil War and the preservation of the Union, a price paid by Maria and countless other women and children. Maria never remarried, and like others of her day she may have been following the custom set by Queen Victoria after Prince Albert's death in 1861. Or perhaps she felt that no man could take the place of Frank Dyer.

In her last years Maria suffered from deafness and lameness as the result of a fall. She died at the Leonard Street house on June 26, 1925, of a cerebral hemorrhage brought on by grippe and bronchitis. The lead story on the front page of the *Gloucester Daily Times* proclaimed the "City's Oldest Resident Dead" and said, "Her death will leave a distinct void in the hearts of many citizens for she was a greatly beloved woman." On the day of her funeral, the paper's front page obituary, "Annisquam's Grand Old Lady Dead," was overshadowed only by the death of fifteen local men when a Cunard liner rammed their fishing boat. Maria Davis Dyer had lived in Annisquam for sixty-eight years and had been a member of its Woman's Benevolent Association from the first year of her residence. [12]

Edward J. Dyer became a landscape photographer, and many of the pictures he took of the Annisquam house have been preserved by the family. He never married and did not long survive his mother, dying on June 7, 1928, of suppurative erysipelas and epileptic psychosis at the state hospital in North Grafton, Massachusetts, where he had been a patient for almost twelve years. His death received prominent coverage. He was a member of the Sons of Union Veterans camp founded in the 1880s and named for his father. On Sunday, June 10, his comrades in J. Franklin Dyer Camp 24 met at Gloucester's G.A.R. hall to attend his funeral. Conducted by the Rev. George H. Lewis, the local Universalist pastor, it was held at "Dyerholm" in Annisquam. [13] Frank and Maria's second child was buried beneath a simple obelisk in Oak Grove Cemetery, where he joined his mother, brother, and father.

The inscription for Dr. J. Franklin Dyer has only the dates and places of his birth and death. There is no mention of his place in Gloucester's history, both as a town and a city; of his generation of service to the community as a physician; or of the part that he played in the war to save the Union. Perhaps Frank Dyer would have wanted it that way, feeling that he had only done what duty required.

APPENDIX 1

Letter from J. Franklin Dyer to H. K. Oliver

Camp near Cumberland, Va.
May 16, 1862

Hon. H. K. Oliver,

Dear Sir,

Yours regarding the case of Horace Lakeman has been received.[1] Upon the evacuation of Yorktown, I was ordered to send all patients in regimental hospital to the division hospital established in the rear and then under the care of three Boston surgeons, Drs. Cabot, Gay, and Homans.[2] Thus I have lost sight of him, as well as some fifty others whom we have been obliged to send to general hospital since landing on the Peninsula. Many of these have been sent farther north, and no doubt all have received the best attention. Lakeman's case was not of such a nature as to preclude his recovery—and I hope ere this he is in improved health.[3]

In all these cases I have acted in accordance with instructions from my superiors in the Medical Department and am bound to believe that they have acted for the best interests of those entrusted to their care.[4]

I am very respectfully,

Your obedient servant,

J. Franklin Dyer, Surgeon, 19th Massachusetts

The Gettysburg Letters

"The Last Assault Was a Desperate One"

Near Poolesville, Maryland, June 27

Dear M—

Here we are back again near old Camp Benton. Crossed the river last night. Left Thoroughfare Gap day before yesterday. Had a small fight at Haymarket; one killed, eight wounded. The army is all across except the VI Corps, which crosses today. We are under orders to march again today, go up toward Pennsylvania. I am well and hope we shall do the right thing with the Rebs. The mail carrier is waiting. Love to all. Goodbye.

Yours always,

Frank

Monocacy Bridge, near Frederick City
June 28, 1863

Dear Maria—

We have had a tiresome march up here. Arrived this afternoon about four o'clock. Left our old campground near Camp Benton, where I saw the old chimneys standing that we left there, and marched over a very bad road through mud and rain to a spot this side of Barnesville just under Sugar Loaf mountain. Arrived there at ten o'clock at night. Got something to eat and slept till six, when we were ordered to march. Did not get our division out until 8 o'clock and then the baggage and supply trains impeded our march very much.

Passed through the neat little village of Urbana, about which time a report came that General Hooker was relieved from the command of the Army of the Potomac and General Meade placed in command. I can really say that no one felt aggrieved, and I heard of no resignations being tendered in consequence. He is said to be a good officer and was in command of the V Corps. General Gibbon is very intimate with him and has gone to Frederick this evening to see him with General Hancock. I am inclined to think that he will want Gibbon either to command a corps or else appoint him his chief of staff, as of course Hooker's staff will be relieved. I shall be sorry to lose him, but I think he is one of the best generals we have. I am inclined to think Hancock may be relieved and also Howard. I like Howard personally, but I do not think he has the *power* and *vim* sufficient for a large command. I don't know of anything that is likely to turn up for my advantage in this overturn.

Well, we have got a big piece of work in hand, but where the fight will take place I cannot tell. The Rebels are well into Pennsylvania, and we shall have to head them off somewhere and fight them. From what I can learn of their position they may march toward either Philadelphia or Baltimore. We are to march in the morning at six o'clock toward Newmarket in the direction of Baltimore. That is the understanding now. We shall not go over South Mountain probably. Yet no one can tell from one hour to another what is to be done, as we have not sources of information here that they have at headquarters of the army. I am in hopes we have now force enough in Pennsylvania to give them a check until we can have time to get up with them.

Major Webb of General Meade's staff, a regular-army officer, was appointed brigadier general and ordered to report to General Gibbon for duty today. He will command the Second Brigade, General Owen's Philadelphia Brigade. Owen is now under arrest for irregular conduct, and General Gibbon doesn't like him. He has had a very good brigade, but his discipline has been so loose that they have become notorious stragglers.

It seems singular to get back on this old ground again after so long a time, but war is very uncertain. I think however we are bound to whip them out at last, and if we do they had better not try it again. Hoping for all things favorable I remain with love to all,

your always,
Frank

Uniontown, Maryland, June 30

Dear M—

I wrote to you from near Frederick yesterday or night before. We started on our march yesterday morning, passing east of Frederick City through Lakesville, Liberty, Union Bridge, and Uniontown, where we arrived just before dark, the troops coming in until ten or eleven o'clock pretty well tired out, having marched from twenty-five to thirty miles during the day, a very long march.[1] The men kept up well too, especially in our division. A new brigade that joined us the other day straggled so that but few were left at night.

We were following pretty close upon the Rebels. Their scouts have been here and taken a good many cattle, horses, and mules. Soon after we arrived our cavalry scouts brought in two buggies in which four secesh gentlemen of Uniontown had driven out from Uniontown to inform the Rebels of our approach. They were brought in and put under guard. The Rebel pickets were within two miles of ours last night, but we are ready for them. However, I think they have gone this morning toward Pennsylvania.

We shall probably remain here today. It is not certain which route we shall take. The Rebs are at Harrisburg, but many are yet threatening Baltimore and Washington. There are many good Union people about here but some violent secesh. In some little one-horse villages the people shut themselves up in their houses or scowled at the windows. While others gave our men what they had and threw bouquets to some officers. A very pretty young lady at Union Mills threw me a bouquet, which act showed remarkable *good taste* on her part. This is a splendid country about here. The fields of wheat are magnificent and they are about reaping. The prospect from the hills over which we pass is splendid.

I saw Smith and Bibber yesterday just as we passed the Monocacy Bridge. They were both well.[2] The First Maine is in Gregg's division, Pleasonton's corps.[3] They have had some fighting lately and lost some men. The colonel was killed the other day at Aldie.[4] Smith will probably be promoted.

Appendix 2

{Note: same letter}
Near Gettysburg, Pennsylvania, July 2, 12 P.M.

You have heard of the battle ere this reaches you. It is over now and thousands lay dead and wounded in the fields and in the hospitals under the trees and about the farm barns. The fight was terrible. We marched from our camp of last night about four miles to the front and took position this morning. Skirmishing and artillery firing occupied nearly all day until we found their position, and the fight began at about four o'clock in earnest. From that time till after eight the roar of battle was terrific.

They came down on our left with a large force and at first over-powered us. We threw in more troops, then they brought more, column after column formed into the gap which they tried to force but were baffled. About dark Sedgwick came up and they were forced back. Several times my heart almost failed me as our men were forced back, but when I saw "Uncle John Sedgwick's" flag advancing, I knew we should check them or the VI Corps would not survive.

We were nearly driven out of our hospital but held on and afterward were relieved by their being driven back. I was so busy I could not indulge curiosity to watch more than I saw before me, but I never saw or heard such fighting. Hour after hour the volleys poured incessantly. I have about five hundred or six hundred in hospital. I have no knowledge of the number killed and wounded. It is to be reckoned by thousands.

In the fight of {the} thirtieth, General Reynolds was killed.[5] Today I heard Sickles was badly wounded and since dead.[6] Some of the regiments of our division have lost heavily. The First Minnesota had colonel, lieutenant colonel, major, and three captains wounded. Colonel Revere of the Twentieth Massachusetts will probably die. Colonel Ward of the Fifteenth will lose his other leg (lost one at Balls Bluff). Colonel Huston of the Eighty-second New York killed and three captains. In fact it was a terrible fight. Captain Dodge and Lieutenant Stone of the Nineteenth wounded.[7]

I have sat down in the kitchen of the little house where we are to write. The family have fled and well they might. All took their children and fled, leaving their homes perhaps not to find them again, as the Rebels burnt several houses. The fight will probably be renewed in the morning. I hope we shall be able to hold our position if nothing more. Sedgwick will be ready to go in with nearly his whole corps.[8] But it is one o'clock. I must get a little sleep and be up at daylight. Good night. God help us and give us the victory. Our army has fought with desperation and will fight tomorrow. I think so far there has been no blundering. We have done the best we could, and if we fail it is because we have not men enough or God is not on our side.

{Note: same letter}
July 3, 12 o'clock

We have been fighting this morning, but all quiet now. A grand attack is to be made by us this P.M., if not by the Rebels. They have so far been repulsed. They are desperate however and will try to cut their way through. The hospital was rather close yesterday, and we are now moving back to be out of the way. Reinforcements are coming. Couch is on the way. Hoping for a joyful fourth of July.

I am as always,

yours,

Frank

Captain Patten of the Twentieth goes to Westminster by the ammunition train and takes this.

Field Hospital near Gettysburg
July 4, 1863

Dear M. I wrote you yesterday and sent by Captain Patten on his way home. Just after he left about one o'clock the enemy fired his artillery, one hundred pieces as we heard afterward, and ours replied.[9] Along the whole line there was a perfect roar. We had probably more guns than they, and the fire was so incessant that it seemed blended together in one roar. For at least four hours it continued without cessation. Batteries fired till all their men were disabled and men from the infantry were detailed to take their places. Guns and caissons were knocked to pieces, wheels replaced and knocked to pieces again. Guns fired till they were heated and taken off to cool while new batteries were put in their places. Horses killed by the hundred. It seemed as impossible for one to escape as it would

215

to escape a drop of rain in a shower. Generals Hancock and Gibbon wounded, some generals killed; Zook of Third Division, Colonel Cross, Fifth New Hampshire, and officers and men by thousands.

Then line after line of the enemy infantry came up in front of our division. They broke through at one point where the Second Brigade were posted. Our old Third Brigade faced around and poured such a fire into them that today I saw the ground fairly covered with their dead. Here twenty-one Rebel colors were taken; our regiment took four. I saw lots of them. They were finally repulsed from every point, and hundreds of prisoners, some say thousands, remained in our hands with all their wounded.

This finished the fight in a manner, though they tried last night, and this morning rather feebly, to force through. Today they are not in sight, except skirmishers, and they are all along the line. We are victorious. For three days they have attempted to force our lines and were three times repulsed. The last assault was a desperate one. Never in the history of the war was known such a fiercely contested fight and such slaughter.

We have a joyful Fourth of July only for the dreadful scenes about us. I am now sitting in a little sheltered tent which one of the men has up while the rain is pouring down in torrents as thousands of wounded men gathered in hospital about two miles from the front. Our corps and some others have no tents, no houses or barns, all exposed to the rain, and thousands of wounded have not yet been brought in. It is impossible to operate fast enough to dress all the wounds in three or four days. I am waiting for the rain to hold up to go to work.

I have had a good deal of outdoor work to do, that is to see to directing matters, especially about bringing in wounded and providing means of feeding the men, etc. We were obliged to leave our hospital near the field quite fast as the shells came bursting among us quite lively. When it was over, however, we brought more wounded in there and now keep both going, though the corps hospital is established here. We ought to have had tents, but the trains were all ordered to be sent to Westminster, and the stupid quartermasters would not allow hospital wagons even to come up. That comes of having the Medical Department interfered with by others. However, it is the fate of war. We shall have them up tomorrow.

We have advanced our lines considerably, but as I finish this at ten o'clock tonight some cannonading is heard, and Lt. Colonel Cunningham of the Nineteenth Maine, who was just here, says they expect an attack tonight. [10] The Rebs are desperate and will attempt anything, but they are terribly whipped now, and we have enough to meet them. The corps is almost fresh yet, and the other corps are collecting their men very well. The II Corps has lost probably 3,000 in killed and wounded. The Nineteenth Massachusetts at least 60, the Nineteenth Maine, 212. [11] They did bravely.

We have tonight about 650 of our own and even 200 Rebels in our hospital. All on the ground but have given them soup and tea and whiskey when needed, and they are doing well generally.

Colonel Revere of the Twentieth is dead. We have lost heavily. I will write more particularly by and by; a clerk is going to Westminster tonight and will take this. The Rebel army is in danger of destruction.

Love to all—

Frank

Headquarters, Second Division, II Corps
Taneytown, Maryland, July 7, 1863

Dear Maria—

We marched today from the vicinity of the battlefield and are encamped just outside the town. We march tomorrow morning at five o'clock, in the direction of Frederick, I suppose. Most of the troops have preceded us. What the plan of operations is I cannot learn yet, but we are daily taking large numbers of prisoners. At least 11,000 have been taken already; 800 passed today. French took 1,500 yesterday.

Lee has got a good-sized army and is a good general, but General Meade will cripple him terribly. I hope now no one will complain of the Army of the Potomac. Those old veterans fight like tigers, and our old Second Division is entitled to a great share of the credit, for in our front the main attack was made, and we lost 1,700 men killed and wounded, while our division buried 800 Rebels in its front. They fight like devils.

Hancock was the man of the day, and Gibbon was a hero. He is quite badly wounded by a ball through the shoulder but not dangerously. Hancock has only a flesh wound. Our men have had to suffer in hospital for want of food and shelter. Through all the rain not a tent was in our corps hospital. All the men, more than 2,000, were lying on the ground in the woods, but the trains were sent back as a military necessity, and it was two or three days before proper supplies could be sent up. They will do better now, however.

No thanks to the people in the neighborhood, however. They are very mean — charged 1.00 a quart for milk and .50 cents a loaf for bread, and one man charged 3.00 for making a crutch for a wounded man who, with many others slightly wounded, were allowed to make their way to the nearest depot to go to Baltimore hospitals. In this neighborhood they are much more liberal and will sell anything they have at a fair price. Officers have to beg for themselves, and the men want a little extra once in a while. Our supply train failed to come up last night, and the men had but little breakfast this morning; the first time I ever knew it to fail in issuing hard bread and coffee at least. But the commissaries had cattle and bought all the supplies in town, and the train arrived before night. So nobody was hurt, but think what the Rebels have to undergo, and where does Lee get his provisions? Gregg destroyed a train of 170 wagons loaded with dry goods and shoes yesterday, which the Rebs were taking off. They are after Lee's ammunition train. This has been as great a battle as Waterloo, and I am thankful I was present. I could tell you all day of deeds of heroism performed by our men, and neither Mac nor Hooker nor any other man but Meade ever fought a battle with such skill as that. The Army of the Potomac is immortal, and our little division, numbering less than three full regiments, is ready if necessary to fight again another such battle. I hope we shall follow them to Richmond. They had the idea that troops from the north, with militia, joined us, but it was the old Army of the Potomac alone that fought them, and we have not seen or heard of any others. I would not give a straw for five million such as Pennsylvania Militia. No army but veterans could have withstood the steady and desperate attacks of Lee. Half a million militia would have been an encumbrance and perhaps our ruin. The Nineteenth has but few left. They lost about seventy killed and wounded and have not more than one company left. What will be done with us I don't know. I am willing to go home after this. Don't be alarmed. I shall get out of it soon perhaps, and I shall care more to go home than to any hospital. I had a paper from George tonight. No letter from you for more than a week; only one since we left Thoroughfare Gap. Will Knapp did very well, I believe. He remained at the hospital near the front all the time, I believe, and did his duty. If so, I shall be glad to give him the credit of it. He very carelessly left his horse for someone to carry off, a thing I warned him of before when he lost another in the same way. It is something to learn to look out for these things. The sun has not been out full and free since we left Thoroughfare Gap. It is now raining, and I am writing in an ambulance.

Love to all,

Frank

Headquarter, Second Division
Taneytown, Maryland, July 7, 1863

Dear M—

We marched from our camp near Gettysburg this morning at five o'clock. Halted here for an hour or two near the town. Part of our surgeons are left at the hospital in the rear, the rest come on. We are bound toward Frederick I suppose. I hear that Sedgwick has taken a number of prisoners. I am well but have not had a very pleasant time. General Harrow is in command of the division. No such man as Gibbon. Gibbon has a pretty severe wound in the shoulder. We are following the Rebs pretty close and hope we shall destroy a good part of Lee's army. He has probably lost from one cause and another 50,000 men since he came across the Potomac. Prisoners are taken every day.

I think I shall go into the town and get something to eat, leaving my letter at the post office. We have had no mail for more than a week, I think.

Love to all,

Frank

I am glad we are out of Pennsylvania. They are the meanest people about Gettysburg that I ever saw. They will sell nothing, only at the most exorbitant prices. Milk, 1.00 a quart, bread .50 cents a loaf, and refused to let us have sheets for bandages except by paying a great price when we happened to get short. The Maryland people are kings to them.

Appendix 2

{Sentence below in ink, probably from some days later.}
Written when we halted, when we did not expect remain tonight.

{Next three pages in pencil on heavy lined paper except for an insertion in ink along the left margin, enclosed below in square brackets; not in letter format, lacks salutation and close.}
On the morning of the fourth I looked over the field where the dead lay unburied. Our own men were carefully collecting the remains of their comrades and marking headboards for their graves. Regiments were sending in to headquarters the captured flags and obtaining receipts for them. Lieutenant Barrows, formerly my hospital steward, aide on the staff of Colonel Hall, commanding Third Brigade, had then about a dozen. The division captured twenty-one, I believe.

Of the number of men in our division and losses, I have not preserved a copy of my report made at the time, but to the best of my recollection we had fifteen regiments numbering 3,600 men. Our killed, wounded, and missing numbered between 1,700 and 1,800, according to field report on the fifth, reduced to perhaps 1,600 in a few days by more correct reports and collecting of stragglers. On the fifth we had in our division hospital some 700 to 800 and 300 Rebel wounded. Many slightly wounded had walked or obtained conveyance to the nearest railroad station and made their way home. [The First and Third Division hospitals adjoined ours, and their numbers were about the same, the First a little less. During the fight on the second, the First Division was driven back with the III Corps and suffered considerably. Their division rallied in the rear of our hospital.] I collected the names of such officers as wish to leave for home, and leave was afterward granted each in general orders.

Eight hundred Rebel dead were buried in front of our division. One could not ask for stronger proof of the fierceness of the attack and the obstinate defense. Riding over a part of the field with Lieutenant Haskell on the sixth, we noted some of the marks of the combat. Toward the right, on {the} hill where the XII Corps was attacked on the night of the second, the trees were completely cut to pieces by bullets. Withered leaves and branches strewed the ground. In an ordinary-sized tree we counted some 150 bullets within six feet of the ground. Passing to the left, the broken and battered monuments of the cemetery told of the severe cannonade on the third, and to the left of that in the line of the II Corps, the dead horses of the batteries covered the ground where Cushing, wounded, fired until he fell in death and the Rhode Island batteries stood their ground until not enough horses remained to draw off the guns. Every artillery officer of the Rhode Island battery but one was hit.

Where the Second Division fought so well the rows of graves were long and the little "clump of trees" so often spoken of was torn and stripped by the storm of shots. The few rails and stones hastily gathered and the little earth scraped up by sticks served but a poor purpose for protection, and these were mostly thrown up after the battle in anticipation of another attack. Indeed, this part of the line was more open and easy of access by the nature of the ground than other parts, and though the attack was intended to be on the whole length of the line, it seemed to center at this point, and the breach at one time seemed to be complete.

General Meade was on the spot immediately after the repulse, and when informed by Lieutenant Haskell that the attack was repulsed, he asked again if it was entirely repulsed, and when informed again that it was so, a fervent "Thank God" broke from his lips, and then in his prompt and business way {he} gave directions for placing reinforcements, which he had ordered up but which were now unnecessary. Hancock and Gibbon were out of the fight. Webb was slightly wounded but on duty. A hero everywhere and the division was under command of General Harrow, a man of no military ability, and in the opinion of some of doubtful courage. Hall, Devereux, and Mallon were still with us, but Ward and Revere were gone, and our little division seemed sadly cut up, though covered with glory.

Working at the operating tables and attending to other duties, my time was fully occupied. The small amount of surgical dressings, chloroform, etc., in one of our wagons was sufficient for immediate use, though we were without shelter and cooking {text continues in ink} apparatus sufficient for use. On the evening of the fifth, our hospital trains arrived and at the same time wagons of the Sanitary Commission, also our commissaries, and henceforth our supplies were sufficient. Tents, however, had to be put up and straw obtained to keep the wounded from the wet ground, ground policed, and preparations for a longer stay completed. In this I was engaged until the evening of the sixth. Details of surgeons were made to remain in hospital, the others to go on with the army. My duty and orders required me to move on, and leaving the hospital on the seventh, I joined the division already on its way.

A Confederate officer remarked that when they came into the state, the whole population seemed to rise in arms. A great mistake however. He did not know that the old Army of the Potomac was all they had to contend with and seemed surprised when told that no other troops had been engaged in the fight. Their officers encouraged the men by telling them there was nothing but Pennsylvania militia before them, but they found to their cost that their old adversaries were there instead.

{Note: New page to what appears to be a journal entry}
It has generally happened that during our greatest battles and immediately afterward, I have been too much engaged to write particulars. During the early part of the battle of Gettysburg, I was engaged in locating and preparing the hospital, after which I must work attending to wounded but frequently had occasion to go to the front and see that all in my department is going on right there. That those surgeons who were ordered to examine wounded and dispatch them to the rear were at their posts and that the ambulance officers were doing their duty. Lieutenant Searles of the First Minnesota, ambulance officer of the division, was very faithful in the performance of his duties. [12] The ambulance horses were worked night and day, and many broke down. Mules were sometimes substituted.

The road just in rear of our lines, where I had occasion to pass frequently, was within range of enemy artillery and at one time of musketry fire. I noticed a group of men sitting down quietly play poker while shells were bursting frequently and unpleasantly near. They sought mental occupation to divert their attention from more serious matters. General Meade's headquarters were at a small home near the road, and as many as seventeen horses of officers and orderlies were killed while standing there. General Gibbon's orderly, John, was killed by a shell while holding horses at the rear. While going up I met Generals Hancock and Gibbon, and Major (now Brevet Major General) Macy coming from the field. I accompanied them to the hospital, where Dr. Dougherty dressed General Hancock's wound. Dr. Hayward, Macy, and I attended to General Gibbon. Lieutenant Haskell, who was slightly wounded, soon came down and reported the attack entirely repulsed. General Gibbon, who sat on the step of an ambulance while I dressed the wounds in his shoulder, was feeling rather faint but on this announcement was so elated that he got up and walked to General Hancock's ambulance to shake hands with him and congratulate him on the victory. After taking some refreshment they kept on to Westminster to take the cars for home. While on the road, about the same time I met Gibbon, Major Rice came walking down with a flesh wound in the thigh, which he called a "good joke," and carrying three Confederate flags. There were none of us who did not fully appreciate the magnitude and importance of this engagement. Men fought with desperation, and each seemed to feel that here in the soil of the North was to be decided the great contest between freedom and slavery.

Gen. Gibbon's Division in the Battle of Gettysburg

A Sketch of Its History

From the *New York Times*, August 1, 1863

No Division of the Union Army bears a better record than the Second Division of the Second Army Corps. It was originally formed at Poolesville, Maryland, under the command of Brigadier General C. P. Stone, in the summer of 1861, and was occupied in picketing the upper Potomac, building block houses, and trying a little fighting at Ball's Bluff. In the latter part of the month of February 1862, it marched, under command of Gen. Sedgwick, who succeeded Gen. Stone, by way of Adamstown to Harper's Ferry, and in March, in the command of Gen. Banks, drove the rebels out of Winchester. Returning by way of Harper's Ferry and Washington, embarked at Alexandria for the Peninsula; at Alexandria being placed in the Second Corps, and under command of the veteran General E. V. Sumner. Landing at Fortress Monroe just after the fight between the Monitor and the Merrimac, the Division was marched by the way of Big Bethel to Yorktown, where it was constantly on duty, building earthworks, corduroy roads, and on picket duty, close up under the enemy's works. From Yorktown, after the evacuation of that place by the enemy, the Division proceeded by transports on the York River to West Point, where part of it was landed in haste while the fight was going on there, under the fire of the enemy's artillery, but was held in reserve.

Our gunboats having opened fire the rebels soon retreated, and the Division marched by the Pamunkey River to Tyler's Farm, near the Chickahominy, whence on the 31st of May, guided by the sound of the enemy's cannon, it marched to Fair Oaks, crossing the Chickahominy on a temporary bridge, which was swept away almost as soon as the troops had passed. It arrived just in time to turn the fortunes of the day. The 82d New York (2d New York State Militia) and 34th New York Volunteers (since mustered out of service, their time having expired), in support of Kirby's Battery, kept up a steady fire in line of battle for more than two hours against a whole Brigade of the enemy. The Second New York, just as night fell, charged the enemy and drove them into the woods. They then rested on their arms amid the dead and dying for the night. For this charge, by the way, the Second Excelsior Regiment has always had the credit, from the fact of the Second New York carrying a stand of colors presented by the corporation of the city of New York years before, with the coat of arms and bearing the motto "Excelsior," with the number of the Regiment. The next day the Division fought the rebels on the left, and drove them beyond the railroad.

Occupying a position in the centre "in front of Richmond," after the battle of Fair Oaks, breastworks were thrown up along the whole line, and here the Division was almost constantly under fire while it held the position. Being the last to leave the front in the "change of base" it participated in all the battles of the "Seven days," meeting the enemy at Peach Orchard Station, and again at Savage Station on the same day that it left the front, hurling the rebel force back in every engagement. At White Oak Swamp, Nelson's Farm, and Malvern Hill it also bore a conspicuous part.

Leaving Harrison's Landing in the latter end of August, again it covered the rear, marching to Newport News, and thence by shipping to Aquia Creek. On the same day it re-embarked for Alexandria, thence to Chain Bridge, and from Chain Bridge to Centreville, marching nearly all night in the rain. Now, for once, it was a day too late for the fight, but not too late to cover the retreat, and it was the last to leave Centreville the night after the battle of Chantilly. By way of Chain Bridge it again crossed out of Dixie to meet the rebels at South Mountain and Antietam. On the battle field of Antietam it changed commanders; Gen. Sedgwick having been seriously wounded, the command fell upon General Howard.

After lying four days on the battle field near Sharpsburg, it marched again to Harpers Ferry to find it evacuated by Stonewall Jackson, after he had dislodged the force under Col. Miles. This time he forded the river, as Jackson had destroyed the railroad bridge more effectually than before, even blasting the granite piers, telling the Superintendent of Repairs of the road, that "it would be more of a job than it was the last time" to rebuild it. Toward the last of October the march was again taken up, by Loudoun Valley to Warrenton Junction and the Rappahannock.

On the 11th of December the Division threw the pontoon bridge across to Fredericksburg, under a severe fire from the enemy's artillery and sharpshooters, yet crossing before dark, in the face of all opposition, and driving the rebels through and out of the city. In the next two days it suffered severely.

On the Union forces evacuating Fredericksburg, it was, strange to say, not the last to leave. It recrossed the river about midnight, reoccupied its old position in and around Falmouth, where it remained while Gen. Burnside led the army out on the mud raid, and while it again crossed the Rappahannock under General Hooker to Chancellorsville. Gen. Howard having been ordered to the command of the Eleventh Corps, he was relieved by General Gibbon, shortly before the battle of Chancellorsville, who was familiar with the ground on both sides of the river, having had a command there in 1862 for several months. He was left in command at Falmouth with the 1st and 3d Brigades, with which he threw across two pontoon bridges and again crossed into Fredericksburg, joining forces with Gen. Sedgwick, and assisted in driving the rebels over the crest that had been so determinedly struggled for in December.

On the march from Falmouth to Gettysburg, the Division was again in the rear, passing again through Centreville to Thoroughfare Gap, which it held for some days, and then by the way of Gum Spring and Edwards Ferry again into Maryland and Pennsylvania, making on the last march but one before reaching Gettysburg, over thirty miles in one day. The Commanding General, Gibbon, was again badly wounded at Gettysburg, having been wounded in the wrist at Fredericksburg in December, at which time he was in command of a Division of the 1st corps.

The First Minnesota, which is the oldest Volunteer Regiment in the service, is also one of the best, and has furnished the Army three General Officers, Generals Gorman, Dana, and Sully. The Fifteenth Massachusetts has also furnished a General Officer, Brigadier General Devens, and has always kept up the reputation of the Old Bay State. The Second Brigade is generally known as the Philadelphia Brigade, and has furnished two general officers, Generals

Wister {Wistar} and Owen, from the Seventy-first and sixty-ninth Regiments. The Brigade is commanded by an able young officer, Brig. Gen. Webb, a son of J. Watson Webb, and a graduate of the Military Academy. The Seventy-first Pennsylvania is better known as the First California, first commanded by Col. Baker, which lost so heavily at Ball's Bluff. The Seventy-second Pennsylvania is also known as Baxter's Fire Zouaves.

In the Third Brigade there are two Regiments, the Nineteenth and Twentieth Massachusetts, perfect as any in the Army in drill and discipline. They are both from Boston. These two Regiments, the Forty-second and Fifty-ninth New York, and the Seventh Michigan, form its Third Brigade. The Colonel of the 7th Michigan has been in command of the Brigade since the summer of 1862. He is an able officer, and should have a star instead of an eagle. It is a singular circumstance that Col. Hall's command has in six engagements met the Brigade of Gen. Barksdale, who fought his last battle at Gettysburg.

The Division has many trophies credited to it in Washington; many stands of colors were taken by its fearless soldiers. In the last Battle, the great Battle of Gettysburg, it took no less than thirteen, making one for each Regiment in the Division.

Roster of Medical Officers, Second Division, II Corps, May 10, 1864

2D DIVISION
J. F. Dyer,   Surgeon 19th Mass. Surgeon in Chief
                               2d Div. 2d Corps. Present.

1ST BRIGADE
G. B. Pratt,   Asst. Surgeon 19th Mass. Present
Nathan Hayward,   Surgeon 20th Mass. Surgeon in Chief
                               1st Brigade. Pres. Since died in St. Louis.
John L. Perry,   Asst. Surgeon 20th Mass.—present
                               Reported dead
G. Chaddock   Surgeon 7th Michigan—present
Wm. J. Burr   Surgeon 42d New York—present
R. P. H. Sawyer   Asst. Surgeon 42d New York—present
F. LeB. Monroe   Surgeon 15th Mass. Detailed to remain in
                               Wilderness, not pres
T. O. Cornish   Asst. Surg. 15th Mass.—present
J. Q. A. Hawes   Surgeon 19th Maine Permitted to go to
                               Fred'bg with Col. Connor, not
                               returned—absent without leave.*
                               * A poor officer—allowed to resign.
B. F. Sturgis   Asst. Surgeon 19th Maine—present
W. F. Randall   Asst. Surgeon 19th Maine—present
S. H. Plumb   Surgeon 82d New York—present
Wm. J. Darby   Asst. Surgeon 82d New York—Detailed
                               to go to F. with train today
John. T. Myers   Surgeon 59th New York—present
J. W. Hughes   Asst. Surgeon 59th New York—present
C. Miller   Surgeon 36th Wisconsin—present
E. A. Woodward   Asst. Surgeon 36th Wisconsin—present
Geo. D. Winch   Asst. Surgeon 36th Wisconsin—present

2D BRIGADE

F. F. Burmeister	Surgeon 69th Pa. detailed on 8th to go to F. with wounded—not returned (sub-detailed at City Pt.)
B. A. McNeil	Asst. Surgeon 69th Pa.—present
John Aiken	Surgeon 71st Pa. detailed to remain at Wilderness with wounded—not returned)
G. R. B. Robinson	Asst. Surgeon 71st Pa.—present
Martin Rizer	Surgeon 72d Pa. Surgeon in Chief 2nd Brigade—present
A. Stokes Jones	Asst. Surg. 72d Pa.—present
Justin Dwinelle	Surgeon 106th Pa.—present—in chg. 2d Div. Hosp—
E. D. Gates	Asst. Surg. 106th Pa.—present
S. A. Ingham	Surgeon 152d New York—present
E. L. Corbin	Asst. Surgeon 152d New York—present

3D BRIGADE

E. W. Morrison	Surgeon 4th Ohio—present
B. Gray	Asst. Surgeon 4th Ohio—present
J. L. Brenton	Surgeon 8th Ohio—present
J. S. Pollock	Asst. Surgeon 8th Ohio, absent in hospital for treatment
Isaac Scott	Surgeon 7th {West} Va.—present
W. T. Hicks	Asst. Surgeon 7th {West} Va.—detailed to go with W. to F. Not ret.
Geo. W. McCune	Surgeon 14th Ind. present
W. B. Squires	Asst. Surg. 14th Ind.—present
J. W. Maull	Surg. 1st Del. Surgeon in Chief 1st Brigade—Present
J. W. McCullough	Asst. Surgeon 1st Del. present
Fred J. Owens	Asst. Surgeon 1st Del. present
A. Satterthwaite	Surgeon 12th N.J. present
S. S. Miller	Asst. Surgeon 12th N.J. present
W. Gilman	Asst. Surgeon 12th N.J. present
F. A. Dudley	Surgeon 14th Conn. present
Charles Tomlinson	Asst. Surgeon 14th Conn. present
Levi Jewett	Asst. Surgeon 14th Conn. detailed to F. 7th not ret.
Francis Wafer	Asst. Surgeon 108th N.Y. present

Bernard Gesner	Surgeon 10th N.Y. present
R. H. Palmer	Asst. Surgeon 10th N.Y. present

4TH BRIGADE

M. F. Regan	Surgeon 164th N.Y. Surgeon in Chief 4th Brig.
J. L. Hasbrouck	Asst. Surgeon 164th N.Y. present
F{arand}	Wylie Surgeon 155th N.Y. present
{L. S. [or C.]} Comstock	Asst. Surgeon 155th N.Y. Absent without leave.
J. A. Spencer	Surgeon 155th N.Y. present
W. F. Nealis	Asst. Surgeon 155th N.Y. present
J. Douglas	Surgeon 170th N.Y. present
S. H. Olmstead	Asst. Surgeon 170th N.Y. present
S. S. Lounsberg	Asst. Surgeon 170th N.Y. present

Notes

ABBREVIATIONS

Atlas   Maj. George B. Davis, U.S. Army, et al., *Atlas to Accompany the Official Records of the Union and Confederate Armies* (Washington: Government Printing Office, 1891–95; reprinted as *The Official Military Atlas of the Civil War*, New York: Arno and Crown, 1978).

BDJ   *Boston Daily Journal* (evening edition).

B&L   Robert Underwood Johnson and Clarence Clough Buel, eds., *Battles and Leaders of the Civil War*, 4 vols. (New York: Century, 1887–88; reprint, New York: Thomas Yoseloff, 1956).

Confederate   Janet B. Hewett, ed., *The Roster of Confederate Soldiers, 1861–1865*, 16 vols. (Wilmington, N.C.: Broadfoot, 1995–96).

CWT   *Civil War Times Illustrated*.

DAB   *Dictionary of American Biography*, 22 vols. (New York: Charles Scribner's Sons, 1943–64).

MOLLUS,   Military Order of the Loyal Legion of the United States,
Register   *Register of the Commandery of the State of Massachusetts* (Cambridge: University Press, 1912).

MSH   U.S. Surgeon-General's Office, *The Medical and Surgical History of the War of the Rebellion*, 6 vols. (Washington: Government Printing Office, 1870–88; reprinted as *The Medical and Surgical History of the Civil War*, 15 vols. Wilmington, N.C.: Broadfoot, 1990–92).

NCAB   *National Cyclopaedia of American Biography*, 53 vols. (New York: J. T. White, 1893–1984).

OR   U.S. War Department, *The War of the Rebellion: A Compilation of the Official Records of the Union and Confederate Armies*, 128 vols. (Washington: Government Printing Office, 1880–1901; reprint, Harrisburg, Pa.: National Historical Society, 1985). References are to series 1 unless otherwise indicated.

233

Abbreviations

OR Supp   Janet B. Hewett et al., eds., *Supplement to the Official Records of the Union and Confederate Armies*, 100 vols. (Wilmington, N.C.: Broadfoot, 1994–2001).

RMV   Adjutant-General's Office, *Record of the Massachusetts Volunteers, 1861–1865*, 2 vols. (Boston: Wright and Potter, 1868–70).

Surgeons   Newton Allen Strait, comp., *Roster of All Regimental Surgeons and Assistant Surgeons in the Late War* (1882; reprinted as *Roster of Regimental Surgeons and Assistant Surgeons in the U.S. Army Medical Department during the Civil War*, ed. F. Terry Hambrecht (Gaithersburg, Md.: Olde Soldier Books, 1989).

Union   Janet B. Hewett, ed., *The Roster of Union Soldiers, 1861–1865*, 33 vols. (Wilmington, N.C.: Broadfoot, 1997–2001).

VMHB   *Virginia Magazine of History and Biography*.

INTRODUCTION

1. Charles Dyer's family numbered eight people, including a boy under five, the future surgeon. U.S. Bureau of the Census, 1830 Census, Washington County, Maine, Eastport, roll 47, frame 304, line 21 [hereafter cited as 1830 Census]. Eastport's population in 1830, frame 309, was 2,450, including 583 aliens and 19 free blacks. F[ranklin] G. Dyer and George Burton Dyer, comps., "Genealogy Snow-Dyer," manuscript without pagination, in family's possession [cited hereafter as "Genealogy"]; *General Catalogue of Bowdoin College and the Medical School of Maine: A Biographical Record of Alumni and Officers, 1749–1950* (Brunswick, Maine: Bowdoin College, 1950), 465 [hereafter cited as *Bowdoin Alumni*]; "Obituary: Dr. Jonah Franklin Dyer," *Cape Ann Bulletin* (Gloucester, Mass.), Feb. 12, 1879 [hereafter cited as "Obituary"].

2. "Genealogy"; Nancy D. Witmer to author, Anderson, S.C., Mar. 19, 1995.

3. "Genealogy"; U.S. Bureau of the Census, 1840 Census, roll 152, p. 87 [hereafter cited as 1840 Census].

4. "Genealogy." Charles Dyer was engaged in manufactures and trades. 1840 Census, p. 88, line 21, p. 73. Eastport's population had grown to 2,876 by that time.

5. William Snow Dyer to J. Franklin Dyer, Machias, Feb. 1, 1846. All letters cited are held by the family in their private collection and were written in Eastport (often Machias in William's case) unless otherwise indicated. Aaron Hayden was in his fifties and headed the family. 1830 Census, p. 296, line 7.

6. "Genealogy." Both of Frank's older brothers appear on the 1840 Census, with their parents and siblings, as males aged fifteen but under twenty. 1840 Census, p. 88, line 21. William's letter of November 15, 1846, was addressed to Mr. J. F. Dyer. It begins "Dear brother" and urges him to pursue medical studies: "So Frank you must go ahead." Earlier letters generally use his first name, Jonah, as do a few after this date. He was known professionally as J. Franklin Dyer or, more rarely, J. F. Dyer. He signed his letters to Maria "Frank."

7. Frank to Maria, Stevensburg, Va., Apr. 25 [26?], 1864.

8. Charles to Frank, Feb. 9, 1848; George B. Dyer to Frank, Apr. 16,

1846; William to Frank, Machias, Nov. 15, 1846. There were two women in the household unaccounted for in the family history, probably servants. 1840 Census, p. 88, line 21. On Stephen Hopkins and his servant problem, see John Demos, *A Little Commonwealth: Family Life in Plymouth Colony* (New York: Oxford University Press, 1970), 109–10.

9. William to Frank, Machias, Feb. 1, 1846.

10. Hannah Snow Dyer to Frank, July 31, 1846, July 24, 1847.

11. Charles to Frank, Aug. 14, 1846.

12. "Genealogy"; J. G. Blanchard to Frank, Feb. 17, 1848.

13. William to Frank, Machias, May 21, 1846.

14. Charles to Frank, July 21, 1846; William to Frank, Machias, Nov. 15, 1846.

15. William to Frank, Milwaukee, Dec. 29, 1847.

16. Charles to Frank, Apr. 15, 1848.

17. "Genealogy"; William to Frank, Mar. 23, 1848, July 17, Aug. 11, 29, 1849; James A. Gleason to Frank, Apr. 24, 1848; J. G. Blanchard to Frank, May 7, 1848; Charles to Frank, June 1, 1849. Both Erastus Richardson and William Billings were under forty. See 1830 Census, pp. 294–95.

18. Charles to Frank, Mar. 19, 1848. This letter announced that he and a partner had bought out the firm of Charles H. Hayden. Both Aaron Hayden, now in his sixties, and the younger Hayden were in commerce along with another family member during this decade. 1840 Census, p. 87, lines 17–18. The "Genealogy" states that Charles bought the Hayden store and wharf when he was twenty-four, which would have been in 1845–46, but this may be in error.

19. Dyer studied medicine in South Berwick under Dr. Charles T. Trafton of the firm S. R. Philbrick and Trafton, which had a Boston store at 160 Washington Street. 1840 Census, York County, Maine, South Berwick, roll 155, p. 206, line 7. Frank's letters mention another Trafton, probably the son, Augustus, who was living in the same household and also worked in the South Berwick pharmacy. It is unclear when Dyer decided to apprentice himself as an apothecary and whether that was his ultimate goal at the time or a step toward medical school and a degree. A Boston merchant and friend, J. D. Beckford, wrote to him as early as January 7, 1846, asking "how goes Medicine?" Hannah S. Dyer to Frank, July 29, 31, 1846; C. T. Trafton to Frank, South Berwick, Maine, Aug. 7, 1847.

20. Dr. Charles Trafton, letter of reference, South Berwick, York County, Maine, Feb. 12, 1848; Dr. Erastus Richardson, letters of reference, Eastport, Jan. 30, Feb. 14, 1849; Medical School of Maine, Historical Records and Files, 1820–1921, Bowdoin College Archives, Brunswick, Maine.

21. Charles C. Tyler to Frank, Sept. 2, 1846.

22. J. F. Dyer to J. Woodman Emery, South Berwick, Aug. 28, 1847.

23. Charles to Frank, Jan. 2, 14, Feb. 9, Mar. 19, Apr. 15, 20, 1848; Hannah to Frank, Jan. 20, 1848; William to Frank, Milwaukee, Jan. 23, 25, 1848; and Eastport, Mar. 23, 1848; Alice Rains Trulock, *In the Hands of Providence: Joshua L. Chamberlain and the American Civil War* (Chapel Hill: University of North Carolina Press, 1992), 37. Harriet Beecher Stowe and three of her children came to Brunswick in May 1850, when Dyer was already in Boston starting his medical practice. Thomas F. Gossett, *Uncle Tom's Cabin and American Culture* (Dallas: Southern Methodist University Press, 1985), 63.

24. J. G. Blanchard to Frank, Feb. 17, 1848. This was the first letter addressed to him at Brunswick.

25. William to Frank, Mar. 23, 1848; George W. Woodhouse to Frank, Dover, N.H., Feb. 12, 1849.

26. Prof. Nathan S. Cleaveland to Frank, Brunswick, Dec. 20, 1848; Susan Ravdin, assistant, Special Collections, The Library, Bowdoin College, to author, Aug. 28, 1995; votes of two doctors on thirteen candidates for M.D., Mar. 21, 1849, and n.d., Bowdoin College Archives. Two years later Cleaveland appeared on the census as a twenty-nine-year-old apothecary living with his seventy-year-old father, Parker Cleaveland, a professor at Bowdoin. U.S. Bureau of the Census, 1850 Census, Cumberland County, Maine, Brunswick, roll 251, p. 241, family 700.

27. Dr. Ephraim Marston, letter of reference, Boston, Aug. 14, 1849, Medical School of Maine Historical Records, Bowdoin College Archives; J. F. Robinson to Dr. J. F. Dyer, Richmond Corner, Maine, July 17, 1849; Charles to Frank, June 1, 1849; William to Frank, Aug. 11, 29, 1849; Prof. N. S. Cleaveland to J. F. Dyer, M.D., Brunswick, Sept. 6, 1849; "Day Book," E. Marston and J. F. Dyer, Boston, May 28, 1849–Oct. 9, 1850, in family's possession.

28. "Obituary"; "Genealogy"; William to Frank, Aug. 11, 1849; correspondence from Elizabeth French to Frank Dyer, June–Dec. 1854.

29. Charles to Frank, July 21, 1846; William to Frank, Nov. 15, 1846; F. P. Philbrick to Frank, Boston, Apr. 11, 1848.

30. Charles C. Tyler to Frank, Sept. 2, 1846; Charles to Frank, Mar. 4, 1847.

31. Charles to Frank, Feb. 9, 1848; Frank to J. Woodman Emery, South Berwick, Aug. 28, 1847; S. R. Byram to Frank, Eastport, June 1, 1846; W. Wilson Deverett to Frank, Durham, N.H., Jan. 16, 1849.

32. "Day Book," July 12, 1851–Dec. 31, 1852; marriage record, 1853, vol. 69, p. 189, roll 7, Massachusetts Archives; "Genealogy"; correspondence

from Elizabeth French to Frank Dyer, June 2, Nov. 9, Dec. 30, 1854, and n.d.

33. Marriage record, 1854, vol. 78, p. 153, marriage 66, roll 8; obituary of Mrs. Maria B. (Davis) Dyer, *Gloucester Daily Times*, June 29, 1925; Frank to Maria, near Morrisville, Va., Aug. 27, 1863; "Genealogy."

34. Frank to Maria, Headquarters, Second Division, II Corps, Stevensburg, Va., Apr. 27, 1864.

35. Frank to Maria, Stevensburg, Va., Apr. 7, 1864; "Obituary"; *Gloucester Daily Times*, June 27, 1925; Maria Dyer, diary, Apr. 26, 1886, Annisquam Historical Society, Annisquam, Mass.

36. Frank to Maria, Baltimore, Mar. 18, 1864.

37. Dyer's service was credited to the adjacent town of Rockport rather than Gloucester, but a large proportion of its military-age males served. *RMV*, 2:300. Perhaps he took the $20 bounty paid by the much smaller town (raised in 1862 to $125 and then to $200), which had a population of 3,237 against Gloucester's 10,904. William Schouler, *A History of Massachusetts in the Civil War*, 2 vols. (Boston: By the author, 1871), 2:191–94, 230–32. Only fourteen other men credited to Gloucester served in the Nineteenth Massachusetts, all but one in Companies F and H. *RMV*, 2:300–331. A broadside compiled by the monumental committee of Grand Army of the Republic Post 45 has the names of 1,262 men and confirms this number. "Gloucester in the Rebellion," Houghton Library, Harvard University. Gloucester's selectmen reported a total of 852 men for the war in 1866, but their figure did not reflect those in the navy or regular army, who are listed on the broadside. See also "Genealogy"; "Obituary"; and Ernest Linden Waitt, comp., *History of the Nineteenth Regiment Massachusetts Volunteer Infantry, 1861–1865* (Salem, Mass.: Salem, 1906; reprint, Baltimore: Butternut and Blue, 1988), 1–5, 383. Waitt assigns Dyer to Companies F and G.

38. George Burton Dyer enlisted in the Ninth Maine September 10, 1862, and was promoted to second lieutenant June 23, 1862, to captain August 22, 1864, and to major October 4, 1864. He mustered out July 13, 1865, with brevets as lieutenant colonel and colonel, U.S. Volunteers, March 13, 1865, "for gallant and meritorious services during the War." MOLLUS, *Register*, 136.

William Snow Dyer does not appear in the *Roster of Union Soldiers* or the *Roster of Regimental Surgeons and Assistant Surgeons*. His compiled service record has not been found, probably because he was a contract surgeon. He appears once in the *Medical and Surgical History of the Civil War* as an acting assistant surgeon who operated successfully on a private in the Thirty-second Missouri but is not in the "Record of Events for Thirty-second Missouri Infantry, August 1862–October 1864." *MSH*, 10:778; *OR Supp*, 37:643–89. Pvt. William Dyer, Company I, a Tennessee native, was not the surgeon's brother; he died of disease March 5, 1863. Compiled Service Records, Record Group 94, National Archives and Record Administration. Dyer's letter of December 6, 1863, reported that William had a farm forty-seven miles from St. Louis near Tyrone.

Heber James Davis enlisted in Company E, First New Hampshire, May 2, 1861, and mustered out August 9, 1861. He reenlisted in the Seventh New Hampshire as a sergeant December 11, 1861, serving in Companies K, I, and B; was promoted to second lieutenant July 19, 1863; and to first lieutenant March 27, 1864. Davis was discharged March 27, 1865. MOLLUS, *Register*, 115; *Union*, 1:408. See also "Genealogy"; and references to all three men in the Dyer family letters.

39. Waitt, *Nineteenth Massachusetts*, 8.

40. See chapter 3, entry dated Sept. 23, 1862.

41. See chapter 6, entry dated May 2, 1863.

42. Waitt, *Nineteenth Massachusetts*, 282–302; Capt. John G. B. Adams, *Reminiscences of the Nineteenth Massachusetts Regiment* (Boston: Wright and Potter, 1899), 78–84; Kenneth C. Turino, ed., *The Civil War Diary of Lieut. J. E. Hodgkins* (Camden, Maine: Picton, 1994), xvii, 71–78.

43. Frank to Maria, near Petersburg, Va., June 23, 1864; *BDJ*, June 30, 1864; Waitt, *Nineteenth Massachusetts*, 326–35.

44. Fielding H. Garrison, *John Shaw Billings: A Memoir* (New York: G. P. Putnam's Sons, Knickerbocker Press, 1915), 1–160; *Personal Memoirs of John H. Brinton, Civil War Surgeon, 1861–1865* (New York: Neale, 1914; reprint, Carbondale: Southern Illinois University Press, 1996); John Michael Priest et al., eds., *One Surgeon's Private War: Dr. William W. Potter of the 57th New York* (Buffalo: n.p., 1888; reprint, Shippensburg, Pa.: White Mane, 1996); James M. Greiner, Janet L. Coryell, and James R. Smither, eds., *A Surgeon's Civil War: The Letters and Diary of Daniel M. Holt, M.D.* (Kent, Ohio: Kent State University Press, 1994); Richard R. Duncan, ed., *Alexander Neil and the Last Shenandoah Valley Campaign* (Shippensburg, Pa.: White Mane, 1996); Peter Josyph, ed., *The Wounded River: The Civil War Letters of John Vance Lauderdale, M.D.* (East Lansing: Michigan State University Press, 1993); Martha Derby Perry, comp., *Letters from a Surgeon of the Civil War* (Boston: Little, Brown, 1906); Paul Fatout, ed., *Letters of a Civil War Surgeon* (West Lafayette, Ind.: Purdue University Studies, Humanities Series, 1961); Spencer Glasgow Welch, *A Confederate Surgeon's Letters to His Wife* (New York: Neale, 1911; reprint, Marietta, Ga.: Continental, 1954); John Allan Wyeth, *With Sabre and Scalpel* (New York: Harper and Brothers, 1914); William R. Scaife, ed.,

Confederate Surgeon: Civil War Record of Dr. William L. Scaife, 4th ed. (Atlanta: By the author, 1985); Glenn L. McMullen, ed., *A Surgeon with Stonewall Jackson: The Civil War Letters of Dr. Harvey Black* (Baltimore: Butternut and Blue, 1995); Peter W. Houck, ed., *Confederate Surgeon: The Personal Recollections of E. A. Craighill* (Lynchburg: H. E. Howard, 1989); Donald B. Koonce, ed., *Doctor to the Front: The Recollections of Confederate Surgeon Thomas Fanning Wood* (Knoxville: University of Tennessee Press, 2000).

45. On Buchanan, see *MSH*, 11:258, case 1088 ("injuries of the lower extremities"); Waitt, *Nineteenth Massachusetts*, 288, 322, 374; and *RMV*, 2:326. On Kennelly, see *MSH*, 10:861, case 1790 ("fatal primary excisions at the elbow").

46. *MSH*, 7:175 (Simms), 8:462, 9:20, 78, 100, 307, 415, 10:496, 632, 709, 713 (two), 722, 751 (two), 767, 848, 935, 969, 11:82, 86, 87, 203, 307, 435.

47. *MSH*, 6:683–87.

48. *MSH*, 6:832–40, 5:249–50, 254–57, 309.

NOTE ON EDITORIAL METHOD
1. See chapter 15, entry dated December 7, 1864.

1. "A BLUNDER HAS BEEN MADE"
   1. Schouler, *Massachusetts in the Civil War*, 1:164–69, 188–90.
   2. Essex County: north of Boston, along the New Hampshire border; its population in 1860 was 165,611. Essex County sent an estimated 20,805 men to the Union army. Schouler, *Massachusetts in the Civil War*, 2:171–72.
   3. William Johnson Dale was "a gentleman who, in civil life, during the Rebellion, was specially distinguished for conspicuous and consistent loyalty. Devoted and earnest in all loyal service. He was surgeon general (colonel), state of Massachusetts, June 13, 1861; surgeon general (brigadier general), October 7, 1863; acting medical director, U.S.A., and acting assistant surgeon, U.S.A., 1861–1865; died at North Andover, Massachusetts, October 7, 1903." MOLLUS, *Register*, 113. Dale supported Dyer's bid for a political post after leaving the army, and attended his funeral.
   4. Lynnfield's population in 1860 was 866.
   5. See Thomas Kirwan, comp., and Henry Splaine, ed., *Memorial History of the Seventeenth Regiment Massachusetts Infantry in the Civil War from 1861–1865* (Salem, Mass.: Salem, 1911); Capt. John G. B. Adams has Col. Lyman Dyke commanding the Seventeenth in July. *Reminiscences*, 3. But he does not appear with that regiment in *Massachusetts Soldiers, Sailors, and Marines in the Civil War* (Norwood, Mass.: Norwood, 1931), 2:270–71.

6. After going to the Seventeenth, Hinds transferred to the Twelfth Massachusetts in May 1863.

7. Colonel Hinks: Col. (later Brig. Gen.) Edward Ward Hinks (1830–94), Eighth Massachusetts Veteran Militia, sent to the Nineteenth when his old unit mustered out and led troops on Harrison's Island during Ball's Bluff and the brigade after Brig. Gen. Frederick Lander's and Col. William Lee's capture. Like Dyer, he was a Maine native and a printer, and he later commanded black soldiers in the Army of the James, 1864–65. In 1860 he was a clerk with $500 in personal property. U.S. Bureau of the Census, 1860 Census, Essex County, Mass., City of Lynn, Sixth Ward, roll 495, p. 427, family 3,650.

A. F. Devereaux: Lt. Col. Arthur F. Devereux.

John C. Chadwick: Capt. John C. Chadwick, Company C, later acting assistant adjutant general at brigade headquarters for a lengthy period; discharged for promotion to Ullmann's brigade, Corps d'Afrique, Department of the Gulf, in spring 1863.

8. Levi Shaw: Joseph Levi Shaw.

9. Dr. J. N. Willard: Dr. Josiah N. Willard, Boston.

10. Mrs. Dyer and Frank: Maria Davis Dyer, his wife, and Frank, their son; Hancock: Maria's home at the time of their marriage, in south-central New Hampshire between Keene and Manchester. She visited her family there.

11. "Traps": the knapsack and other gear of a Civil War soldier.

12. Meridian Hill, between Fifteenth and Sixteenth and W and Euclid Streets, due north of the White House, was the site of Columbian College. Its main building became a military hospital.

13. The regiment traveled by rail down the coast to Boston.

14. Massachusetts regiments usually departed from Boston, often going to New York via steamship from Fall River down Narragansett Bay to Long Island Sound.

15. Amboy: a New Jersey rail junction just west of Staten Island; poor cars: railway passenger coaches, common period usage.

16. Many accounts by Union soldiers praise the reception offered them in Philadelphia.

17. A pro-Confederate mob attacked the Sixth Massachusetts as it marched through Baltimore between railroad stations; troops and civilians died. Brig. Gen. Benjamin F. Butler occupied the city May 13, 1861. It had been under martial law since then.

18. Dyer's attitude toward and concern for enlisted men, including the need for a supply of fresh vegetables to prevent scurvy, changed significantly during the Peninsula campaign. See chapter 2, entries starting June 14, 1862.

19. Poolesville: a small town in Montgomery County, Maryland, northwest of Washington and due east of Leesburg, Virginia, and Ball's Bluff, less than three miles from the Potomac River.

Brig. Gen. Frederick West Lander (1821–62) of Salem, Second Brigade, Stone's division was wounded at Ball's Bluff. After recovering, he died later in the war of pneumonia. See Gary L. Ecelbarger, *Frederick W. Lander: The Great Natural American Soldier* (Baton Rouge: Louisiana State University Press, 2000).

20. He had malaria, which accounted for six percent of Union patients by this time. George Worthington Adams, *Doctors in Blue* (New York: Henry Schuman, 1952), 14. By 1864 he had stopped taking quinine, the accepted treatment, and was dosing himself with tea and fresh vegetables.

21. Dr. Crosby: Alpheus B. Crosby was brigade surgeon. *OR*, 5:86, 89, 11:916.

22. Dr. Bryant: Henry Bryant, forty-one, of Boston, promoted to brigade surgeon September 19, 1861. George A. Bruce, *The Twentieth Regiment of Massachusetts Volunteer Infantry* (1906; reprint, Baltimore: Butternut and Blue, 1988), 445 [hereafter cited as Bruce, *Twentieth Massachusetts*].

23. Camp Benton: near Edwards Ferry; probably named for Thomas Hart Benton (1782–1858), Jacksonian Democrat and Missouri Unionist.

24. A distinguished unit organized August 1861, the Seventh Michigan had an epidemic of measles, which Dyer was later credited with curtailing. It was in the Third and then the Second Brigade, Second Division, II Corps and served throughout the war.

25. Lieutenant Bishop: Second Lt. Edward P. Bishop, Company K, Tiger Fire Zouaves, Boston.

26. Dyer describes the regiment in a letter home, apparently for a newspaper: "Through the untiring exertions of Colonel Hinks, who is emphatically a working man, the general condition of the regiment has vastly improved: cleanliness and order are strictly enforced. Under the superintendence of Lieut. Col. Devereux, the companies have acquired a proficiency in drill not surpassed by many older troops. Under charge of Major Howe, the important guard duties of the guard are well attended to. Other department are in good hands, and a system of strict accountability is rigidly enforced." Quoted in Waitt, *Nineteenth Massachusetts*, 16.

27. The Seventeenth Massachusetts served in Baltimore and on the Delmarva Peninsula under Maj. Gen. John A. Dix during the latter part of 1861. *OR*, 5:425, 428, 666.

28. The men were on picket duty along the Potomac. Second Lt. Henry L. Abbott, Twentieth Massachusetts, wrote from Camp Benton September 24 that the Confederate "pickets are very friendly" and Septem-

ber 26 that "the pickets are very friendly & don't fire on each other." Robert Garth Scott, ed., *Fallen Leaves: The Civil War Letters of Major Henry Livermore Abbott* (Kent, Ohio: Kent State University Press, 1991), 48, 54.

29. General Banks: Maj. Gen. Nathaniel P. Banks (1816–94); General Stone: Brig. Gen. Charles P. Stone (1824–87), blamed for the disaster at Ball's Bluff.

30. Selden's Island: a long narrow island in the Potomac below Edwards Ferry and due south of Poolesville also known as Lee's Island.

31. Edwards Ferry: opposite the point where Goose Creek joins the Potomac.

towpath: this is the towpath of the Chesapeake and Ohio Canal.

Andrews Sharpshooters: First Company, Massachusetts Volunteer Sharpshooters, Capt. John Saunders, attached to the Fifteenth, Nineteenth, and Twentieth Massachusetts; named for Governor Andrew. George Bruce refers to them as the First Massachusetts. *Twentieth Massachusetts*, 17. Dyer always calls them "Andrews Sharpshooters." In addition, see Turino, *Diary of Lieut. J. E. Hodgkins*, 91 n.141.

32. See Byron Farwell, *Ball's Bluff* (McLean, Va.: EPM Publications, 1990).

33. Fifteenth Massachusetts: organized in Worcester County, it left the state August 8, 1861. See Gregory A. Coco, ed., *From Ball's Bluff to Gettysburg* (Gettysburg: Thomas, 1994).

Baker's California regiment: California senator and Lincoln friend Col. Edward D. Baker, whose First California became the Seventy-first Pennsylvania and was recruited mainly in Philadelphia.

Tammany regiment: Forty-second New York, Col. Milton Cogswell commanding.

Vaughn's Rhode Island guns: Capt. Thomas Vaughan, Battery B, First Rhode Island Artillery.

34. Some men of the Nineteenth helped pole the scows to bring survivors back across the river, but many in the regiment were demoralized by the sight of hundreds of dead and wounded.

35. Colonel Lee: William R. Lee (ca. 1804–91).

Adjutant Revere: Maj. Paul Joseph Revere. Bruce, *Twentieth Massachusetts*, 446. Byron Farwell lists Lt. Charles (Lawrence) Peirson as adjutant. *Ball's Bluff*, 75, 109.

Asst. Surgeon Revere: Dr. Edward H. R. Revere. Both he and Major Revere were grandsons of the Revolutionary War hero.

36. Second Lt. James G. C. Dodge of Boston, Company F, Nineteenth Massachusetts.

37. Colonel Burt: Erasmus R. Burt, wounded October 21, died five days later. Farwell, *Ball's Bluff*, 35, 86, 142.

38. Capt. Thomas W. Thurman, Thirteenth Mississippi, Company D, was reported dangerously wounded and captured by his colonel on December 11, 1862, at Fredericksburg. His commanding officer at Ball's Bluff was Col. William Barksdale. Dyer errs about the unit; the Twentieth Mississippi was not at Fredericksburg. *Confederate*, 15:249.

39. General Evans: Col. Nathan George "Shanks" Evans (1824–68), made brigadier general, ranking from the date of the battle.

40. Lieutenant Young: Lt. Francis G. Young.

41. Farwell, *Ball's Bluff*, 125–26.

42. Colonel Devens: Charles Devens Jr. (1820–91), original colonel of the Fifteenth Massachusetts.

Lt. Colonel Palfrey: Lt. Col. Francis Winthrop Palfrey (1831–89), Twentieth Massachusetts.

Mr. Howard: Joseph Howard Jr. (1833–1908), a controversial reporter for the *New York Times*. Louis M. Starr, *Bohemian Brigade: Civil War Newsmen in Action* (1954; reprint, Madison: University of Wisconsin Press, 1987), 43, 355.

Mr. William D. Miller: has not been identified.

Colonel Bruce: Lt. Col. Robert Bruce, Second Maryland Potomac Home Brigade, VIII Corps, Middle Department, on detached service commanding a post at Springfield, Virginia. Other companies of his command were scattered along the upper Potomac. Field and Staff Muster Roll, Dec. 31, 1861, Compiled Service Records, Record Group 94, National Archives and Record Administration; *OR*, 19(2):338, 523.

43. Darnestown is between Rockville and Poolesville, Maryland.

44. Seneca: a Potomac village midway between Poolesville and Rockville; the regiment's nearby camp was Muddy Branch.

45. A Virginia town south of the Potomac along the Leesburg-Washington Road.

46. Van Alen cavalry: Col. James H. Van Alen, Third New York Cavalry.

47. Judge Bowie: Richard Jones Bowie (1807–81), a leading Montgomery County lawyer and Whig, served in the Maryland senate (1836–38), U.S. Congress (1849–53), and state court of appeals (1861–67) as its chief judge. *NCAB*, 13:152.

Mrs. Hinks: Anne R. Hinks, a Massachusetts native, was almost twenty-four. U.S. Bureau of the Census, 1860 Census, Essex County, Mass., City of Lynn, Sixth Ward, roll 495, p. 427, family 3,650. Their son, Anson B. Hicks, was nearly five.

48. The original chaplain, Rev. Joseph C. Cromack, went to the Twenty-second Massachusetts, November 8, 1861; Rev. Ezra D. Winslow joined the regiment December 1.

49. Captain Wass: Capt. Ansel Dyer Wass eventually commanded the

Nineteenth Massachusetts, though in name only as far as Dyer was concerned. He was nearly always sick or on sick leave and missed some of the heaviest fighting of the war. In fairness to him, Wass was wounded during the Seven Days, at Gettysburg, and at Bealeton (a minor wound) in 1864. Dyer may have been critical of him if the two men were related. Henry Abbott called Wass a "rowdy with a dyed mustache" who liked to tell dirty stories, "devlish green and devlish saucy." Scott, *Fallen Leaves*, 209; Waitt, *Nineteenth Massachusetts*, 97, 257, 327.

"Tigers": Company K (Boston Tiger Fire Zouaves), Nineteenth Massachusetts.

50. Rimback: Lewis Rimback (or Rimbach) of Boston, newly appointed bandmaster.

51. McClellan ordered Stone's arrest February 8, 1862.

52. Brig. Gen. "Uncle" John Sedgwick (1813–64) led the Second Division, II Corps, during the Peninsula Campaign and was a favorite with the troops.

53. Napoleon Jackson Tecumseh Dana (1822–1905), Third Brigade, Second Division, II Corps.

54. Dr. Alexander N. Dougherty, later brevet lieutenant colonel, U.S. Volunteers, and medical director of the Right Grand Division and I Corps.

55. General Gorman: Brig. Gen. Willis Arnold Gorman (1816–76), First Brigade, Second Division, II Corps.

56. Capt. Charles Stewart: Adolphus Frederick Charles William Vane-Tempest, late of the Scots Fusilier Guards, a Crimean War veteran. Farwell, *Ball's Bluff*, 98.

57. Secretary Stanton's letters: probably the widely circulated public letters Secretary of War Edwin Stanton sent to Charles A. Dana, managing editor of the *New York Tribune*, at least one of which appeared there, and possibly in the *Washington Star* as well, February 18–23, 1862. Stanton applauded then Brig. Gen. Ulysses Grant's determination at Fort Donelson and criticized McClellan. See Benjamin P. Thomas and Harold M. Hyman, eds., *Stanton* (New York: Knopf, 1962), 174 and n. 5.

58. The Loudoun County, Virginia, seat, close to Ball's Bluff.

59. Maj. Gen. Thomas "Stonewall" Jackson had evacuated Winchester earlier; Kernstown was fought March 23.

60. Berryville: the Clarke County, Virginia, seat, due west of Loudoun County.

2. "WE HAVE BEEN OBLIGED TO RETREAT"

1. Bolivar: a village on the Baltimore and Ohio Railroad across the Potomac from Harpers Ferry.

2. This was the first battle of Kernstown, fought March 23 south of Winchester, the beginning of Jackson's Valley campaign. Maj. Gen. Nathaniel Banks had the V Corps, which was detached from McClellan's army.

3. The *North America* was a U.S. Army transport in regular service on the Potomac used during the Peninsula campaign. Its captain told a man in the Nineteenth Massachusetts that the ship would have sunk in two hours had he not turned back. It nearly sank again in May 1863 off North Carolina. Cpl. Horace Lakeman to mother [Mrs. E. K. Lakeman], camp near Hampton, Va., Apr. 2, 1862, Horace Lakeman (1840–62) Letters, 1859–62, Phillips Library, Peabody Essex Museum, Salem, Mass.

4. The hotel was erected as the centerpiece of a seaside resort by William Cost Johnson in 1857, mortgaged at the start of the war, and offered to the government for hospital use in 1862. Lakeman called it "a very stylish hotel" with "fifty or more snug little buildings calculated for sleeping apartments for the guests . . . the best quarters we have enjoyed yet." Lakeman to mother, Apr. 2, 1862.

5. Hampton's own residents burned the town in August 1861 to prevent occupation by troops from Fort Monroe.

6. The css *Virginia*, the former uss *Merrimac*, had been destroyed to prevent her capture when the Confederates evacuated Norfolk, March 9, 1862.

7. Little Bethel: a church northwest of Hampton along the road to Big Bethel and Yorktown.

Heintzelman's division: Maj. Gen. Samuel Heintzelman now led the III Corps; two of the brigades in his old division, plus the 63d and 105th Pennsylvania were in Brig. Gen. Charles S. Hamilton's division. *OR*, 5:718, 11(1):282.

8. Howard's Branch: an arm of the Poquoson River.

9. General Porter: Brig. Gen. Fitz John Porter (1822–1901), First Division, III Corps, until assuming command of the V Corps in May, was a favorite of McClellan.

General Sumner: Brig. Gen. Edwin V. Sumner (1797–1863) led the II Corps in 1862.

General Keyes: Brig. Gen. Erasmus D. Keyes (1810–95) led the IV Corps.

10. Maj. Gen. John B. Magruder's line ran along the Warwick River, a tributary of the James that rises on the far side of the Peninsula near Yorktown. Ship Point on the Poquoson's northwest bank was well outside the Rebel works.

11. Brig. Gen. William T. H. Brooks (1821–70) led the Second, or Vermont, Brigade, Second Division, VI Corps; originally comprising the

Second through Sixth Vermont. Mark Boatner calls it the only brigade in the war to maintain its original organization, one of the few made up of men from one state, and one that suffered the war's highest losses. Boatner, *Dictionary*, 869.

12. Another bout with malaria.

13. Maj. Gen. Irwin McDowell, I Corps, with his recently created Army of the Rappahannock, was to move south from Washington toward Richmond while McClellan advanced up the Peninsula.

14. William Francis Bartlett (1840–76) of Haverhill, Harvard class of 1862, enlisted April 14, 1861, was wounded three times, led black troops, and was captured at the Crater. Retired with a brevet as major general, U.S. Volunteers. See Bruce, *Twentieth Massachusetts*, 84–85; and Scott, *Fallen Leaves*, 112.

15. McClellan claimed credit, reporting to Stanton that Company H, First Massachusetts (Hooker's division, III Corps) had taken an outpost by assault, capturing twelve prisoners and losing three killed, one mortally wounded, and twelve wounded. *OR*, 11(1):382–83. For McClellan's Peninsula plan, which started at Fort Monroe (as opposed to his overland plan from northern Virginia, based at Urbana), see Stephen W. Sears, *To the Gates of Richmond* (New York: Ticknor and Fields, 1992), chaps. 1–2.

16. George Bruce claimed the honor for his unit, but Dyer is supported by Henry Abbott of the Twentieth Massachusetts. Bruce, *Twentieth Massachusetts*, 85–86; Scott, *Fallen Leaves*, 113.

17. Yorktown peaked as a tobacco port about 1700 but remained the seat of York County. The town was the site of the siege of Cornwallis's army in 1781 and his surrender to Washington.

18. On Confederate land mines at Yorktown and on the retreat to Richmond, see Milton F. Perry, *Infernal Machines* (Baton Rouge: Louisiana State University Press, 1965), 20–27.

19. The *Vanderbilt*: rated as a coastal steamer by Frederick Law Olmsted of the Sanitary Commission and not to be sent outside the Chesapeake Bay. Katharine Prescott Wormeley, *The Other Side of War: On the Hospital Transports with the Army of the Potomac* (1889; reprint, Gansevoort, N.Y.: Cornerhouse, 1998), app. D.

West Point: a town in King William County at the head of the York River, situated between its tributaries, the Pamunkey and the Mattaponi, and a port of entry since 1691. Called the Point in the late colonial era, "West" was added in honor of a local family.

20. Eltham was a large plantation house in New Kent County inland beyond West Point. Paul Wilstach, *Tidewater Virginia* (Indianapolis: Bobbs-Merrill, 1929), 223.

21. A "heavy skirmish" rather than a full battle, Maj. Gen. William B.

Franklin's caution May 7, along with the larger action at Williamsburg, allowed the Rebel army to continue its retreat to Richmond. Union casualties were 186, Confederate, 48. Sears, *Gates of Richmond*, 85–86.

22. At Williamsburg May 4–5 the Union advance caught the Confederate rear guard. Dyer's estimate of Union losses is close to McClellan's figure of 2,239. See David and Earl C. Hastings Jr., *A Pitiless Rain: The Battle of Williamsburg, 1862* (Shippensburg, Pa.: White Mane, 1997), 117.

23. Cumberland: a village on the Pamunkey north of New Kent Court House. See appendix 1 for Dyer's letter to Massachusetts treasurer H. K. Oliver, written from this location the previous day.

24. Mayo: a prominent local family; an ancestor laid out the site of Richmond for William Byrd II. Dr. Mayo lived northwest of the courthouse near Cedar Hill. *Atlas*, plate 92:1.

25. White House: the home of Martha Custis and site of her marriage to George Washington, it passed to the Lee family and burned during the Union occupation. McClellan allowed Mrs. Lee to go to Richmond. The plantation was several miles upriver from West Point, on the south bank of the Pamunkey, a short distance below the tracks of the Richmond and York River Railroad. It became a major supply depot for this phase of the campaign.

26. He went southwest. Bottom's Bridge was a major crossing of the Chickahominy River, the only vehicular bridge in a span of ten miles, and twelve miles east of Richmond.

27. Maj. Gen. Fitz John Porter, the new V Corps commander, led a reconnaissance in force to Hanover Court House, fourteen miles north. He claimed almost 1,000 Confederate casualties against 355 Union.

28. Fair Oaks, or Seven Pines, May 31–June 1, 1862.

29. "Grape vine bridge": an ingenious structure that briefly spanned the Chickahominy about three miles north of Seven Pines, Dyer called it Sumner's because that general insisted on crossing it as it was about to collapse. Sears, *Gates of Richmond*, 135–36.

30. Maj. Gen. Silas Casey (1807–82), Third Division, IV Corps, suffered heavy casualties at Fair Oaks, May 31, 1862, at least partly because of a surprise night attack by the Confederates. Waitt, *Nineteenth Massachusetts*, 76.

31. The Adams house was near the Gaines' Mill battlefield.

32. Maj. Gen. Edwin Sumner reported 1,185 total casualties at Fair Oaks. *OR*, 11(1):758.

33. The army's medical director, Dr. Charles S. Tripler, reported to the surgeon general that there was no scurvy in the army:

But three weeks later, on June 14, there were discovered in the 19th and

20th Massachusetts six men showing symptoms of scurvy and others "acquiring a disposition to the disease." Surgeon J. F. Hammond, U.S.A., Medical Director of Sumner's Corps . . . stated that the 19th had become generally, indeed almost universally, affected with scorbutic symptoms, and reported on medical authority that similar cases had been observed in another brigade of the corps. . . . At the end of the month Surgeon J. F. Dyer, 19th Mass., furnished a report of the condition of his command, showing 18 cases of pronounced scurvy, 100 of the scorbutic taint, and many of diarrhoea which he attributed to the causes of scurvy, inasmuch as it was controlled when the patients had access to a free supply of vegetables. MSH, 6:683–90; OR, 11(1):186–89, 207–10, 214.

34. Brig. Gen. J. E. B. Stuart hit this Richmond and York River Railroad station, a line completed just before the war connecting the capital to West Point, June 13 during his ride around the Army of the Potomac. Sears, *Gates of Richmond*, 170–72.

35. Apparently a reference to civilian contract surgeons like John G. Perry. See Perry, *Letters from a Surgeon*, 1–19.

36. The battle of Mechanicsville, or Beaver Dam Creek, one of the first of the Seven Days battles.

37. Brig. Gen. Daniel E. Sickles (1825–1914) raised the Excelsior Brigade (Second Brigade), Second Division, III Corps.

38. Lieutenant Warner: Second Lt. Charles B. Warner, Company H; Lieutenant Rice: First Lt. James H. Rice, Company F, who suffered a severe hip wound.

39. The Nineteenth Massachusetts lost nine killed and thirty-four wounded. Waitt, *Nineteenth Massachusetts*, 80–82.

40. Harrison's Landing became McClellan's headquarters along the James, after shifting from White House, until his withdrawal from the Peninsula began.

41. Porter retreated at Gaines' Mill, June 27, 1862.

42. Orchard Station: east of Fair Oaks and northeast of Seven Pines, about two miles from Savage's Station. Sears, *Gates of Richmond*, 263, 265.

43. Lieutenant Lee: First Lt. David Lee, twenty-two, Company E.

44. Only one has been identified. In a long passage apparently written between July 7 and 10 (see appendix 1), Dyer refers to Lt. William E. Barrows, twenty-two, his former hospital steward from Andover, then an aide to Colonel Hall, commanding Third Brigade. Edward N. Schoff, Charles W. Tibbetts, and James B. Wiggin were also on the Nineteenth Massachusetts roster as hospital stewards, who did the work of pharmacists. They were noncommissioned officers with the same rank as an

ordnance sergeant and paid thirty dollars a month. RMV, 2:302. See Frank R. Freemon, *Microbes and Minie Balls: An Annotated Bibliography of Civil War Medicine* (Cranbury, N.J.: Associated University Presses, 1993), 141–42; Joseph Janvier Woodward, *The Hospital Steward's Manual* (Philadelphia: J. B. Lippincott, 1862); and John Michael Priest, ed., *Turn Them Out to Die like a Mule: The Civil War Letters of Hospital Steward John N. Henry, 49th New York, 1861–1865* (Leesburg, Va.: Gauley Mount, 1995).

45. Lee's army had total casualties of 20,204; McClellan's, 15,855. Sears, *Gates of Richmond*, 343, 345.

46. A comment supporting the argument that Lincoln began to win the support of soldiers early in the war. See William C. Davis, *Lincoln's Men: How President Lincoln became Father to an Army and a Nation* (New York: Free Press, 1999), 66–69.

47. Dr. John E. Hill was hit by friendly fire from the rear guard of the II Corps on the retreat from Second Bull Run, dying several days later. See Waitt, *Nineteenth Massachusetts*, 124; and chapter 3, entry for September 4, 1862.

48. Willard later transferred to the Fourteenth Massachusetts (First Heavy Artillery).

49. General Order 21, reprinted in Waitt, *Nineteenth Massachusetts*, 113.

50. Colonel Ruffin: if captured at Bristoe Station, October 14, 1863, he was almost certainly a grandson, Thomas Ruffin, who wrote to Edmund Ruffin in 1864 and was exchanged that spring.

The "Venerable Edmund Ruffin": the noted fire-eater (1794–1865) was one of several alleged to have fired the first shot at Fort Sumter.

51. Westover (1730), in Charles City County, overlooks the James and was the seat of the Byrd family.

52. The attitude of many Union soldiers toward Confederate civilians had begun to change long before Sherman's March to the Sea, despite McClellan's stated wish to wage a Christian war based on civilized principles. See Albert Castel, *Decision in the West* (Lawrence: University Press of Kansas, 1992), 44–45; Charles Royster, *The Destructive War* (New York: Knopf, 1991), 85–86; and Mark Grimsley, *The Hard Hand of War* (New York: Cambridge University Press, 1995), 67–78, 85–95.

53. Lysander J. Hume, Company K, captured on the move to the James and exchanged, lived to march in the Grand Review in Washington in 1865; he was also called Josiah L. Hume. Turino, *Diary of Lieut. J. E. Hodgkins*, 92 n.142; Waitt, *Nineteenth Massachusetts*, 88, 118.

54. Newport News: a small fishing village at the Peninsula's tip; the duel of the ironclads was fought offshore. Pvt. James B. Wiggin, Company

K, Nineteenth Massachusetts, wrote to his siblings Sarah and Willard in Boston the next day: "I am here at Newport News. The doctor sent me here to recruit up. . . . [T]here is about 2,000 sick and disabled soldiers here now, lame and crippled in all shapes. They don't die off very fast." James Wiggin to Sarah and Willard, Aug. 24, 1862, James B. Wiggin (1838?–65) Letters, 1862–63, Peabody Essex Museum, Salem, Mass.

55. Charles City: settled in 1613 and established (1634) as one of the eight original shires in the Virginia colony. The courthouse dated from 1730.

Place belonging to John Tyler: Sherwood Forest, built in the late colonial era and enlarged in the 1840s, was the estate of the former president, who died January 17, 1862, in Richmond as a member of the Confederate House of Representatives.

56. The Chickahominy flows into the James.

57. Williamsburg: founded in 1633 and renamed in honor of King William III in 1699, the town was the colony's capital until 1780.

58. Founded in 1693, it remains the second oldest college in the United States.

59. Virginia's Eastern Lunatic Asylum, founded in 1773, treated whites, free blacks, and slaves.

60. *Atlantic*: a large steamer, its deep draft would not allow it to come upriver to Harrison's Landing, according to McClellan, and this played a bit part in the commander's dispute with Halleck over his withdrawal. *OR*, 11(1):87.

61. The Fifty-ninth New York is not listed in the *OR* for the Peninsula campaign nor mentioned by historian Stephen Sears. Neither of the New York regiments played a role in Second Bull Run and are not mentioned in John J. Hennessy, *Return to Bull Run* (New York: Simon & Schuster, 1993).

62. Aquia Creek's mouth is located in Stafford County north of Fredericksburg. After Antietam, Asst. Surgeon T. J. McMillan, medical purveyor of the army, moved his depot from near Harpers Ferry to the major Union base and medical receiving point established here for much of the war. There was a medical subdepot at the Falmouth railway station. Capt. Louis C. Duncan, *The Medical Department of the United States Army in the Civil War* (Washington, D.C., 1910; reprint, Gaithersburg, Md.: Olde Soldier Books, 1985), 178–79.

63. The Tammany regiment was one of the most unpopular units in the army because of its Democratic affiliation, its largely Irish flavor, and the regional rivalry between its members and New Englanders. They fled at Ball's Bluff but fought well at Fair Oaks. Scott, *Fallen Leaves*, 73, 127. From

June 25 to July 2, its total casualties were 57 men, the lowest in the Third Brigade, Second Division, II Corps. The Nineteenth Massachusetts lost 196 during the same period. *OR*, 11(2):25.

3. "INTO THE FIGHT WITH OUR REGIMENT"

1. Maj. Gen. Philip Kearny (1814–62) had commanded the First Division, III Corps.

2. Sibley tents: designed by Henry Hopkins Sibley; a conical tent on a tripod, with a single pole, that held twelve men. Boatner, *Dictionary*, 760.

3. Fort Ethan Allen: part of the western outer defenses of Washington, south of the Potomac at the Chain Bridge near Fort Marcy.

4. For a favorable account, see Robert G. Carter, *Four Brothers in Blue* (1913; reprint, Austin: University of Texas Press, 1978), 86–90. The Fourteenth's experience was repeated on a larger scale in 1864 when Lt. Gen. U. S. Grant ordered all of the "heavies" out of the capital's defenses. Unused to field service and with no infantry experience, they fought bravely but suffered high casualties.

5. Dyer refers to Porter's failure to launch a night attack at Bull Run August 29. The general claimed that orders from Maj. Gen. John Pope came too late to act on them. Hennessy, *Return to Bull Run*, 464–65.

6. First Minnesota: one of the great regiments, part of the First Brigade, Second Division, II Corps. See Richard Moe, *The Last Full Measure: The Life and Death of the First Minnesota Volunteers* (New York: Henry Holt, 1993).

7. The chaplain was Ezra Winslow, discharged for disability December 12, 1862.

8. On Georgetown's Union Hospital, see Louisa May Alcott, *Hospital Sketches* (Boston: Roberts Brothers, 1892); and Hannah Ropes [Alcott's supervisor], *Civil War Nurse: The Diary and Letters of Hannah Ropes*, ed. John R. Brumgardt (Knoxville: University of Tennessee Press, 1980).

9. Here and elsewhere Dyer was frustrated by the Medical Corps bureaucracy and military red tape, feelings shared by many other surgeons.

10. Chain Bridge: a Potomac River bridge above Georgetown; Tenleytown: a village northwest of Washington; Fort Gaines: a fort between Tenleytown and the Chain Bridge.

11. Howard had lost his right arm, and Kearny had lost his left arm. Kearny was killed at Chantilly, Virginia, September 1, 1862.

12. Keedysville was a village northeast of Sharpsburg where McClellan issued early dispatches; also the II Corps arrival point, with nine hospitals in the vicinity. The "great fight" was the battle of Antietam fought the previous day.

13. Captain Batchelder: George W. Batchelder, commander of Company C.

Captain Hale: Henry A. Hale, captain of Company H.

Lieutenant Thorndike: Albert Thorndyke, Company H.

Lieutenant Hinks: Lt. Elisha A. Hinks, Company B, rose to brevet colonel, March 1865.

Lieutenant Reynolds: John P. Reynolds Jr., Company D, credited with designing the II Corps badge, a trefoil or club, each division denoted by a different color; the Second Division was white.

Captain Rice: Edmund Rice, Company F, was the only one of the original thirty-seven officers to come home with the regiment, by then its colonel. Captured at Spotsylvania, he escaped from prison the next month, making his way back to the regiment via West Virginia and Ohio. He mustered out June 30, 1865, but rejoined the army, serving until his retirement in 1903, when he was promoted to brigadier general. BDJ, June 20, 1864; Adams, *Reminiscences*, 186; MOLLUS, *Register*, 371; Waitt, *Nineteenth Massachusetts*, 136.

14. Valley Mills was the hospital at Pry's gristmill, a three-story brick building along the Little Antietam just above its junction with Antietam Creek; home of Samuel and Mary Ann Cost Pry. A wagon full of wounded from the Sunken Road overturned at the Pry Ford, spilling the men into the creek. Doctors at the hospital were reprimanded for using the whiskey intended for the wounded. John W. Schildt, *Antietam Hospitals* (Chewsville, Md.: Antietam, 1987), 19–24; Kathleen A. Ernst, *Too Afraid to Cry: Maryland Civilians in the Antietam Campaign* (Mechanicsburg, Pa.: Stackpole, 1999), 121; *Atlas*, plates 28:2, 29:2. Dr. Thomas T. Ellis used the term "Valley Mills," but it has not been found in the MSH, OR, or modern sources. Ellis, *Leaves from the Diary of an Army Surgeon; or, Incidents of Field, Camp, and Hospital Life* (New York: John Bradburn, 1863), 277. Dyer visited the site July 13, 1863, calling it "Pry's Mills."

15. Maj. Gen. Jesse L. Reno (b. 1823), IX Corps.

16. Kirby's battery: Lt. Edmund Kirby's (d. 1863) Battery I, First U.S. Artillery, Sedgwick's division, II Corps. Led by Capt. James B. Ricketts at Bull Run and by Lt. George A. Woodruff at Antietam. General Howard reported that Sedgwick himself put it in position. It was the only battery to go into the West Woods; when Sedgwick retreated, it stopped the Confederate advance before being ordered to retire. OR, 19(1):306, 309–10; Curt Johnson and Richard C. Anderson Jr., *Artillery Hell: The Employment of Artillery at Antietam* (College Station: Texas A&M University Press, 1995), 63; Stephen W. Sears, *Landscape Turned Red: The Battle of Antietam* (New Haven: Ticknor and Fields, 1983), 225–26; Kent Masterson

Brown, *Cushing of Gettysburg* (Lexington: University Press of Kentucky, 1993), 64–65, 103, 121, 186.

17. Possibly the Seventy-first Pennsylvania. See John Michael Priest, *Antietam: The Soldiers' Battle* (Shippensburg, Pa.: White Mane, 1989), 116 (map); and the confusing report in *OR*, 19(1):318–19. Col. Joshua T. Owen, Sixty-ninth Pennsylvania, Second Brigade, said Maj. Gen. Edwin Sumner ordered the retreat and that the Seventy-first Pennsylvania fell back in good order, unlike the Seventy-second Pennsylvania and other, unnamed, units.

18. The hospital established at the John Hoffman farm house, across the creek and north of the Upper Bridge.

19. Dr. Palmer: Gideon Stinson Palmer, Third Maine, promoted to brigade surgeon, October 1861, was in the First Brigade, First Division, II Corps under Howard in June 1862 on the Peninsula. *Surgeons*, 68. *OR*, 11(1):770.

20. There were seventy hospitals in and around Sharpsburg and Keedysville. *Atlas*, plate 28:2.

21. Most hospital doctors were contract surgeons, who might wear officers' uniforms and were called "acting assistant surgeons" but held no commission. The Union hired 5,500 such physicians, but many served for only three or six months. Adams, *Doctors in Blue*, 174–75.

22. Asst. Surgeon Revere: Edward H. R. Revere.

Dr. Hayward: Nathan Hayward, of Roxbury, at thirty-two was eight years older than Dr. John G. Perry and known as "Uncle Nathan" to his friends. He succeeded Dyer as the Third Brigade's surgeon. *RMV*, 2:332; Perry, *Letters from a Surgeon*, 23, 152.

Dr. Kendall: Asst. Surgeon Albert A. Kendall, Twelfth Massachusetts, Second Brigade, Second Division, I Corps.

Dr. White: Dr. William J. H. White, surgeon and medical director, VI Corps.

23. The casualty report in his journal listed 1,959 casualties for Second Division, II Corps. At Gettysburg the death rate of the wounded was 13.9 percent. John W. Busey, *These Honored Dead: The Union Casualties at Gettysburg* (Hightstown, N.J.: Longstreet House, 1988), 6.

24. Smoketown: a small village 3.5 miles north of Sharpsburg. See Bob Zeller, "Smoketown Hospital," *CWT* 35 (May 1996): 37–43.

25. An opinion shared by the more enlightened doctors during the war, as indicated by various accounts and secondary sources.

26. Captain Russell: James D. Russell, Company D, resigned November 20, 1862; Charles Mudge: Capt. Charles R. Mudge, Second Massachusetts.

27. Brig. Gen. J. E. B. Stuart's Chambersburg raid, October 9–12. Sears, *Landscape Turned Red*, 327–28.

28. A common practice complained of by officers and men.

29. Paris: a Fauquier County village southeast of Ashby's Gap.

30. Enoch O'Rear owned eleven slaves in 1850 and twelve by 1860, when he was fifty-nine and a farmer reporting $10,000 in real and $8,200 in personal property. His wife, Catharine, was forty-five. Two older daughters, Mary F., eighteen, and Harriet H., sixteen, had moved out by 1860, but three others remained: Louisa, twenty; Adelaide, seventeen; and Elizabeth, thirteen. Dyer met the youngest and one of the others. U.S. Bureau of the Census, 1850 Census, Free Schedule, Fauquier County, roll 943, p. 204, family 76; and Slave Schedule, roll 986, p. 724, Ashby District, July 31, 1850; 1860 Census, Free Schedule, roll 1344, p. 6, family 35, Southwest Revenue District, Post Office, Paris; and Slave Schedule, roll 1390, p. 3, June 15, 1860.

31. Shinplasters: paper money issued in values under one dollar. These bills were often called fractional currency or stamp money because the notes were tiny, resembling the small pieces of paper soaked in a home remedy and plastered on a sore leg.

32. Dyer was surgeon in chief of the Third Brigade, Second Division, II Corps. He was appointed surgeon in chief of the Second Division December 3, 1862.

4. "SUCH A ROW IN WASHINGTON"

1. For the events of the Fredericksburg campaign, see Jay Luvaas and Harold W. Nelson, eds., *Guide to the Battles of Chancellorsville and Fredericksburg* (Carlisle, Pa.: South Mountain, 1988); and Daniel E. Sutherland, *Fredericksburg and Chancellorsville: The Dare Mark Campaign* (Lincoln: University of Nebraska Press, 1998).

2. Burnside reorganized the army into three "Grand Divisions"; Sumner's Right Grand Division comprised the II and IX Corps.

3. 300-dollar men: men who had enlisted for a cash bounty of three hundred dollars.

4. Vertulan R. Stone, appointed by Gov. John A. Andrew November 6, 1862, discharged May 11, 1863, for disability.

5. Colonel Hall: Col. Norman J. Hall, Seventh Michigan, led the Third Brigade at Chancellorsville and Gettysburg. Waitt, *Nineteenth Massachusetts*, 158.

6. Even when he was acting medical director of the II Corps, Dyer continued to treat wounded from the Nineteenth Massachusetts. Many of his reported cases were from his old regiment, like Capt. Elisha A. Hinks, Company C, on whom he operated June 3, 1864. MSH, 10:496.

7. Engineers laying the pontoon bridge suffered heavy casualties from sharpshooters in the town. The three regiments were ordered across the river in small boats to dislodge them.

8. Lt. Col. Henry Baxter (1821–73), wounded in the lung.

9. Harrison G. O. Weymouth, Company G, lost a leg; honorably discharged April 4, 1863.

10. Lacy house: called by Union soldiers after its Confederate owner, Maj. J. Horace Lacy, Chatham Manor was built after 1750 and was Sumner's headquarters. See Duncan, *Medical Department*, 192.

11. Brig. Gen. William A. Hammond (1828–1900) had been appointed surgeon general in April 1862.

12. Samuel Foster Haven Jr., thirty-one, of Worcester, was hit in the leg by a shell December 11 as his regiment occupied the town. *OR*, 21:271; *RMV*, 2:202; Duncan, *Medical Department*, 189.

13. Mark Boatner's estimate of Union casualties is 12,700; Jay Luvaas and Harold Nelson, as well as George Rable, 12,653. Boatner, *Dictionary*, 313; Luvaas and Nelson, *Guide*, 349; George C. Rable, *Fredericksburg! Fredericksburg!* (Chapel Hill: University of North Carolina Press, 2001), 288 (citing Thomas L. Livermore, *Numbers and Losses in the Civil War in America, 1861–65*, and the *OR*). Dyer reported 809 casualties in the Second Division, II Corps, December 11–13, 1862.

14. The house was built about 1754 and bought by George Washington for his mother in 1772. She died there in 1789. The monument was later completed and at the time was said to be the largest erected for any American woman.

15. Edgar M. Newcomb, Company F, wounded during an assault on Marye's Heights.

16. Captain Mahoney: Andrew Mahoney, commander of Company E; Captain Palmer: William L. Palmer, commanding Company I, suffered the first of his three wounds during the war at Fredericksburg.

17. Dr. Alexander N. Dougherty was medical director of the Right Grand Division as well as chief surgeon, Sedgwick's division. Note Waitt's variant, "Doherty." *Nineteenth Massachusetts*, 75–76.

18. F. Beardslee, Capt.: Frederick E. Beardslee, assistant quartermaster, U.S. Army, and acting signal officer. *OR*, 21:157–59.

19. The Sanitary Commission was a civilian organization that helped sick and wounded soldiers, despite friction with the army and particularly some surgeons, including Dyer. Its relief station, with a kitchen staffed by attendants, helped compensate for the lack of an evacuation hospital at Aquia. It supplied thousands of blankets and underclothing to an army unprepared for the cold. Duncan, *Medical Department*, 206.

20. A Massachusetts senator and prominent Republican, Wilson took an active interest in Bay State soldiers, especially the sick and wounded. See Adams, *Doctors in Blue*, 35–36, 95, 167; and Ropes, *Civil War Nurse*. Walt Whitman visited Dyer's hospital the next day, writing his mother, "One of the first things that met my eyes in camp was a heap of feet, arms, legs, etc., under a tree in front of a hospital, the Lacy house." Whitman, *The Wound Dresser* (1897; reprint, New York: Bodley, 1949), 48.

21. Dr. Justin Dwinelle began the war with the 71st Pennsylvania, transferring to the 106th Pennsylvania in September 1861 and serving until September 1864.

22. Jonathan Letterman (1824–72), medical director, Army of the Potomac, 1862–64.

23. Burnside wrote Halleck December 17, "For the failure in the attack I am responsible." Luvaas and Nelson, *Guide*, 119.

24. North Carolina: a Federal expedition from New Berne, North Carolina, had moved inland from the coast and achieved minor goals.

Banks will not accomplish much: possibly a reference to Maj. Gen. Nathaniel Banks's orders to open up the Mississippi, resulting in the Port Hudson campaign of 1863. He took command of the Department of the Gulf, with headquarters in New Orleans, December 16, 1862, replacing Maj. Gen. Benjamin Butler.

25. Pvt. James Wiggin, Company K, Nineteenth Massachusetts, wrote his sister Sarah: "I got through the battle of Fredericksburg safe and sound and unhurt glory to God for that. I never was so sick of anything in my life as I am of the war. We are all played out intirely [*sic*] but there will be a forward movement again soon. . . . Tell Willard I am a bold soldier boy." James Wiggin to Sarah, "Camp near Falmouth," Jan. 10, 1863, James B. Wiggin (1838?–65) Letters, 1862–63, Peabody Essex Museum, Salem, Mass.

26. O. O. Howard taught school during vacations to pay his tuition at Bowdoin College, graduating in 1850 and then from West Point four years later. Ezra Warner, *Generals in Blue* (Baton Rouge: Louisiana State University Press, 1964), 237. Mark Boatner says Howard wrote on many subjects but nothing on the war. The school tie may explain Dyer's high opinion of this rather unsuccessful general, but this changed after Chancellorsville. Boatner, *Dictionary*, 414.

27. Captain Wittlesey: Bowdoin professor Eliphalet Whittlesey (1822–1909), close friend and contemporary of Howard, joined the army in 1862 as a chaplain, transferred to the general's staff as an aide, and returned to Bowdoin for a year after Chancellorsville, but he was back with Howard by 1864, staying with him into their days with the Freedmen's Bureau. *OR*,

21:264; William S. McFeely, *Yankee Stepfather* (New York: W. W. Norton, 1970), 15, 78–83.

Lieutenant Howard: Charles Henry Howard, also of Maine, later a colonel of U.S. Colored Infantry and brevet brigadier general.

28. A. D. Richardson: Albert Deane Richardson (1833–69), Massachusetts-born war correspondent and friend of Horace Greeley, was captured at Vicksburg, spent time in Confederate prisons, and escaped. See George Cooper, *Lost Love* (New York: Random House, 1994).

29. The *Richmond Enquirer* was a major paper in the Confederate capital, one of six dailies published there, and read by Lincoln in the antebellum era.

30. Murfreesboro: Gen. Braxton Bragg's Confederate army withdrew January 3, 1863, after the battle of Stones River (Dec. 31, 1862–Jan. 2, 1863).

31. Galveston: Maj. Gen. John B. Magruder recaptured the Texas port January 1, 1863.

32. One of the great "what ifs" of the war is what might have happened if only the pontoons had arrived in time for a quick crossing of the river before Lee massed his entire army on Marye's Heights.

33. General Couch: Maj. Gen. Darius N. Couch (1822–97), commanding II Corps.

34. Mr. Alvord: John W. Alvord, Congregational minister, colonel, and a close friend of Howard. McFeely, *Yankee Stepfather*, 140, 245.

Rev. Dr. Childs: Frederick L. Childs's family befriended Howard while a junior ordnance officer at the Kennebec Arsenal in Augusta, Maine. This minister may have been related. O. O. Howard, *Autobiography of Oliver Otis Howard*, 2 vols., (1907; reprint, Freeport, N.Y.: Books for Libraries, 1971), 1:69.

35. James Gordon Bennett's *New York Herald* was generally Democratic and more conservative than Horace Greeley's *New York Tribune*.

36. Lincoln's Emancipation Proclamation took effect January 1, 1863.

37. January 20–23, 1863.

38. Dr. Socrates N. Sherman, surgeon, Thirty-fourth New York (Herkimer regiment). *Surgeons*, 131.

5. "A FAR BETTER STATE OF THINGS"

1. General Owen: Brig. Gen. Joshua T. Owen (1821–87), Sixty-ninth Pennsylvania, Second Brigade, Second Division.

2. In the East, Hooker often rode a white horse, as at Antietam. Unlike many generals, he grew no beard.

3. Thomas Francis Meagher's Irish Brigade in Sumner's division suffered heavy casualties at Fredericksburg.

4. Many soldiers recorded such improvements under Hooker. It was also the beginning of a new era for the Medical Department, starting with earlier changes like Letterman's division hospitals instead of regimental ones. Adams, *Doctors in Blue*, 88; Duncan, *Medical Department*, 209, 317–18.

5. Howard ranked from November 29, 1862.

6. Dr. Benjamin F. Taft transferred from the Twentieth to the Nineteenth Massachusetts in January 1863.

7. Captain Gosson: John J. Gosson, "a foxhunting squireen from Swords, county Dublin," with varied military service in Europe. Cited by Meagher after the Peninsula campaign and by Maj. Gen. Winfield S. Hancock after Antietam. *OR*, 11(2):72, 19(1):282; Paul Jones, *The Irish Brigade* (Washington: Robert B. Luce, 1969), 102, 163–66.

8. General Caldwell: Brig. Gen. John C. Caldwell (1833–1912), First Brigade, First Division, II Corps.

9. General Berry: Maj. Gen. Hiram G. Berry (1824–63), Second Division, III Corps.

10. Count Blucher: Lt. Gustav von Blucher, Twenty-ninth Battery, New York Light Artillery, active at Chancellorsville and Gettysburg.

11. An innovation meant to lift morale and foster corps' identities, it was a great success.

12. Maj. Gen. David B. Birney (1825–64), First Division, III Corps.

13. George W. Von Schack (?–1887), colonel of the Seventh New York, "Steuben Rifles," was on a leave of absence from the Prussian army. *OR*, 21:236.

14. Prince Salm Salm: Prince Felix Salm-Salm (1828–70) of Prussia, Eighth New York.

Mrs. Salm Salm: Princess Agnes Salm-Salm (1842–81), a colorful figure, would soon steal a kiss from Lincoln, causing a rift between Maj. Gen. Daniel Sickles and Mrs. Lincoln. Frank L. Byrne and Andrew T. Weaver, eds., *Haskell of Gettysburg* (Madison: State Historical Society of Wisconsin, 1970), 85; John Bigelow Jr., *The Campaign of Chancellorsville* (New Haven: Yale University Press, 1910), 129, 131–32.

15. Howard led his new command at Chancellorsville and Gettysburg. Called "the German Corps" because of its many ethnic regiments, it was an unlucky organization that suffered heavy casualties from Stonewall Jackson's flank attack at Chancellorsville.

Lieutenant Stinson: Maj. Harry Stinson, for whom the general named a son after the war, was the nephew of Mrs. James G. Blaine, wife of Maine's Republican boss and newly elected congressman. McFeely, *Yankee Stepfather*, 15.

16. Brig. Gen. John Gibbon (1827–96), Second Division, II Corps.

17. Asst. Surgeon William D. Knapp, twenty-two, of Boston; dismissed, December 2, 1863.

18. Lieutenant Haskell: First Lt. Frank Aretas Haskell (1828–64), Sixth Wisconsin, Gibbon's closest friend; Lieutenant Moale: Edward Moale, Nineteenth U.S. Infantry, brother-in-law of General Gibbon. *OR*, 21, 481; *DAB*, 7:237.

19. The Mormon, or Utah Expedition, 1857–58, of U.S. troops to pacify followers of Brigham Young, allowing for westward expansion and free passage of wagon trains to California.

20. Curtis was probably a fugitive slave who did chores. There were hundreds if not thousands who served both officers and regiments in most Union armies.

21. Governor Ramsey: Alexander Ramsey (1815–1903), a Pennsylvania Whig, territorial governor of Minnesota, and its second elected governor. A strong Unionist, he offered ten thousand troops to Secretary of War Simon Cameron two days after the firing on Fort Sumter. Elected to the U.S. Senate as a Republican in 1863.

22. Lieutenant Hildreth: Gibbon cited James H. Hildreth for service at South Mountain and Antietam; Captain Wood: J. P. Wood, Nineteenth Indiana, adjutant general. John Gibbon, *Personal Recollections of the Civil War* (1928; reprint, Dayton, Ohio: Morningside, 1988), 37.

23. Dyer was not well informed on home front sentiment, particularly in cities. There would be major riots against the draft in the coming summer, especially in New York City, with smaller ones in Boston and elsewhere. See Iver Bernstein, *The New York City Draft Riots* (New York: Oxford University Press, 1990).

24. A joint congressional committee organized in December 1861, chaired by Sen. Benjamin Wade of Ohio and dominated by Radical Republicans. It was critical of the Democrat McClellan and others, including Lincoln, who did not push the war aggressively enough for their liking. Mark Boatner says it investigated all of the leaders of the Army of the Potomac except Grant. Boatner, *Dictionary*, 168. See Bruce Tap, *Over Lincoln's Shoulder: The Committee on the Conduct of the War* (Lawrence: University Press of Kansas, 1998).

25. There is no mention of a woman companion in the most detailed accounts. See Carl Sandburg, *Abraham Lincoln: The War Years* (New York: Harcourt, Brace, and World, 1939), 2:84–92; and Bigelow, *Chancellorsville*, 127–32.

26. Thomas "Tad" Lincoln (1853–71), the president's youngest son.

27. These were the opening preparations for the Chancellorsville campaign.

28. Potomac Creek: a tributary just north of the Rappahannock. The hospitals were moved closer to the scene of probable fighting.

29. Hooker wired Lincoln that the rain was slowing the departure of Maj. Gen. George Stoneman's cavalry on its Richmond raid. Bruce Catton, *Glory Road* (Garden City, N.Y.: Doubleday, 1952), 159.

30. 140,000 men: Dyer's estimate was high by perhaps six to ten thousand; 30,000 at Manassas: this force guarded an approach to Washington.

31. The unlucky XI Corps.

32. The opposing troops were close enough to see each other and dignitaries like Lincoln distinctly.

33. Dr. John Hurley, Sixty-ninth New York. *MSH*, 7:30 (introduction).

34. Robert Ware of Boston, serving with a nine months' regiment based chiefly in North Carolina, died April 10, 1863, of disease.

35. Edwin F. Denyse's letter to his paper, describing preparations for the army's movement, appeared March 14, 1863; he was arrested two days later. Sentenced to six months, Hooker then commuted the penalty to transportation beyond the lines. J. Cutler Andrews, *The North Reports the Civil War* (Pittsburgh: University of Pittsburgh Press, 1955), 343.

36. Major Beard: Thomas W. Baird, cited by Gibbon after Gettysburg. *OR*, 27(1):418.

Captain Embler: A. Henry Embler, Eighty-second New York, cited by Gibbon, November 7, 1864, for Grant's Overland campaign. *OR*, 36(1):435.

Captain Owen: Frederick W. Owen, commissary of subsistence, First Brigade, Second Division. *OR*, 33:809.

Captain Crombarger: Thomas S. Crombargar, commissary of subsistence, Second Division, cited by Gibbon, November 7, 1864. *OR*, 33:809.

Lieutenant Steele: William R. Steele, Fifteenth Massachusetts, First Brigade, was Dyer's tentmate on occasion and still on the staff as of March 23, 1864.

37. Capt. John M. Garland of the Tammany regiment, Third Brigade, had been cited for meritorious service with the ambulance corps at Antietam by Jonathan Letterman and by Maj. Gen. Edwin Sumner for Fredericksburg. After Ball's Bluff he was one of the officers who conferred with Confederates for General Stone about Union prisoners. General Couch wrote that one of the Garland family's slaves made his way from the Rebel lines to II Corps headquarters after the battle of Fredericksburg and reported on Confederate movements. Dr. Garland, father of the Union officer, vouched for the slave's reliability. *OR*, 5:306, 19(1):110, 21:166, 220.

38. Copperheads were Northern Democrats, also known as Peace Democrats, bitterly opposed to both the war and the Lincoln administration.

39. Near the northeastern Maine coast below Lubec, the school was Washington Academy.

40. The general's eldest daughter was Frances Moale Gibbon, named for her mother; John was her younger brother. An older boy has not been identified, and a second daughter came in 1864.

6. "THOSE DUTCHMEN WOULD NOT FIGHT"

1. See Stephen W. Sears, *Chancellorsville* (Boston: Houghton Mifflin, 1996); and Ernest B. Furgurson, *Chancellorsville, 1863: The Souls of the Brave* (New York: Knopf, 1992).

2. The crossing is well to the northwest of Fredericksburg on the North Fork of the Rappahannock, east of Culpeper Court House, and was the site of a cavalry fight March 17.

3. XII Corps: smallest corps in the Army of the Potomac, claimed never to have lost a color or a gun. Boatner, *Dictionary*, 194; General Slocum: Maj. Gen. Henry W. Slocum (1827–94).

4. Many of the army's bridges had guardhouses or redoubts at each end, even huge doors as barricades.

5. These were Hancock's and French's divisions.

6. Third Brigade, First Division, led by the 95th and 119th Pennsylvania.

7. Dyer was correct. The plan was to flank the Confederates holding the heights above Fredericksburg from both sides.

8. Lee's men were indeed on half rations at this time. See Sears, *Chancellorsville*, 35–38, 95–96, 145.

9. The XI, XII, and V Corps.

10. The dispute arose because six companies felt their enlistment dated from the time they signed up, but the army standard was from the time they were mustered in to Federal service, which for the New Yorkers was June 1861. Furgurson, *Chancellorsville*, 122–23.

11. Sully was restored to command but then sent west.

12. Gibbon apparently felt this regiment to be the most reliable in a brigade with the First Minnesota, Nineteenth Maine, and Eighty-second New York.

13. First Corps: created from the III Corps; previously led by Hooker, George Meade, and Brig. Gen. James Wadsworth (briefly); and now commanded by Maj. Gen. John F. Reynolds.

Banks' Ford: a crossing due west of Fredericksburg just above a sharp bend in the Rappahannock.

One brigade of our division: Second Brigade, Second Division. *OR*, 25(1):248, 350.

14. It comprised the 19th and 20th Massachusetts, 7th Michigan, 42d and 59th New York, and 127th Pennsylvania.

15. Captain Holmes: Oliver Wendell Holmes Jr. was hit in the heel and treated at the Lacy house; Captain Murphy: James Murphy, Company F. Holmes called him a former first sergeant who had served at Fort Pickens, Pensacola Bay, Florida, during the secession crisis.

16. Only Maj. Gen. Jubal Early's division and Brig. Gen. William Barksdale's brigade held the town. Sedgwick was pushed back across the river at day's end. Furgurson, *Chancellorsville*, 258.

17. Lt. Gen. James Longstreet's arrival was reported by Confederate prisoners, and the rumor spread through Hooker's army during the battle. Furgurson, *Chancellorsville*, 185.

18. Due north of Chancellorsville; the main crossing point for the army (also Mine Ford).

19. Lt. Benjamin E. Kelley; Lts. Crawford Allen Jr. and Otto L. Torslow were the two officers wounded. *OR*, 25(1):251, 310.

20. A dwelling on Stafford Heights above and about a mile northeast of the Lacy house.

21. Maj. Gen. George Stoneman (1822–94). Dyer's judgment of his Richmond raid was largely correct.

22. The XI Corps had its flank "in the air" and took the brunt of Stonewall Jackson's attack the evening of May 2.

23. General Berry: Berry died May 3 trying to stop the renewed Rebel assault. His demise has been attributed both to a bayonet and a sharpshooter.

Captain Dessauer: Capt. Francis A. Dessauer died next to Howard while the general and his staff were trying to stop their panicked men.

24. Dyer's first appraisal of the raid was more accurate. Stoneman reached the outskirts of Richmond and damaged miles of railroad and canal but failed to distract Lee, and Stoneman's absence cost Hooker vital cavalry support.

25. Maj. Gen. John J. Peck (1821–78) had been reinforced to almost 25,000 men and defended a strongly fortified position at Suffolk, Virginia, southwest of Portsmouth and Norfolk. He managed to hold off the divisions of Maj. Gens. John Bell Hood and George B. Pickett under Longstreet's command, but Peck was not expected to launch an offensive against Richmond. He was severely injured during the operation.

26. XI Corps misbehaved: Sears, *Chancellorsville*, 432–33.

27. Sedgwick blamed: Sears, *Chancellorsville*, 437.

28. Indeed, Lincoln was depressed after the battle. David Herbert Donald, *Lincoln* (New York: Simon and Schuster, 1995), 435–38.

29. Maj. Gen. Darius Couch asked to be relieved and urged Hooker's removal.

30. Hooker was relieved of command at his request June 27, 1863.

31. Jackson died May 10, 1863. Pneumonia has usually been given as the cause of death. For the case that sepsis caused by Group A *Streptococcus* killed Jackson, and a rebuttal to it, see Marvin P. Rozear and Joseph C. Greenfield Jr., " 'Let Us Cross over the River': The Final Illness of Stonewall Jackson," *VMHB* 103 (January 1995): 29–46; (July 1995), 389–91.

32. Except Sickles: Sears, *Chancellorsville*, 420–22.

33. Mrs. Barlow: Arabella Wharton Griffith, of Somerville, New Jersey, married Brig. Gen. Francis C. Barlow, Second Brigade, Second Division, XI Corps, April 20, 1861, the day after he enlisted in the Twelfth New York. After her husband was wounded at Gettysburg, she nursed him back to health for ten months but herself died July 27, 1864, of a fever caught while working at the front. See entries for June 1, 1863, and July 29, 1864. *Sanitary Commission Bulletin* 1 (Aug. 15, 1864): 615–17.

34. Fraternization between troops of the two armies was a problem for officers for much of the war.

35. Mrs. John Harris, secretary of the Ladies' Aid Society of Philadelphia, followed the army to the Peninsula and Antietam and wrote from the Lacy house May 18. Frank Moore, *Women of the War* (Hartford, Conn.: S. S. Scranton, 1866), 176–77, 196–99.

36. There was a Washington property north of Falmouth and west of the Richmond, Fredericksburg, and Potomac Railroad and another just north of the pontoon bridge near the river.

37. Duff Green (1791–1875) served in Pres. Andrew Jackson's Kitchen Cabinet and actively supported the Confederacy.

38. A premature rumor following Maj. Gen. U. S. Grant's first two assaults, May 19 and 22.

39. A theme explored by Michael C. C. Adams, *Our Masters the Rebels* (Cambridge: Harvard University Press, 1978); and Richard McMurry, *Two Great Rebel Armies* (Chapel Hill: University of North Carolina Press, 1989).

40. Of Simon Cameron's three daughters, the oldest, Rachel, married a Pennsylvania judge but was widowed in 1859. This woman was probably one of the younger daughters, Virginia Rolette or Margaretta; both also married prominent men in their state, in 1866 and 1870 respectively.

41. Lt. Col. Jo Smith: Joseph S. Smith. *OR*, 25(1):308.

42. Perhaps a rumor, but Lee's army began to move June 3; Griffin's division: Brig. Gen. Charles Griffin (1825–67), First Division, V Corps.

43. First Brigade, First Division, II Corps.

44. Col. Edward E. Cross (1832–63), Fifth New Hampshire, wounded at Seven Pines, Antietam, and Fredericksburg. A friend of Nathaniel Hawthorne, he was killed July 2 at Gettysburg.

45. General Sykes: Maj. Gen. George Sykes (1822–80), V Corps.

46. Also called the Old Richmond Stage Road, it went south to Bowling Green, seat of Caroline County.

47. Banks launched three unsuccessful assaults in May and June before besieging Port Hudson.

48. Grant settled down to a siege of Vicksburg too. On June 15 Gen. Joseph E. Johnston told Richmond authorities that saving Vicksburg was impossible.

49. General Pleasanton: Brig. Gen. Alfred Pleasonton (1824–97), soon to be a major general, led the cavalry corps through the Gettysburg campaign.

50. Brandy Station, June 9, 1863, the largest cavalry battle ever fought in the Western Hemisphere. Union casualties were almost twice those of the Confederates, but Hooker now knew that Lee was moving north, and his cavalry gained confidence against Stuart. Dyer was usually right on specifics, but he sometimes failed to see the big picture.

51. Col. Benjamin Franklin "Grimes" Davis (1832–63), an Alabama-born officer loyal to the Union.

52. Couch's headquarters were actually in Harrisburg, where he organized Pennsylvania home-guard units during Lee's invasion and assisted Secretary of War Edwin Stanton.

53. See David M. Jordan, *Winfield Scott Hancock* (Bloomington: University of Indiana Press, 1988), 75.

54. Stoneman was relieved of command and took over the cavalry bureau in Washington. Hooker blamed his defeat at Chancellorsville on him and others.

7. "MY HEART ALMOST FAILED ME"

1. Sangster's Station was along the Orange and Alexandria Railroad between Fairfax Station and Bull Run.

2. John, his youngest son, sick for months, had seemed to recover in May. Dennis Sherman Lavery, "John Gibbon and the Old Army: Portrait of an American Professional Soldier, 1827–1896" (Ph.D. diss., Pennsylvania State University, 1964), 103.

3. Brig. Gen. William Harrow (1822–72).

4. General Abercrombie: Brig. Gen. John J. Abercrombie (1798–1877) led a division in the Washington defenses; troops who were surrendered: troops under Col. Dixon S. Miles surrendered September 15, 1862, to Jackson during the Antietam campaign.

5. The Second Wisconsin lost 298 of its 500 men, the brigade at least 751. Alan T. Nolan, *The Iron Brigade: A Military History* (Bloomington: Indiana University Press, 1961), 95.

6. Ailing and bedridden, widow Judith Carter Henry, eighty-five, was killed, probably by fire from Ricketts's battery during First Bull Run. Her house was on Henry Hill, near the turning point of the battle.

7. With infantry support from Maj. Gen. Joseph Hooker, they tried to break Maj. Gen. J. E. B. Stuart's force and reach Ashby's Gap. Edward G. Longacre, *The Cavalry at Gettysburg* (1986; reprint, Lincoln: University of Nebraska Press, Bison Books, 1993), 125–29.

8. Dr. John G. Perry, of Boston, describes his injury in Perry, *Letters from a Surgeon*, 47–56.

9. General Owen: his confirmation as general was never made, according to Ezra Warner; Mark Boatner says it was renewed March 30, 1863. Owen angered Gibbon again at Cold Harbor the following year. Warner, *Generals in Blue*, 354; Boatner, *Dictionary*, 614.

10. Divisions of Lt. Gen. Ambrose P. Hill's corps reached the town June 23 and crossed the Potomac the next day. Edwin B. Coddington, *The Gettysburg Campaign* (New York: Scribner's, 1968), 113.

11. Stuart briefly engaged the Second Division, rear of the II Corps column. Francis A. Walker, *History of the Second Army Corps in the Army of the Potomac* (New York: Charles Scribner's Sons, 1886), 259 [hereafter cited as Walker, *Second Corps*].

12. The V Corps was one of the army's original organizations under McClellan. In his letter of June 28, Dyer speculated that Meade would make Gibbon either a corps commander or his chief of staff and that Hancock and Howard might be relieved along with the rest of Hooker's staff. He wrote, "I like Howard personally, but I do not think he has the *power* and *vim* sufficient for a large command." His excerpt from his letter of October 17, 1863, was very brief in the journal. In the original letter Dyer wrote: "General Howard is out west with his corps. I am sorry his corps has such a reputation, but I really think he is not the best man to command a corps. He is not a good disciplinarian and as fine a man as he is, and as brave, he cannot inspire his men with the same ideas. I think he was not made for such a position." In his close to the June letter, he remarked: "It seems singular to get back on this old ground again after so long a time — but war is very uncertain. I think however we are bound to whip them out at last."

13. Brig. Gen. Alexander S. Webb (1835–1911) led the 69th, 71st, 72d, and 106th Pennsylvania. Bradley M. Gottfried, *Stopping Pickett: The History of the Philadelphia Brigade* (Shippensburg, Pa.: White Mane, 1999), 150–54.

14. Union Bridge: along Little Pipe Creek south of Taneytown. An extension of the Western Maryland Railroad ran here from Westminster, unknown to Maj. Gen. Daniel Butterfield, Meade's chief of staff. Coddington, *Gettysburg Campaign*, 329.

15. Third Brigade, Third Division, II Corps, commanded by Col. George L. Willard, including four companies of the Thirty-ninth New York (Garibaldi Guard), which stopped Barksdale's Mississippians July 2.

16. In his letter of June 30, written from Uniontown, Dyer wrote: "Soon after we arrived our cavalry scouts brought in two buggies in which four secesh gentlemen . . . had driven out . . . to inform the Rebels of our approach. They were brought in and put under guard."

17. Confederates reached the outskirts of Harrisburg and Baltimore but were not close enough to threaten the other cities, though there was concern in Philadelphia.

18. The VI Corps was not heavily engaged at Gettysburg. Compare Coco, *Ball's Bluff to Gettysburg*, 192.

19. The hospital was on the Sarah Patterson farm, directly behind the lines.

20. Col. William Colvill Jr., Lt. Col. Charles Adams, and Maj. Mark W. Downie were wounded. Capt. Henry C. Coates, commanding the regiment after the battle, reported August 3 that Captain Muller, Company E, was killed; and Captain Periam, Company K, mortally wounded July 2. Capt. Nathan S. Messick, leading the regiment, and Capt. W. B. Farrell, Company C, were killed July 3. Byrne and Weaver, *Haskell of Gettysburg*, 125–26; *OR*, 27(1):425.

21. Revere died July 5 from a shell wound suffered during Maj. Gen. Richard Anderson's attack late in the day July 2. Bruce, *Twentieth Massachusetts*, 282.

22. As Dyer states, Col. George H. Ward died of his wounds. Bruce, *Twentieth Massachusetts*, 279. See Private Bowen's extensive comments on Ward in Coco, *Ball's Bluff to Gettysburg*.

23. Lt. Col. James Huston died. His regiment, from the same brigade as the First Minnesota, was the first to help that unit. Capt. Jonah C. Hoyt and Lt. John H. McDonald were killed, and Lt. John Cranston, mortally wounded. *OR*, 27(1):189, 191.

24. The stone house on the Patterson farm. Dr. Dwinelle estimated that there were five hundred wounded that night, most from the Second Division. Gregory A. Coco, *A Vast Sea of Misery* (Gettysburg: Thomas, 1988), 67.

25. Henry L. Patten, Company D, Twentieth Massachusetts, wounded July 2. Scott, *Fallen Leaves*, 186 n. 4.

26. Flags of the Fourteenth, Fifty-third, Fifty-seventh, and probably Nineteenth Virginia. Waitt, *Nineteenth Massachusetts*, 247.

27. Generals Hancock and Gibbon: both generals were severely wounded on the third but recovered; General Zook: Brig. Gen. Samuel K.

Zook (1823–63), Third Brigade, First Division, II Corps, wounded in the Wheatfield, died the next day.

28. Lt. Col. George N. Macy (1837–75), Twentieth Massachusetts, had his left hand amputated after it was shattered by a minié ball.

29. Second Corps: reports of II Corps casualties include 4,383 and 4,369 men. See, respectively, *OR*, 27(1):112; and Jay Luvaas and Harold W. Nelson, eds., *The U.S. Army War College Guide to the Battle of Gettysburg* (Carlisle, Pa.: South Mountain, 1986), 231.

Nineteenth Massachusetts: other sources report the regiment's losses at seventy-seven. See Waitt, *Nineteenth Massachusetts*, 247; and *OR*, 27(1):176.

Nineteenth Maine: this was the only Maine regiment in Gibbon's division or in the entire II Corps, which explains Dyer's interest. It was recruited primarily in Kennebec, Knox, Sagadahoc, and Waldo Counties. Part of Harrow's brigade, the Nineteenth Maine had over 200 casualties among 405 effectives. *OR*, 27(1):176; *Maine at Gettysburg* (1898; reprint, Gettysburg: Stan Clark, 1994), 290–91, 310.

30. Our hospital here: from its first creek location in a bend on the west bank, due east of the Round Tops, to (July 3) " 'the bank of Rock Creek, at its junction with White Creek' "; "about a mile and a half down stream from the Baltimore Pike bridge." *Atlas*, plate 95:1; Coco, *Vast Sea of Misery*, 92–94; and Coco, " 'A Laborious and Vexatious Task': The Medical Department of the Army of the Potomac from the Seven Days through the Gettysburg Campaign," in *Mr. Lincoln's Army: The Army of the Potomac in the Gettysburg Campaign* (Gettysburg NMP: National Park Service, 1997), 309.

Nathaniel Davidson wrote on July 17: "To the southeast [of XII Corps hospital], is the Second army corps hospital, a portion of it upon a wooded hill, near a muddy creek, and the Third division across the creek and upon another hill, half a mile removed. . . . Here there were in all some three thousand cases, four to five hundred of them being rebels." *New York Herald*, July 24, 1863.

Capt. John G. B. Adams recalled: "They laid us on the ground on the side of the hill, near a stream called Cub Run. This was the field hospital of the 2d corps, Dr. Dyer, my regimental surgeon, in charge. He soon visited me, and found that one bullet had entered my groin and had not come out, the other had passed through my right hip. I asked him what he thought of it and he said, 'It is a bad wound, John, a very bad wound.' " *Reminiscences*, 69.

31. Dr. Justin Dwinelle of the II Corps later asserted, " 'Nothing but to gain victory should ever prevent these wagons from following the ammunition train.' " Quoted in Gerard A. Patterson, *Debris of Battle: The Wounded of Gettysburg* (Mechanicsburg, Pa.: Stackpole, 1997), 45–50.

32. In his letter of August 8, 1863, Dyer refers to the battle account written by a member of the division. A clipping found in one of his scrapbooks from the *Baltimore American* of August 6 has a letter dated July 23, headlined "The Pinch of the Fight at Gettysburg." It appeared to be an eyewitness report by a soldier but was written by Baltimore lawyer John H. B. Latrobe based on what General Gibbon, recuperating at his house, had told him of the battle. Gibbon, *Personal Recollections*, 173–83.

33. The Codori house. Coddington, *Gettysburg Campaign*, 412.

34. On the left of us: actually Brig. Gen. Elon J. Farnsworth's cavalry fight.

35. Haskell was hit on the thigh by a bullet that bruised and numbed his leg. Byrne and Weaver, *Haskell*, 189–92.

36. See Edmund Rice, "Repelling Lee's Last Blow at Gettysburg," *B&L*, 3:387–90.

37. William E. Barrows. Waitt, *Nineteenth Massachusetts*, 258.

38. A *New York Times* article (see appendix 3) credited the division with thirteen captured flags, one for each regiment; the II Corps took a total of thirty-three. Bruce, *Twentieth Massachusetts*, 295.

39. The three brigades of the Second Division had thirteen regiments plus the Second Company Minnesota Sharpshooters.

40. Dyer reported 356 killed, 1,156 wounded, and 94 missing, a total of 1,606 in the Second Division and close to the figure of 1,651 reported in the *OR*.

41. See Byrne and Weaver, *Haskell of Gettysburg*, 193 n. 103. Charles Fairchild described the battlefield tour but did not mention Dyer. Charles Fairchild, Gettysburg, July 6, 1863, to his mother, Lucius Fairchild Papers, State Historical Society of Wisconsin, Madison. I am indebted to Harold L. Miller, reference archivist, for a copy of this letter.

42. See Brown, *Cushing of Gettysburg*; two Rhode Island batteries: Batteries A and B, First Rhode Island Artillery.

43. The Fifty-ninth New York, Seventh Michigan, and Twentieth Massachusetts had but one shovel each with which to throw a bit of dirt over the rail fence. Bruce, *Twentieth Massachusetts*, 291; Coddington, *Gettysburg Campaign*, 511.

44. Maj. Henry L. Abbott said Harrow was "a western col. promoted for a bloodless skirmish out west ostensibly, but really for cursing rebels." Scott, *Fallen Leaves*, 191.

45. Mallon: Col. James E. Mallon, Forty-second New York (Tammany Regiment).

46. Surgeon Burmeister: Dr. Frederick F. Burmeister, Sixty-ninth Pennsylvania, transferred as assistant surgeon from the Seventy-third Pennsylvania.

8. "I HAVE FAITH IN MEADE"

1. Chief correspondent Lorenzo Livingston Crouse condemned the citizens' " 'craven-hearted meanness' " and was blasted by local clergy in a letter to the publisher, Henry J. Raymond, printed in the rival *New York Tribune*, July 24, 1863. Andrews, *North Reports*, 435–36; Patterson, *Debris of Battle*, 53–55, 70–71, 115–18, 149.

2. After Gettysburg the regiment mustered about eighty-three officers and men. Waitt, *Nineteenth Massachusetts*, 247.

3. Strength estimates vary widely, from "no more than 80,000 officers and men available for combat" to 95,000 for Meade—and a maximum of 35,000 excluding his cavalry—to "at least 50,000" for Lee. Coddington, *Gettysburg Campaign*, 569; Kenneth P. Williams, *Lincoln Finds a General* (New York: Macmillan, 1952), 2:753; Stephen Z. Starr, *The Union Cavalry in the Civil War* (Baton Rouge: Louisiana State University Press, 1981), 2:1–2 n. 2.

4. Edwin Coddington writes of the Pennsylvania militia, "none of them, especially those in Couch's department, dared to confront any significant portion of Lee's army for fear of annihilation." *Gettysburg Campaign*, 561.

5. Comments reflecting prevalent thinking in the army, and certainly at Meade's level. There was criticism from Lincoln, Congress, the press, and the public that the army moved too slowly. Some historians have agreed, but for a measured assessment see Coddington, *Gettysburg Campaign*, 535–74.

6. Rather than replenish veteran regiments with new men, many new regiments were created during the war, offering more jobs for officers seeking posts and for politicians eager to reward supporters.

7. A former editor and publisher, Dyer expressed repeated skepticism about correspondents yet told Maria that she would know the results of events before he would—from the newspapers. His attitude shows his innate conservatism and his acceptance of the army's view about an issue that still divides the military and the media. Journalistic coverage was strongly colored by the political affiliation of each paper, as seen in the reporting of events after Gettysburg by the Republican *New York Times* and *New York Tribune* and the Democratic *New York Herald*. In his letter of July 10, Dyer singled out for criticism war correspondent Charles C. Coffin of the *Boston Journal*, who had ridden rode north with the II Corps from Frederick, Maryland. Dyer also dismissed a story about the capture of Lt. Gen. James Longstreet at Gettysburg, claiming that reporters had confused him with Brig. Gen. Lewis Armistead. See Andrews, *North Reports*, 406, 417–30.

8. Dyer was defensive about officers' drinking, denying the problem

again in his letter of August 23 despite his origins in the temperance state of Maine, but the complaints of men on both sides about this abuse are too common to ignore.

9. Both a contradictory statement and an accurate one since Meade was indeed criticized for moving very slowly.

10. See Chester G. Hearn, *Six Years of Hell: Harpers Ferry during the Civil War* (1996; reprint, Baton Rouge: Louisiana State University Press, 1999), 222–30. Harpers Ferry was the reverse of a choke point, changing hands several times, and could not be defended by either Yanks or Rebs if the other side held the surrounding heights.

11. Dyer's final figures were 1,156 wounded, 356 killed, and 94 missing, a total of 1,606. Of the 3,200 patients in the II Corps hospital, 437 died—one out of nine Federals, one out of five Confederates. Patterson, *Debris of Battle*, 70. In his letter of July 17, before giving the casualty figures, Dyer wrote: "The account of Col. Devereux's death was a mistake. He was not hurt."

12. Gerard Patterson is critical of Meade, arguing that if a hundred more doctors had been left behind, many deaths might have been prevented, but the commander took 85 percent of them when the army moved south, leaving the II Corps hospital especially undermanned. *Debris of Battle*, 46, 100, 110, 167, 189–92.

13. Many of the army doctors had the same attitude toward civilian physicians shown by Dyer. It may be that there were simply not enough surgeons willing and competent to serve, either in a military or civilian role, with the army or in the town after a battle with unprecedented casualties. Patterson, *Debris of Battle*, 99–100.

14. A *New York Times* correspondent reported July 20 that "General Meade is in active pursuit, and will soon be heard from" and then quoted the *Springfield (Mass.) Republican* (same date) that "Lee's army is moving leisurely down the valley toward Richmond." *New York Times*, July 21, 1863. The *New York Tribune* was more critical, with a Maryland dispatch of July 16 headlined "The Escape of Lee." "The army is today congregating . . . preparatory to crossing the Potomac for another campaign in Virginia. For this it awaits pontoons. We are afflicted with another pontoon delay at a momentous period. . . . There is a sense of the ludicrous experienced by all in being precisely where we were last year, with Richmond as far off as ever."

15. On May 27 Capt. Bernard McMahon of the Seventy-first Pennsylvania shot and killed Capt. Andrew McManus of the Sixty-ninth Pennsylvania in his tent after his victim had repeatedly accused him of cowardice, orally and in writing. Bradley M. Gottfried, *Stopping Pickett: The History*

of the Philadelphia Brigade (Shippensburg, Pa.: White Mane, 1999), 148, 248 n. 2. Robert I. Alotta argues that field commanders often lacked the expertise to deal with criminal offenses and that there may have been an ethnic and religious bias affecting their decisions. *Civil War Justice: Union Army Executions under Lincoln* (Shippensburg, Pa.: White Mane, 1989).

16. Confederates held the Blue Ridge gaps long enough for Lee's army to escape. E. B. Long, *The Civil War Day by Day: An Almanac, 1861–1865* (Garden City, N.Y.: Doubleday, 1971), 390–91.

17. The *New York Times*, July 23, proclaimed "The Pursuit of Lee. . . . Gen. Meade's Army in a Position to Intercept Him. A Battle Expected Soon" and concluded, "We may expect stirring news from Gen. Meade's army soon." That day's *New York Herald* compared Antietam and Gettysburg and the respective performances of McClellan and Meade in a lengthy article, arguing: "There is little cause to find fault with Meade for not immediately following up the fruits of his victory, there is assuredly less for censuring McClellan for acting on the same prudential considerations. . . . No competent military critics have been found to condemn the respite given by Meade to his army. . . . The results of his present operations will . . . justify the wisdom of his course. He will cut up and capture Lee's army." The *Times* and *Tribune* remained optimistic for four more days; the *Herald* reported July 26 that Lee had escaped.

18. Brig. Gen. Alexander Hays (1819–64), Third Division, II Corps. Dyer wrote in his letter of July 27, "The people, the high *minded* and *elegant* ladies of the South, beg for protection and then make signals to Rebel guerillas to come and capture them {Union guards}." The next day he wrote, "The people are leagued with the guerillas, and their houses should be burnt rather than protected if they are to aid the capture of their safeguards."

19. I. Harris Hooper, thirty-one, of Boston later commanded the Fifteenth Massachusetts. Coco, *Ball's Bluff to Gettysburg*, 240.

20. The doctor's younger brother, George Burton Dyer, Ninth Maine, and Maria's brother Lt. Heber James Davis, Seventh New Hampshire, were both near Charleston. In his letter of July 21, Dyer said he had read of heavy losses in the Ninth Maine after the first day's attack on Morris Island, and although George was no doubt involved, he told Maria that Heber's regiment had not been. Their regiments lost 117 and 216 men respectively in the second assault on Fort Wagner, but both Dyer and Davis survived. *OR*, 28(1):210.

21. Maj. S. Octavius Bull, Fifty-third Pennsylvania. Walker, *Second Corps*, 406.

22. Lee's escape surprised editors at the *New York Times*: "We had been told it so often, that at last even the incredulous became convinced, that we held all these Blue Ridge mountain passes. But it was not the case. We probably held securely all the passes as far west as Manassas Gap. But beyond that, unfortunately, our cavalry only made their advance *after* the rebels had seized Chester and Thornton's Gaps. We cannot help thinking that there was a very fatal oversight here." *New York Times*, July 28, 1863.

23. Brig. Gen. William Hays (1819–75) "made little impression" on the II Corps. Coddington, *Gettysburg Campaign*, 558. In his letter of August 1, just before mention of William Hays, Dyer commented: "General Howard is to have the II Corps I see. I don't want him to bring any of his Dutchmen here." On August 7 Dyer confirmed this to be "a false report."

24. Maj. Gen. Gouverneur K. Warren (1830–82), II Corps, won fame while the army's chief engineer on July 2 at Little Round Top. Dyer wrote on August 16: "He is a small man, a West Point man, and was first colonel of the 5th New York—a Zouave regiment, and a splendid one too." But after Mine Run Dyer wrote of Warren (on December 8, 1863): "I think he has got ahead rather too fast. I have no great regard for him as a man, and that is perhaps why I have no great sympathy for him in his trouble: for he is in some trouble about his part in the recent movement. He undertook something which he did not perform—whether it was his fault or not I don't feel prepared to say." For a sympathetic treatment, see David M. Jordan, *"Happiness Is Not My Companion": The Life of General G. K. Warren* (Bloomington: Indiana University Press, 2001).

25. The Seventh Michigan and First Minnesota were ordered to New York City, as another round of conscription was carried out, to prevent a repetition of the July draft riots. The latter unit took fifty-five casualties July 3 at Gettysburg, twenty-three of them killed or mortally wounded and at least eighty killed or mortally wounded for the two days it was engaged in that battle. See Moe, *Last Full Measure*, 295–96, 298–99. New York governor Horatio Seymour (1810–87) was a Democrat.

26. There were many complaints during the last two years of the war about the poor quality of new men in the Army of the Potomac, complaints confirmed by Confederate observations, particularly on Union deserters. By this time many new recruits had to be paid to enlist; bounty jumpers took the money, enlisting with the intention of deserting and repeating the process. Waitt, *Nineteenth Massachusetts*, 260; Eugene C. Murdock, *One Million Men: The Civil War Draft in the North* (Madison: State Historical Society of Wisconsin, 1971), 334–35; Murdock, *Patriotism Limited, 1862–*

1865: The Civil War Draft and the Bounty System (Kent, Ohio: Kent State University Press, 1967), 81–82. Dyer wrote on September 3, 1863, that two substitutes for the Twentieth Massachusetts had deserted the day before after stealing six hundred dollars from their comrades.

27. Jesse Mayberry, Company M. *Union,* 2:507; Henrietta Stratton Jaquette, ed., *Letters of a Civil War Nurse: Cornelia Hancock, 1863–1865* (1971; reprint, Lincoln: University of Nebraska Press, 1998), 22. Of deserters such as Mayberry, Dyer wrote on August 21, 1863: "The Fifteenth and Nineteenth {Massachusetts} have had about 150 conscripts or substitutes each. They desert every chance they get—when they are fully aware what the consequences *may* be, but they *think* they will come out all right. Some of them have enlisted and deserted over and over again."

28. Richard Napoleon Batchelder (d. 1901). Walker, *Second Corps,* 207, 209. For the presentation to Sedgwick, see Walker, *Second Corps,* 317–18.

29. George B. Corkhill, Second Brigade, Second Division. *OR,* 33:809.

30. Dr. Dwinelle, Third Division, II Corps, had two hundred wounded in his Culpeper hospital. Jaquette, *Civil War Nurse,* 25–26. In a postscript dated August 30 to his letter of the twenty-ninth, Dyer wrote that he went with General Webb to Sunday services at the Seventy-second Pennsylvania, which had the only chaplain in the division, "a poor stick."

31. Lt. John Taylor Wood, CSN, and a small force had captured the USS *Satellite* and *Reliance* August 23. Union cavalry destroyed the vessels September 2, 1863. Long, *Day by Day,* 404.

32. Brig. Gen. Hugh Judson Kilpatrick (1836–81), Third Division, Cavalry Corps.

33. Brig. Gen. George A. Custer (1839–76), Second Brigade (Michigan), Third Cavalry Division.

34. In an addition to his letter of September 9, actually written the next evening, he told Maria that one of their substitutes had been arrested for rape the previous night, would be tried on the eleventh, and if convicted, which seemed likely, would be executed as soon as the sentence could be sent to army headquarters and approved. "There will be no respite for him. It is the first time any such charge was made against a man of this division, and all the old soldiers will gladly see him strung up. He will not have the privilege of being shot."

35. *Failure:* probably a reference to the cavalry commander's attempt to destroy enemy gunboats on nearby rivers, which began August 4.

36. Lincoln's remark was widely repeated at the time and quoted by historians since. Dyer's opinion of Maj. Gen. Abner Doubleday was shared by Frank Haskell and some other hardcore veterans. Coddington, *Gettysburg Campaign,* 690–91; Byrne and Weaver, *Haskell,* 165.

37. Dyer's comment again shows his innate conservatism as a Maine man, as a doctor, and as a military surgeon who had become thoroughly imbued with the values of the old army. It may also suggest that William A. Hammond, and perhaps Jonathan Letterman, were not as popular among field surgeons as recent works suggest. Hammond's friends in the Sanitary Commission had helped him get the position of Surgeon General with the rank of brigadier general in April 1862, jumping over many senior surgeons, and he in turn appointed his friend Letterman as medical director of the Army of the Potomac. Hammond offended first many older surgeons, including respected civilians, by condemning the use of calomel, then army doctors by banning heavy doses of mercury. His colleagues did not help him when he ran afoul of Secretary of War Edwin Stanton (in a bureaucratic fight with the Quartermaster Department over removal of dead and wounded from the field at Second Bull Run, during which he recklessly accused Stanton of being indirectly responsible for much suffering and death) and was later unfairly court-martialed for discrepancies in his handling of liquor supplies, among other charges. One of Hammond's medical colleagues said, " 'those who knew him rarely found him anything but captious, irritable, and pompous,' " an opinion echoed by an assistant surgeon in Philadelphia who wrote, " 'a more arrogant and pompous individual had never visited the hospital.' " As for Letterman, by the fall of 1863, Dyer thought well of him, writing on September 7 that Letterman, "who has been Medical Director of the Army of the Potomac for two years, understands the wants of armies better than one who has had no experience."

Most historians of Civil War medicine have praised Hammond and Letterman, but such feelings were hardly universal during the war, from Stanton on down. See Thomas and Hyman, *Stanton*, 266–68; Garrison, *John Shaw Billings*, 21–22, 30, 213; Frank R. Freemon, *Gangrene and Glory: Medical Care during the American Civil War* (1998; reprint, Urbana: University of Illinois Press, 2001), 70–76, 142–46, 215; Coco, " 'A Laborious and Vexatious Task,' " 290–324; Jonathan Letterman, M.D., *Medical Recollections of the Army of the Potomac*, and Lt. Col. Bennett A. Clements, *Memoir of Jonathan Letterman* (1866, 1883; reprint ed. of both works in one vol., Knoxville: Bohemian Brigade, 1994), 220–26; and Harris D. Riley Jr., "Medical Activities," in Steven E. Woodworth, ed., *The American Civil War: A Handbook of Literature and Research* (Westport, Conn.: Greenwood, 1996), 438.

38. The French emperor Napoleon III was preparing to install a relative, Archduke Ferdinand Maximilian of Austria, as puppet ruler of Mexico, a violation of the Monroe Doctrine.

39. Gregg: Brig. Gen. David M. Gregg (1833–1916), Second Division, Cavalry Corps; Buford: Brig. Gen. John Buford (1826–63), First Division, Cavalry Corps.

40. The transfer west of Lt. Gen. James Longstreet's corps weakened Lee's army, leading to fighting. Long, *Day by Day*, 408–9.

41. In his letter of September 15, Dyer mentioned that William Douglas Wallach, Copperhead owner of the *Washington Star*, lived near the division's camp with his family; his wife was in Washington. Culpeper Court House was "a dirty place and rats are as plenty as blackberries."

42. In his letter of September 18, Dyer wrote that the cavalry was armed with newly arrived Spencer's seven shooters, with which they were pestering Rebel pickets.

43. Cedar Mountain was the opening battle of the Second Bull Run campaign, on August 9, 1862. Maj. Gen. Nathaniel Banks attacked Stonewall Jackson's forces, under Maj. Gen. Richard S. Ewell and Brig. Gen. Winder, but was defeated by a flank attack from Maj. Gen. A. P. Hill.

44. Slaves were more than half the population of Culpeper County in 1860, and more than 10 percent of the farms were five hundred acres or larger, two indices of concentrated wealth and a plantation economy. Sam Bowers Hilliard, *Atlas of Antebellum Southern Agriculture* (Baton Rouge: Louisiana State University Press, 1984), maps 38, 52.

45. Chickamauga, September 19–20. Aided by most of Longstreet's corps, Gen. Braxton Bragg defeated Maj. Gen. William S. Rosecrans, driving his army back into Chattanooga, which the Confederates had recently evacuated. The Union Signal Corps had been able to read Confederate flag messages since November 1862. Edwin C. Fishel, *The Secret War for the Union: The Untold Story of Military Intelligence in the Civil War* (Boston: Houghton Mifflin, 1996), 321.

46. Maj. Gen. Joseph Hooker was ordered west with the XI and XII Corps.

47. Col. James B. Fry, the provost marshal general, claimed that the number of deserters in September and October 1863 was half of what it had been in May and June 1863. Executions, at first held on Fridays, came to be almost a daily occurrence. Dr. John G. Perry, assistant surgeon, Twentieth Massachusetts, wrote on October 1, "These conscripts, or rather substitutes, behave disgracefully, deserting at every possible chance, even to the enemy," adding that two deserters in the regiment were shot, and thirty-four men deserted immediately afterward. Another was caught while attempting desertion and shot off a finger, hoping to be sent to the hospital, but instead would serve with one less digit. Perry, *Letters from a Surgeon*, 77–78; Ella Lonn, *Desertion during the Civil War* (1928; reprint, Gloucester: Peter Smith, 1966), 174, 178, 180–82.

48. One of a series of cavalry actions, probably the reconnaissance across the Rapidan River, September 21–23, as reported by Brig. Gen. John Buford. *OR*, 29(1):140–41.

49. Henry Rockwood, thirty-one, from either Westford or South Weymouth. *RMV*, 2:202; *Surgeons*, 80. For more serious disciplinary cases involving army surgeons, see Thomas P. Lowry, M.D., and Jack D. Welsh, M.D., *Tarnished Scalpels: The Court-Martials of Fifty Union Surgeons* (Mechanicsburg, Pa.: Stackpole, 2000).

50. He meant that Longstreet's corps was fresh from fighting the Army of the Potomac. His comments reflect the rivalry between the two great Union armies, and the resentment of Ulysses Grant by some Army of the Potomac veterans. Yet Dyer may well have been correct about the respective casualties of the II Corps and Grant's army at Vicksburg, where he suffered a loss of perhaps five thousand in the fighting around the city and ten thousand for the entire campaign. At Antietam, the II Corps lost 5,138. Bruce Catton, *Grant Moves South* (Boston: Little, Brown, 1960), 479; Samuel Carter, *The Final Fortress: The Campaign for Vicksburg, 1862–1863* (New York: St. Martin's Press, 1980), 302; Walker, *Second Corps*, 120.

9. "CERTAIN DEATH AWAITED SO MANY BRAVE MEN"

1. "Lee's difficulty is Meade's opportunity. There are yet two months before him of good campaigning weather in Virginia. . . . Here, surely, is margin enough for the march of the Potomac army to Richmond over all impediments." *New York Herald*, Sept. 30, 1863. "In Gen. Meade's army everything remains the same, nor are there any indications of immediate active operations. . . . [W]ith the army of Rosecrans still confronting him, supported by Burnside's column, and daily receiving reinforcements, Bragg is not in a condition to send back even his Virginia divisions in support of Lee. . . . [E]ven with the loss of two corps, or three for that matter, the army of General Meade is still superior to that of his adversary, and has nothing to fear from him." *New York Herald*, Oct. 2, 1863.

2. Probably E. L. Sproat, a civilian volunteer aide on Brig. Gen. Alfred Sully's staff, first with the First Minnesota, then the First Brigade, Second Division, II Corps in July 1862. Dyer may have given him an honorary rank, as he seems to do with Meade below.

3. Jefferson P. Kidder (1815–83), Vermont Democrat and lieutenant governor, who became a leading Minnesota Republican.

4. In his letter of this date, Dyer calls Meade, of Tarrytown, the brother-in-law of Brig. Gen. Alexander Webb and says a lieutenant's commission in the Forty-second New York arrived the day after his departure. He read of Meade's death in the *Washington Chronicle* the same day.

5. Captain MacKay: Thomas M. McKay was "assassinated." Asst. Surgeon John G. Perry describes the incident in detail. See Perry, *Letters from a Surgeon*, 80–98. See also Bruce, *Twentieth Massachusetts*, 446; and Walker, *Second Corps*, 317.

6. After advancing, Meade withdrew behind the Rappahannock. Lee's advance then led to the battle of Bristoe Station. Walker, *Second Corps*, 321–24.

7. John Minor Botts (1802–69), prominent Whig, congressman, and Virginia Unionist. His house was just west of Brandy Station above the Orange and Alexandria Railroad. The headquarters of the Third Brigade, First Division, III Corps was nearby; one of Botts's daughters became pregnant by a Massachusetts sergeant. Daniel E. Sutherland, *Seasons of War: The Ordeal of a Confederate Community, 1861–1865* (New York: Free Press, 1995), 286, 306. For his hospitality, Rebels took all his provisions, burned his fences, shot his cattle, and rearrested Botts, taking him as far as Culpeper Court House before releasing him. Bruce, *Twentieth Massachusetts*, 326; *Atlas*, plate 87:3; Theodore Lyman, *With Grant and Meade* (1922; reprint, Lincoln: University of Nebraska Press, 1994), 46–47.

8. Sears, *Gates of Richmond*, 44–52, 87–88.

9. News of Lincoln's acceptance of William Harrow's resignation reached II Corps headquarters October 3. Walker, *Second Corps*, 320. The general resigned April 20, 1865, having been transferred west after Mine Run, where he led the Fourth Division, XV Corps until his command was broken up. Maj. Gen. O. O. Howard refused to give him another and sent him to Maj. Gen. William T. Sherman, who sent him to Washington. Boatner, *Dictionary*, 381; Warner, *Generals in Blue*, 211.

10. A soldier with two years' service received $402 for reenlisting, $100 more than a new recruit. Units where two-thirds of the enlisted men resigned were designated as "veteran" regiments, and its members received a service chevron on their uniform and a thirty-day furlough, officers included. James W. Geary, *We Need Men: The Union Draft in the Civil War* (DeKalb: Northern Illinois University Press, 1991), 112; Perry, *Letters from a Surgeon*, 151.

11. This fighting led to the battle of Bristoe Station October 14.

12. Colonel Murray: Edward Murray (1819–74), Lee's assistant adjutant general, December 30, 1862–August 31, 1863, was a farmer in 1860 with $6,900 in real and $2,218 in personal property. Louisa Murray, his wife, was ten years younger. Both were Marylanders as were their first two children. Having moved to Virginia in the mid-1850s, their house in late 1863 was on the II Corps line of march to Bristoe Station, near the Warrenton Branch Railroad. Freeman, *Lee*, 1:643; *Staff Officers*, 119; U.S., Eighth Census,

1860, Fauquier County, Va., Northeastern Revenue District, p. 108, family 762, roll 1344; *Atlas*, plate 45:6.

13. The rear-guard fight at Auburn (Catlett's Station). Walker, *Second Corps*, 330–34; Boatner, *Dictionary*, 132.

14. The battle of Bristoe Station, fought October 14.

15. Capt. S. Newell Smith, acting assistant inspector general, 7th Michigan; Capt. Francis Wessells, judge advocate, 106th Pennsylvania; Col. James E. Mallon, 42d New York. Walker, *Second Corps*, 358–59; Charles H. Banes, *History of the Philadelphia Brigade* (Philadelphia: J. B. Lippincott, 1876), 205.

16. McClellan's letter of October 12 endorsed Democrat George W. Woodward (1809–75), Pennsylvania supreme court judge, for governor. With another prominent Copperhead and gubernatorial candidate, Ohio lawyer Clement L. Vallandigham (1820–71), they united with New York governor Horatio Seymour against Lincoln and Congressional Republicans after the campaign, but Gettysburg changed the course of state elections held on various dates. *NCAB*, 11:517; Stephen W. Sears, ed., *The Civil War Papers of George B. McClellan* (New York: Ticknor and Fields, 1989), 524, 558–59; James M. McPherson, *Battle Cry of Freedom* (New York: Oxford University Press, 1988), 684–88.

17. No documentation for this story has been found.

18. Lincoln's third call for volunteers. Geary, *We Need Men*, 80.

19. One of the accomplishments of Lee's Bristoe campaign. He had not only pushed Meade back some distance but also destroyed miles of railroad with Shermanesque methods and captured or destroyed quantities of supplies.

20. Ewell: Lt. Gen. Richard S. Ewell (1817–72), II Corps, Army of Northern Virginia.

Leading the first part of Lee's army to reach the area, and eager to get at the III Corps, Hill failed to note the presence of the II Corps on his flank and suffered heavy casualties, but he was not arrested. James I. Robertson Jr., *General A. P. Hill* (New York: Random House, 1987), 239–40.

21. Maj. Gen. George Thomas took command from Rosecrans at Chattanooga October 17. Long, *Day by Day*, 423.

22. See Jordan, *Warren*, 107–11, 120. Sykes was known as "Tardy George" in the old army, and Meade removed him in December 1863. Warner, *Generals in Blue*, 493.

23. The spur linked Warrenton to the Orange and Alexandria at Warrenton Station. *Atlas*, plate 8:1.

24. Union surgeons wore a distinctive green sash.

25. Brig. Gen. Seth Williams of Maine (1822–66).

26. *OR*, 29(1):338, 418, 29(2):385–92.

27. Victor A. Yorke; Atkinson remains unidentified. Lyman, *Grant and Meade*, 42.

28. Berry Hill, a Culpeper County estate off the Fredericksburg Plank Road north of Stevensburg near Brandy Station, was looted by Maj. Gen. John Pope's troops in 1862. William Alexander Thom was a Confederate surgeon. II Corps headquarters was next to one of two Thom houses. Mrs. Taylor's house was just south of Stevensburg. Sutherland, *Seasons of War*, 123, 250, 298; *Confederate*, 15:165; *Atlas*, plates 44:3, 87:3.

29. Lieutenant Harmon: Lt. William Harmon, Company C, First Minnesota. Moe, *Last Full Measure*, 282.

Belle Isle: for an account of this prison camp in the James River at Richmond, see Don Allison, ed., *Hell on Belle Isle: Diary of a Civil War POW* (Bryan, Ohio: Faded Banner, 1997). Sgt. Jacob Osborn Coburn, Sixth Michigan Cavalry, was captured at Harpers Ferry October 18, 1863, the same month as the provost guards.

30. The Mine Run campaign began November 26. Like Bristoe, it was a flanking attempt by one of the commanding generals. Meade had five corps, about 85,000 men, against Lee's 48,500. It was the end of major offensive operations by the army until Ulysses Grant's Wilderness campaign in May 1864. Long, *Day by Day*, 439.

31. In his letter to Maria of August 8, Dyer referred to the account of the Second Division, II Corps, from the *New York Times* (reprinted as appendix 3), writing: "Many of the letters from correspondents are perfectly ridiculous. Some generals keep a lot of reporters with them to record their deeds and I know of an officer who agreed to pay $100 for a good notice in the *N.Y. Herald*—but he paid only $25 and the reporter told of it."

32. After Grant's victory at Chattanooga, Lt. Gen. James Longstreet ended his campaign against Knoxville because of the approach of Federal reinforcements.

33. Theodore Hesser, Seventy-second Pennsylvania, died leading a charge. George C. Joslin, Fifteenth Massachusetts, of Worcester, survived the war. Gottfried, *Stopping Pickett*, 186–87; Walker, *Second Corps*, 389; Coco, *Ball's Bluff to Gettysburg*, 147, 251.

34. Lieutenant Simms: William T. Simms, Eighty-second New York, later major. Wounded during May 1864, he could not talk at first and suffered mentally. Simms transferred to the Fifty-ninth New York and mustered out April 18, 1865, the wound still open with partial paralysis of the left side of his face. Walker, *Second Corps*, 697; *MSH*, 7:175.

10. "HANCOCK AND MYSELF RUN THIS MACHINE"

1. Brig. Gen. Gustavus A. DeRussy (1818–91), XXII Corps, commanded the defenses south of the Potomac.

2. Captain Gale: Capt. W. Gale, judge advocate, Fifteenth Massachusetts, cited by Maj. Gen. John Gibbon, November 7, 1864, for his performance in the spring campaign.

3. Colonel Carroll: Col. Samuel Sprigg Carroll (1832–93), Third Brigade, Second Division, II Corps. Wounded at the Wilderness and Spotsylvania, he was promoted to brigadier general.

4. Grant ordered the "heavies" (the heavy artillery regiments) out of the Washington defenses. The Second New York later fired a volley into the First Massachusetts, which lost 398 men to musket fire in its first fight, at Harris's Farm, May 19, 1864. William D. Matter, *If It Takes All Summer* (Chapel Hill: University of North Carolina Press, 1988), 325.

5. Dr. James T. Calhoun, surgeon, Seventy-fourth New York (Fifth Excelsior). *Surgeons*, 139.

6. A mild form of smallpox for those vaccinated or previously exposed.

7. John M. Norvell became Gibbon's assistant adjutant general, having filled the same office for Maj. Gen. William H. French, III Corps. *OR*, 29(1):738, 36(1):435.

8. Kilpatrick returned from his Richmond raid a month earlier, losing 340 men, 1,100 horses, and dozens of modern small arms while achieving little, but he served General Sherman well in the West. Pleasonton was replaced March 25 and sent to Missouri. The two cavalrymen were "pernicious influences." Longacre, *Cavalry at Gettysburg*, 275. The cavalry had been an overall disappointment but did better under Sheridan and Custer.

9. Dr. Henry Lawrence (b. 1830), assistant surgeon of the Grenadier Guards, February 1854, served in the Crimean War until the British withdrawal in 1856, was a member of the Crimean Medical Society of military doctors and surgeons, and retired in 1885 as brigade surgeon. John Shepherd, *The Crimean Doctors: A History of the British Medical Services in the Crimean War*, 2 vols. (Liverpool: Liverpool University Press, 1991), 2:582, 589 n. 37.

10. The division was led by Lt. Col. Edmund Rice and Maj. Henry L. Abbott. Others attending the review included Generals Hancock, A. A. Humphreys, Warren, Gibbon, and Sheridan.

11. The Letterman system of division instead of regimental hospitals was being fully implemented. Although Dyer had weighty responsibilities, including decisions about what to bring in the thirteen wagons and what to leave behind, he could rely upon the army being resupplied, not only from

Aquia Creek but also from Port Royal, White House, Harrison's Landing, and City Point as Grant moved south over the next two months. The parallel rivers that formed defensive barriers also allowed naval support for an invading army. See chapter 11, entries dated May 22 and 26, 1864.

12. Sheridan transformed the cavalry. Discipline was lacking in this arm on both sides at various times, as was attention to uniforms and grooming. Compare the somewhat similar views on aviators held by other branches in twentieth-century armed forces. Starr, *Union Cavalry*, 2:208–33.

13. Walker mentions 25,000 were reviewed and additional details. *Second Corps*, 405–6. See also Waitt, *Nineteenth Massachusetts*, 301.

14. Compare Lyman, *Grant and Meade*, 80–81, 156; Horace Porter, *Campaigning with Grant* (1897; reprint, New York: Time-Life, 1981), 1–2, 13–15; and Perry, *Letters from a Surgeon*, 163.

11. "WE SHALL HAMMER AT THEM"

1. Dyer reported 5 killed, 23 wounded, and 5 missing from the Nineteenth and 19 killed, 95 wounded, and 75 missing from the Twentieth Massachusetts during the battle of the Wilderness, May 5–7, 1864. His total casualties for the Second Division, II Corps, were 168 killed, 1,037 wounded, and 251 missing from an aggregate present for duty of 5,968—a 24 percent loss.

2. Scott, *Fallen Leaves*, 250–55.

3. Dyer operated May 6, the date Col. Selden S. Connor (1839–1917) was wounded in the leg. Later governor of Maine, Connor was discharged April 7, 1866, as a brigadier general and pensioned with anchylosis of the knee joint, his injured limb useless. *MSH*, 11:203. The Nineteenth Maine had 20 killed, 110 wounded, and 10 missing.

4. In his report Hancock cited Capt. Edward P. Brownson, son of writer and philosopher Orestes A. Brownson and an aide to Maj. Gen. Gouverneur Warren at Bristoe. Like his brother, Lt. Leonard J. Brownson, First Vermont, the captain died that summer. Dyer had frequent dealings with Captain Brownson, commissary of musters for the II Corps, in July and August 1864 and wrote of that officer's death shortly before the doctor himself was discharged. Arthur M. Schlesinger Jr., *Orestes A. Brownson* (Boston: Little, Brown, 1939), 250.

5. See Brooks D. Simpson, *Ulysses S. Grant: Triumph over Adversity, 1822–1865* (Boston: Houghton Mifflin, 2000), 284–87.

6. John Aiken, Seventy-first Pennsylvania, served from April 1863. F. LeB. Monroe, of Brooklyn, went to the Fifteenth Massachusetts in January 1863. R. P. H. Sawyer, Forty-second New York, from Bedford, served from July 1863 and, unlike the two others, rejoined the Second Division by May 10. *Surgeons*, 80, 132, 196. See also appendixes 3 and 4.

7. For the battle of Po River Dyer reported 14 killed, 174 wounded, and 17 missing; a total of 205 from an aggregate present for duty of 4,292 in the Second Division, II Corps.

8. Major Generals William F. "Baldy" Smith and Benjamin Butler were to attack Richmond from the south up the James River. William G. Robertson, *Back Door to Richmond: The Bermuda Hundred Campaign* (Newark: University of Delaware Press, 1987).

9. Hancock's preparations for his assault on the Mule Shoe Salient and the fighting at the Bloody Angle.

10. Dyer's letter of May 12 describes the fighting in more detail, along with an anecdote from headquarters: "I had just dressed Gen. Webb's wound and sent him off in an ambulance when Gen. H. was impatiently calling for his pencil, which he had probably lost. I lent him mine, with which he wrote a dispatch to Gen. Meade, one of the proudest things he has done during this war, saying he had taken 3,000 prisoners, from 30 to 40 pieces of artillery, and had 3 lines of their rifle pits. This number was afterwards increased to 5,000 and the guns to 46." Maria asked if he had gotten the pencil back as a souvenir of the battle. On May 30 he responded: "The pencil you spoke of I shall never see again. No one ever lent anything to Hancock and got it again."

11. Brig. Gen. Cullen Andrews Battle's brigade, Rodes's division, Ewell's corps.

12. The Twentieth: Lt. Col. Edmund Rice was wounded and captured but lived until 1906. John J. Ferris enlisted as a private. John B. Thompson was killed June 3, 1864. Charles B. Brown, Company G, was hit in both thighs. Waitt, *Nineteenth Massachusetts*, 322. Dyer listed 6 killed, 30 wounded, and 5 missing among 165 present for duty, while the OR gives a total of 50. For the Twentieth Massachusetts he reported 6 killed, 71 wounded, and 38 missing, from 365 present; the OR gives total casualties as 102.

13. Burnside's IX Corps officially became part of the army May 25. Maj. Gen. Christopher C. Augur (1821–98) helped Halleck get troops out of Washington to Grant. OR, 36(2):696.

14. Col. Samuel S. Carroll (1832–93), Third Brigade, Second Division, II Corps.

15. One of two Beverley houses northeast of Spotsylvania Court House off the Fredericksburg road.

16. There is no mention of Wass in the regimental history from March until June 22, 1864. The silence of Ernest Waitt and John Adams on this is suggestive. See Waitt, *Nineteenth Massachusetts*, 300, 327; and Adams, *Reminiscences*, 82–103. A member of Company K wrote on June 19, 1864, describing events in the regiment since its crossing of the James, and

ended: "Col. Ansel D. Wass is at the Corps Hospital sick. Tiger." *BDJ*, June 24, 1864.

17. Corcoran Legion: a brigade of four New York regiments raised by Brig. Gen. Michael Corcoran (1827–63) in November 1862.

18. At Spotsylvania, May 12–19, Dyer reported 145 killed, 774 wounded, and 170 missing—1,089 from an aggregate of 7,764.

19. On the north side of the Ni River.

20. Recently organized, the regiment became a legendary unit as part of the First Brigade, Second Division, II Corps.

21. John D. Starbird, twenty-one, Company K, enlisted September 3, 1861. He had most recently deserted at Laurel Hill, May 10–11. Waitt, *Nineteenth Massachusetts*, 412; Adams, *Reminiscences*, 94; Turino, *Diary of Lieut. J. E. Hodgkins*, 88 n.136.

22. The Richmond, Fredericksburg, and Potomac Railroad ran north from the Confederate capital via Ashland and Hanover Junction and was a major logistical link for Lee's army.

23. Seringas: seringa trees, or mock oranges. Compare Turino, *Diary of Lieut. J. E. Hodgkins*, 88.

24. For casualties during the battle of North Anna River, Dyer reported 47 killed, 229 wounded, and 44 missing, a total of 320 out of 5,806 effectives.

25. Hanover Junction, at the intersection of the Richmond, Fredericksburg, and Potomac, and the Virginia Central Railroads, was renamed for the Doswell family after the war. Bernard Doswell's rank was probably honorary, for he does not appear in standard references. But for a statement by two of his slaves to Hancock, sent on to Meade, see *OR*, 36(3):148–49.

26. After inconclusive fighting at Drewry's Bluff, Butler withdrew his two corps of the Army of the James onto the Bermuda Hundred peninsula. Gen. P. G. T. Beauregard built earthworks across the neck, hemming in the Federals.

12. "VERY FEW WOUNDED HAVE BEEN BROUGHT IN"

1. Grant moved toward Cold Harbor, fighting there June 1–3.

2. Dudley C. Mumford, Company G, killed May 31. Adams, *Reminiscences*, 97–98.

3. Dyer recorded 161 division casualties out of 7,211 present for duty at Totopotomoy Creek, May 30–June 1, most of them from the Thirty-sixth Wisconsin.

4. The house was on a hill between branches of the creek. Waitt, *Nineteenth Massachusetts*, 317; *Atlas*, plate 96:6.

5. General Tyler: Brig. Gen. Robert O. Tyler, Fourth Brigade, Second Division, II Corps, was seriously wounded at Cold Harbor, June 3, 1864.

Article on doing housework: "House and Home Papers," a monthly series by "Christopher Crowfield." Number six concerned "The *lady who does her own work*." *Atlantic Monthly* 13 (June 1864): 754–61. Maria's domestic management, overexertion, and the hiring of a servant were frequent topics in the couple's letters.

6. Gibbon cited Dyer in his report on the operations of the Second Division, May 3–June 12, as "unremitting" in attention to his duties and said that "the sick, wounded, and well wanted for nothing." *OR*, 36(1):435.

7. See Robertson, *Back Door to Richmond*, 231–32.

8. Lieutenant Thompson: John B. Thompson, Company F; Captain Hinks: Elisha A. Hinks, Company C, badly wounded, discharged for disability October 1864; Captain Hale: Henry A. Hale, Company B.

9. George: the doctor's brother, George B. Dyer.

10. Maria's brother, Heber James Davis.

11. The XVIII Corps, in the Department of North Carolina since December 1862, joined Maj. Gen. Benjamin Butler's Army of the James in July 1863 when the Departments of Virginia and North Carolina merged and fought at Bermuda Hundred before moving under Maj. Gen. William F. "Baldy" Smith to aid Grant. The X Corps was in the Department of the South around Charleston in the fall of 1862 and later in Florida before assignment to Butler. The Second and Third Divisions were sent to Cold Harbor to assist the XVIII Corps at the end of May, led by Maj. Gen. Quincy A. Gillmore.

12. A comment reflecting the view still held by many on both sides that the war would end with a big battle rather than by attrition, or with a siege of Richmond rather than Petersburg.

13. A dispute arose between Grant and Lee over a truce to care for the wounded, mostly Union, between the lines near Cold Harbor. They corresponded for several days, and by the time the demands of military etiquette were met, all but two were dead. *OR*, 36(3):599–600, 603–4, 608, 638–39, 666–67, 669–70; Emory M. Thomas, *Robert E. Lee* (New York: W. W. Norton, 1995), 334–35; Simpson, *Grant*, 328–30; William S. McFeely, *Grant* (New York: W. W. Norton, 1981), 171–73.

14. Dr. Tyler has not been identified but was the *former* owner of the house, called by Cornelia Hancock "a Virginia mansion." Jaquette, *Civil War Nurse*, 99. The doctor was a cousin of ex-President John Tyler. John Michael Priest, ed., *One Surgeon's Private War: Dr. William W. Potter of the 57th New York* (Shippensburg, Pa.: White Mane, 1996), 106. No Tyler listed as a physician appears on the 1850 or 1860 census for Hanover County, but the house is shown on many maps, both those of Cold Harbor and of the Peninsula Campaign, and is mentioned in the *New York Times*

account of the Second Division, II Corps during McClellan's campaign as well as a number of times in the *OR* and *OR Supp.* See *Atlas*, plates 92:1-1, 97:2.

15. He reported 1,494 casualties (267 killed, 964 wounded) in the Second Division, June 2–12, the Nineteenth Massachusetts accounting for 21 of them.

16. Lincoln was renominated by the National Union party at a coalition convention in Baltimore June 8, 1864.

17. Captain Gray: Robert J. Gray, Ninth Maine, Second Brigade, Third Division, XVIII Corps. *OR*, 36(3):429.

18. Dyer was on the north bank of the James below Charles City Court House. Windmill Point, on the south shore of the river, was in Prince George County.

19. Gunboats protected McClellan's army near the same spot, close to the Berkeley and Westover plantations, after Malvern Hill.

20. The bridge was north of Harrison's Landing.

21. Dr. Wilcox's house is shown east of the landing on many maps. *Atlas*, plates 92:1-1, 93:1.

22. The longest pontoon bridge ever built in wartime, it stretched two thousand feet across a channel ninety feet deep with a four-foot tidal range; completed June 15. Boatner, *Dictionary*, 434.

23. Dyer's letter of this date called the plantation "Flowery Hundred." Flowerdew Hundred, established before 1619, was one of the original settlements in the Virginia colony. Mrs. M. J. Wilcox was forty-two in 1860, a farmer with $40,000 in real estate and $50,000 in personal property and the owner of 91 slaves, wealth that made her one of the richest people in the Old South. Four years later she was living in relative poverty. Her two sons of military age were J. V. Wilcox Jr., twenty-three, and William, seventeen. J. V. Wilcox owned 27 slaves in 1860. U.S. Bureau of the Census, 1860 Census, Prince George County, Va., roll 1372, p. 71, family 585; and Slave Schedule, roll 1396, pp. 42–43; see also *Atlas*, plate 93:1. Four different Wilcoxes in Charles City County owned a total of 203 slaves and reported $85,000 in real and $129,000 in personal property. 1860 Census, Charles City County, Va., roll 1340, pp. 27, 65–66, families 204, 206, 503, 523; and Slave Schedule, roll 1388, pp. 1, 12, 30–31, 33–34.

24. Dyer's comment echoes those of Theodore Lyman and Horace Porter and is supported by recent scholarship. Despite much damage to civilian property, historian Mark Grimsley argues that by war's end the Union army's policy in Virginia differed little from McClellan's. Lyman, *Grant and Meade*, 117, 119, 122, 129–32; Porter, *Campaigning with Grant*, 109–10, 133–34, 137–39; Grimsley, *Hard Hand of War*, 1, 212, 222–25.

13. "A MASS OF EARTH ROSE IN THE AIR"

1. Grant stole a march on Lee, not merely outflanking him but moving his entire army across the James to threaten Petersburg, a rail hub crucial to Richmond's safety. Old men and boys held the lines until Gen. P. G. T. Beauregard brought in regular troops. It was several days before Lee was convinced that the entire Army of the Potomac was there.

2. Dyer counted 1,987 casualties in the Second Division, June 16–30, including 136 in the Nineteenth Massachusetts.

3. Petersburg had direct rail links with Richmond, twenty miles to the north, and with Norfolk and Portsmouth until Union occupation of eastern Virginia. Vital now were ties to the lower Confederacy along the South Side Railroad via Lynchburg or Danville and on the Weldon Railroad leading to Wilmington, one of the last major ports open to blockade runners.

4. City Point: Petersburg's port, at the junction of the Appomattox River with the James, now the city of Hopewell. It was the last major supply depot for the Army of the Potomac.

5. At Fort Pillow, Tennessee, Maj. Gen. Nathan Bedford Forrest's troops attacked when the Union commander refused to surrender April 12, 1864. For examples of black troops shooting Rebels who had surrendered and the reverse at Plymouth, North Carolina, and the Crater, see Joseph T. Glatthaar, *Forged in Battle: The Civil War Alliance of Black Soldiers and White Officers* (New York: Free Press, 1990), 157–58. For German Americans shooting Rebels who had surrendered, see Peter Cozzens, *The Shipwreck of Their Hopes* (Urbana: University of Illinois Press, 1994), 338–39. For a similar comment on the contrast between black Union soldiers and Confederate prisoners, see Lyman, *Grant and Meade*, 162.

6. The photographs of dead boys in the Petersburg trenches (even those posed by photographers) document a practice that Lee referred to as the Confederacy using up its "seed corn."

7. His letter of June 20, 1864, not copied into his journal, mentions the execution of a black soldier, William Johnson, accused of raping a white woman and hanged between the lines. William A. Frassanito, *Grant and Lee: The Virginia Campaigns, 1864–1865* (New York: Macmillan, 1983), 216–22.

8. For more on the capture of these veteran regiments west of the Jerusalem Plank Road, see *BDJ*, June 25, 28, 30, July 1; Adams, *Reminiscences*, 102–3; Turino, *Diary of Lieut. J. E. Hodgkins*, 96–97; Waitt, *Nineteenth Massachusetts*, 326–35; and Noah Andre Trudeau, *The Last Citadel: Petersburg, Virginia, June 1864–April 1865* (Boston: Little, Brown, 1991), 73–76. The unsuccessful operations of June 22–23 resulted in three thousand Union casualties. There were many attempts to cut the Weldon line south of Petersburg, but it was not accomplished until December.

9. Wass was mustered out July 28, 1864, a month after his account of the regiment's capture appeared in the *Boston Daily Journal*. Dyer blasted him, writing Maria July 4 that "Col. Wass's story is a regular byword. The idea of his going to join his Regt. just in time to see it captured, was so laughable. He must have had a wonderful glass to see through the side of a house, and through woods, fields, &c three or four miles. Bah!" The same issue carried an item claiming that Rebel troops had draped their earthworks with the regimental flag the next day. Dyer may have written or telegraphed his letter to Boston because of the Wass story. He said that the Nineteenth now had about 150 men, the Fifteenth only about 60. *BDJ*, June 28, 30, 1864.

10. Westbrook's house: east of the Jerusalem Plank Road between it and the Norfolk and Petersburg Railroad, north of Second Swamp. *Atlas*, plate 40-1.

11. Hancock was in almost constant pain from his Gettysburg wound and not himself. See Jordan, *Hancock*, 148.

12. Comments like this one, and his remark of June 28 about the unwillingness of troops to charge, can be found in many other accounts for this period. See, for example, Porter, *Campaigning with Grant*, 210–11; and Lyman, *Grant and Meade*, 207–9.

13. J. Warner Johnson, superintendent of field relief based at City Point, visited each army division, ordering supplies of fresh vegetables from the Sanitary Commission's depot. *Sanitary Commission Bulletin* 1 (Aug. 15, 1864): 618–19, 635–36. In his letter of October 25, 1863, Dyer identified him as superintendent of the commission for the Army of the Potomac.

14. Next to the story about Dyer's letter ran one taken from the *New York Herald* claiming that Capt. H. L. Patten, Twentieth Massachusetts, had single-handedly tried to repel the Confederate charge with volleys from his regiment. The next day Quartermaster Thomas F. Winthrop's report to Adjutant General Schouler appeared. Six officers and 165 men surrendered. Two officers and 41 men were left. Twelve officers (including Dyer) and 55 men were on detached service; one officer, no doubt Wass, and 163 men were absent on sick leave. *BDJ*, June 30, July 1, 1864.

15. Finley Anderson, close to Hancock, had been captured and held for a year and was wounded May 10. His dispatch of June 29 said all the railroads running south from Petersburg had been cut by Wilson's cavalry; that the VI Corps had rescued him and been relieved by the II Corps; and that "Gibbon's division . . . has just taken position in the line vacated by the Sixth. The countermarching of the troops was a splendid spectacle. . . . All is quiet along the lines to-night." *New York Herald*, July 2, 1864. Dyer may have had a personal dislike for Anderson because of

his dispatch, censored by Secretary of War Stanton, reporting casualties in the II Corps during the first assaults on Petersburg. Andrews, *North Reports*, 67, 386–87, 537, 550.

16. He confused Lt. Gen. Richard Ewell with Lt. Gen. Jubal Early in his letter this date and did not correct his journal. Some Rebels made the same mistake, crediting Ewell with the Washington raid. See Michael B. Chesson and Leslie J. Roberts, eds., *In Exile: The Confederate Journal of Henri Garidel* (Charlottesville: University Press of Virginia, 2001), 154 n.2, 182 n.1. Grant sent Brig. Gen. Ricketts's Third Division, and then the rest of the VI Corps, to repulse the Confederates in Maryland.

17. Dyer probably read advance news of the president's proclamation, issued July 18. Abraham Lincoln, *The Collected Works of Abraham Lincoln*, ed. Roy P. Basler et al., 8 vols. (New Brunswick, N.J.: Rutgers University Press, 1953–55), 7:448–49.

18. The black troops of the Fourth Division, IX Corps, under Brig. Gen. Edward Ferrero, were training for what would be the battle of the Crater.

19. North of the Westbrook place, between the Norfolk Railroad and the Jerusalem Plank Road. *Atlas*, plate 40:1.

20. Nova Zembla are islands in the Arctic Ocean north of Archangel, Russia. Dyer's hyperbole is a tribute to Lee's army, whose lines would break at the end of March 1865.

21. The uss *Mendota*, a side-wheel steamer that entered service in February 1864, carried two 100-pounder Parrott rifles, one of which broke in this action, and other cannon. The other vessel was probably the *Agawam*. U.S. Navy Department, *Official Records of the Union and Confederate Navies in the War of the Rebellion*, 31 vols. (Washington: Government Printing Office, 1894–1927; reprint, Harrisburg, Pa.: National Historical Society, 1987), ser. 1, vol. 10, 319.

22. Barlow's health failed, and he took a long European leave of absence, returning to command at war's end.

23. The battle of the Crater, or the Petersburg Mine Assault, July 30, 1864.

24. The IX and X Corps suffered 3,798 casualties. *OR*, 40(1):246–49. Dyer meant troops formerly assigned to the XVIII Corps. Black troops specially trained to lead the assault had been pulled out at the last moment. They followed up the initial attack after the explosion but were slaughtered in the Crater by Confederates who refused to accept their surrender. Mark Boatner estimates 1,500 Confederate casualties. Confederates dug shafts of their own trying to intercept the Pennsylvania coalminers at work on the Union tunnel. Boatner, *Dictionary*, 647–49.

14. "THE PROSPECT OF QUARTERS IN LIBBY"

1. General Burnside, Edward Ferrero, James H. Ledlie, and others were all at fault.

2. A diversionary movement to Deep Bottom and back.

3. The use of "fortress" has been a common error; Monroe was designated a fort in 1832 by the secretary of war. David A. Clary, *Fortress America* (Charlottesville: University Press of Virginia, 1990), 58.

4. Lt. Gen. Jubal Early's burning of Chambersburg, Pennsylvania, July 30, 1864.

5. Early August 1864 was a low point in Union morale just before the fall of Atlanta at month's end.

6. Lieutenant colonel commanding: Lt. Col. Henry Pleasants (1833–80).

7. Surgeon Evarts: Orpheus Evarts of College Hill, Ohio, Twentieth Indiana, First Brigade, Third Division, II Corps, served from July 1861 to July 1865. *Surgeons*, 35.

8. Confederate ordnance clerk Henri Garidel referred to Beauregard's mine in his diary entry for August 6 as did Dr. Perry two days later. See Perry, *Letters from a Surgeon*, 220; Chesson and Roberts, *In Exile*, 193 n. 4.

9. "Old Hundred" was based on the One Hundredth Psalm. "Kathleen Mavourneen" (1837) by William Nicholas Crouch, First Company, Richmond Howitzers, was very popular with Union troops. An undated arrangement of "No One to Love" by H. H. G. Richardson was included in *Heart Songs Dear to the American People* (New York: World Syndicate, 1909). "Haggerty's Breeches" has not been identified, but may have been a variant of "Paddy's Leather Breeches," a four-step jig.

10. Thomas A. Smyth (1832–65), a Wilmington coach maker promoted to brigadier general October 1 for Cold Harbor. Hit by a sharpshooter while leading the Third Brigade, Second Division, II Corps at Farmville, he died April 9, 1865, the last Union general killed during the war. Boatner, *Dictionary*, 777.

11. Jacob P. Gould led the First Brigade, First Division, IX Corps. The Dyer-Snow genealogy lists other Goulds.

12. John Hodges Jr., Fifty-ninth Massachusetts, had served under Gould but resigned before the Seven Days. Ernest Waitt lists him as major of the Fiftieth Massachusetts. *Nineteenth Massachusetts*, 79, 112.

13. Confederate agents placed a bomb aboard a Union vessel. The explosion killed 43 men and wounded 126. Grant was showered with debris at his headquarters tent but unhurt. William A. Tidwell et al., *Come Retribution* (Jackson: University Press of Mississippi, 1988), 163; *OR*, 42(1):17.

14. A movement that was part of a week of Union diversions north of the James. Long, *Day by Day*, 555.

15. Macy had been convalescing from a wound received during the Wilderness. Bruce, *Twentieth Massachusetts*, 415–17.

16. Henry L. Patten died September 10, 1864. Scott, *Fallen Leaves*, 186 n.4; Perry, *Letters from a Surgeon*, 173.

17. Miles's brigade: Brig. Gen. Nelson A. Miles (1839–1925), First Division, II Corps.

18. Victor Jean Baptiste Girardey (b. 1837, France), newly promoted to brigadier general from captain for his exploits at the Crater, died August 16 at Fussell's Mill on the Darbytown Road. Brig. Gen. John R. Chambliss died the same day fighting Union cavalry on the Charles City Road. Both deaths came in a series of engagements, August 14–20, north of the James. *OR*, 42(1):18, 81; Ezra Warner, *Generals in Gray* (Baton Rouge: Louisiana State University Press, 1959), 47, 106.

19. A side-wheeler ferryboat carrying 100-pounder Parrotts and other cannon, the *Hunchback* had been engaged by Rebel batteries at Four Mile Creek just east of Deep Bottom August 13, 1864.

20. Sergeant Meahan (perhaps Meehan or Mihan) has not been identified.

21. Warren's V Corps went to Globe Tavern on the Weldon Railroad to destroy track and was attacked August 18–21.

22. Southall house: southeast of the junction of the Norfolk and Petersburg and military railroad from City Point. *Atlas*, plates 40:1, 77:2.

23. Hancock took two divisions to destroy the Weldon Railroad below Reams' Station, working until attacked August 25.

24. The beginning of his journal entry for this date. The notes that follow are to the concluding pages of his journal. Four letters to Maria, dated November 5, 6, 8, and 18, 1864, have survived. The first three he sent from Chesapeake Hospital, Hampton, Virginia, where he went to care for Heber Davis, her brother, who had been severely wounded after Dyer mustered out near the end of August.

25. Sleeper's battery: Capt. J. Henry Sleeper, Tenth Massachusetts Battery.

26. Colonel Walker: Francis A. Walker, later president of the Massachusetts Institute of Technology, was serving as a courier after dark and rode into the enemy's lines. Walker, *Second Corps*, 600 n.1.

27. Confirmed by Bruce, *Twentieth Massachusetts*, 421–23.

28. Levi Jewett, of New York City, served until January 1865. *Surgeons*, 6.

29. Libby prison: named for Maine native Luther Libby, Richmond ship

chandler and slave trader, whose warehouse was seized by the Confederate government and used as a prison for Union officers.

30. Mark Boatner gives Union casualties of 2,742 for Reams' Station, including 2,073 captured or missing, against 720 Confederate losses as reported by Lt. Gen. A. P. Hill. *Dictionary*, 683.

31. David W. Maull, of Wilmington, served to April 1865. *Surgeons*, 8; *OR*, 46(1):758; Jaquette, *Civil War Nurse*, 76.

32. Captain Embler: A. Henry Embler, acting assistant adjutant general. Waitt, *Nineteenth Massachusetts*, 350.

33. Dr. Chaddock: Gilbert Chaddock, from Muskegon, Seventh Michigan, served to January 1865. *Surgeons*, 91.

Dr. Aiken: surgeon John Aiken of the Seventy-first Pennsylvania served from April 1863. He was listed in Dyer's roster of medical officers, Second Division, II Corps, as detailed to remain at the Wilderness with the wounded but not returned as of May 10. Aiken's regiment mustered out July 2. For many references, see Jaquette, *Civil War Nurse*, 72, 74; and *Surgeons*, 196. Cornelia Hancock said he suffered from consumption and coughed terribly.

34. Frederick F. Burmeister, of Philadelphia, originally assistant surgeon, Seventy-third Pennsylvania, transferred to the Sixty-ninth Pennsylvania in December 1862 and was about to lose his post as head of the II Corps hospital. Jaquette, *Civil War Nurse*, 153, 156, 159.

35. Both sides used vessels fitted with nets ahead of the bow designed to catch underwater mines.

15. "THIS GOVERNMENT OF THE PEOPLE"

1. General Hawley: Brig. Gen. Joseph Roswell Hawley (1826–1905), Second Brigade, First Division, X Corps; Chesapeake Hospital: a Fort Monroe hospital, used as early as the Peninsula campaign, in a four-story building that had been a school for young women. Freemon, *Microbes and Minie Balls*, 93–94; Robert E. Denney, *Civil War Medicine* (New York: Sterling, 1994), 118, 134–35.

2. Fort Harrison, on the outer Richmond defenses below Chafin's Bluff, was renamed for Brig. Gen. Hiram Burnham, who died September 29, 1864, while leading the Second Brigade, First Division, XVIII Corps at New Market Heights.

3. Friend House: an entry based on a letter written at the Friend House, Second Division, II Corps headquarters, as shown by the contents and letterhead. The building was northeast of Petersburg, just south of the Appomattox River and City Point Railroad. *Atlas*, plate 40:1.

"Petersburg Express": another nickname for "The Dictator," a thirteen-inch seacoast mortar originally mounted on a railroad car before it was given a fixed site. Boatner, *Dictionary*, 240.

4. Grant's railroad: this military railroad connected the Army of the Potomac's extended lines with City Point, speeding transport of supplies, and eventually stretched far to the south and southwest of Petersburg, even crossing the Weldon line.

5. Hotel at 9 Pleasant Street, above Main Street, near the post office, custom house, and town center. *Gloucester Directory, 1882–83* (Boston: Sampson, Davenport, 1882).

6. B. H. S.: Benjamin H. Smith, whose law firm was across from the Gloucester post office and who represented Gloucester in the House of Representatives of the Massachusetts General Court, 1863–64, became surveyor of customs. *Acts and Resolves Passed by the General Court of Massachusetts* (Boston: Wright and Potter, 1863–64); *Gloucester Directory for 1870–71.*

7. Hon. John B. Alley: Lynn merchant and Republican John Bassett Alley (1817–1896), in Congress, 1859–67. *Who Was Who in America: Historical Volume, 1607–1896* (Chicago: A. N. Marquis, 1963), 21.

Mr. Pew: William A. Pew, of a large, wealthy, and prominent family, was twenty-eight and a merchant with $9,000 in real and $10,000 in personal property in 1860. He was one of the town's three selectmen in 1864, collector at the custom house in 1869, president of the First National Bank of Gloucester by 1870, and a member of the House of Representatives of the Massachusetts General Court from Gloucester, Essex County's eighth district, in the sessions of 1870–71. U.S. Bureau of the Census, 1860 Census, Essex County, Mass., Gloucester, roll 499, p. 245; Schouler, *Massachusetts in the Civil War*, 2:191; *Acts and Resolves*, 1869–71, 1875; Joseph E. Garland, *Eastern Point: A Nautical, Rustical, and Social Chronicle of Gloucester's Outer Shield and Inner Sanctum, 1606–1950* (Peterborough, N.H.: Noone House, 1971), 122–23, 300; *Gloucester and Rockport Directory for 1869*, 155; *Gloucester Directory for 1870–71.*

8. The brevity of Hancock's endorsement may indicate that Dyer had not been as close to him as he thought. More likely the general was overwhelmed with requests for recommendations, and Dyer was a Republican, whereas Hancock was a Democrat.

9. Dr. H.: Dr. Charles H. Hildreth (1825–84) was the popular acting assistant surgeon at Eastern Point fort. He resigned soon after the war ended. Dyer and Hildreth had served on the town's school committee in 1859–60. Garland, *Eastern Point*, 106; *Gloucester Directory for 1870–71*; *Annual Report of the School Committee of the Town of Gloucester* (Gloucester, Mass.: John S. E. Rogers, 1860), 5.

10. Mr. Haskell: It is unclear which member of this large and prominent family Dyer is referring to. There is a gap in Gloucester directories between 1860 and 1869. In the latter year Charles A. Haskell was listed as assistant postmaster and Henry C. L. Haskell as postmaster of West Gloucester. *Gloucester Directory for 1869*, 50. When they lived in town at 13 Spring, corner of Water Street, Maria and Frank's butcher was Benjamin Haskell and Sons (Otis L. and Howard). Otis lived at 58 Spring and was mentioned in Frank's letter of August 27, 1863, as a deserter from the army on the Peninsula.

Papers of that date: I have not found a Gloucester paper for August 3, but the *Boston Evening Transcript* ran "Changes among Massachusetts Postmasters" the next day: "The President has made the following appointments of Postmasters in this State: Major J. Franklin Dyer, at Gloucester, vice Haskell." Two of the three other appointees listed were former Union officers.

EPILOGUE

1. Journal afterword; Dyer to Gen. Oliver O. Howard, Gloucester, Aug. 10, 1867, Oliver Otis Howard Papers, Special Collections, The Library, Bowdoin College, Brunswick, Maine.

2. "Obituary." One of his first cases was a joint examination with Drs. Herman E. Davidson and Joseph Garland of the brain of J. Sydney Allen's late brother, George, who died July 5, 1866, a thirty-four-year-old trader. They pronounced the cause of death as "softening of the brain" of a year's duration. In the late nineteenth century, softening of the brain, also called "yellow softening," was described as pus forming after a contusion or laceration. It could spread and apparently changed the color of the brain matter from gray to yellow. It was likely paresis, a disease of the brain caused by syphilis and usually occurring five to fifteen years after the primary infection. J. Sydney Allen Diary, July 5, 1866, Peabody Essex Museum, Salem, Mass.

3. Journal afterword; Dyer to Howard, Aug. 10, 1867.

4. The cause was pulmonary tuberculosis. Death record, 1879, 310:172, death no. 3, roll 58, Massachusetts Archives; "Obituary"; "Genealogy"; death notice, "Dr. J. Franklin Dyer," *Boston Daily Advertiser*, Feb. 10, 1879; "Inaugural Address of J. Franklin Dyer, Mayor of Gloucester, to the City Council, January 7, 1878"; James Robert Pringle, *History of the Town and City of Gloucester* (Gloucester, Mass.: By the author, 1892), 247.

5. "Obituary"; "Genealogy"; *Bowdoin Alumni*, 148.

6. "Obituary."

7. Dyer to Howard, Aug. 10, 1867.

8. James A. Cunningham: Lt. Col. James Adams Cunningham, Thirty-second Massachusetts, brevet brigadier general, earned brevets for Peebles' Farm, Cox Road, the Richmond campaign, and "especial gallantry" at Five Forks. He died July 17, 1892, at Chelsea, Mass. MOLLUS, *Register*, 107.

Dyer had been elected: "Obituary"; MOLLUS, *Register*, 137.

9. "In Memoriam," City Document 6, 1879, Gloucester Archives.

10. Waitt, *Nineteenth Massachusetts*, 8.

11. Maria D. Dyer, Cash Book, Sept. 1, 1881–Dec. 30, 1884; diary excerpts, Annisquam Historical Society; "Genealogy"; Dyer family scrapbook and picture album; Maria D. Dyer, secretary's report, The Reading Circle, Feb. 15, 1880–Jan. 7, 1881, Annisquam Historical Society; *Gloucester Daily Times*, June 29, 1925; U.S. Bureau of the Census, 1890 Census, NARA no. 123, roll 15, Supervisor's District 67, Enumeration District 181, p. 1, Special Schedule, Surviving Soldiers, Sailors and Marines, and Widows, Gloucester, Essex County, Mass.

12. *Gloucester Daily Times*, June 27, 29, 1925.

13. Certificate of Death, A767797, Registry of Vital Records and Statistics, Commonwealth of Massachusetts; *Gloucester Daily Times*, June 7, 9, 11.

APPENDIX 1

The original document is found in Horace Lakeman (1840–62) Letters, 1859–62, Phillips Library, Peabody Essex Museum, Salem, Mass. Henry Kemble Oliver (1800–85) joined the Salem Light Infantry in 1821; was colonel of the Sixth Massachusetts, serving in the Mexican War; had been adjutant general of the Massachusetts Militia (1844–48); and was elected treasurer of the state in 1860, serving throughout the war. He wrote to Dyer, probably on behalf of Lakeman's widowed mother, a Salem resident. *DAB*, 14:18–19.

1. Horace Lakeman of Salem enlisted at twenty-one in Company H, Nineteenth Massachusetts, October 25, 1861, and was mustered in December 10. He made corporal and served during the Peninsula campaign. *RMV*, 2:321.

2. Drs. Samuel Cabot, George H. Gay, and Charles D. Homans were three of the "six eminent surgeons" sent to the Peninsula by Massachusetts governor John Andrew, acting on the secretary of war's authority. They arrived April 13, 1862, to care for Massachusetts volunteers and established a hospital for Maj. Gen. Edwin Sumner's corps, including the Nineteenth Massachusetts. "Report of Surgeon Charles S. Tripler, Medical Director, Army of the Potomac, for operations from March 17 to July 3," *OR*, 11(1):181, 184–85.

3. Lakeman went from Yorktown aboard the *State of Maine* to Washington, where he arrived May 1, 1862, and then to the Mount Pleasant General Hospital more than two miles outside the city. He provides no details of his illness or disease in his letters, except for a lack of strength. Lakeman was discharged for disability May 24, 1862. A family friend brought him home to Salem. He seemed to rally at first, but with a racking cough he slowly declined and died after two weeks, probably from tuberculosis. Horace Lakeman to mother, Camp Winfield Scott, Yorktown, Va., May 2, 1862; Lakeman to mother, Mt. Pleasant General Hospital, Washington, D.C., May 15, 1862; and his sister, Lissie, Salem, June 15, 1862, to their brother, Lt. John R. Lakeman [Company C, Twenty-third Massachusetts], Port Royal, South Carolina, Lakeman Letters. The latter contains details of Horace's death.

4. Although care of the sick and wounded improved as the war continued, Tripler's report seems to support Dyer's assertion here. See "Report of Surgeon Charles S. Tripler."

APPENDIX 2

This is the first of Dyer's surviving letters.

1. Lakesville: not Lakesville on Maryland's Eastern Shore. He wrote "Johnsville" in his journal, a small town north of Liberty, erring slightly about the order of march. *Atlas*, plate 136.

2. Smith: Lt. Col. Charles H. Smith (from Eastport), First Maine, Third Brigade; Bibber: Second Lt. Andrew H. Bibber (from Eastport), Company D, First Maine Cavalry, Third Brigade, Second Division. Dyer mentions him several times. *Maine at Gettysburg*, 474.

3. Col. J. Irvin Gregg, Third Brigade, Second Division, Cavalry Corps.

4. Col. Calvin S. Douty was killed June 17, 1863.

5. Maj. Gen. John Reynolds was killed July 1, hit by a sharpshooter as he relieved Brig. Gen. John Buford's cavalry.

6. Maj. Gen. Daniel Sickles lost a leg July 2 but lived a half century more.

7. Captain Dodge: Capt. James G. C. Dodge was wounded on the third; Lieutenant Stone: Lt. William Stone, Company F.

8. The VI Corps was not heavily engaged in the battle.

9. This letter was written in pencil. Dyer appears to have changed the number of cannon in ink, replacing "sixty-seven" with "one hundred." The artillery bombardment started about 1:10 P.M. Hancock said it lasted one hour, forty-five minutes, but it seemed much longer to Dyer. See George R. Stewart, *Pickett's Charge* (Boston: Houghton Mifflin, 1959), 127–29, 159.

10. Lt. Col. Henry W. Cunningham, Nineteenth Maine, First Brigade, Second Division, II Corps. He was an older man and led the brigade in August. See Harry W. Pfanz, *Gettysburg: The Second Day* (Chapel Hill: University of North Carolina Press, 1987), 375–80.

11. In the statistical appendix to his journal, Dyer reports 356 killed, 1,156 wounded, and 94 missing, for a total of 1,606 in the Second Division; the OR gives 1,651. 27(1):112. The Second Division mustered only 1,037 on noon of the third of the 3,730 reported present before the battle. The Nineteenth Massachusetts had 77 casualties among 160 officers and men. Waitt, *Nineteenth Massachusetts*, 247.

12. Lt. Jasper N. Searles, First Minnesota, survived the war, leaving the army as a captain. Moe, *Last Full Measure*, 307–8.

Index

Numbers in boldface refer to photographic inserts; the first number is that of the text page preceding the insert, the second that of the page in the insert.

299

Index

Index

Index

Chain Bridge, 38, 226
Chamberlain, Joshua L., xviii
Chambersburg PA, 84
Chancellor house, 147
Chancellorsville, 132; battle of, xxvi, 74–77, 82, 147, 227; campaign of, 63, 73–78
Chantilly VA, 226
chaplains, 11–12, 37, 187
Charles City Court House VA, 33
Charleston SC: casualties at, 108–9; resists capture, 106, 115
Charlestown MA, xxv, xxix
Charlestown VA: execution of John Brown at, 13; residents of, 13
Chesapeake Bay, xxv, 34
Chesapeake Hospital (Hampton VA), xxxiii, 198
Chickahominy River, 22, 33, 122, 166, 168, 225; dead in swamps of, 47
Childs, Rev. Dr., 60
City Point VA, 180, 185, 187, 189, 192, 194; explosion at, 185, 188; mustered out surgeons sent to, 177; sick and wounded sent to, 173–74
civilians: at Antietam, 35, 39, 41; at Gettysburg, 101–2, 219; in Maryland, 90, 102, 219; in Virginia, 101, 120, 127
Cleaveland, Nathan S., xviii–xix, xix
"clump of trees," 99; Second Division, II Corps at, 221
Coddington, Edwin B., 101
"coffee boilers," 164
Cold Harbor: battle of, xxvi, 163–67; camp life at, 163–64, 166
College of William and Mary, 33
Commissary Department, 178
Committee on the Conduct of the War, 69
Committee on Reconstruction, 203
Comstock, Dr. L. C., 231
Confederate draft, 122
Confederate mine, 187–88
Confederates, xxvi; Dyer's feelings toward, xxxi
Congregational church (Gloucester MA), xxiii, 205

Connecticut troops, 128, 152
Connor, Col. Selden S., 149
conscripts, 120
contrabands, 122
contract surgeons, 41
Copperheads, xxii, 119, 120, 124; Dyer's feelings toward, xxxi, 71, 88–89, 108, 124
Corbin, Dr. E. Lyon, 230
Corcoran Legion, 155, 161
Corkhill, Capt. George B., 112–13
Cornish, Dr. Theodore O., 229
corps badges, 63, 67
Couch, Gen. Darius N., 60, 64, 76; Dyer's views on, 84; at Gettysburg, 92, 102, 215; ordered to Department of the Susquehanna, 84; resigns, 78, 81
Crampton's Gap, 104
Crater, battle of the, 171; explosion at, xxvi, 183; failure of assault at, 183; investigation of, 185–87
Crombarger, Capt. Thomas S., 71
Crosby, Dr. Alpheus B., 5
Cross, Col. Edward E., 82, 216
CSS Virginia, 16
Culpeper County VA, 121–23, 146
Culpeper VA: cavalry fight at, 84, 115–16; court house at, 115, 120; destruction in, 146; Ford, 134
Culp's Hill, 99
Cumberland VA, 21
Cunningham, Lt. Col. Henry W., 217
Cunningham, James A., 205
Curtis, 68, 141
Cushing, Lt. Alonzo H., 99, 221
Custer, Gen. George A., 101; Dyer's views on, 114

Dale, Dr. William J., 49, 57, 61, 199, 205; as surgeon general of Massachusetts, 2, 57–58
Dana, Gen. Napoleon J. T., 12, 32, 227
Darby, Dr. William J., 229
Darnestown MD, 9–10
Davis, Col. Benjamin F., 84

Index

Davis, Heber James (brother-in-law), xxv, 109; reported wounded, 165; tended by Dyer, 197–98

Davis, James (father-in-law), xx, xxiii

Davis, Rebecca Symonds (mother-in-law), xx

Deep Bottom VA, xxix, 183, 190–91

Democrats, rivals in mayoral election, 204

Denyse, Edwin F., 71

DeRussy, Gen. Gustavus A., 138

deserters, 63, 101, 120, 123; desertion and, 60, 101, 111; executions of, 111–14, 118, 147

Dessauer, Capt. Francis A., 76

Devens, Gen. Charles, 9, 227

Devereux, Col. Arthur F., 2, 9, 12, 42, 100, 108, 221; resigns, 138; wounded, 27

diseases, xxx, 9"

Dixie," 19

Dodge, Lt. James G. C., 7, 54, 91, 214

Doswell, Bernard, 159

Doubleday, Gen. Abner, 114

Dougherty, Dr. Alexander N., 12, 24, 26, 187, 189; I Corps, 200; after Gettysburg, 106; on leave, 135, 139; as medical director in Right Grand Division, 54–56, 69–70; operates on Hancock, 97, 222; praises Dyer, 194; as surgeon of volunteers, II Corps, 141, 143; wounded, 150–51; writes letter for Dyer, 200

Douglas, Dr. J., 231

draft, 69; riots, xxii, 111

Dranesville VA, 10

drummer boys, 171, 174–75

Dudley, Dr. Frederick A., 230

Dutch Gap, 190

Dwinelle, Dr. Justin, 230; xxiii–xxiv, 55–56, 81; stays at Gettysburg, 100

Dyer, Adelaide (sister), xv–xvi, xxv

Dyer, Charles (father), xv

Dyer, Charles Henry (brother), xv, and advice on women, xix–xx; characterizes daguerreotyping, xvii; congratulates Frank on medical degree, xix; as head of family, xv;

helps widowed Maria raise son, 205; marriage of, xx; remains at home, xxv; servant problems of, xvi; struggles in Eastport, xvii

Dyer, Edward James (son), 204–6

Dyer, Franklin "Frankie" (son), xxi–xxii, xxvi, 2, 62, 204

Dyer, George Burton (brother), xv; at Cold Harbor (XVIII Corps), 165, 167, 185; enlists in Ninth Maine, xxv, 109; Frank seeks, 194–95; helps widowed Maria raise son, 205; letters from, xxxiii, 218; at Petersburg, 173, 179, 180, 183, 191; studies Latin, xvi

Dyer, Hannah Snow (mother), xv–xvi, xxv; arranges loan for, xviii; consents to various careers for, xvi; thinks of best profession for, xvii

Dyer, Capt. Jonah (grandfather), xv

Dyer, Dr. Jonah Franklin, 70, as alderman, 204; ancestry of, xv; antebellum letters of, xxxiii; appointed acting surgeon, Nineteenth Massachusetts, xxiv–xxvi, 2; army service, xxiv–xxvi, xxviii; attends medical school, xvi; bond with brothers, xvi; buys Leonard Street house, 203, 206; casualty reports, 23, 148–49; childhood of, xv–xvi; cited by compilers of *Medical and Surgical History*, xxx; compiles journal, xxxi–xxxiv; conservatism of, xxiii; copies letters of recommendation into journal, xxxiii, 197–201; courtship and marriage of, xix–xxi; death of, 205; decides to become a druggist, xvii; defends Nineteenth Massachusetts, xxvi; details of operations by, xxviii–xxix; dreams of Rebels, 72; earns M.D., xix; edits *Eastport Sentinel*, xvii; and Edward James (son), 204–6; and election to Military Order of the Loyal Legion, 205; epitaph for, 207; escape at Reams' Station, xxviii, 193; escapes death in no man's land, xxviii, 195; expertise of, xxix–xxx;

Index

Index

Eastport ME, xv, xx, xxv; as Dyer's birthplace, xv; as residence of Snows, xv

Eastport Sentinel, xvii

Edwards Ferry MD, 227; Ball's Bluff campaign at, 6–8, 13; 38, 88–89

Eleventh Corps, Army of the Potomac, xxviii, 68, 73, 77–78

Eltham's Landing VA, 15, 20

Emancipation Proclamation, 45

Embler, Capt. A. Henry, 71; prepares Dyer's discharge papers, 193–94

England: intervention by, 115

English visitors, 129–30

Essex County MA, xix, xxiv, 2

Evans, Gen. Nathan G., 8

Evarts, Dr. Orpheus, 187

Everett, Edward: Dyer's views on, xxxi

Ewell, Gen. Richard S., 156; Dyer credits Washington raid to, 179

Exeter Academy, 204

Fairfax Court House VA, 36–37

Fairfax Station VA, 88

Fair Oaks VA, battle of, xxviii, 15, 22–26, 38, 60, 225; Howard loses arm at, 82; return to, 161

Falmouth VA, 51–56, 58–59, 61, 63–71, 73–84, 88, 114, 227

Farrowsville VA, 107

Fayetteville VA, 123

Ferrero, Gen. Edward, 180

Ferris, Lt. John J., 152

Fessenden, William P., 199–201

fevers, xxx, 5, 9, 18, 25, 30, 111, 182

flags: Nineteenth Massachusetts's captured, 175; of truce, 53, 56, 77, 190

food: civilian prices of, 20, 51, 102, 127, 218, 219; foraged, 34, 51, 88, 107; for men, 24, 29, 30–31, 34, 51, 58, 64, 102, 110, 128, 130, 134, 173–74; officers', 51, 127, 128, 167, 179, 218

Forrest, Gen. Nathan Bedford, xxvii

Fort Burnham, 198

Fort Donelson, 12

Fort Ethan Allen, 36

Fort Gregg SC, 115

"Fort Hell," 187

Fort Monroe VA, xxv, 15–16, 185, 195, 198, 225; Lincoln's meeting with Grant and Butler at, 186

Fort Pillow TN, 174

Fort Sumter SC, 32

Fort Wagner SC, 115

Fort Warren MA, 156

Fort Whipple, 138

Foster, Gen. John G., 118

Fourth of July, 93, 215–16

Franklin, Gen. William B., 50, 61

Frederick MD, 10, 39, 89–90, 103, 212–13, 217, 219; wounded sent to, 40–42

Fredericksburg, battle of, 52–55; campaign of, 49–56, 227; defeat of, 56

Fredericksburg and Richmond Railroad, 157, 158

Fredericksburg VA, xxiv, xxvi, 8, 50–52, 75, 79, 132, 148–50; bombardment of, 52–53; hospitals at, after Spotsylvania, 156–57; residents of, 56, 71, 79–80

Freedmen's Bureau, 204

French, Caleb (father-in-law), xx

French, Maria Haskell (first wife), xx

French, Nancy Parmenter (mother-in-law), xx

French, Gen. William H., 217

French: intervention by, 115; surgical knapsacks, 57–58

Friend House, 198

friendly fire, 35, 37

Front Royal VA, 107

Gainesville VA, 87, 125

Gale, Capt. W., 139

Galveston TX, 59

Garland, Lt. John M., 71

Gates, Dr. E. D., 230

Gay, Dr. George H., 209

"Gen. Gibbon's Division in the Battle of Gettysburg," 225–28

Georgia surgeon, xxviii, 23

Georgetown DC, 38

305

153–54, 171, 176, 179, 182, 188, 212; at Angle, 151–52; censures officers, 177; Dyer's views on, 84; endorses Dr. Dougherty's letter for Dyer, 200; at Gettysburg, 91–97, 99; investigates failure at Crater, 186; leads First Division, 81; reviews Caldwell's division, 81; rumored command of cavalry corps, 84; staff of, captured, 193; takes II Corps, 137, 139–40; talks to wounded, 81–82; temperament of, 163, 169, 182; visits Meade, 89; wounded, 216–17, 221–22

Hanover VA, 22

Hanover Junction, 158

Hanovertown, 160, 165

Harmon, Lt. William, 130

Harpers Ferry VA, xxii, 1, 12–13, 15, 41–44, 49, 86, 104–6, 225–26; residents of, 13

Harris, Mrs. John, 79

Harrisburg PA, 90, 213

Harrison's Island, 7

Harrison's Landing VA, 15, 26–34; Dyer's return to, 168, 177

Harrow, Gen. William, 86, 99, 104, 108, 111, 114–15, 219, 221; resignation of, accepted, 123

Hartwood Church VA, 114

Hasbrouck, Dr. Joseph L., 231

Haskell, Mr., 201

Haskell, Lt. Frank A., 68, 71; battlefield tour with Dyer, 220–21; at Gettysburg, 96–97, 99, 222; at Spotsylvania with 36th Wisconsin, 156

Haven, Dr. Samuel Foster, Jr., 53

Hawes, Dr. J. Q. A., 229

Hawley, Gen. Joseph R., 197

Hayden family, xv

Haymarket VA, 87, 211; skirmish at, 89

Hays, Gen. Alexander, 108, 113, 138

Hays, Gen. William, 110

Hayward, Dr. Nathan, 189; 194, 229; captured at Antietam, 41–42; operates on Maj. Macy, 97, 222; stays at Gettysburg, 100, 106

Heintzelman, Gen. Samuel P., 16, 70

Henry, Judith, 87

Hesser, Lt. Col. Theodore, 132

Hicks, Dr. W. T., 230

Hildreth, Lt. James H., 69, 71

Hill, Gen. Ambrose P., 119; blamed for Bristoe, 125; corps of, 123

Hill, Dr. John E., xxv, 30, 35, 37–38

Hill, Capt. William A., 196

Hinds, Dr. William H. W., 2

Hinks, Col. Edward W., 2–3, 12, 42; and Ball's Bluff, 7, 9; and division of black troops, 172; praises Dyer, 58; wounded, 27, 38, 40–41; Dyer operates on, 40; writes for Dyer, 201; writes Dr. Warren, 57–58

Hinks, Capt. Elisha A., 38, 165

Hodges, Lt. Col. John, Jr. 188

Hoffman house hospital: Dyer directs, 40–42; relatives seek wounded at, 43

Holmes, Capt. Oliver W., Jr., 75

Homans, Dr. Charles D., 209

Hooker, Maj. Gen. Joseph, xxvi, 29, 35, 39, 48, 61, 63–64, 66–69, 73, 74–75, 77, 81, 88, 147, 227; dissatisfied with Stoneman, 84; Dyer's views on, 64, 76–78; removed from command, 85, 89, 211–12; report criticized by Grant, 143; reviews II Corps, 64

Hooper, Maj. I. Harris, 108–9; escapes capture, 175; leads First Brigade at Spotsylvania, 153

Hopkins, Constance (ancestor), xv

Hopkins, Stephen (ancestor), xv

horse races, 66–67, 83

hospital flag, 53

hospitals: cooking in, 171, 173–74; field, 39–42; general, 38, 131; at Gettysburg, 217–18, 220–23; raided by guerrillas, 149; regimental, 209; Second Division, 64, 82, 84, 110, 113, 142, 147–49, 152, 167, 172–73, 175, 209; Spotsylvania wounded sent to Fredericksburg, 151

hospital stewards, 38, 98

Howard, Lt. Charles H., 59, 68; Dyer's views on, 59–60

Howard, Joseph, Jr., 9

Index

Howard, Gen. Oliver O., xxv, 37–38,
46, 64, 66–67, 69, 73, 77, 82, 104,
203, 226–27; at Bowdoin College,
59; corps of, 76, 78; Dyer assesses,
212; Dyer joins, 52, 58–60; Dyer
visits, 81; early career of, 60; gets
artificial arm, 63; at Gettysburg,
91; to lead XI Corps, 68–69,
70; and newspaper reporters, 73;
presentation to, 64–65; staff of,
59–60, 64–65
Howard's Branch VA, 17
Howe, Maj. Henry J., 2, 7, 27
Hughes, Dr. James W., 229
Hume, Lt. Lysander J., 32
Hunter, Gen. David, 171, 178
Hurley, Dr. John, 70
Huston, Lt. Col. James, 91, 214

Ingham, Dr. Silas A., 230
insects, 18, 30, 33, 81
Irish Brigade, 65

Jackson, Gen. Thomas J., xxvii, 73,
226–27; Dyer's views on, xxxi, 32,
35, 78
James River, xxvi, 33, 168–69, 186, 191;
Rebel mines in, 195
Jefferson MD, 104
Jerusalem plank road, 177
Jewett, Dr. Levi, 193, 230
"John Brown's Body," 13
Johnson, President Andrew, 197, 201,
203
Johnson, J. Warner, 178
Johnsville MD, 90
Jones' Neck VA, 181
Jones, Dr. A. Stokes, 230
Jones, Washington, 163
Joslin, Lt. Col. George C., 132

"Kathleen Mavourneen," 187
Kearny, Gen. Philip, 35, 38
Keedysville MD, 38–39; hospitals at, 40
Kelley, Lt. Benjamin E., 76
Kelly's Ford VA, 73–74, 110, 128–29
Kendall, Dr. Albert A., 42

Kennelly, Pvt. J., xxix
Kettle Run, 125
Keyes, Gen. Erasmus D., 17; reinforce-
ments from, 103
Kidder, Jefferson P., 120
Kilpatrick, Gen. Hugh J., 101, 115, 118,
121, 129, 138; appearance of, old
division, 144; Dyer's views on, 114;
sent west, 137, 141
Kirby's Battery: at Antietam, 39, 41; at
Fair Oaks, 225
Knapp, Dr. William D., xxii, 68, 219

Lacy house (Fredericksburg VA), xxiv,
xxvi, 52–56, 75–76, 79–80
Lakeman, Cpl. Horace, xxv, 209
Lakesville (Johnsville) MD, 213
Lander, Gen. Frederick W., 5, 6, 8, 12
land mines, 20
Landrum house (Spotsylvania VA), 152,
155
Latrobe, John H. B., 85, 94–97
Lawrence, Dr. Henry, 142
Lee, Lt. David, 27
Lee, Gen. Robert E., xxvi, 119; Dyer's
views on, xxxi, 80, 88, 104, 111, 124,
126, 130, 139, 155, 165, 204, 217;
pursuit of, 85, 101–8, 219
Lee, Col. William R., 7
Leeds ME, 60
Lee mansion (Arlington VA), 138–39
Leesburg VA, 88; occupied by Federals,
12
Leonard Street, xxi, 126–6, 203, 206
Letterman, Dr. Jonathan, 56, 80
letters of recommendation for Dyer,
xxxiii, 199–201
Lewis, Rev. George H., 206
Libby, Lt. Joseph, 196
Libby prison (Richmond VA), 185, 193
Liberty MD, 90, 213
Lincoln, Abraham, 1–2, 29, 114, 119,
124, 180, 186; and Emancipation
Proclamation, 45; and Gettysburg
Address, xxxi; 202; removes
McClellan, 46, 49; renominated, 163;
and pursuit of Lee, 101; and Second